21ST CENTURY MONETARY POLICY

21ST CENTURY MONETARY POLICY

∎

The Federal Reserve from the Great Inflation to COVID-19

BEN S. BERNANKE

W. W. NORTON & COMPANY
Independent Publishers Since 1923

For information about permission to reproduce selections from this book, write to
Permissions, W. W. Norton & Company, Inc., 500 Fifth Avenue, New York, NY 10110

For information about special discounts for bulk purchases, please contact
W. W. Norton Special Sales at specialsales@wwnorton.com or 800-233-4830

Manufacturing by Lakeside Book Company
Book design by Ellen Cipriano
Production manager: Anna Oler

Library of Congress Cataloging-in-Publication Data

Names: Bernanke, Ben, author.
Title: 21st century monetary policy : the Federal Reserve from the great inflation to
COVID-19 / Ben S. Bernanke.
Other titles: Twenty-first century monetary policy
Description: First edition. | New York, NY : W. W. Norton & Company, [2022] |
Includes bibliographical references and index.
Identifiers: LCCN 2021055322 | ISBN 9781324020462 (hardcover) |
ISBN 9781324020479 (epub)
Subjects: LCSH: United States. Federal Reserve Board. | Monetary policy—
United States. | United States--Economic policy—2009–
Classification: LCC HG2563 .B419 2022 | DDC 332.1/10973—
dc23/eng/20211201
LC record available at https://lccn.loc.gov/2021055322

W. W. Norton & Company, Inc., 500 Fifth Avenue, New York, N.Y. 10110
www.wwnorton.com

W. W. Norton & Company Ltd., 15 Carlisle Street, London W1D 3BS

1 2 3 4 5 6 7 8 9 0

CONTENTS

PART IV. 21st CENTURY MONETARY POLICY

What Lies Ahead

INTRODUCTION

On January 29, 2020, Jay Powell strode briskly to the podium to begin the first press conference of his third year as chair of the Federal Reserve. He flipped open a white binder, looked up briefly to welcome the assembled reporters, and then looked down to read his prepared statement. His demeanor was low-key, almost somber. But his message was upbeat: The U.S. economy had entered the eleventh year of a record-long expansion, unemployment remained at a half-century low, and people in lower-paying jobs were seeing wage gains after years of stagnation. The trade tensions that had roiled financial markets for the past two years had diminished and global growth seemed to be stabilizing.

In passing, he noted "uncertainties" affecting the economic outlook, "including those posed by the new coronavirus."[*1] A follow-up question on the virus, from Donna Borak of CNN, did not come until 21 minutes into the 54-minute press conference. At that point, only a few cases had been reported outside China. The virus, Powell cautiously acknowledged, was "a

---

* The Note on Sources at the end of the book provides links to official Federal Reserve documents, including transcripts of press conferences and FOMC meetings, policy statements, press releases, meeting minutes, projections, and congressional testimonies. Endnotes throughout the book provide additional information as needed, including page references for direct quotes and references to older or less accessible materials. Speeches by Federal Reserve officials are separately cited.

very serious issue" that could cause "some disruption to activity in China and possibly globally."[2]

Five weeks later, on March 3, Powell walked to the same podium and in the same calm tone read a much darker statement to reporters. He offered his sympathy to people the virus had harmed around the world, noted that it had disrupted the economies of many countries, and predicted that measures to contain the virus "will surely weigh on economic activity both here and abroad for some time." The Fed, he said, was cutting interest rates "to help the economy keep strong in the face of new risks."[3] He hinted at more to come. The state of the world had changed dramatically—and the Fed's policy had changed with it.

Between the January 29 and March 3 press conferences, the virus had evolved from a localized problem to an incipient global crisis. Reported cases of the disease that would become known as COVID-19 had risen from fewer than 10,000, almost all in China, to more than 90,000 worldwide. Italy had quarantined towns in its Lombardy region and Iran had reported a surge of infections. In the United States, the first virus death was reported on February 29—a man in his 50s, near Seattle. U.S. cases, and deaths, grew exponentially from there, threatening to overwhelm healthcare systems in New York City and other hot spots.

Meanwhile, virus fears triggered the worst week in U.S. financial markets since the 2007–2009 financial crisis, signaling trouble ahead for the economy. The Dow Jones Industrial Average, which had hit a record high earlier in the month, plunged more than 12 percent during the week ending February 28. In March the turmoil spread to bond markets. Sellers of even ultrasafe U.S. Treasury securities had difficulty finding buyers, who showed little interest in holding anything other than cash. The markets for private credit, where corporations, home buyers, and state and local governments borrow, threatened to freeze entirely as lenders and investors grappled with coronavirus-induced uncertainty.

The market's panic attack did, in fact, presage economic trauma. With businesses and schools closing, either voluntarily or under lockdowns imposed by local governments, economic activity contracted at an unprecedented rate. In February 2020, following a long recovery from the Great Recession, only 3.5 percent of the labor force was unemployed. Two months later, in April, the official unemployment rate stood at 14.8 percent, a shocking increase that likely understated the damage to the labor market. More than 20 million jobs were lost in April, by far the largest drop recorded since the data series began in 1939. The Business Cycle Dating Committee of the National Bureau of Economic Research, the arbiter of the timing of recessions and expansions, would later date the start of the pandemic recession to February.

Having served as Fed chair during the 2007–2009 global financial crisis, I had some idea of the stress that Powell and his colleagues at the Fed were experiencing. But, unlike the crisis we faced a dozen years earlier—which played out over nearly two years—this one seemed to happen all at once. On the principle that it's better to get ahead of a crisis when you can, the Powell Fed quickly took a remarkable range of actions to calm the financial turmoil and protect the economy. It took its short-term interest rate target close to zero and promised to hold it there for as long as needed. To help restore normal functioning in money markets and Treasury debt markets, it lent to cash-strapped financial firms and bought hundreds of billions of dollars' worth of Treasury and mortgage-backed securities on the open market. It reinstituted financial crisis–era programs to support business and consumer credit markets. Working with foreign central banks, it ensured global markets an adequate supply of dollars, the world's reserve currency. And it would ultimately promise to continue its large-scale purchases of securities—a policy known as quantitative easing—until economic conditions improved substantially.

All of those measures were drawn from a playbook developed during the 2007–2009 crisis. But the Powell Fed did not stop there. It worked with Congress and the Treasury Department to establish new programs to backstop corporate and municipal bond markets and to finance bank loans to medium-sized businesses and nonprofit organizations. And in August 2020 it announced important changes to its monetary policymaking framework—the outcome of a process begun before the pandemic struck—aimed at making policy more powerful when interest rates are already low. In the ensuing months, it fleshed out its monetary approach by making more explicit its promises to keep interest rates low for as long as needed.

Of course, the Federal Reserve could do nothing to affect the course of the virus, the ultimate source of the crisis. Nor could it tax and spend to support the people and businesses most affected by the disease, as the administration and Congress could. But it could use both monetary policy and its lending powers to provide stability to the financial system, smooth the flow of credit to the economy, support consumer and business spending, and promote job creation. In doing so, it would play a substantial role in bridging the economy to the recovery that would follow the pandemic.

As I often remarked when I led the Fed, monetary policy is not a panacea. But money matters—a great deal. And, as the responses of the Powell Fed to the pandemic illustrate, monetary policy in the 21st century—and central banking more generally—has been defined by remarkable innovation and change. The Fed's varied and sweeping actions during the pandemic, and the speed at which they were decided upon and announced, once would have seemed inconceivable—not only to the Fed of the 1950s and 1960s, chaired by the first modern Fed leader, William McChesney Martin Jr., but even to the Fed of the 1990s, led by one of history's most influential central bankers, Alan Greenspan. As Powell himself would acknowledge, "We crossed a lot of red lines that had not been crossed before."[4]

The aim of this book is to help readers understand how the Federal Reserve, the steward of U.S. monetary policy, got to where it is today, what it has learned from the diverse challenges it has faced, and how it may evolve in the future. Although my account focuses on the Fed, the central bank I know best, I also draw on the experiences of other major central banks, which have faced many of the same challenges and have made important innovations of their own. I hope this book will be useful to my fellow economists and their students, but I have tried to make it accessible to anyone with an interest in economic policy, finance, or central banking. As the role played by the Powell Fed in the pandemic crisis makes clear, an appreciation of the goals of the Federal Reserve, and of the tools and strategies it uses to meet those goals, is essential for understanding the contemporary global economy.

THE HISTORICAL LENS

This book examines today's (and tomorrow's) Federal Reserve primarily through an historical lens. That's how I came to the subject, and I see no other way to understand completely how the Fed's tools, strategies, and communication have evolved to where they are today.

A conversation I had as a graduate student at the Massachusetts Institute of Technology (MIT) in the late 1970s kindled my interest in monetary policy. I went to a young professor, Stanley Fischer—then a rising academic star, later a governor of the Bank of Israel and vice chair of the Federal Reserve—looking for advice on a dissertation topic. Stan, who would become my adviser and mentor, handed me a copy of the 860-page *A Monetary History of the United States, 1867–1960*, by Milton Friedman and Anna Schwartz.[5]

"Read this," Stan said. "It may bore you to death. But if it excites you, you might consider doing monetary economics."

The book fascinated me. It got me interested not only in monetary economics, but also in the causes of the Great Depression of the 1930s, a topic that I would return to frequently in my academic writings. As Friedman and Schwartz showed, central bankers' outmoded doctrines and flawed understanding of the economy played a crucial role in that catastrophic decade, demonstrating the power of ideas to shape events. It's in the spirit of Friedman and Schwartz that this book uses history to explain the evolution of the Fed's policies and role in the economy. And since Friedman and Schwartz left off their history in the decades after World War II, the immediate postwar era seems an appropriate place to start this narrative. Learning the lessons of the Fed's history prepares us to speculate about the future as well, as I do in the final part of the book.

Indeed, in many ways, the 1950s and early 1960s mark the beginning of modern central banking. By that time, the Fed was no longer constrained by the gold standard of the 1920s and 1930s, or by the responsibility, assumed during World War II, to help finance wartime debts by keeping interest rates low. It was also a time when the ideas of the British economist John Maynard Keynes were becoming increasingly influential in the United States. Keynes died in 1946, but his followers built on his Depression-era writings to highlight the potential of macroeconomic policies, including monetary policy, to fight recessions and control inflation. So-called Keynesian economics, in a modernized form, remains the central paradigm at the Fed and other central banks.

The 1960s also saw the beginning of one of the most traumatic economic events of postwar U.S. history, as well as one of the signal failures of economic policymaking—what we now call the Great Inflation. Until it was conquered (at a high cost in lost jobs) by Paul Volcker's Fed in the 1980s, the Great Inflation threatened U.S. economic and even political stability. What policymakers learned, or thought they learned, from the Great Inflation shaped the evolution of monetary policy, and continues to shape it, even today.

THE FEDERAL RESERVE: SOME BACKGROUND

To lay some groundwork, I'll sketch here some early history of U.S. central banking and provide background on the Fed—its structure, how it is governed, and how it implements its monetary policy decisions. I'll then preview the critical factors that, this book will argue, shaped the modern Fed and motivated the remarkable changes in its tools and policies in recent decades.

Early Years

America has a strong populist tradition, and populists—from President Andrew Jackson to, more recently, members of the Tea Party and Occupy Wall Street—have always been hostile to perceived concentrations of power in finance and government. Populist influences help explain why the United States lacked a well-established central bank until the creation of the Federal Reserve in 1913, later than many other advanced economies (the Bank of England dates back to 1694, Sweden's central bank even earlier). Alexander Hamilton—the country's first Treasury secretary and a modernizer who understood that America would one day be an industrial and financial power—initiated a central bank in 1791, but only over the bitter opposition of Thomas Jefferson and James Madison, who had more-pastoral visions for the U.S. economy. The charter of Hamilton's First Bank of the United States was allowed to lapse in 1811, on a narrow congressional vote. Another attempt at establishing a central bank, the Second Bank of the United States, also was dashed when, in 1832, President Jackson—who distrusted banks in general and feuded with the Second Bank's leader, Nicholas Biddle—vetoed Congress's renewal of its charter. (It's ironic that Jackson's likeness remains on the $20 Federal Reserve note. He would have objected.)

The political environment of the Progressive Era, from roughly the 1890s to the 1920s, was more conducive to the establishment of a central bank. President Woodrow Wilson did just that by signing the Federal Reserve Act on December 23, 1913. Consistent with progressive views of the time, which advocated scientific, rational policies to improve the economy, the new Federal Reserve System was intended to oversee and help stabilize America's lightly regulated and often-dysfunctional banking system. The 19th century American banking system had been afflicted by frequent runs and panics, which were almost always associated with recessions, some of them quite severe. The panic of 1907—ended by the intervention of the famed financier J. Pierpont Morgan and his allies, not the government—was the last straw. Congress grew determined to revisit the idea of a central bank.

The Bank of England, the world's most important central bank at the time, provided a model. It had two primary responsibilities. First, it managed Great Britain's money supply consistent with the gold standard. The pound, like other major currencies, had a fixed value in terms of gold, and the Bank adjusted short-term interest rates to ensure the pound's gold value remained stable. Second, and particularly relevant to the United States, it served as a *lender of last resort* during runs and panics. If depositors lost confidence in British banks or other financial firms and lined up to withdraw their money, the Bank of England stood ready to lend the banks the cash they needed to pay off depositors, taking the banks' loans and other assets as collateral. So long as a bank was fundamentally solvent, the Bank of England's loans would allow it to remain open and avoid selling off their assets at fire sale prices. Great Britain thus avoided the pattern of recurring financial crises and economic instability that had plagued the United States in the 1800s and early 1900s.

Like the Bank of England, the newly created Federal Reserve was given the critical roles of managing the money supply (as dictated by the gold standard) and serving as lender of last resort for banks that chose to join the Federal Reserve System—so-called member banks.[*] Since only solvent banks were eligible to borrow from the Fed, the new central bank was also given authority to examine member banks' books, authority it shared with the Comptroller of the Currency (established during the Civil War to oversee nationally chartered banks) and state banking regulators (who supervised state-chartered banks). To this day, monetary policy, bank supervision, and responding to threats to financial stability are a pretty good description of the Fed's main responsibilities.

There had been an ongoing debate about whether the new central bank would be managed from Washington (as advocated by most bankers) or in a more decentralized way that gave greater power to regional branches of the central bank (the model preferred by midwestern farmers and others who feared the concentrated power of eastern financial interests). Wilson backed a compromise: The Federal Reserve System would consist of both a Board of Governors in Washington with general oversight powers and up to twelve regional Federal Reserve Banks, each with considerable

---

[*] Banks with national charters were required to join the System but state-chartered banks could choose whether to join. The U.S. banking system today still has three types of banks: national banks, state-chartered banks that are members of the Federal Reserve System, and state nonmember banks, each with a different mix of regulators.

autonomy, located in major cities across the country. Cities campaigned to be the sites of Reserve Banks, which were ultimately established in Boston, New York, Philadelphia, Cleveland, Richmond, Atlanta, Chicago, St. Louis, Minneapolis, Kansas City, Dallas, and San Francisco. These cities remain the locations of the Reserve Banks today, despite the westward shift of economic activity since the Fed was founded. (The San Francisco Fed's district now includes more than one-fifth of U.S. economic activity.)

The Great Depression

The U.S. economy prospered, on balance, during the Fed's first fifteen years, but in 1929 the world entered a global depression. The origins of the Great Depression are complex, but the international gold standard, which had been reinstituted following its suspension by most countries during World War I, was a principal cause. The war had been accompanied by substantial inflation, as the government finances of belligerent countries crumbled and shortages of critical commodities multiplied. As countries returned to the gold standard after the war, reestablishing the link between the supply of money and the quantity of available gold, it became evident that there was not enough gold in the world, nor was it distributed evenly enough among countries, to sustain the prices of goods and services at their new, higher levels.

One solution would have been to reduce the official values of currencies relative to gold, allowing the available gold to support higher money supplies and price levels, but in many countries currency devaluation was seen as inconsistent with the spirit of the gold standard. (Purchasers of government bonds were particularly opposed to devaluation, since it would reduce the real value of their bonds.) Instead, jury-rigged arrangements were developed to compensate for the shortage of gold. For example, some countries agreed to hold gold-backed currencies, like the British pound, in lieu of actual gold. The Bank of England itself, as had long been its practice, held a gold stock that was small compared to the number of paper pounds outstanding, relying on investor confidence in England's commitment to the gold standard rather than actual gold to back the pound.

International political and financial conditions remained highly unstable after the war, however, exacerbated by disagreements over how much Germany should pay in reparations and American demands for the full repayment of its wartime loans to Great Britain and France. These conflicts in turn shook confidence in the reconstructed global monetary system, which relied heavily on mutual trust and cooperation. As fear and uncertainty grew, governments and investors stopped holding pounds and other gold surrogates and tried to obtain physical gold instead, resulting in a global "scramble for gold," including runs on the gold held by central banks. As the global shortage of gold began to reassert itself, money supplies and prices collapsed in the gold-standard countries. The prices of U.S. goods and services, for example, fell by 30 percent from 1931 to 1933.

The deflation of the price level in turn bankrupted many debtors—think of farmers trying to pay their mortgages when crop prices were plummeting—which helped bring down the financial system and, with it, the economy.[6] Runs by frightened depositors led to increasingly severe waves of bank failures—in the United States, thousands of mostly small banks closed their doors—which worsened financial distress, further reduced the money supply, and constricted credit to businesses and farmers. With few exceptions, the Depression was global although, consistent with the view that the gold standard was a major cause of the downturn, the economies of countries that chose or were forced to abandon the gold standard earlier also recovered more quickly.[7]

In 1933, newly elected President Franklin Roosevelt launched a barrage of new policies to try to end the Depression. Two were particularly important: First, FDR broke the link between the dollar and gold, which ended the U.S. deflation and allowed a nascent recovery, until premature monetary and fiscal tightening led to a new recession in 1937.[*] Second, Roosevelt declared a banking "holiday," closing all banks and vowing to reopen only those banks that were solvent. Together with the creation of federal deposit

---

[*] Vestiges of the international gold standard remained until the 1970s, but after 1933 the gold standard placed essentially no constraints on Federal Reserve policies.

insurance by Congress, which protected small depositors from losses from bank failures, the holiday decisively ended the banking panics.

Friedman and Schwartz's *Monetary History* underscored the role of the collapse in money and prices in creating the Great Depression. Shortly after I joined the Federal Reserve, as a member of the Board of Governors, I spoke at Friedman's ninetieth birthday party. I concluded my remarks by apologizing for the Federal Reserve's role in the catastrophe: "I would like to say to Milton and Anna: Regarding the Great Depression. You're right, we did it. We're very sorry. But thanks to you, we won't do it again."[8]

Blaming the Depression entirely on the Fed is an exaggeration, but the relatively new and unseasoned central bank did perform poorly. Its interest-rate increases in the 1920s, aimed at cooling speculation in the stock market, contributed to both the 1929 stock crash and the initial global downturn. Its commitment to the gold standard prevented it from responding adequately to the destructive deflation of the early 1930s. And it did too little to stem the waves of banking panics, even though ending panics had been one of the motivations for its creation.[*] The Fed's failure to preserve either monetary or financial stability made the Great Depression much worse than it might otherwise have been.

A flawed intellectual framework—including adherence to the gold standard beyond its point of viability—was a key reason the Fed and other policymakers failed to avert the Depression. But another explanation for the Fed's relative passivity during the 1930s crisis, stressed by Friedman and Schwartz, was its decentralized structure and lack of effective leadership. (Benjamin Strong, the influential governor of the Federal Reserve Bank of New York, and the *de facto* leader of the Fed system, had died of tuberculosis in 1928.) Congress addressed this weakness by revamping the organization of the central bank. As part of the Banking Act of 1935, it increased

---

[*] The reasons for the Fed's failure to stop the banking panics of the 1930s are debated. Most banks at the time were small and undiversified and quickly became insolvent; they thus lacked collateral against which to borrow from the Fed. Many others were not members of the Federal Reserve System and thus were not eligible for Fed loans. Nevertheless, most historians agree that the Fed could have done more to stabilize the banking system.

the power of the Federal Reserve Board in Washington and reduced the autonomy of the regional Reserve Banks, creating what remains today the Fed's basic decision-making structure.

The reforms also increased the Fed's independence from the executive branch by removing the Treasury secretary and the Comptroller of the Currency (the regulator of nationally chartered banks) from the Fed Board and—in an important symbolic step—by moving the Board from its previous location in the Treasury Department to a grand new headquarters— a Works Progress Administration project—on Constitution Avenue in Washington, facing the Mall. The building was later named for Marriner Eccles, Board chair from 1934 to 1948. Eccles was instrumental in crafting the Banking Act of 1935 and would ultimately fill the leadership void left by the death of Strong. In contrast to many of his predecessors at the Fed, Eccles recognized that forceful government action was necessary to counter the Depression, and his ideas—some of which anticipated the theories of Keynes—helped form the basis of Roosevelt's New Deal.

The Depression lasted until the massive war effort of 1941–45 pushed the American economy to full employment and beyond. During and immediately after the war, at the Treasury's request, the Fed held interest rates at low levels to reduce the government's cost of financing the war. After the war, and facing new hostilities in Korea, President Truman pressed the Fed to keep rates low. But the Fed's leaders worried that very low rates would stoke inflation, which had surged when the end of wartime rationing spurred demand for consumer goods. As we'll see in Chapter 1, the Fed rebelled, and in March 1951 the Treasury and the Fed agreed that the Fed would phase out its interest-rate peg, leaving it free to use monetary policy to advance macroeconomic goals, including the stabilization of inflation. This historic agreement, known as the Treasury-Fed Accord of 1951, helped set the stage for modern monetary policy.

The Federal Reserve's Structure

The Federal Reserve's structure today largely reflects congressional choices made at its founding in 1913 and in the 1935 reforms.

As at its inception, the Federal Reserve System consists of a Board of Governors in Washington and twelve Reserve Banks. The seven members of the Board are nominated by the president and confirmed by the Senate to fourteen-year, staggered terms. The Board chair and vice chair—plus, since the passage of regulatory reforms in 2010, a second vice chair responsible for the oversight of bank supervision—are also nominated by the president and confirmed by the Senate to four-year terms. Unlike Cabinet secretaries, by law, Board members cannot be fired by the president for policy differences, but only for malfeasance or through impeachment by Congress.

Reflecting compromises made when the Fed was created, the twelve Reserve Banks are technically private institutions, though with a public purpose. Each has a board of directors, drawn from local bankers, businesspeople, and community leaders. These boards help oversee the operations of their Reserve Bank and, importantly, the directors (excluding, since 2010, the bankers) choose its president, subject to the approval of the Board in Washington.

Reflecting the 1935 reforms, as well as the fact that members of the Board—unlike Reserve Bank presidents—are presidential appointees, the Board today holds much of the Federal Reserve's policymaking authority. Importantly, the Board is in charge of lender-of-last-resort policy; it sets the *discount rate*—the interest rate at which the Fed lends to banks—and determines whether to invoke the Fed's emergency lending powers. The Board also establishes rules, such as capital requirements, for the banks and bank holding companies (companies that own banks and possibly other financial firms) that the Fed regulates and supervises.* Staff at the regional Reserve Banks do the actual hands-on supervision of banks, ensuring that the banks in their district follow the rules set by the Board.

There is one very important exception to the principle that the Board sets Federal Reserve policies: *monetary policy*, which includes the setting

---

* A bank's capital is, roughly, the excess of its assets over its liabilities, which in turn equals the equity of its shareholders. Capital is available to absorb losses on loans and other investments without triggering bankruptcy, so a bank with a large amount of capital is at less risk of failing.

of short-term interest rates and other measures aimed at affecting overall financial conditions and, through them, the health of the economy. By law, monetary policy is made by a larger group called the *Federal Open Market Committee* (the FOMC or the Committee, for short). The FOMC's meetings are attended by nineteen policymakers (when there are no vacancies)—the seven Board members and twelve Reserve Bank presidents—along with staff from the Board and each of the Reserve Banks. By tradition, the Committee each year elects the Board chair as its chair. The FOMC meets eight times each year around a massive mahogany and black granite table in the boardroom of the Eccles building in Washington. The chair can also call unscheduled meetings, formerly held by phone and now by videoconference.

The voting rules of the FOMC are convoluted. Of the nineteen governors and presidents who attend and participate, only twelve vote at any given meeting. The seven Board members and the president of the Federal Reserve Bank of New York (who also by tradition serves as the vice chair of the FOMC) vote at every meeting. The remaining four votes rotate annually among the other eleven Reserve Bank presidents. This complex design allows the regional Reserve Bank presidents a voice but gives the majority (depending on Board vacancies) to the politically appointed Board members. In Fed lingo, the nineteen policymakers who attend FOMC meetings are called *participants*, while voters are called *members*.

The Fed chair, in his or her capacity as chair of the FOMC, has only one vote on monetary policy, but the ability to set the agenda and recommend policy actions, together with the Committee's tradition of consensus decision-making, makes the chair a highly influential first among equals. The Board vice chair and the president of the Federal Reserve Bank of New York are also usually quite influential and work closely with the chair.

Ultimately, of course, the administration and Congress, through legislation, set the Fed's goals, structure, and authorities. The cornerstone of congressional oversight of the Fed's monetary policy, formally laid out in the Federal Reserve Reform Act of 1977, is the so-called *dual mandate*:

Congress's instruction to the FOMC to pursue the economic goals of maximum employment and stable prices. Although the Fed's monetary policy objectives are enshrined in law, Fed policymakers are responsible for managing interest rates and other policy instruments to achieve those objectives. In a distinction popularized by Stanley Fischer, the Fed does not have *goal independence*—its objectives are set by the president and Congress, through legislation—but it does have, at least in principle, what I'll call *policy independence*, the ability to use its policy instruments as it sees fit to best achieve those mandated goals.[9] Various aspects of the Fed's structure—including the long, overlapping terms of governors; the provision that governors cannot be fired by the president for policy differences; the fact that Reserve Bank presidents are not political appointees; and the Fed's ability to pay for its operations out of the returns from the securities it owns rather than relying on congressional appropriations—help insulate it from short-term political pressures, allowing it to act more independently than Cabinet departments and with a greater focus on longer-term outcomes.

The Federal Reserve's Balance Sheet and Monetary Policy

Like any bank, the Federal Reserve has a balance sheet with assets and liabilities.* It has two principal liabilities: currency—cash, known as Federal Reserve notes—and bank reserves. A remarkably large amount of U.S. currency is in circulation—about $2.15 trillion in 2021, or more than $6,000 per each American. (Of course, few Americans hold that much cash; many dollars are held overseas, often as a hedge against inflation or instability of the local currency.)

Bank reserves are deposits that commercial banks hold at the Fed. (Cash held by banks in their vaults also counts as reserves.) Banks no longer have to hold reserves to satisfy regulatory requirements, as they did in the past,

---

* More precisely, each regional Federal Reserve Bank has its own balance sheet, a relic of the time when each Reserve Bank served as an independent lender of last resort to banks in its district. Taken together, the regional Fed balance sheets make up the collective balance sheet of the Federal Reserve System.

but they nevertheless find them useful. For example, if a bank in San Francisco needs to transfer funds to a bank in New York, it can do that easily by instructing the Fed to move reserves from its account to the account of the New York bank. Bank reserves are also safe and liquid, and can be quickly converted into cash to meet the needs of depositors.

A bank that wants additional reserves can borrow them from another bank, usually overnight. The interest rate that banks charge each other to borrow reserves is called the *federal funds rate*. Despite its name, the federal funds rate is a market-determined rate. However, the funds rate, for short, is a key interest rate for monetary policymakers. Throughout most of its modern history, the FOMC has implemented monetary policy through its ability to influence the funds rate, although at times the discount rate has also been used to signal monetary policy changes.

On the asset side of its balance sheet, the Fed's principal holdings are U.S. Treasury securities (federal government debt) of varying maturities, as well as mortgage-backed securities (securities that bundle together large numbers of individual mortgages). The mortgage-backed securities held by the Fed are issued by the *government-sponsored enterprises*, or GSEs. The GSEs—organizations with the nicknames Fannie Mae, Freddie Mac, and Ginnie Mae—were created by the federal government to facilitate the flow of credit into the housing market. All the securities issued by the GSEs, which the Fed is allowed to buy and hold, are currently government-guaranteed. In addition, any loans the Fed makes—say, to a bank, in its role of lender of last resort—count as assets.

The Fed's balance sheet typically provides substantial income. On the asset side, the Fed receives interest on the securities it holds. On the liability side, it pays interest on bank reserves but not on currency. It uses some of its income to pay for its own operations but remits most of it to the Treasury, thus reducing the government's budget deficit.

Importantly, the Fed uses its balance sheet to implement its monetary policy decisions. Suppose higher interest rates are needed to achieve the FOMC's economic goals. Having made that decision, the Committee would increase the target level (or, more recently, target range) for the federal funds rate.

In recent years, the Fed has influenced the funds rate by varying two administered rates, including the interest rate it pays banks on the reserves they hold at the Fed. Throughout most of its modern history, though, the Fed raised the funds rate by creating a shortage of bank reserves, which, in turn, caused the banks themselves to bid up the funds rate. To reduce the supply of bank reserves, the Fed, through the Open Market Desk at the Federal Reserve Bank of New York, sold Treasury securities to private investors, using a designated set of private financial firms called *primary dealers* as its agents. As investors paid for the securities, reserves in the banking system declined in equal measure. (Think of the purchasers of the securities as writing checks to the Fed; to settle those checks, the purchasers' banks must draw down their reserves.) With fewer reserves available, the rate (price) that banks paid to borrow reserves from each other naturally rose, as intended by the FOMC. Likewise, to lower the federal funds rate (the price of borrowing reserves), the Open Market Desk bought Treasury securities on the open market, increasing the supply of reserves in the banking system. Other forms of monetary policy, including the large-scale securities purchases that constitute quantitative easing, also employ changes in the Federal Reserve's balance sheet.

Because financial markets are closely linked, the Fed's ability to change the federal funds rate allows it to affect financial conditions more broadly. Easy financial conditions promote borrowing and spending and thus economic activity. To ease financial conditions, the FOMC lowers its target for the funds rate, which then affects other financial variables. For example, a lower funds rate would normally be associated with lower rates on mortgages and corporate bonds (supporting spending on housing and capital investment), higher stock prices (increasing spending by raising wealth), and a weaker dollar (which encourages exports by making the prices of U.S. goods cheaper). To tighten financial conditions, the FOMC would raise its target for the funds rate, reversing the effects of easy policy.

THE THESIS OF THIS BOOK

As the response of the Powell Fed to the pandemic showed, the Fed's tools, policy framework, and communications have changed radically since the 1951 Treasury-Fed Accord freed the central bank to pursue macroeconomic objectives. The unifying thesis of this book is that these changes have, for the most part, been the result not of changes in economic theories or in the Fed's formal powers, but of three broad economic developments that, in combination, have shaped how the central bank sees its goals and constraints.

The first of these developments is *the ongoing change in the behavior of inflation and, in particular, its relationship to employment.* Since the 1950s, U.S. monetary policy has been heavily influenced by economists' and policymakers' views about the relationship between inflation and the labor market. Policymakers of the 1960s and 1970s both misjudged this relationship and failed to consider the destabilizing effects of what economists call "inflation psychology," twin mistakes that contributed to a decade and a half of rapid price increases—the Great Inflation.

The restoration of the Fed's inflation-fighting credibility in the 1980s and 1990s under chairs Volcker and Greenspan would have important benefits, and the control of inflation became central to the Fed's policy strategy during that time. However, as we will see, subsequent years saw significant changes in the behavior of inflation, including an apparent marked weakening in the relationship between inflation and unemployment. Monetary policymakers also recognized, after 2000, that inflation can be too low as well as too high. These changes led to new policy strategies and tactics, including a new framework from Chair Powell's Fed in August 2020. Then, in 2021, shortages and bottlenecks associated with reopening after the pandemic helped spark a sharp increase in inflation, despite the fact that employment remained well below pre-pandemic levels. Why has the behavior of inflation, including its relationship with employment, changed over time? What implications does this have for monetary policy and the economy, now and in the future?

The second development is *the long-term decline in the normal level of interest rates*. In part because of lower inflation, the general level of interest rates—even when monetary policy is not adding stimulus to the economy—is much lower than in the past. Importantly, that reduces the scope of the Fed and other central banks to cut interest rates to support the economy during downturns. In 2008, during the global financial crisis, and again in 2020, with the economy shut down by a pandemic, the federal funds rate hit zero, but the economy needed much more stimulus. How can the Fed and other central banks support the economy when short-term interest rates remain relatively close to zero? What tools have been used, how have they worked, and what new tools might be used in the future? What role should fiscal policy—government spending and taxation—play in stabilizing the economy?

The third and final long-term development is *increased risk of systemic financial instability*. The Fed was founded to help keep the financial system stable, to avoid panics and crashes that endanger the economy. It failed to achieve that during the Depression. Between World War II and the 2007–2009 global financial crisis, the United States faced periodic, but ultimately limited, threats to financial stability. The global financial crisis showed, however, that severe financial instability is not an historical curiosity or something that can happen only in emerging markets. It can happen in, and do terrible damage to, even the most advanced economies and the most sophisticated financial systems. The 2007–2009 crisis forced the Fed, during my term as chair, to develop new tools for fighting financial instability, and the Fed further expanded its crisis-fighting toolkit during the pandemic-era crisis of March 2020. Increased instability also motivated significant regulatory reforms and more-intensive monitoring of the financial system. Are those measures enough? What else can be done? To what extent, if any, should monetary policy take financial-stability risks into account?

These three factors are primarily economic, but understanding the Fed's policy choices also requires attention to its political and social environment. Among the most important political determinants of Fed decision-making is the degree of independence the institution enjoys. As we've seen, aspects of the Fed's structure, like the long terms of governors and budgetary autonomy, promote its policy independence. On the other hand, Congress could change the Fed's structure and authorities at any time, and the Fed's democratic legitimacy requires that it respond to the popular will as expressed through the legislative and executive branches. What is the modern case for central-bank independence? When should the central bank cooperate with the Treasury or other parts of the government? Should monetary and fiscal policy be more coordinated? Should the Fed have a role in the pursuit of broader social goals, such as reducing economic inequality or mitigating climate change?

The critical questions raised here cannot be answered in the abstract, but only by understanding the historical context in which these issues arose and in which Fed policy was made. Parts I to III of this book look at the evolution of Federal Reserve policies, as the Fed responded to a changing economic and political environment, from the early postwar period through the present. Part IV is forward looking, drawing on the lessons of this experience to consider current controversies and the future prospects of U.S. monetary policy and policies to maintain financial stability.

PART I

20TH CENTURY MONETARY POLICY

■

The Rise and Fall of Inflation

1

THE GREAT INFLATION

THE WORD "GREAT" USUALLY HAS a positive connotation. In economics—
not so much. Unemployment soared and incomes fell sharply during both
the Great Depression of the 1930s and the Great Recession of 2007–2009.
America's Great Inflation, which lasted from the mid-1960s until the mid-
1980s, inflicted less economic distress than the other two "great" episodes.
Nevertheless, the era—symbolized by gas lines and the Ford administration's famously futile Whip Inflation Now (WIN) buttons—eroded Americans' confidence in their economy and their government. For the Federal
Reserve, the period had both low and high points. Facing political pressures and evolving views about the appropriate role of monetary policy,
the Fed responded hesitantly and inadequately to the building inflation of
the late 1960s and 1970s. But, under Paul Volcker, it took up and won the
battle against inflation in the 1980s. The victory was costly, but it helped
to restore confidence in economic policymaking and set the stage for two
decades of strong economic performance.

As a childhood trauma shapes an adult's personality, the Great Inflation shaped the theory and practice of monetary policy for years to come,
both in the United States and around the world. Critically, central banks
incorporated the lessons of the period in a policy framework focused on
controlling inflation and managing inflation expectations—a framework

that remained highly influential, even as inflation receded. The experience of the Great Inflation, which showed how political pressure can distort monetary policy, also convinced many that monetary policymakers should make their decisions, to the extent possible, independently, based on objective analysis and in the long-run interest of the economy.

THE GREAT INFLATION: AN OVERVIEW

Before the 1960s, except during wartime and subsequent demobilizations, inflation had only rarely been a problem in the United States. Out of living memory, the worst inflations on American soil were during the Revolutionary War—when individual colonies issued their own currencies—and after the collapse of the Confederate currency during the Civil War. But neither of those episodes involved a currency issued by the federal government. During the Great Depression, the concern had been deflation—rapidly falling prices—not inflation. Inflation surged briefly at the end of World War II and again at the start of the Korean War. But it was largely quiescent from the early 1950s until the mid-1960s. The consumer price index (CPI)—a measure of the cost of a standard basket of consumer goods—rose on average only about 1.3 percent per year between 1952 and 1965.

That began to change around 1966, when consumer prices rose a surprising 3.5 percent. The pace picked up from there, ushering in what would become a decade and a half of high and variable inflation. From the end of 1965 to the end of 1981, inflation averaged more than 7 percent annually, peaking at nearly 13 percent on average in 1979 and 1980. Americans had never experienced a sustained inflation this severe, and they didn't like it. By the late 1970s, high inflation regularly polled as the top economic concern, and people increasingly expressed little or no confidence in government economic policies.

Why did inflation rise so much after 1965? The economic doctrines of the time seemed to explain the rise, at least at first. A paper published in 1958 by A. W. Phillips, a New Zealander who spent most of his career at the London School of Economics, laid out the key idea. Using nearly a century's worth of data from the United Kingdom, Phillips studied the relationship between average wage growth and the amount of slack in the labor market, as measured by the unemployment rate. Phillips found that low unemployment rates tended to be accompanied by more-rapid wage growth. This empirical relationship became known as the *Phillips curve*.[1]

The Phillips curve captured an intuitive idea: If the demand for workers is high relative to the supply—that is, if employers have difficulty attracting and retaining workers—then workers should be able to command higher wages. Moreover, as many economists were quick to point out, the same basic idea should apply to the prices of goods and services.[2] If demand is so strong across the board that firms are having trouble filling their customers' orders, they will have more scope to raise prices. (Economists now distinguish between the wage Phillips curve, which links wage growth to unemployment as in the original Phillips paper, and the price Phillips curve, which ties consumer price inflation to unemployment or other measures of economic slack.) Basically, the logic of the Phillips curve is that inflation should accelerate when total demand from the private and public sectors persistently outstrips the capacity of the economy to produce.

That straightforward insight seemed to describe the late 1960s, when the economywide demand for goods and services grew rapidly. The main driver of demand growth was *fiscal policy*, the tax and spending policies of the federal government. Dissatisfaction with the economy had helped John F. Kennedy narrowly win the 1960 election. The economy had recovered only slowly from a recession in 1957–58, and another brief recession began as the election campaign was underway in 1960, pushing up unemployment through the year and into 1961. Kennedy had promised voters that he would "get America moving again."[3] To follow through on his promise, he filled his administration with a new generation of advisers who, in the spirit of Keynes's writings of the 1930s, advocated active management of the economy to promote employment. Among the economic luminaries who served in the Kennedy White House were future Nobel laureates James Tobin, Kenneth Arrow, and Robert Solow. Walter

Heller, a well-regarded economist from the University of Minnesota, led the economic team as chair of the president's Council of Economic Advisers (CEA).

Keynes had advocated active use of fiscal policy to fight unemployment. The new president, following his advisers' recommendations, proposed a wide-ranging tax cut to stimulate consumer and business spending. Kennedy was assassinated before his proposal could become law, but his successor, Lyndon B. Johnson, saw the tax cut through in 1964.

The tax cut was widely seen as a success. It helped bring down unemployment, which had peaked at 7.1 percent in mid-1961, early in Kennedy's term, to 4.0 percent by the end of 1965.* From a macroeconomic policy perspective, it would have been a logical moment to ease up on the accelerator, but foreign policy and social goals took priority over economic stability. Under Johnson, fiscal policy revved up further to accommodate both increased spending on the Vietnam War and new spending for the president's ambitious Great Society programs—a case of choosing both guns and butter. American troops deployed in Vietnam rose from 23,000 in 1964 to 184,000 in 1965, and to more than a half million by 1968.[4] Meanwhile, Johnson announced his War on Poverty in January 1964, and both Medicare and Medicaid were introduced in 1965, committing the government to pay medical costs for retired and low-income Americans. Many Great Society programs would ultimately have important benefits, including a significant reduction in poverty rates among over-65 Americans, but they also had the effect of adding further to government spending.

As the economy heated up and unemployment fell (to about 3.5 percent in 1968–69), wages and prices began to accelerate, much as simple Phillips-curve reasoning would have predicted. Health care provides an example: With the advent of Medicare and Medicaid boosting the demand for medical services, the rate of increase in the price of health care jumped

---

* Both Keynesians, who focused on the demand-side effects of the tax cut, and supply-siders, who believe that lower marginal tax rates induce more economic activity, have claimed credit for this success. Because the tax cut was followed by higher inflation, a sign of strong demand, the Keynesians probably have the better case.

from about 4 percent in 1965 to about 9 percent in 1966, led by increases in physicians' fees.[5] Meanwhile, nominal defense spending rose 44 percent between 1965 and 1968, leading military contractors to ramp up production and employment. The economywide inflationary impact might have been mitigated if higher taxes had paid for at least some of the increased spending, thereby reducing private-sector purchasing power. But the war was unpopular, and Johnson resisted any significant tax increase for fear that it would further diminish public support. (The president did approve, in 1968, a one-year 10 percent surcharge on personal and corporate income taxes, but—probably because it was understood to be a purely temporary measure—it did little to slow private spending.)

Fiscal policy, through tax increases or spending cuts, is not the only tool that can cool an overheating economy. Monetary policy can too. In the 1960s, a tighter monetary policy—in the form of higher interest rates— might have reduced housing construction, capital investment, and other private-sector spending by enough to compensate for the expansion in federal spending. However, for reasons we will explore shortly, the Fed did not tighten monetary policy sufficiently or persistently enough to offset the building inflationary forces.

Richard Nixon, Johnson's successor in 1968, recognized the growing inflation problem but, like his predecessor, wanted to avoid the political costs of tighter fiscal or monetary policies, especially after the economy suffered a mild recession in 1970. The economist Ray Fair would a few years later document the powerful effect of economic growth on presidential election outcomes, but Nixon understood this connection intuitively without having to consult an econometric model.[6]

Was there a way to deal with rising inflation—without slowing the economy? With an eye on the approaching 1972 election, Nixon, after some initial reluctance, used authority provided by Congress in 1970 and approved direct controls on wages and prices. The program began on August 15, 1971, with a ninety-day freeze, known as Phase I. The freeze was followed by evolving rules for wage- and price-setters. Phase II of the program, which lasted until January 1973, limited most wage increases to

5.5 percent and required most price increases to be justified to a Price Commission. Phase III was intended to be a transitional stage between controls and voluntary wage-price restraint, but after a sharp increase in food and fuel prices boosted inflation again, the administration ordered a second freeze in June 1973, this time for sixty days. The second freeze was followed by Phase IV, a period of selective decontrol of some prices. Wage-price controls finally expired in April 1974.[7]

The controls were initially popular. They were seen as a sign that the government was finally taking strong action on inflation. But they would ultimately be a costly failure. In a market economy, wages and prices provide crucial information, coordinating the decisions of workers, producers, and consumers. A high relative price for a commodity, for example, incentivizes producers to produce more and consumers to use less of that good. By short-circuiting this coordination mechanism, wage-price controls can be highly disruptive. Following the imposition of Nixon's controls, shortages developed for consumer goods and for critical inputs to production. For example, farmers, trapped between rising prices for feed (set, uncontrolled, in world markets) and limits on the retail prices of beef and poultry, slaughtered their herds and flocks rather than raising them at a loss. Meanwhile, supermarket shelves were empty. Evasion of the controls became increasingly common. Firms found ways around the rules or lobbied for exceptions.

Nor did the controls have a lasting effect on inflation, which fell modestly in 1971 and 1972 but then rose again as the controls were lifted. The controls, as applied, were analogous to dealing with an overheating engine by disabling its temperature gauge. To have had any chance to work, the controls would have to have been accompanied by measures to cool overall demand, such as reduced government spending or tighter monetary policy. Wartime price controls, for example, are usually accompanied by rationing (you need a ration ticket to buy certain goods) and measures to reduce consumer purchasing power (higher taxes, sales of war bonds). In wartime, compliance inspired by patriotism may also help. But, with the 1972 election campaign already in progress, no action was taken to limit aggregate demand. To the contrary, both fiscal and monetary policy were expansionary in the run-up to the election, focused on bringing down unemployment.

Nixon's strategy succeeded in one respect: He was resoundingly reelected. But inflation grew worse as the 1970s progressed. Beyond the inflation rebound after the expiration of controls, two key developments drove the rate yet higher: oil prices and human psychology.

In October 1973, in response to the Yom Kippur War between Israel and its neighbors, Arab oil producers imposed an embargo on exports. From 1972 to 1975, the price of oil more than quadrupled.[8] Higher prices for oil imports led to higher prices for gasoline and heating fuel. But higher oil prices also pushed up the prices of goods and services whose production required a lot of energy. For example, taxis and trucking services added surcharges to help cover their extra fuel costs.

Some wage-price controls remained at the time of the embargo, and, in November 1973, the administration placed additional controls on selected petroleum-related prices. Predictably, the price ceilings led to shortages, among them the infamous gas lines, which (along with disco and Watergate) came to symbolize the era. In 1974 many drivers could buy gas only on odd or even days of the month, depending on the last digit of their license plate. Fistfights sometimes erupted among frustrated drivers waiting for their turn at the pump. World oil prices remained high during the next few years, despite a significant slowdown in global growth that dampened demand in the mid-1970s. In 1979, the Iranian revolution and the overthrow of the Shah disrupted supplies again, leading to a more-than-doubling of oil prices and yet another inflation surge.

Meanwhile, in an even more worrisome development, a new inflation psychology took hold. In the 1950s and early 1960s inflation had been so low that people could safely ignore it in their everyday decision-making. But as inflation ratcheted higher and government attempts to contain it proved inadequate or even counterproductive, people came to see high and volatile inflation as the new normal. Workers routinely began to demand compensation for inflation in wage negotiations, often informally but in some cases through automatic-indexing mechanisms (COLAs, or cost-of-living adjustments), which proliferated in the 1970s. Employers had little incentive to resist wage increases, focusing instead on passing their rising costs on to consumers. In a self-reinforcing loop, higher inflation expectations gave inflation new momentum, which in turn ratified those expectations. The term "wage-price spiral" entered the popular lexicon.

Unstable inflation expectations also reinforced the effects of oil price shocks. A one-time increase in the price of oil or another critical commodity, on its own, creates only a temporary boost in inflation. However, if an initial inflation surge causes people to infer that inflation will be persistently higher, that expectation can become self-confirming, as workers and firms begin to incorporate expectations of continuing price increases into their own wage and price demands. That pattern was evident during the 1970s.

Expectations of rapid inflation are a problem, but perhaps even worse is uncertainty about inflation. In principle at least, adjusting to, say, an 8 percent inflation rate—if it were truly stable and predictable—might not be so difficult. Wages and prices set by individual firms could adjust smoothly at a rate that took into account the 8 percent increase in overall prices, and interest rates could include an 8 percent premium to compensate investors and lenders for the anticipated loss in the purchasing power of their investments.

In practice, people may be confused by even relatively stable inflation, particularly over long time horizons, as when planning for retirement. But in any case, when inflation is high it is also typically *not* stable, but volatile and hard to predict. That was certainly the case during the Great Inflation. Over one stretch in the 1970s, CPI inflation swung wildly from 3.4 percent in 1972, to 12.3 percent in 1974, to 4.9 percent in 1976, then back up to 9.0 percent in 1978. Hard-to-predict inflation creates confusion and economic risk. People become unsure about the future buying power of their wages or savings. Lower-income households are particularly vulnerable, because they keep much of any savings they have in cash or checking accounts and are less able to protect themselves against price changes. The economic insecurity and uncertainty generated by high inflation help

FIGURE 1.1.   INFLATION, 1950–1990

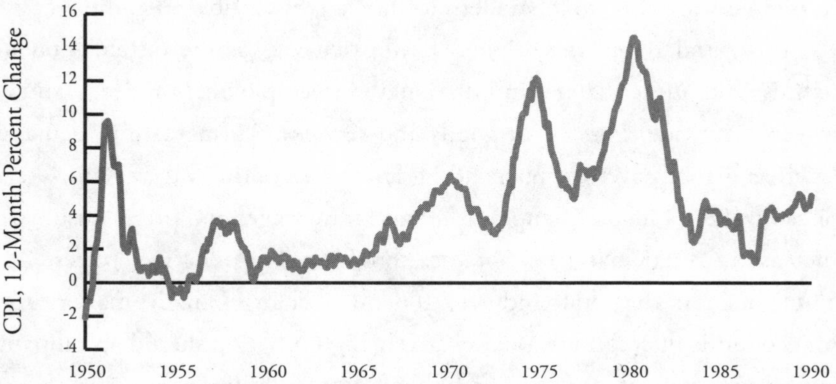

Inflation, stable in the 1950s and early 1960s, rose in the late 1960s and was high in the 1970s. It was finally brought under control in the 1980s. Source: Bureau of Labor Statistics and FRED.

explain why, by the late 1970s, so many people saw inflation as a devastating problem.

The combination of oil price shocks and destabilized inflation expectations was powerful. Inflation seemed increasingly out of control, reaching 13.3 percent in 1979 and 12.5 percent in 1980. Along with the 12.3 percent rate in 1974, these were the highest rates since 1946.

THE EVOLVING PHILLIPS CURVE

The inflation of the 1970s would have puzzled an economist familiar only with the original, 1958-vintage Phillips curve, which would have predicted high inflation only in combination with extremely low unemployment rates. However, unemployment, on average, was not particularly low in the 1970s, and indeed it rose as high as 9 percent after the sharp 1973–75 recession. The distressing combination of high inflation and stagnating economic growth was dubbed *stagflation*. By the mid-1970s the Phillips curve, at least as it was understood at the time, appeared to have broken down.

Critically, however, economists of the period showed that the core of the Phillips curve idea could be saved, and recast the theory of inflation into something close to its modern form, via two sensible amendments.

First, underlying the original Phillips curve was the (often implicit) premise that most changes in inflation and unemployment reflect changes in economywide *demand* for goods and services. An increase in demand (such as higher government spending for the Vietnam War and the Great Society) should increase employment and raise wages and prices, just as an increase in the demand for potatoes should raise production, prices, and employment in the potato industry. If demand changes are the main reason for economic fluctuations, then relatively high inflation should accompany low unemployment, as predicted by the original Phillips curve.

However, sometimes the economy experiences shocks to supply rather than demand, the sharp increases in oil prices in 1973–74 and 1979 being classic examples. Rising oil prices in the 1970s added to inflation by increasing the costs of producing and transporting many goods and services. Just as a blight that kills potatoes reduces output and employment in the potato industry while raising potato prices, a macroeconomic supply shock is stagflationary, raising both inflation and unemployment. For the Phillips curve to explain the data, therefore, it's necessary to separate inflation caused by supply shocks from inflation arising from demand shocks. Economists developed methods to make this distinction.

A rough-and-ready approach is to focus on *core inflation*, a measure of inflation that excludes energy and food prices, which are volatile and particularly subject to supply disturbances. Because it excludes some important sources of supply shocks, core inflation may be a better indicator of how increases and decreases in demand are influencing the inflation rate. The behavior of core inflation during the 1970s suggests that, even as supply-side shocks became more prominent, inflation continued to respond to demand as well. For example, core inflation declined significantly after the recessions of 1969–70, 1973–75, and 1980, suggesting that slower growth and higher unemployment still had the ability to slow the rate of price increases, despite the influence of supply factors.

Besides adding supply shocks, the second amendment to the traditional

Phillips curve was to allow an explicit role for inflation expectations. Presciently, future Nobel laureates Milton Friedman and Edmund Phelps had, in the late 1960s, each anticipated the possibility of the self-reinforcing inflation psychology that prevailed in the 1970s. Friedman, in his December 1967 presidential address to the American Economic Association, predicted that the traditional Phillips-curve relationship between inflation and unemployment would become unstable if inflation expectations rose, as they were bound to do if actual inflation remained high.[9] If people expect inflation to rise, Friedman argued, they will try to protect their purchasing power by increasing their demands for wage and price rises roughly in proportion. Thus, a 1 percent increase in the rate of inflation expected by households and firms should lead over time to a 1 percent higher rate of actual inflation. Phelps made similar points in a 1968 paper.[10] The 1970s would demonstrate the relevance of the Friedman-Phelps theory.

What causes people's inflation expectations to change? Debates about the determinants of inflation expectations and about how central banks can affect those expectations have been central to the analysis and practice of monetary policy since at least the 1960s, if not earlier. However, no one doubts that people learn from experience, so it's hardly surprising that the government's failure to control inflation in the late 1960s and early 1970s dashed expectations that inflation would remain low. Higher inflation expectations in turn helped push up actual inflation, in what would become a vicious circle. Restabilizing inflation and inflation expectations at a reasonably low level would prove to be a major challenge.

As modified by the experience of the 1970s and the insights of Friedman, Phelps, and others, the Phillips curve remains a centerpiece of economists' thinking about inflation today. To summarize, in its contemporary form, the Phillips curve makes three assertions:[11]

First, economic expansion, when driven by increases in demand not matched by increases in supply, will ultimately lead to higher inflation, in both wages and prices. This is the message of the original 1958 Phillips curve and of the research that followed Phillips's paper.

Second, supply shocks are stagflationary, raising inflation but lowering output and employment, at least for a time. This was the experience following the oil price shocks of the 1970s.

Third, holding constant the level of unemployment and the effects of supply shocks, increases in the inflation expectations of households and firms ultimately raise the actual inflation rate roughly one for one. Higher inflation can in turn justify the higher level of inflation expectations, in what can become a vicious circle.

The updated version of the Phillips curve offers a reasonably good explanation of America's Great Inflation. Fiscal policy—tax cuts, war spending, and social spending—was easy for too long under Presidents Kennedy and Johnson, leading to overheating and the beginning of an inflation problem. President Nixon continued stimulating demand, hoping to cool inflation through direct controls on wages and prices, but was unsuccessful. Nixon's controls led to shortages and misallocated resources, and inflation still returned as the controls were lifted. Global oil price increases and other adverse supply shocks worsened the Phillips curve trade-off, pushing the economy into stagflation. And, increasingly, inflation psychology took hold, leading to a self-perpetuating spiral of higher inflation and higher inflation expectations.

Though a modernized version of the Phillips curve helps explain the Great Inflation, the question remains: Where was the Federal Reserve? Why did the Fed let inflation get out of control, and, once that happened, why didn't it do more to stop the inflationary cycle? The short answer is that a brew of raw politics and flawed views of the inflation process prompted Fed leaders to hold back at crucial moments, avoiding the painful steps that would have brought inflation under control.

WILLIAM MCCHESNEY MARTIN, LYNDON B. JOHNSON, AND THE BEGINNINGS OF THE GREAT INFLATION

As is the case today, Fed chairs in the 1960s and 1970s heavily influenced the institution's policies. During a twenty-seven-year period that included both the onset and the peak of the Great Inflation, just two individuals led the Fed: William McChesney Martin Jr. (chair from 1951 to 1970) and Arthur Burns (chair from 1970 to 1978). To see why the Fed failed to contain the Great Inflation, we have to understand the ideas and political forces that shaped the decisions of these two men.

Martin Jr., the longest-tenured Fed chair in history, served under five presidents. He had Federal Reserve bloodlines. His father, William McChesney Martin Sr., helped write the law that created the Fed and later served as president of the Federal Reserve Bank of St. Louis. Martin Jr. studied English and Latin at Yale, and seriously considered becoming a Presbyterian minister—he would always abstain from smoking, drinking, or gambling. But he also retained his father's interest in business and finance. His first job was working for his father as a bank examiner at the St. Louis Fed.[12] His subsequent career included time both as a financier and a public servant. In 1938, at age 31, he became president of the New York Stock Exchange, where he worked to restore confidence in the stock market. He later served as head of the Export-Import Bank and as an assistant secretary in the Treasury Department.

While at the Treasury, Martin became a principal negotiator in the landmark 1951 Treasury-Federal Reserve Accord, taking over the negotiations when Treasury Secretary John Snyder was hospitalized for a cataract operation. Since 1942, at the Treasury's request, the Fed had capped both short- and long-term interest rates to reduce the government's cost of servicing war debts. A burst of inflation that followed the end of wartime controls and rationing was short lived. Nevertheless, over the next few years the Fed became increasingly concerned that keeping interest rates pegged at low levels would overstimulate the economy. It consequently sought to end the peg.

With a new war heating up in Korea, the White House and Treasury resisted the Fed's proposed change in its policy. A remarkable public battle ensued, including an episode in which President Truman summoned the entire Federal Open Market Committee to the White House for a lecture. Following that meeting, Truman released a statement that claimed the

FOMC had agreed to maintain the peg. However, the FOMC had made no such agreement, and Marriner Eccles—the former chair, then serving as a Board member—leaked a contradictory account to the press. With the Fed intransigent and with little support forthcoming from Congress or the media, the administration conceded.[13] The subsequent Accord with the Treasury allowed the Fed to phase out the peg, freeing it to set interest rates as needed for economic stabilization, including inflation control.*[14]

The change in the Fed's role implied by the Accord was consistent with the growing political and intellectual consensus of the time, which—reflecting fears of a new Depression after the war and the influence of Keynesian thinking—held that government policies should actively seek to stabilize the economy, including inflation, rather than accepting booms and recessions as natural and inevitable. Legislatively, the Employment Act of 1946 reflected this view. It required the federal government to use all practicable means to achieve "maximum employment, production and purchasing power." Indeed, Congress's desire to enlist the Federal Reserve in the quest for a stronger, more stable economy likely strengthened the Fed's hand in its dispute with the Treasury.[15] From the Fed's perspective, the Accord was a turning point in its drive for greater monetary policy independence, meaning in this case the freedom to set policy to advance broad economic goals rather than serving the Treasury's financing needs.

Shortly after the Accord was reached, Truman appointed Martin to replace the outgoing Fed chair, Thomas McCabe, who had resigned because—following the sometimes-bitter Treasury-Fed dispute—he believed he could no longer work with the administration. Truman hoped that Martin, given his previous role at the Treasury, would serve the president's political ends at the Fed by keeping monetary policy easy. But Martin would prove to be a straight shooter who refused to accept White

---

* The brief statement released by the two parties was actually rather vague, stating only that the Treasury and the Fed "had reached full accord with respect to debt-management and monetary policies to be pursued . . . to assure the successful financing of the Government's requirements and, at the same time, to minimize monetization of the public debt." The Fed interpreted the last phrase as releasing it from the obligation to peg rates on Treasury securities.

House instruction at the expense of the Fed's newly won policy freedom. (Truman, in a later chance encounter with Martin, said only one word: "Traitor.")[16] Paul Volcker, who served as Fed chair in the 1980s and was no pushover himself, would later write that Martin, "for all his friendly manner and personal modesty, had an iron backbone when it came to policy and the defense of Federal Reserve independence."[17] That backbone would be tested.

Martin did not identify strongly with any particular school of economic thought. His basic approach was simple: He believed that monetary policy should lean against the business cycle, working to counter both recessions and unsustainable economic booms and avoiding inflationary excesses.[18] In practice, that meant raising interest rates during expansions, before inflation could become a problem, while allowing rates to fall during recessions or when growth slowed. He famously likened the Federal Reserve to a chaperone who orders "the punch bowl removed just when the party was really warming up."[19] Martin believed low inflation promoted healthy economic development, at least in the longer term, rather than being a trade-off against growth and employment: "Price stability is essential to sustainable growth," he said in 1957.[20]

In managing monetary policy to promote economic stability and low inflation, rather than—as in earlier eras—to maintain the dollar's value in gold, counter speculative excesses, or facilitate the financing of government debt, Martin helped create the template for modern central banking. Economic historians Christina Romer and David Romer have argued that Martin's monetary policy in the 1950s, in its focus on leaning against cyclical winds and pre-empting inflationary pressures when necessary, was more similar to the policies of the 1980s and 1990s than to the policies of the late 1960s or 1970s.[21] No doubt it helped that President Eisenhower, elected in 1952, was also persuaded of the importance of keeping inflation low and did not resist Martin's anti-inflationary rate increases—punch-bowl removals—during that decade.

During the Kennedy administration the political and policy environment changed markedly, and even more so once Johnson took office after

Kennedy's assassination. Before 1960, the Employment Act of 1946, which held the government responsible for achieving "maximum employment," had been mostly aspirational. In contrast, the Kennedy administration, particularly the White House's Council of Economic Advisers—an agency itself created by the Employment Act—sought to make the act operational, by quantitatively defining maximum employment. Attaching a number to maximum employment—or full employment, the phrase that became more common—would provide an explicit target for economic policy and thus a benchmark for policy success.[22]

But then, as now, defining full employment was more art than science. In 1962, using Phillips-curve reasoning, Arthur Okun, an influential economist who advised both Kennedy and Johnson, defined full employment as the highest level of employment achievable "without inflation pressure."[23] Because, outside of recessions, the unemployment rate had often been at or below 4 percent during the 1950s, a period without high inflation, CEA economists estimated that, in practice, full employment corresponded to an unemployment rate of about 4 percent. This estimate became widely accepted by policymakers and by economists generally.[*]

The actual unemployment rate had exceeded 7 percent shortly after Kennedy's inauguration and remained around 5.5 percent at the end of 1962, suggesting that considerable slack remained in the labor market. Put another way, the country was seen to be suffering an *output gap*, a shortfall in production relative to what could be produced at full employment. Okun estimated that each percentage point increase in unemployment corresponded to about a 3 percent loss in output, a rule of thumb that became known as *Okun's Law*.[24] The CEA argued that eliminating the output gap should be a central goal of policy; and that this could be done without creating inflation pressures, so long as unemployment was near 4 percent.

Full or maximum employment as defined by Okun, and the

---

[*] Taken literally, the unemployment rate corresponding to full employment might be thought to be zero, but economists recognized that—even in the strongest of labor markets—there will always be some unemployment, as people switch jobs, move between jobs and other activities such as schooling, or lack the skills they need to qualify for available jobs.

unemployment rate that signals full employment, remain important concepts in contemporary macroeconomics. Today, economists typically refer to the lowest unemployment rate consistent with stable inflation as the *natural rate of unemployment*—sometimes abbreviated as u*, pronounced u-star. The term "natural rate" is a bit misleading since it suggests that u* is unchanging. In fact, u* can vary over time—due to changes in the demographic makeup of the labor force or the structure of the economy, for example. And lowering u*, say through policies that improve skills or the matching of employers and workers, can lead to better labor market outcomes. Still, the term "natural rate" has been widely adopted.

Although the natural rate concept has not much changed since the 1960s, experience has shown that, in practice, estimates of u* may be quite uncertain, implying the need for great care when using them in policymaking. This uncertainty is relevant to our story because—despite the wide acceptance of the CEA's 4 percent estimate of the natural rate of unemployment during the 1960s and 1970s—in retrospect, the unemployment rate that could be sustained "without inflation pressure," in Okun's phrase, proved to be significantly higher than 4 percent at the time, a fact that would have profound implications. The Congressional Budget Office (CBO), which constructs retrospective estimates of potential output and the corresponding natural rate of unemployment, today estimates that u* was actually in the vicinity of 5.5 percent in the 1960s and 6 percent during the 1970s.* If the modern estimates—made with the benefit of hindsight—are correct, then the output gap in the '60s and '70s was not only much smaller than policymakers at the time believed, it was often negative, with output well above the economy's sustainable potential. At a minimum, it's clear that policymakers of that period were too confident of their estimate of u*, sticking with it even as inflation increased.[25]

---

* According to the CBO, the rise in u* in the late 1960s and 1970s relative to the 1950s reflected shifting demographics of the labor force and structural changes in the economy that increased the time needed to match unemployed workers with jobs. See Brauer (2007). Orphanides (2003) argues that 1970s policymakers did not recognize the slowing of productivity growth in that decade in a timely way and thus overestimated the economy's potential output.

Following the Keynesian consensus at the time that fiscal policy should take the lead in stabilizing the economy, a position supported by the fact that massive wartime spending had decisively ended the Great Depression, the Kennedy administration had focused on tax cuts—a fiscal measure—rather than monetary policy to help close the perceived output gap. However, the administration presumed, backed by many in Congress, that the Fed would support the government's efforts to stimulate growth. Starting in 1961, regular meetings began of a group dubbed the Quadriad, which included the Fed chair, the Treasury secretary, the White House budget director, the CEA chair, and sometimes the president.[26] Its purpose was to coordinate economic policies, which the White House interpreted as keeping the Fed on board. Presidents Kennedy and Johnson also appointed to the Fed's Board of Governors people sympathetic to their expansionist view, moves which further hemmed in Martin.

Martin was skeptical of the new Keynesian orthodoxy, seeing it as overoptimistic about what policy could achieve in practice, but inflation remained modest during the early 1960s. Nevertheless, in May 1965, in the wake of the Kennedy-Johnson tax cut and the growing commitment of troops to Vietnam, Martin publicly expressed concern about the possible inflationary consequences of "perpetual deficits and easy money."[27] In December 1965, with the unemployment rate at the critical level of 4 percent—full employment, even by the White House's estimates—Martin won the support of his Board, on a 4–3 vote, to take a very public preemptive action against inflation by announcing a half-percentage-point increase in the Fed's discount rate.* As in the 1950s, Martin saw his role as taking away the punch bowl.

President Johnson reacted furiously. Following the Fed's decision, the president summoned Martin to his Texas ranch and dressed him down. "Martin, my boys are dying in Vietnam, and you won't print the money I

---

* The Fed had allowed the federal funds rate to rise over 1965, but at the time changes in the Fed's funds rate target were not publicly announced, as discount rate changes were. The discount rate was thus often used to signal changes in the stance of monetary policy.

need," Johnson reportedly said.[28] Further pressure came from Democrats in Congress, who argued that Fed tightening would unnecessarily slow job creation. Indeed, some legislators argued that 4 percent unemployment should be viewed as the maximum, rather than the minimum, level that policymakers should accept.

Martin, seeking a compromise, consulted with Johnson's CEA.[29] The economy was in an inflationary danger zone, he believed. If Congress and the administration would tighten fiscal policy, slowing the overheated economy and limiting inflation pressures, Martin suggested, a restrictive monetary policy might not be needed. The CEA's members were open to Martin's arguments and agreed that, if tightening was necessary, it would be preferable for fiscal policy to take the lead. However, the president was unwilling to back legislation that increased taxes or reduced spending.

Accordingly, the Fed continued rate increases in 1966 and, using its influence as a regulator, pressed banks to tighten lending standards. The results were more dramatic than Martin had expected. The economy slowed almost immediately—particularly the housing market, which is especially sensitive to interest rates and the availability of credit. The possibility of a broader recession sounded alarm bells at the Fed and the White House. In response to assurances from the CEA that Johnson would ask Congress for a tax increase to help cool inflation risks, Martin backed off, reversing the Fed's earlier tightening. However, seeing a rise in taxes as a political loser, Johnson failed to follow through.

In 1967 the growth scare abated and inflation worries increased, renewing the game of chicken between the Fed and the White House. In the fall Martin's Fed began to tighten again. The White House in turn again agreed to pursue a tax increase. The political environment in 1968—a year that included the assassinations of Martin Luther King Jr. and Robert F. Kennedy, intense protests and civil disorder, as well as a presidential election—was not conducive to congressional compromise. Still, with concerns about inflation and the stability of the dollar rising, in June the president signed a bill that included a temporary 10 percent income-tax surcharge. Assuming that the surcharge would slow the economy, Martin's Fed once again paused its tightening campaign, cutting the discount rate in August.

This would prove to be a miscalculation. Although the surcharge led to a short-lived government budget surplus, it restrained overall demand by much less than either the Fed or the CEA expected. Knowing that the tax increase was temporary, most people and businesses paid the increase out of their savings and maintained their spending. By the end of 1968, the unemployment rate had fallen to 3.4 percent and inflation was rising further. Reversing itself once more, the Fed swung back to tightening, but Martin's time at the Fed was coming to an end. As his term wound down, in January 1970, Martin called the other governors to the Board library and told them, "I've been a failure."[30] Inflation in 1969 came in just under 6 percent.

Did Martin fail? The Great Inflation did begin on his watch, in part because the Fed—in the hope that a more-restrictive fiscal policy would do the heavy lifting—was inconsistent and late in raising interest rates. However, overall, Martin was an unwilling co-conspirator who, under intense political pressure, resisted the overexpansion of the economy when he could. The inflation of the latter half of the 1960s was mostly the result of guns-and-butter fiscal policies and, as Martin had worried, overoptimism about the natural unemployment rate and the ability of the new Keynesian policies to fine-tune the economy.

The 1970s were a different story. Under Martin's successor, Arthur Burns, the Fed made only limited efforts to maintain policy independence and, for doctrinal as well as political reasons, enabled a decade of high and volatile inflation.

2

BURNS AND VOLCKER

IN NOVEMBER 1969 PRESIDENT RICHARD NIXON appointed Arthur Burns
to succeed Martin as Fed chair, effective in February 1970. Burns (born
Burnseig, in 1904) emigrated with his parents from Galicia (Austrian
Poland) to the United States as a boy.* Tweedy and pipe-smoking, Burns—
a professor at Columbia University, where a later Fed chair, Alan Greenspan, was one of his students—looked like the distinguished academic
economist that he was. As a young scholar, Burns published some of the
earliest and most influential empirical analyses of booms and recessions,
together with economist Wesley C. Mitchell, his mentor at Columbia. The
index of leading economic indicators, still in use, originates from Burns's
and Mitchell's historical studies of business cycles, as do the principles for
dating the beginnings and ends of recessions. Burns had also been the president of the American Economic Association and led the National Bureau
of Economic Research, which remains a leading center for research on a
wide range of economic topics.

Burns was not just an ivory-tower academic, however. He served
on many business boards and was a trusted adviser in the Eisenhower

---

* My paternal grandparents, Jonas and Lina Bernanke, also were born in that region and immigrated
to the United States in 1921.

administration, heading the Council of Economic Advisers. He prided himself on his forecasting skills, honed by his long immersion in the economic data. Indeed, his accurate forecasting as an Eisenhower adviser helped him gain the confidence of Nixon, Eisenhower's vice president. And, like Martin, Burns frequently warned of potential damage from too-high inflation. Burns was particularly concerned about the effects of inflation on business confidence, which he believed to be a driving force of the business cycle.[1] Yet, despite Burns's professional qualifications and frequently stated aversion to inflation, as chair he proved reluctant to tighten monetary policy enough to control inflation.

ARTHUR BURNS AND THE "ANGUISH OF CENTRAL BANKING"

Burns's approach became apparent soon after he took office. The economy was slowing—a mild recession occurred in 1970, partly because of Martin's tightening of monetary policy the previous year—but inflation remained a significant concern, with prices rising 5.6 percent over the year. Burns, prioritizing near-term growth, responded by easing monetary policy. The federal funds rate, at 9 percent when Burns took the reins at the Fed, fell to about 5 percent by the fall of 1972. Lower rates provided support for the economic recovery—the unemployment rate fell from a peak of about 6 percent in mid-1971 to less than 5 percent in late 1973—but did nothing to help limit inflation, which rose after the Nixon wage and price controls were lifted. Why did Burns accept this trade-off?

Politics was certainly part of the story. Like Martin before him, Burns was pressured by the president, in this case Nixon—the man who appointed him and would reappoint him in 1973. Burns had served as Nixon's economic adviser during the 1968 presidential campaign and became an important player in the White House after the election. Once Burns was installed at the Fed, Nixon had no reservations about using their relationship to his political advantage. With unemployment having risen during the 1970 recession, the president wanted a strong economy going into the 1972 election. White House tapes reveal Nixon appealing to Burns's personal and party loyalties, pushing him to keep monetary policy easy in the run-up to the vote, with Treasury Secretary George Shultz reinforcing the message.

I know of no hard evidence that Burns explicitly agreed to Nixon's demands, but monetary policy was eased before the election, as was fiscal policy. In his diary, Burns acknowledged Nixon's arm-twisting: "I am convinced that the President will do anything to be re-elected," he wrote. "The harassing of the Fed by the President and his pusillanimous staff will continue and may even intensify." He added an assertion of independence: "Fortunately, although I am no longer sure whether the President fully knows this, I am still his best friend. By standing firm, I will serve the economy—and thereby also the President—best." Still, the recordings do reveal that Burns called the president in advance of Fed decisions and discussed policy considerations with him to an extent that would be considered extremely inappropriate today.[2] Burns's diary also shows him acting more like a member of the administration—plotting political strategy in White House meetings and discussing policy initiatives unrelated to Fed responsibilities—than the head of an independent central bank.[3]

That said, Nixon's machinations do not fully explain Burns's reluctance to tackle inflation, particularly since Burns's reticence continued after Nixon resigned in 1974. As argued by economic historian Robert Hetzel and others, Burns's own views about the causes of inflation and the proper role of monetary policy would likely have inclined him toward a more passive approach, even without Nixon's influence.[4]

Although he did not identify as a Keynesian, Burns shared the view of many Keynesians of the time that the U.S. economy had become more disposed to inflation, for reasons unrelated to monetary policy. This greater tendency to inflation, in Burns's view, reflected the growing ability of large corporations and labor unions to insulate themselves from market forces, a power they used to push up prices and wages at will. The government's commitment to maintain full employment—which Burns supported—increased the market power of these actors further by reducing the painful discipline of periodic recessions.

Because he saw inflation as driven primarily by "cost-push" forces (like the power of corporations and unions to raise prices and wages) rather than by "demand-pull" pressures (like rising government and consumer spending), Burns viewed monetary policy, which operates primarily by slowing demand growth, as a costly and inefficient way to bring down inflation. He argued that monetary policy alone could end inflation only by causing a recession deep enough that powerful wage- and price-setters would have no choice but to pull back. In the process, he argued, many workers would lose their jobs, and smaller firms lacking market power would be hit especially hard. Moreover, Burns believed, the effects of restrictive monetary policy would fall unevenly, putting unfair burdens on certain sectors of the economy. Tight money would crush interest-sensitive construction and real estate, for example, while having much less effect on consumer spending or capital investments by large corporations.

Burns's cost-push theory of inflation led him to believe that government-imposed controls, which directly limited the ability of unions and firms to raise wages and prices, were a less costly way to stop inflation than tight monetary policy, or tight fiscal policy for that matter. He was accordingly a strong early advocate of wage-price controls, or what were termed at the time incomes policies.[5] Indeed, it is unlikely that Nixon would have put the controls in place without Burns's advice and encouragement. Thus, while Nixon influenced Burns, Burns also influenced Nixon. Burns also rejected the idea that wage-price controls must be paired with restraints on overall spending. He saw instead a division of labor: Controls would constrain the behavior of wage- and price-setters, which would free monetary and fiscal policy to support growth and employment. Importantly, Burns's cost-push theory of inflation also explains how he could observe sustained increases in inflation without concluding that the economy was operating above its potential, and that monetary and fiscal policy were accordingly too expansionary.

Burns's view that inflation was largely caused by nonmonetary factors was only reinforced by the 1973 oil price shock and the resulting inflation spike. After all, the jump in oil prices looked largely to be the result of geopolitics and global economic conditions, not easy money or an over-heated domestic economy in the United States. Burns's preferred response to this new bout of inflation was to reimpose comprehensive wage-price controls, but the failure of the earlier rounds of controls to end inflation had discredited them in the minds of most Americans. In an effort to con-tain the rise in inflation, the Fed did begin a sequence of rate increases in 1973, but these were largely reversed when the economy fell into recession. This "stop-go" pattern—tightening policy when inflation surged but then easing as soon as unemployment began to rise—proved ineffectual and allowed inflation and inflation expectations to ratchet up.

Burns recognized that the state of the economy in the stagflationary 1970s was far from satisfactory. He believed that inflation was costly and destabilizing, but then, so was unemployment. He did not think that the public would tolerate unemployment high enough to fully control infla-tion using monetary policy alone, or that it was the Fed's place to make that decision. That was certainly the message that Burns was getting from Congress. In 1976, even though the Fed was easing and the economy was in recovery, Senator Hubert Humphrey (D-Minnesota) and his allies com-plained that the central bank was not doing enough to boost employment. Humphrey argued for explicit employment goals for the government—including governmental job guarantees if necessary—and a greater role for the president in determining monetary policy. His proposals did not pass, but Humphrey, with his House colleague Augustus Hawkins (D-California), continued to push for legislation.

An important consequence of the ongoing legislative debate was the passage, in 1977, of amendments to the Federal Reserve Act that instructed the Fed to manage monetary policy so as to pursue "stable prices, maximum employment, and moderate long-term interest rates." Since stable prices and maximum employment normally result in moderate long-term interest rates, the third objective is usually ignored as redundant, and Fed leaders ever since have frequently referred to the institution's dual mandate, to promote stable prices and maximum employment. The dual mandate was itself a compromise, with Democrats—who held majorities in both the House and Senate throughout the 1970s—pushing for greater emphasis on employment and Republicans insisting that price stability be given equal status.

The logic of the Phillips curve implies that, at times, monetary policymakers will have to make trade-offs between inflation and unemployment. The 1977 law did not say specifically how the two goals should be weighed in policy decisions. Through the decades, borrowing from the language of diplomacy, Fed policymakers putting greater weight on the employment mandate have been called *doves* and policymakers more focused on inflation have been called *hawks*. Of course, the definitions are fluid, with policymakers sometimes shifting from hawk to dove and back again, depending on economic conditions.

Although Senator Humphrey died in January 1978, congressional debate on his proposals continued. Later that year Congress passed, and President Carter signed, the Full Employment and Balanced Growth Act, better known as the Humphrey-Hawkins Act. The 1978 Act (which applied to the entire government, not just the Fed) set ambitious goals for employment, including that the unemployment rate for people 20 years or older should not exceed 3 percent—an even lower number than the 4 percent full-employment benchmark of the Kennedy CEA. Goals were also set for inflation, including bringing inflation down to zero within a decade, but the bill gave precedence to the employment goal.[6] The law also required that the Federal Reserve Board submit a semiannual monetary policy report to Congress, describing the Fed's progress toward the central bank's mandated goals.[*] Burns certainly knew that the quantitative goals of the Humphrey-Hawkins Act were infeasible, at least within any reasonable time, but likely he would have seen the bill, together with the approval of the dual mandate the previous year, as confirmation that Congress would not condone an approach to inflation control that involved significant increases in unemployment.

---

[*] The chair's testimony to the Fed's House and Senate oversight committees that accompanies this report is still known as the Humphrey-Hawkins testimony.

In short, Burns's motivations during the Great Inflation were complex. He was influenced by politics, possibly in the narrow sense of succumbing to pressure from President Nixon and certainly in the broader sense that he believed that the country would not tolerate monetary policies that created high unemployment. But Burns's policies also reflected his own views about the causes of inflation. Unlike his predecessor Martin (and, for that matter, his successor Volcker), he did not believe that inflation was caused primarily by monetary forces, and, consequently, he saw tight monetary policy as an indirect, costly, and largely ineffective tool for controlling inflation. The stop-go policies of the Burns Fed, alternating between monetary tightness and ease, achieved neither low inflation nor consistently low unemployment. Instead, inflation continued its upward spiral.

In 1979, shortly after he left the Fed, Burns gave a lecture titled "The Anguish of Central Banking," which was partly *mea culpa* and partly self-defense.[7] He acknowledged that the failure to control inflationary psychology had greatly worsened inflation: "Nowadays, businessmen, farmers, bankers, trade union leaders, factory workers, and housewives generally proceed on the expectation that inflation will continue in the future, whether economic activity is booming or receding. Once such a psychology has become dominant in a country, the influence of a central-bank error that intensifies inflation may stretch out over years." He also acknowledged that Fed policymakers, along with many others, had been too optimistic about how low unemployment could be pushed without triggering inflationary pressures. In retrospect, Burns thought that what we now call the natural rate of unemployment, u^*, was not the 4 percent (or less) that was the conventional wisdom of his time, but more like 5.5 to 6 percent, consistent with current estimates for that period. And he admitted that, in principle, central bankers, by restricting the growth of the money supply, could have stopped the inflation "with little delay," albeit by methods that would have created "strains" in financial markets and the economy.

So why didn't the Burns Fed do that? "It did not do so," Burns said, "because the Federal Reserve was itself caught up in the philosophic and political currents that were transforming American life and culture." In short, Burns believed that the social compact by which the government had effectively promised full employment made it politically impossible for the Fed, acting on its own, to inflict the significant and prolonged pain that a successful war on inflation would require. Action to fight inflation would have to wait for both a new political consensus, driven by the growing popular conviction that inflation was the nation's greatest economic challenge, and a new perspective and personality at the Fed. Sitting in Burns's audience that day was the person who would provide that new perspective. His name was Paul Volcker.

PAUL VOLCKER: THE TRIUMPH OF PERSISTENCE

Like William McChesney Martin, Volcker had a career that spanned both the public and private sectors. Born and raised in New Jersey, where his father was the city manager of Teaneck, Volcker spent his undergraduate years at Princeton University, where he majored in economics. Foreshadowing his later policy views, his senior thesis criticized the Fed for allowing inflation to flare briefly after World War II. His first job, from 1952 to 1957, was as an economist at the Federal Reserve Bank of New York. He subsequently moved back and forth between private-sector employment at the Chase Manhattan Bank, where he eventually became a vice president, and positions in the U.S. Treasury. From 1969 to 1974, he was the undersecretary for international affairs at the Treasury, where he played a role in the Nixon administration's decision to cut the dollar's remaining formal ties to gold.*

In August 1975, with support from Burns, Volcker was appointed

---

* The "closing of the gold window," as the episode was called, was the last step in the dismantling of the post–World War II Bretton Woods system, which established fixed exchange rates between the dollar and other major currencies. Some accounts attribute some or all of the 1970s inflation to America's abandonment of even a symbolic connection to gold, but in reality, the causality went in the opposite direction. Because other currencies were tied to the dollar, U.S. inflation led to misalignment between official exchange rates and the exchange rates that would have been set by a free-market system. U.S. inflation thus led to the collapse of Bretton Woods and the closing of the gold window, rather than the other way around.

president of the Federal Reserve Bank of New York—a position that gave him a vote on the FOMC and, by tradition, made him the Committee's vice chair. The president of the New York Fed arguably wields the second-greatest influence on the Committee after the chair and functions as the Fed's eyes and ears on Wall Street, overseeing the New York district's large banks and providing intelligence from participants in key financial markets and institutions. Volcker's experience in finance and in the Treasury prepared him for that role, and his seat on the FOMC would expose him to monetary policy debates during a difficult period. For four years, Volcker sat at the chair's elbow and watched with frustration as inflation worsened. He argued for tighter policy but was constrained by the tradition that the vice chair of the FOMC votes with the chair on final policy decisions.

In March 1978, at the end of Burns's second term, President Carter appointed G. William Miller, a former aerospace executive, to lead the Fed. Volcker had been on the short list for the job but was passed over.[8] Miller, who like Burns was reluctant to tackle inflation, was in any case a questionable choice for Fed chair. He was not a monetary expert, and, culturally, he was a bad fit with the consensus-oriented Fed. He could not order FOMC members around in the way he could his employees in the business world. (He was not even successful at banning smoking in the boardroom; after he had the ashtrays removed from the room, several heavy smokers on the Board began to bring their own.) After only seventeen months at the Fed, as part of a Cabinet shake-up, Miller was nominated by Carter to be Treasury secretary. Fed staff lore later depicted Miller's transfer as an unsuccessful Fed chair being "kicked upstairs" after a short tryout. However, Volcker told an interviewer that Carter regarded the Treasury position as more important and viewed the transfer as a promotion.[9] In any case, the shake-up portended a major shift in Fed policy.

Inflation was rising to yet greater heights and, with Miller on his way to Treasury, Carter needed to find a replacement quickly. Recommended by some of Carter's economic advisers (but not his political advisers), Volcker met with Carter and told the president that he believed that a tighter monetary policy was urgently needed to fight inflation.[10] "I would have a tighter policy than that fellow," Volcker said, pointing to Miller, who was at the interview. Volcker says in his autobiography that he expected that that would kill the appointment. But the next morning, still in bed, he received a call from the president, offering him the job.[11]

Carter's decision to appoint Volcker was fateful. The president presumably understood that Volcker was likely to launch an attack on inflation, because Volcker told him so. He also must have known that tight money policies—higher interest rates—could well result in increased unemployment and slower growth and that, even if inflation subsided, the political costs could be heavy. Indeed, that's what happened. A weak economy helped ensure that Carter lost his reelection bid in 1980. As Vice President Walter Mondale recalled, Volcker's policy "did wring inflation out of the economy eventually but it also helped wring us out of the White House."[12] So why did Carter—in a 180-degree turn from the approach taken by Nixon, and from his own approach in picking Miller—choose the hawkish Volcker?

For the economy's benefit, if not necessarily for Carter's personal political fortunes, Volcker or someone like Volcker was a logical choice. The Fed had lost its credibility as an inflation-fighter, and the challenge for the new chair was to restore it. Credibility—a reputation for following through on commitments—is critical for policymaking in general, as in everyday life. But credibility can be especially important for fighting inflation, because of the role of public psychology. In 1979, with inflation in double digits, any new Fed chair would say that inflation must be brought down, but would market participants, business leaders, and consumers believe such statements? If not, then inflation expectations would remain stubbornly high, making the defeat of inflation more difficult and costly. But if the new chair had a reputation for toughness and aversion to inflation, then people might be more likely to believe that a war on inflation would be sustained, allowing inflation expectations—and thus inflation itself—to fall more quickly. Arguably, Volcker, with his hawkish reputation—not to mention his imposing six-foot-seven frame and gravelly voice—would be more credible on inflation than an evidently less hawkish appointee.[13]

It's a subtle argument, and it's not clear that Carter was thinking along those lines. We know that he settled on Volcker in haste, and that several prominent bank executives declined to be considered before Volcker was approached. Carter did not know Volcker well and was not even sure what political party he belonged to (he was a Democrat, like Carter). It may be that Carter made one of the most important decisions of his presidency without fully considering its ramifications. Miller at Treasury opposed the appointment and Mondale recalled he was uneasy about it. But on the other hand, the president surely did appreciate that the country was on the brink of an economic and financial crisis, and that Wall Street was demanding someone with a reputation for toughness and political independence at the Fed. Volcker filled that bill.

For his part, Volcker understood what was needed. He would lay out his philosophy in his first semiannual congressional testimony as chair, in February 1980.[14] It was a very different approach from Burns's. "In the past," Volcker said, "at critical junctures for economic stabilization policy, we have usually been more preoccupied with the possibility of near-term weakness in economic activity or other objectives than with the implications of our actions for future inflation." He continued with a swipe at stop-go policies: "As a consequence, fiscal and monetary policies alike too often have been prematurely or excessively stimulative, or insufficiently restrictive. The result has been our now chronic inflationary problem. . . . The broad objective of policy must be to break that ominous pattern. That is why dealing with inflation has properly been elevated to a position of high national priority. Success will require that policy be consistently and persistently oriented to that end. Vacillation and procrastination, out of fears of recession or otherwise, would run grave risks." Consistency and persistence became Volcker's hallmarks.*

Despite his hawkish inclinations, Volcker took time to set a new course for policy and to bring along his FOMC colleagues, some of whom doubted his approach, and his early steps as chair were perceived by many as halting.

---

* Appropriately, the subtitle of William Silber's biography of Volcker is *The Triumph of Persistence*. Volcker's autobiography is titled *Keeping At It*.

A trip to Yugoslavia to attend the fall 1979 meeting of the International Monetary Fund (IMF), together with Treasury Secretary Miller, stiffened his resolve. Volcker got an earful from the Europeans there—especially in Germany, where he stopped on the way—about their concerns about the effects of inflation on the stability of the dollar, the global reserve currency. He also attended the "anguish of central banking" lecture given by Burns in conjunction with the IMF meeting. It sounded to Volcker like a counsel of despair, an admission that, given economic and political realities, the Fed was helpless against inflation. The new chair would not accept that conclusion and returned to Washington determined to act.[15]

A New Approach

Volcker and his colleagues took a critical step at a rare (and unannounced) Saturday meeting of the FOMC on October 6, 1979, in Washington. Volcker had begun the deliberations in a meeting of the Board of Governors on Thursday, continuing them in a conference call with the whole Committee on Friday. Pope John Paul II's visit to Washington that weekend helped distract the media from what was happening at the Fed.

The discussions were superficially—but only superficially—about technical issues of monetary policy implementation. As had been true for most of the Fed's history since World War II, when Volcker took office the Fed's key monetary policy tool was its ability to influence short-term interest rates—primarily the federal funds rate, the interest rate at which banks lend to each other overnight. The Fed at the time managed the funds rate by varying the quantity of reserves in the banking system, creating a shortage of reserves when it wanted to force the funds rate up, and a surplus when it wanted to push the rate down. So, effectively, at the time that Volcker called the fateful meeting, the standard approach to implementing monetary policy involved targeting the price of money—the federal funds rate—at the level needed to achieve the desired economic outcomes. The Fed would then adjust the money supply—more precisely, bank reserves, an important determinant of the money supply—as needed to achieve the target interest rate.

At the October 6 meeting, Volcker proposed, and the Committee supported, turning the standard approach on its head. Instead of choosing a target level of the funds rate and adjusting bank reserves and the money supply as needed to enforce that rate, Volcker suggested setting a target for growth in the quantity of money and letting the funds rate adjust freely as needed to be consistent with the money-growth target. The purported rationale for the switch was *monetarism*, the doctrine espoused by Milton Friedman and followers, which held that money growth was closely linked to inflation. If money growth and inflation were indeed as closely tied as monetarists believed, then making money growth the focus of policy should allow for more precise control of inflation than the traditional practice of targeting interest rates. Similar ideas were influential in the United Kingdom during the government of Margaret Thatcher, a time when that country was also battling inflation and economic stagnation.

More cynically, a possible advantage of the new operating procedure was that the focus on money growth might help the Fed deflect political criticism for the behavior of short-term interest rates, which would soon soar toward 20 percent. In particular, the new strategy shattered the traditional practice of moving the policy interest rate in small increments, which had proved insufficient to contain inflation. As veteran Board member Henry Wallich put it: "I think the main argument in favor of the reserve strategy is that it allows us to take stronger action than we probably could by the other technique. . . . In the new strategy interest rates become almost a by-product of a more forceful pursuit of the [monetary] aggregates." [16]

Ultimately, it should be said, Volcker's experiment would not do much to improve the reputation of monetarism. Although growth in the money supply and inflation bear some relation in the long run, at least in certain circumstances, in the short run the connection can be unstable and difficult to predict, as the FOMC would quickly learn after adopting the new approach. Indeed, even defining the money supply proved challenging. In principle, the money supply should include any asset usable in ordinary transactions, including for example checking account balances as well as currency. However, in practice, some types of assets are more convenient for transacting than others. How should alternative forms of payment be counted in the money supply, and with what weight? Ongoing financial deregulation during this period, which phased out interest-rate ceilings on bank deposits and allowed new types of deposit accounts to be offered, further complicated the measurement of money. In part because of these practical difficulties, the Committee would abandon its monetarist framework after only three years, in October 1982, returning to its traditional approach of targeting the funds rate.

Although the shift to a monetarist approach would not stick, the October 6, 1979, meeting was nevertheless significant because it publicly signaled a break in the Fed's approach, aimed at showing Wall Street—and the rest of America—that the Fed was determined to defeat inflation. By revamping its tactics, in an emergency meeting, the FOMC had told the world that the status quo was no longer acceptable. That was the signal that Volcker had intended.

To underscore the significance of the FOMC's decision, Volcker followed the meeting of the Committee with a rare (for a Fed chair at the time) press conference—even more unusual for being held on a Saturday evening. Besides the change in the procedures for implementing monetary policy, Volcker was also able to announce that the Board raised the discount rate by a full percentage point, to 12 percent. Moreover, the Board and other members of the FOMC supported the new policy unanimously. Clearly, something had changed.

Volcker's War on Inflation

These dramatic signals notwithstanding, support for Volcker's war on inflation waxed and waned, both within the Federal Reserve and outside. Volcker himself often had doubts. But he persisted, often against intense opposition, and he succeeded in bringing inflation down. Inflation dropped from about 13 percent in 1979 and 1980 to about 4 percent in 1982, where it stabilized for the rest of Volcker's time at the Fed. Thus, in only a few years, the Fed largely reversed the increase in inflation built up over a decade and a half.

The conquest of inflation was a landmark accomplishment with enduring benefits, but it came with heavy costs. After a brief recession in 1980 and short rebound, the economy slumped deeply in 1981 and 1982, with the unemployment rate peaking at a painful 10.8 percent in November and December 1982. The traditional Phillips curve, which predicted that a sharp drop in inflation would be accompanied by significant increases in unemployment, had returned with a vengeance.

The first, relatively short recession, in 1980, was tied to an ill-advised experiment with credit controls.[17] In March 1980 the Fed, at the Carter administration's request and with its authorization, imposed the controls on banks and other lenders. (Volcker initially objected to the policy but then agreed to cooperate.) Banks were asked to keep their annual loan growth between 7 and 9 percent and would be penalized for making certain types of loans. The aim of the program was to restrain overall loan growth and especially consumer borrowing, other than for cars or homes. If credit could be directed away from so-called unproductive uses, the rationale ran, then perhaps spending and inflation could be reduced in a manner that was less disruptive to the economy. However, the program, which provided only general guidance, confused both banks and the public about what types of loans were permissible. People became reluctant to borrow in any form, and spending slowed more sharply than expected. When the economy fell into recession, the administration and the Fed quickly abandoned the strategy, and the economy recovered.

High interest rates—partly the result of increased government borrowing to finance deficits run up during the Reagan administration but mostly driven by Volcker's tight-money policies—were unambiguously the major reason for the second, deeper recession that officially began in July 1981, according to the National Bureau of Economic Research. That fall, for example, thirty-year mortgage rates exceeded 18 percent, devastating the housing industry. Arthur Burns had not been wrong when he predicted that restraining inflation would create major economic and financial strains. A silver lining was that, after the Fed abandoned its money-targeting regime in October 1982 and eased policy a bit, a strong recovery ensued and continued for the rest of the decade. The growth of real (inflation-adjusted) gross domestic product (GDP) in 1983 was nearly 8 percent, and the unemployment rate fell from 10.8 percent in December 1982 to 8.3 percent a year later. President Reagan was among those who benefited from these developments; he was easily reelected in 1984. By the end of Volcker's tenure, in 1987, the unemployment rate had fallen to about 6 percent.

Although the public certainly wanted something to be done about inflation, high unemployment and high interest rates were, inevitably, a politically toxic combination. Volcker had to face contentious congressional hearings, as well as an impeachment threat from Democratic Texas congressman Henry Gonzalez, a regular critic of the Fed. Farmers protested high interest rates by rolling their tractors down Constitution Avenue in Washington and gathering outside the Fed's headquarters. Home builders mailed pieces of two-by-fours to the Fed inked with messages imploring the chair for relief. Some of these missives still decorated my office when I was chair. They were mementos of a critical period in Fed history, as well as reminders of the costs of controlling high inflation.

It helped a great deal that, when the chips were down, the White House usually supported Volcker. President Carter had openly criticized Volcker's policies only once, in the heat of his 1980 reelection race.[18] President Reagan's support was more erratic. Although Reagan rarely criticized the Fed publicly, Volcker clashed with senior administration officials. In his memoir, Volcker reports a meeting at the White House in the summer of 1984 at which James Baker, by then Reagan's chief of staff, in the presence of the president, told Volcker not to raise interest rates before the election. Volcker, determined to avoid another Nixon-Burns scenario, walked out without replying.[19] And when Reagan appointees, at a Board meeting in February 1986, voted over his objections to cut the discount rate, he nearly resigned, only withdrawing the threat after the Board reconsidered its decision later that day.[20] Still, for the most part Reagan accepted that controlling inflation was essential to a healthy economy. According to Volcker, Reagan once explained to him "that a professor at his small college in Illinois had impressed upon him the dangers of inflation."[21] In the end, when it counted, Reagan did not stand in Volcker's way, reappointing him to a new term as chair in 1983. Signaling its confidence in Volcker and his inflation fight, the Senate voted 84–16 to confirm him.

Besides high interest rates and the spike in unemployment, Volcker's war on inflation had other significant side effects. High interest rates in the United States attracted funds from foreign investors and pushed the foreign exchange value of the dollar up sharply; and even as U.S. rates declined, the dollar remained very strong. That made imports cheaper—thereby helping to curb inflation—but it also priced some U.S. exporters out of foreign markets. Volcker, whose early experiences at the Treasury included dealing with a weak dollar, now had to manage a strong one. Along with James Baker, then Reagan's Treasury secretary, Volcker participated in international meetings aimed at curbing the dollar's rise. Following a 1985 agreement with France, Germany, the United Kingdom, and Japan—which came to be known as the Plaza Accord, after the New York hotel where it was negotiated—the Fed and the Treasury coordinated in selling dollars in the open market, putting downward pressure on the dollar's exchange rates with other currencies.

High interest rates and the U.S. economic slump also worsened global financial stresses. Oil exporters during the 1970s had earned massive profits from high oil prices. Some of these funds eventually flowed into major American banks, which lent them to emerging-market economies in Latin America. Many hoped that this process, known as "recycling petrodollars," would help countries like Mexico develop their own oil reserves. However, the strong dollar and high U.S. interest rates made those loans (which were denominated in dollars) difficult to repay, even as the weakness of the U.S. economy and falling prices of oil and other commodities reduced the income of the Latin American debtors. The result was an international debt crisis.

In August 1982, Mexico ran out of international reserves—its official holdings of dollars—and was on the brink of defaulting on its bank loans. The debt of Mexico and other troubled Latin American countries represented a large fraction of the capital of the major U.S. banks, so the countries' potential default threatened American financial stability as well. Volcker pushed the banks to extend additional credit to Mexico until it could borrow from the IMF, which had been created after World War II to make such loans. Volcker's skillful management of the crisis, through a combination of arm-twisting and working with bankers to find solutions, helped cement his reputation as an accomplished central banker. On the other hand, as congressional critics were quick to point out, as president of the New York Fed from 1975 to 1979 he had been the supervisor of many of the banks that had made the Latin American loans. In Volcker's defense, at the time, the Fed's legal authorities to second-guess banks' lending decisions or require them to hold more capital against possible losses were limited.

More financial problems followed the Latin American crisis, this time at home. In 1984, inadequate capital and concentrated lending—in this case, both to developing countries and to speculative domestic oil and gas projects—nearly brought down Continental Illinois, the nation's seventh largest bank by assets and its largest commercial and industrial lender. After facing a run by its depositors, the bank was bailed out by the U.S. government, with the Federal Deposit Insurance Corporation (FDIC) injecting capital and protecting even uninsured creditors. The Federal Reserve provided discount-window loans to the bank and worked closely with the FDIC and other regulators in the salvage operation.[22] The episode gave rise to the phrase "too big to fail" to describe institutions whose bankruptcy could endanger the stability of the financial system.[23]

The savings and loan (S&L) industry in the United States was another financial victim of the Great Inflation and the Volcker Fed's policy response. The S&Ls used federally insured, short-term deposits to finance long-term mortgage lending. Federal law dating to the 1930s capped the interest rates S&Ls and banks could pay on their deposits, with the goal of preventing what was perceived as destructive interest-rate competition among depository institutions. When the Fed's battle against inflation led short-term rates to soar, depositors withdrew their money to seek higher returns elsewhere. Legislation in 1980 phased out the interest-rate controls on deposits, allowing S&Ls to pay the higher rates needed to retain depositors. But these deposit rates exceeded what the S&Ls earned on the old mortgages on their books, which had been made when rates were much lower.[24] At the same time, the higher rates created by the Fed's policies depressed the demand for new mortgages. Many S&Ls became effectively insolvent.

In 1982, in the hope of giving the institutions more breathing space, Congress passed legislation that allowed S&Ls to invest in riskier, higher-return assets. But, for those close to bankruptcy, S&Ls had little incentive to be cautious, and many gambled for redemption by engaging in extreme risk-taking or even fraud in the hope of returning to solvency. Many were unsuccessful. Because their deposits were government-insured, their losses—amounting over time to about $124 billion—were passed to taxpayers. Debates about the relationship between monetary policy and financial stability often assume that easy money and low interest rates are financially destabilizing. The Volcker era showed that tight money and high interest rates can also have destructive side effects.

Volcker and the Fed's Credibility

Although President Carter's motivations for appointing Volcker were not entirely clear at the outset, a plausible rationale was that Volcker's reputation as an inflation hawk might help restore the Fed's credibility. If people were more inclined to believe that the Fed would persist in its war on inflation, the argument goes, they might moderate their inflation expectations, allowing inflation to be brought down more quickly and at a lower cost in jobs and output. Volcker and other FOMC members certainly understood this point: Notably, Volcker stage-managed the dramatic meeting and the change in policy procedures in October 1979 to signal a decisive turn in the Fed's strategy, with the hope of shoring up the institution's credibility and breaking the public's inflation psychology.

In retrospect, was there in fact a "credibility bonus" that made Volcker's fight against inflation less costly than it might have been otherwise? The evidence is mixed. On the one hand, inflation did come down quickly after 1980, accompanied by a notable drop in inflation expectations as well, at least as measured by surveys of households and professional forecasters. For example, the University of Michigan's survey of consumers found that one-year-ahead inflation expectations fell from about 10 percent in 1980 to less than 3 percent in 1982. The output costs of Volcker's war on inflation were also less than some economists predicted. For example, in 1978, Arthur Okun, using standard Phillips-curve models, estimated that controlling inflation through tight monetary policy would induce a downturn comparable to the Great Depression. The actual output losses under Volcker were much lower than those predictions.[25]

Yet, the losses of output and jobs that occurred during the 1980 and (especially) the 1981–82 recessions were hardly small; the 1982 peak in the unemployment rate would not be exceeded until the pandemic of 2020. Moreover, even after inflation fell, long-term interest rates remained high for some time, with mortgage rates still above 10 percent in 1987, for example. Evidently, investors were skeptical that inflation was truly vanquished and remained nervous that it could flare up again, reducing the purchasing power of their bonds and loans. They accordingly demanded extra compensation to hold those assets.

Overall, it appears that Volcker's promises to control inflation, at least in the early stages of his campaign, were not viewed as fully credible, dashing any hope of ending inflation without serious costs. Those costs, however, must be set against substantial future benefits. Inflation and inflation expectations remained low and stable for decades after Volcker's tenure, suggesting that the Fed's anti-inflation credibility had been restored. That credibility would not only make controlling inflation easier; it would also increase the Fed's scope to respond to declines in output and employment, without worrying that a temporary easing of monetary policy could destabilize inflation expectations. Ultimately, Volcker's conquest of inflation helped underpin several decades of strong and stable growth, a period which became known among economists as the Great Moderation. Perhaps the broader lesson is that, in monetary policymaking, credibility is a valuable asset, but one that is earned primarily through deeds and results, not words alone.

In September 1990, three years after leaving the Fed, Volcker delivered a lecture in Washington in the same series in which Arthur Burns had described the "anguish of central banking" a decade earlier. Except that Volcker titled his lecture, "The Triumph of Central Banking?"[26] (Note the question mark.) In contrast to Burns, Volcker was able to say that "central banks are in exceptionally good repute these days," having brought down inflation and navigated the resulting financial and economic currents. Unsurprisingly, he emphasized that good economic performance required low inflation as well as "the importance of dealing with inflation at an early stage," before it develops momentum and becomes embedded in expectations. He also stressed that a flexible, independent central bank was better suited to control inflation. Coining a phrase, he called the central bank "the only game in town" when it came to inflation.

Volcker's lecture well summarized the lessons that central bankers, economists, and even politicians at the time took from the Great Inflation. First, that moderate inflation is an essential cornerstone of a healthy and stable economy. Second, that central banks can keep inflation low, if they are sufficiently credible and persistent enough to counter inflation psychology and anchor inflation expectations at a low level. And finally, that central banks, to be credible, need the scope to make monetary policy decisions with a reasonable degree of independence from short-term political pressure—an independence that Volcker, with the backing of Carter and Reagan, had enjoyed to a degree that his immediate predecessors had not. Volcker's successor, Alan Greenspan, accepting these principles, would make the control of inflation, and the maintenance of the anti-inflation credibility painfully won by Volcker, the centerpiece of his monetary strategy.

After leaving the Fed, Volcker remained engaged in public service, such as when he chaired a commission to help Holocaust victims recover assets from Swiss banks. His views influenced financial reforms after the 2007–2009 global financial crisis, including the adoption of the so-called Volcker rule, intended to prevent banks from speculating with government-insured deposits. He died in 2019 at the age of 92.

3

GREENSPAN AND THE NINETIES BOOM

In August 1987 President Reagan appointed Alan Greenspan chair of the Fed. He would serve for eighteen and a half years, falling only four months short of William McChesney Martin's record.

Greenspan was born in 1926 in the Washington Heights section of New York City. He studied the clarinet at Julliard after high school, during World War II, and had a short career as a jazz musician, playing with luminaries like saxophonist Stan Getz. But, even then, he showed a proclivity for money and finance. He did his bandmates' tax returns.

He left the band to attend New York University, earning undergraduate and master's degrees in economics. He worked as a business analyst and also enrolled in Columbia University's doctoral program, studying under Arthur Burns. Greenspan dropped out as the demands of his job grew but, more than two decades later, at the age of 51, he earned a doctorate in economics by submitting as a dissertation to NYU a compilation of articles he had written over the years. During his career as a business consultant, much of it as the president and CEO of a firm called Townsend-Greenspan, he picked up a fine-grained and often idiosyncratic knowledge of the U.S. economy.

A Republican and a deficit hawk, Greenspan served in the mid-1970s as chair of Gerald Ford's Council of Economic Advisers. In his younger years he had been a devotee of Ayn Rand, the libertarian philosopher and author of *Atlas Shrugged*—creating some consternation among liberals when Reagan nominated him to the Fed. However, as chair, Greenspan proved to be pragmatic and politically savvy. A fixture in the Washington social scene, he was able to forge close relationships with presidents and legislators of both parties. His views on policy issues outside the usual domain of the central bank were widely sought. His willingness to engage on a range of issues, especially fiscal policy, at times created political risks for the Fed. Greenspan largely navigated those risks, however, and during his tenure the Fed's reputation and policy independence reached new heights.

As chair, Greenspan had two principal policy challenges. The first was to consolidate Volcker's gains against inflation while maintaining strong economic growth. On this count he was eminently successful. Inflation rose briefly in 1990, due mostly to a temporary spike in oil prices, but it subsequently remained relatively low and stable, averaging about 3 percent over Greenspan's long tenure. Impressively, in contrast to the 1960s, inflation stayed comparatively low even as the economy grew rapidly, with real output expanding at a heady 3.3 percent annual rate over the 1990s. Economic policymakers of the 1960s had aspired to tame the business cycle, to moderate the swings from recession to boom and back while keeping inflation controlled. With a deft touch informed by his knowledge of economic data, Greenspan succeeded where his predecessors had not. He engineered a difficult "soft landing" of the economy, developed new thinking about the management of macroeconomic risks, and managed monetary policy through a decade in which structural and technological change rendered obsolete much of the received wisdom about inflation. The decade-long economic expansion of the 1990s stands as the second longest in U.S. history, eclipsed only by the 2009–2020 expansion that followed the global financial crisis.

Greenspan's second policy challenge was to ensure financial stability during a time when financial markets had become more complex, more interconnected, and more international. Developments in Mexico, southeast Asia, and Russia sparked a series of foreign financial crises during the

1990s. Greenspan played a constructive role in each, working closely with the Treasury and the International Monetary Fund, while setting monetary policy to avoid collateral damage to the American economy. The U.S. stock market, which seemed to go in only one direction in the 1990s—up—raised particularly difficult questions. Here, some commentators have been more critical of Greenspan. Sebastian Mallaby, in a comprehensive and broadly sympathetic biography, *The Man Who Knew: The Life and Times of Alan Greenspan*, has criticized Greenspan for implicitly choosing to target the rate of inflation of consumer goods and services prices without paying adequate attention to asset prices, especially stock prices.[1] In Mallaby's view, economic stability requires monetary policy to "lean against the wind" to avoid excessive swings in asset markets, much as central bankers since Martin have leaned against inflationary winds.

The preservation of financial stability is, of course, a core responsibility of central banks. However, the traditional tools for limiting systemic financial risks are regulation, supervision of financial institutions and markets, and, when a crisis happens, liquidity provision by the lender of last resort. Whether monetary policy should be set with financial stability in mind, in addition to pursuing price stability and maximum employment, remains a difficult and controversial question. Greenspan, a sophisticated observer of markets, was at least initially open to Mallaby's side of the argument. During his term he tried on several occasions to lean against what he saw as a potential bubble in stock prices, using both monetary actions and the power of his words. However, he became increasingly frustrated by his inability to simultaneously rein in market exuberance and promote good economic performance, and over time he increased his focus on consumer price inflation and employment.

In retrospect, as Greenspan would acknowledge, he did have a blind spot with respect to financial-stability risks—but it was not a lack of attention to asset values, but rather overconfidence in the power of market forces to discipline risk-taking in financial institutions and markets. That shortcoming would ultimately have significant consequences, for the world and for Greenspan's reputation as a central banker.

BLACK MONDAY AND THE 1990–91 RECESSION

Greenspan's close encounters with the stock market began shortly after he arrived at the Fed. In October 1987 U.S. stock prices fell sharply, culminating in a mind-bending, single-day, 23 percent plunge in the Dow Jones average on October 19—Black Monday. The decline in stock prices was global, with severe drops recorded from Japan to Britain to Mexico. Although concerns about the economy had been percolating for months, the crash had no clear trigger. Some observers blamed the unprecedented speed of the decline on early versions of computerized trading, particularly "portfolio insurance" programs that issued sell orders whenever prices declined—a recipe for self-feeding instability. Greenspan himself thought that the market had been too high in the months before the crash, although like everyone else he was shocked by the size of the drop.[2]

In the years that followed, traders referred to the "Greenspan put," the idea that, at least sometimes, the Fed cuts interest rates to protect stock investors rather than to stabilize the broader economy. (The phrase is tongue-in-cheek. A put is an option to sell a stock or other asset at a predetermined price, used by investors as protection against price declines.) The Fed's response to the 1987 crash doesn't support the put notion. Rather than trying to reverse the stock decline or target stock prices at a particular level, Greenspan's Fed focused on cushioning the impact of the crash on the financial system and the economy.

To contain the fallout, Greenspan and his team followed the standard central-bank playbook. First, as it had been originally created to do, the Fed stood ready to serve as lender of last resort, ensuring that panicky withdrawals from financial institutions would not exacerbate the crisis. In that spirit, Greenspan approved the terse but effective announcement on the morning after the crash: "The Federal Reserve, consistent with its responsibilities as the nation's central bank, affirmed today its readiness to serve as a source of liquidity to support the economic and financial system." In his memoir, Greenspan wrote that he thought the statement "was as short and concise as the Gettysburg Address . . . though possibly not as stirring."[3]

In effect, the statement affirmed that the Fed was prepared to lend cash through its discount window (taking loans and securities as collateral) to help banks meet their near-term obligations, thus preventing short-term illiquidity (the unavailability of sufficient cash to meet creditor demands) from morphing into much-more-dangerous default and insolvency of the banks themselves.

The second element of the traditional crisis playbook is *moral suasion*— the polite term for official arm-twisting—to persuade key financial players to work with, rather than against, each other. In 1987 Greenspan delegated most of this responsibility to Gerry Corrigan, the gruff president of the New York Fed. Corrigan, a Fed veteran and former special assistant to Volcker, pressured firms to continue to transact with and lend to customers on the usual terms despite the market disruptions. The Fed's response helped prevent the stock-market swoon from spreading through the rest of the financial system. Stock investors who sold during the crash suffered losses, but no major financial institution defaulted, no exchanges closed (even temporarily), and financial markets soon returned to normal functioning.

In anticipation of a possible economic slowdown, the Fed did cut the federal funds rate by a relatively modest three-quarters of a percentage point in the months immediately after the crash. But the economy didn't need much help and by early 1988 the Federal Open Market Committee started to reverse its rate cuts. The Dow recovered more than half its losses in two days and surpassed its precrash peak in less than two years, as the economy continued to grow rapidly. As Greenspan would recollect: "Today, that market collapse is a distant memory of no ongoing interest, because it had no visible lasting effect on the economy overall, but we did not know that at the time. . . . In the end, much to my surprise, the effect of the crisis was minimal."[4] Greenspan concluded that the stock-market decline did little economic damage, because—in addition to the Fed's prompt and reassuring response—most stockholdings were not financed by debt. As a consequence, falling prices did not force stock investors to default or to dump other financial assets on the market.[5] And, as it turned out, rather than having to respond to a slowdown, by the spring of 1988 the FOMC became concerned about increasing inflation pressures. Going beyond its reversal of the postcrash cuts, the Committee initiated a sequence of additional rate increases, raising the funds rate by about 3 percentage points over the next year.

Although the 1987 crash did not damage the economy, Greenspan's tenure marked the beginning of a shift in the sources of U.S. recessions. From the 1950s to the 1980s, recessions typically followed Fed tightening that had been spurred by too-high inflation. The clearest example was the deep 1981–82 recession that followed Volcker's war on inflation. But the 1970 recession and the deep 1973–75 downturn also were partly the result of monetary policymakers' attempts to rein in inflation, even though ultimately the Fed did not do enough in those cases to bring inflation down permanently. In contrast, since 1990, with inflation well controlled, financial disruptions have played an increasingly important role in economic downturns. The increased size and complexity of the financial sector, the globalization of financial markets, financial innovation, and deregulation, whatever their benefits, have all increased both the risk of financial instability and its economic consequences.

The moderate recession that began in July 1990, lasting eight months, was something of a transitional case. Its causes included both monetary restraint and financial stresses. The Fed's precautionary tightening in the spring of 1988 had helped to cool the economy, and a decline in bank lending—which became known as the credit crunch—added to the downdraft. The credit crunch was the culmination of a boom and bust in commercial real estate lending during the 1980s, which in turn reflected multiple factors, including changes in the tax treatment of real estate.[6] When, in the late 1980s, losses on banks' real estate holdings began to eat into their capital, they became less willing and able to lend. The last stages of the S&L crisis, which saw about half of those institutions disappear between the mid-1980s and mid-1990s, further reduced the supply of credit. The crunch was particularly severe in New England, where banks were enmeshed in risky real estate lending.[7]

To its credit, the Fed anticipated the recession, ending its tightening in February 1989 as job growth slowed and then commencing a long series of rate cuts in June. The funds rate—which had reached almost 10 percent in 1989—fell to 3 percent by September 1992. Even though the recession was short, the sustained rate-cutting seemed necessary because the labor market remained sluggish. The unemployment rate, which had averaged 5.3 percent in the first half of 1990, peaked at 7.8 percent in June 1992 and remained at 7.0 percent in mid-1993, more than two years after the end of the recession. (Recessions officially end when economic activity stops contracting and begins to grow again, not necessarily when unemployment begins to fall or economic conditions return to normal.) A "jobless recovery" following a recession would become a familiar pattern in subsequent economic cycles.*

In July 1991 President George H. W. Bush nominated Greenspan to a second four-year term.[8] The decision was far from open-and-shut. Although the Fed had performed well in the wake of the 1987 crash, much of the leadership had come from Gerry Corrigan and the New York Fed. And Greenspan had angered then-presidential-candidate Bush with a rate hike just before the 1988 election, even after Bush had publicly cautioned the Fed against actions that might slow the economy.[9] The Fed's about-face to rate-cutting in 1989, after Bush took office, mitigated but did not prevent the 1990–91 recession or the jobless recovery that followed.

More conflict between the Fed and the administration would follow. In March 1990, the *Los Angeles Times* had quoted an anonymous source who said Greenspan would not be reappointed because his slowness in cutting rates had made the president "mad as hell."[10] In an unusual move, Bush called for lower rates in his January 1991 State of the Union Address: "You know, I do think there has been too much pessimism. Sound banks should be making sound loans now, and interest rates should be lower, now," he said, to applause.[11]

---

* The decline in the employment share of manufacturing may help explain slower job recoveries. In the past, workers who were laid off when plants were idled could be quickly recalled when demand recovered. Temporary layoffs from idled plants are a smaller share of unemployment fluctuations today.

Greenspan had also asserted himself on issues outside of monetary policy. He successfully resisted a 1991 plan by the Treasury to create a new consolidated federal banking agency, which would have taken away most of the Fed's authority to regulate and supervise banks. Greenspan had good reasons to resist the proposal. Substantively, the Fed's ability to supervise banks helps it to promote financial stability and serve as lender of last resort. And information provided by bank supervisors helps the Fed better understand the economy. From a bureaucratic perspective, losing bank supervision would have been a disaster for Greenspan and the Fed. The supervision of banks within their districts is a principal function of the regional Reserve Banks, and Greenspan needed to protect it (and the associated jobs) if he wanted the Reserve Bank presidents' support in other matters, including monetary policy. Greenspan's successful lobbying helped defeat Treasury's plan.

Greenspan also strayed from monetary policy by carving out a prominent role in the debate on fiscal policy, supporting deficit reduction. Greenspan was strongly interested in fiscal issues well before his time at the Fed; he had chaired a 1981 commission that recommended reforms to improve the long-run finances of Social Security. However, getting involved in fiscal policy, the domain of Congress and the administration, can be politically risky for a Fed chair, especially when seen as aligning with one party or the other.

Greenspan evidently thought the risk was worth taking to get the policies he thought were needed. He worked closely with White House insiders to craft deficit-reduction legislation and publicly advocated federal belt-tightening. In a move with echoes of William McChesney Martin's negotiations with Johnson's advisers in the 1960s, Greenspan also appeared willing to reward with lower interest rates politicians who accomplished deficit reduction. When President Bush broke his famous "read my lips, no new taxes" pledge by announcing a deficit-reduction plan on September 30, 1990, Greenspan followed on October 2 by persuading his FOMC colleagues, over a highly unusual four dissenting votes, to authorize him to announce up to two quarter-point rate cuts after Congress passed the deal.

After Congress approved the budget agreement, Greenspan cut the federal funds rate by a quarter percentage point.[12] From today's perspective, Greenspan's involvement in fiscal matters looks not only like a political overreach but also like an analytical error, as recent experience, as well as academic research, suggests that, in an advanced economy like the United States, the economic risks of moderate government deficits are low.[13]

So why did Bush reappoint Greenspan? Greenspan was evidently competent and had many supporters on Wall Street and in Congress. He actively courted politicians of both parties and would be easily confirmable by the Senate. In a period of uncertainty, continuity at the Fed would support confidence. At the same time, when the chips were down, Bush's advisers expected the chair to remain supportive of the Republican agenda.

However, keeping Greenspan in his post did not bode as well for Bush's reelection bid as the White House hoped. The Fed did continue cutting rates during 1992, but relatively slowly, and unemployment remained high, above 7 percent. Confronted by Bill Clinton's campaign theme, "It's the economy, stupid," Bush lost in a three-way race that included independent candidate H. Ross Perot. In a 1998 interview with British television journalist David Frost, Bush blamed Greenspan. "I think that if interest rates had been lowered more dramatically that I would have been reelected president. . . . I reappointed him, and he disappointed me," he said.[14]

The election of a Democratic president did not change Greenspan's operating style. He quickly established a personal relationship with Bill Clinton, again pushing for deficit reduction. Greenspan's public support of Clinton's belt-tightening plan included not only the positive reviews he gave it in congressional testimony, but also a more symbolic endorsement: When Clinton announced a commitment to deficit reduction in his 1993 State of the Union Address, Greenspan sat prominently between Hillary Clinton and Tipper Gore.

Greenspan's forays outside of monetary policy, particularly into fiscal issues, drew criticism from Congress and even from Fed colleagues, but he believed that the importance of the issues in which he engaged justified the risk of backlash. And, though he knew that he often came across as shy and nerdy, he had confidence in his political skills. Ultimately, Greenspan's close relationship with Clinton worked to the Fed's, and his own, benefit. Clinton, like most presidents, preferred more-dovish policies, and he appointed governors he hoped would push Greenspan in that direction. But, acknowledging the chair's growing influence in Washington, he would reappoint the Republican Greenspan twice.

THE SOFT LANDING, 1994–96

Taming double-digit inflation had required persistence and courage from Volcker but perhaps not so much subtlety or theoretical sophistication. Compared to his predecessor, Greenspan had the politically easier but technically more difficult task of guiding inflation to a sustainably low level without derailing economic growth. He succeeded. Between 1994 and 1996, Greenspan helped the U.S. economy make a *soft landing*, meaning the Fed tightened policy enough to restrain inflation but not so much as to cause a recession.

The idea of a soft landing is closely tied to Phillips-curve reasoning. According to the standard Phillips curve, when the economy is in recession, with significant slack in labor and product markets, inflation pressures should be low. In response, the Fed normally eases monetary policy to put unused labor and capital back to work. But in an expanding economy with strong demand, wages and prices tend to rise more quickly. To avoid too-high inflation, at some point the Fed must end the monetary-policy easing—by the right amount at the right time. Too much tightening too fast could abort the recovery. On the other hand, too little tightening, or too-slow tightening, would risk an inflation rebound, which could require additional policy tightening, and thus more unemployment, later. For policymakers, the Goldilocks response first helps the economy recover and then slows it just enough to allow it to grow steadily, with full employment and low and stable inflation. A soft landing seems straightforward enough in principle, but the difficulty of forecasting or even accurately measuring the current economy, together with uncertainty about the effects of monetary policy changes and of key parameters like the natural rate of unemployment, make a soft landing tricky in practice.

Greenspan's chance to engineer a soft landing came during the protracted recovery from the 1990–91 recession. Because the recovery did not initially generate much job growth, the Fed delayed tightening. But by early 1994 the case for action was strengthening. When the FOMC gathered on February 4, 1994, the unemployment rate had fallen from 7.8 percent to 6.6 percent and was moving decisively downward, as economic growth picked up. At 3 percent, the federal funds rate was relatively low—about zero in real terms, after subtracting inflation. The Reserve Bank presidents relayed reports from their district contacts of building price pressures, but measured inflation had recently been stable, between 2.5 and 3 percent. Should the Fed act?

For most Committee participants, the answer was yes. Many around the FOMC table wanted to increase the funds rate by half a percentage point. Greenspan agreed that the Fed needed to get ahead of inflation before it accelerated; he also worried about signs that inflation expectations might be drifting higher. However, concerned that a too-sudden move would shock financial markets, he got the Committee to agree to a more moderate quarter-point increase.[15] Unusually for the time, Greenspan issued a press release announcing the decision. Since it was the first rate increase in five years, he wanted to be sure that the markets got the message.

Why begin to raise rates when inflation was still low and unemployment was still high? Greenspan explained the Committee's reasoning in congressional testimony a few weeks later: "[M]onetary policy affects inflation only with a significant lag," he said. "That a policy stance is overly stimulative will not become clear in the price indexes for perhaps a year or more. Accordingly, if the Federal Reserve waits until actual inflation worsens before taking countermeasures, it would have waited far too long. At that point, modest corrective steps would no longer be enough. . . . Instead, more wrenching measures would be needed, with unavoidable adverse side effects on near-term economic activity." To Greenspan, the last point was important. Inflation pre-emption was not antigrowth, as he saw it, if it avoided the need for more extreme tightening later. By acting early, the Fed hoped to "preserve and protect the ongoing economic expansion by forestalling a future destabilizing buildup of inflationary pressure," he said.[16] The notion of tightening in advance of actual inflation—the tactic that became known as the *pre-emptive strike*—echoed the punch-bowl approach of Martin in the 1950s.

The February 1994 rate increase was just the start of a new tightening cycle. By February 1995, with an eye on inflation pressures, the Committee had doubled the funds rate—from 3 percent to 6 percent. The policy looked to be slowing the economy, as desired, but it had side effects. The bond market responded sharply to the policy shift, with long-term interest rates rising in sympathy to the rise in the funds rate and the expectation of still further increases to come. Ten-year Treasury yields, which had been less than 6 percent at the end of 1993, shot up to nearly 8 percent by the end of 1994. Since the prices of bonds move inversely with their yields, bondholders—including banks, insurance companies, and pension funds—took large losses in what became known as the bond massacre of 1994.* Among the casualties was Orange County, California, which went bankrupt after suffering losses on bond-related derivative contracts.

The Fed's tightening also had political ramifications. In 1993, newly inaugurated President Clinton had gone along with a Greenspan-endorsed plan to reduce the budget deficit, partly on the promise from his economic advisers and Greenspan that stabilizing the federal fiscal outlook would increase the confidence of bond investors and lower longer-term interest rates. Long-term rates did decline after the plan was announced. But the Fed's actions and the ensuing bond massacre were sending long rates back up. Democratic politicians expressed their displeasure. Senator Paul Sarbanes of Maryland likened the Fed to "a bomber coming along and striking a farmhouse."[17] However, Greenspan and Treasury Secretary Robert Rubin

---

* To see that bond yields and prices move in opposite directions, consider a bond that pays $1 per year, and which trades at a price of $10. This bond has an annual yield of 10 percent ($1/$10). However, if a reduced supply of that bond leads investors to bid its price up to $20, its yield falls to 5 percent ($1/$20).

persuaded Clinton that criticizing the Fed would be counterproductive: The purpose of Greenspan's policy was to control inflation, they argued; in the long run, despite the short-term bump in bond yields, lower inflation would bring lower interest rates. (And indeed, longer-term rates did decline in 1995 and subsequent years.) If, on the other hand, markets believed that the president was trying to obstruct the Fed's efforts to avoid sustained inflation, longer-term rates might ultimately rise further rather than fall. Clinton set an important precedent by declining to pressure or criticize Greenspan publicly, a new standard for Fed policy independence. George W. Bush and Barack Obama would follow his example.

When the funds rate reached 6 percent in February 1995, Greenspan judged that enough tightening had occurred and hinted in congressional testimony later that month that further rate hikes were unlikely. Subsequent cuts in July and December 1995 reduced the funds rate to 5½ percent. The economy responded well, with unemployment continuing to fall gradually and inflation remaining stable, under 3 percent. It looked like the soft landing had been achieved, and the expansion would continue. Greenspan would write in his memoir that pulling off this difficult feat was his proudest moment as Fed chair. The strength of the economy would help to reelect Bill Clinton in November 1996, rewarding the president for his forbearance.

THE MEXICAN PESO CRISIS

Paul Volcker's interest-rate increases in 1982 had helped touch off a financial crisis in Mexico and other Latin American debtor nations. Alan Greenspan's 1994 tightening likewise pressured Mexico, which, as in 1982, teetered on the brink of default. The 1994 Mexican crisis was different, though, reflecting major changes in the international financial system over the previous decade. In 1982, the creditors of Mexico and other Latin American countries had been large American banks, so that the debt crisis was also potentially a crisis of the U.S. banking system. In 1994, however, Mexico's borrowing was not in the form of bank loans—evidently, the banks had learned from 1982—but mostly in the form of bonds sold to creditors around the world. Importantly, many Mexican bonds—like most bonds sold abroad by emerging-market countries—were effectively denominated in dollars, a measure intended to spare creditors the risk of changes in the peso-dollar exchange rate. The exchange-rate risk did not disappear, however. Instead, the Mexican government bore the risk that it would be forced to repay in more-expensive dollars if the peso lost value. Moreover, much of the dollar-linked Mexican debt—called *tesobonos*—was short term, meaning that the lenders, like the depositors in a troubled bank, could pull their funding if they lost confidence.

Mexico had signed the North American Free Trade Agreement with the United States in 1994 and had, in the prior few years, undertaken pro-market reforms, including increasing the independence of the Mexican central bank and assigning it a formal target for inflation. Optimism about a newly reformed Mexico's prospects had attracted foreign money.

But confidence can be fragile. The dollar's value rose as the Fed tightened, raising the real cost of Mexico's debt payments. Beyond that, in 1994 Mexico suffered severe political shocks, including a rebellion in the state of Chiapas and the assassination of a presidential candidate. In response to political pressures, the government eased its monetary and fiscal policies in the run-up to the election. These policy moves were intended to strengthen the economy in the short term but also cast doubt on the country's longer-term commitment to reform, in particular to control of the government budget deficit and inflation. This combination of events spurred investment outflows, forcing the Mexican central bank to use its limited supply of dollar reserves in an effort to support the peso's value.* By December, the central bank did not have enough reserves to maintain the peso's fixed exchange rate, forcing the new president to announce a surprise devaluation of the currency. Foreign investors, fearful that Mexico would be unable to pay back its dollar-linked debt, began pulling their money out at

---

* Investment outflows, including the sale of peso-denominated assets like stocks, flooded the foreign exchange market with pesos. To support the value of the currency, the central bank used its dollar reserves to buy up the excess pesos.

an even more rapid pace. Without help, Mexico would soon default on its international obligations.

The simple free-market solution that Greenspan might have embraced in his libertarian days would be to let Mexico default, avoiding the *moral hazard* of a bailout: If Mexico and its creditors thought that the U.S. government would always protect them from the consequences of their mistakes, they would be encouraged to take excessive risks. However, in his role as Fed chair, Greenspan worried that a Mexican default could imperil the international financial system by causing investors to lose confidence in other emerging-market economies, precipitating more runs. Also, because Mexico is a large U.S. trading partner, the collapse of its economy could restrain U.S. growth. Finally, an argument that appealed to the central banker in Greenspan was that, like an otherwise sound bank facing a run of depositors, Mexico's problem arguably was more a temporary lack of liquidity than fundamental insolvency. Overall, a case could be made for the United States to serve as an international lender of last resort to Mexico, thereby avoiding the default and the losses that would flow from it. And moral hazard issues could be at least partially ameliorated by ensuring that Mexico and its investors suffered costs in the process.

Greenspan, Treasury Secretary Rubin, and Treasury Undersecretary Larry Summers agreed that preventing a Mexican default was in the United States' best interest, and they convinced President Clinton. They could not, however, convince Congress to put up the necessary funds for what seemed likely to be an unpopular bailout of a foreign country. The Rubin-Summers-Greenspan troika arrived at an alternative solution. With Greenspan's support, the Treasury used its Exchange Stabilization Fund to help finance a package for Mexico. The fund had been created by Congress during the Depression to give Treasury the ability to buy and sell dollars as needed to stabilize the dollar's value in foreign exchange markets. However, since any crisis was likely to have implications for the dollar, in practice the use of the fund was quite flexible. The IMF and the Bank for International Settlements in Switzerland, a multilateral institution that helps coordinate the activities of central banks, contributed to what would become a $50 billion bailout of Mexico—$20 billion of which came from the United States.

Mexico ultimately fully repaid the aid, and it was required to undertake economic reforms and tighter monetary and fiscal policies under the eye of the IMF. Although Mexico avoided a default, it suffered a severe recession in 1995. Unfortunately, from a moral hazard perspective, Mexico's bond investors did better, with holders of dollar-linked debt being largely made whole. However, other foreign investors—including investors in Mexico's stock market and peso-denominated debt—took significant losses.

Greenspan's role in the bailout of Mexico enhanced his reputation as a financial fixer and as a policymaker whose influence extended beyond setting interest rates. The larger significance of the episode was that it would become a prototype for financial crises later in the decade.

"MUMBLING WITH GREAT INCOHERENCE": GREENSPAN AS COMMUNICATOR

Central bankers have historically been a secretive bunch. The first central banks, including the three-centuries-old Bank of England, began as private institutions, and their governors maintained the discretion and secrecy expected of professional bankers. Over time, central banks took on a more public role, but for many years the standard view held that preserving a mystique, a sense that central bankers knew more than they were letting on, was important both for policy flexibility and for maximizing the market impact of any announcements. Montagu Norman, the eccentric governor of the Bank of England from 1921 to 1944, reputedly took as his personal motto, "Never explain, never excuse."[18] He routinely rebuffed as presumptuous requests to testify before Parliament.

Internationally, central-bank secrecy began to go out of style in the 1980s and 1990s. A key date was 1990, when the Reserve Bank of New Zealand, which had battled double-digit inflation in the 1980s, announced, in cooperation with the government, a formal inflation target of zero to 2 percent. Many central banks followed New Zealand's lead, in both advanced economies and emerging markets.[19] Along with setting official targets, transparency initiatives included the publication of other information, such as central banks' economic forecasts and analyses.

Two rationales underlay the new openness. The first was that monetary policy would be more effective if financial market participants better understood policymakers' thinking. After all, monetary policy works to an important extent by affecting market returns and asset prices, and a better understanding of the policy committee's goals and strategies should help financial markets better reflect policymakers' intentions. Second, following the Great Inflation, which was seen as having resulted at least partly from political influence on monetary policy, the Fed and other central banks had become more independent from short-term political pressures. But if unelected officials are given the discretion to make consequential monetary policy decisions, they should be expected to explain themselves. That accountability can only be achieved through transparency.

Greenspan was a transitional figure in the global shift toward greater central-bank transparency. His inclinations were old school. He valued flexibility and unpredictability, kept information close, and—as he joked soon after taking office—"I've learned to mumble with great incoherence."[20] He was indeed a master at saying little, at great length. At the same time, he appreciated that communication about policy was often necessary, and sometimes even useful. So, although the Federal Reserve generally lagged other central banks in transparency—in particular, Greenspan resisted the idea of a formal inflation target—the institution took important steps under his leadership. Many of these steps involved the evolution of the statement that accompanies FOMC decisions.

Remarkable as it may seem to modern Fed-watchers, who parse the FOMC's post-meeting statements for every change in wording or tone, before February 1994 changes in the stance of monetary policy were not routinely announced on the day they were made.* (Nor, for that matter,

---

* An exception occurred when the Board of Governors changed the discount rate. Since banks that might want to borrow through the discount window had to know the rate, there was no option but

were any changes enacted right away—the FOMC gave the chair discretion over the precise timing.) Instead, financial journalists would consult Wall Street analysts who tracked movements in short-term market interest rates and would opine on whether a change in policy had occurred. It was not unheard of that a financial reporter would quote analysts saying that a Fed policy action had occurred when in fact none had.

However, the February 1994 rate increase that kicked off the soft-landing sequence was special. It was the first policy change since September 1992 and the first tightening since 1989. Greenspan wanted to ensure that the change was very visible to the markets and it thus deserved a formal announcement after the FOMC meeting.[21] At the same time, preserving his treasured flexibility, Greenspan proceeded in small steps. The post-meeting statement was from Greenspan himself, not the Committee as a whole, which had no chance to edit or approve it. Its wording was opaque and indirect, indicating only that a "small increase in short-term money market interest rates" was expected, with no number given. And Greenspan indicated to the FOMC that statements would not follow every future meeting, especially meetings when no action was taken. Still, the February 1994 statement was an innovation with consequences.

Besides his desire to emphasize the change in policy direction, Greenspan had another motivation for increased transparency—pressure from Capitol Hill. The chair of the House Committee on Banking, Housing, and Urban Affairs, Henry B. Gonzalez (D-Texas), had for some time led congressional demands for greater disclosure of the FOMC's policy deliberations. In response, the FOMC in March 1993 had agreed to begin releasing minutes summarizing each meeting after the subsequent meeting of the Committee—that is, with about a seven-week delay.[22] Unsatisfied, Gonzalez scheduled a hearing on a bill that would have required the FOMC

---

to announce it. Discount rate changes often accompanied changes in the federal funds rate and thus served as a signal of changing monetary policy, as when Paul Volcker's Fed announced a discount rate change at the critical October 1979 meeting. Changes in the discount rate were a strong signal and were thus sometimes referred to as "banging the gong."

to release a full transcript and videotape of each meeting within 60 days. He invited all nineteen FOMC participants (Board members and Reserve Bank presidents) to testify jointly. In the remarkable hearing on October 19, 1993, five Board members and ten Reserve Bank presidents had joined Greenspan, with other FOMC participants submitting statements.

The hearing became even more remarkable when Greenspan revealed that FOMC meetings had been recorded for many years and transcribed to help the staff create minutes. The tapes were routinely erased but the unedited transcripts still existed, going back seventeen years. Most FOMC participants were not aware of the transcripts, and Greenspan wrote in his memoir that he learned of them only in his preparation for the testimony. But the Fed was clearly on the defensive. In the eventual compromise, which still holds, the FOMC agreed to release full, lightly edited transcripts of all its meetings with a five-year lag. (The transcripts are on the Board's website.) This material is valuable for historians, certainly, and it provides some accountability for policymakers, if only with a long lag. But the release of the transcripts has reduced give-and-take and spontaneous discussion at the meetings.

The experience with the transcripts may have persuaded Greenspan that decisions about Fed transparency would not always be up to him, and that allowing a peek behind the curtain might serve political as well as policy purposes. After February 1994, post-meeting statements, though still spare and generally released only after meetings at which action had been taken, began to evolve. As time passed, the FOMC provided more-explicit information about the change in the federal funds rate target, first in terms of its relationship to the discount rate, then (in July 1995) in terms of the target for the funds rate itself. Over time, statements also offered more information about the rationale for the policy action. Indeed, the August 1994 statement included what we would today call forward guidance. Having noted an increase of a half percentage point in the discount rate, which would be allowed to "show through completely" to market rates, Greenspan's post-meeting statement said that "these actions are expected to be sufficient, at least for a time," signaling an expected pause. (The guidance would prove faulty, though, as the Committee raised rates by an additional three-quarters of a point in November.)

Two issues simmered through the rest of the 1990s. The first was whether to provide systematic guidance about the likely future direction of policy, beyond informing the markets of the current action. The Committee, in a directive, already instructed the Federal Reserve Bank of New York about the likely direction of interest rates. (The Open Market Desk at the New York Fed was responsible for implementing monetary policy, buying and selling Treasury securities as needed to manage the supply of bank reserves and the funds rate.) This guidance was called the policy "bias." The bias could be upward (meaning rates were likely to rise), downward, or neutral. Obviously, the bias was potentially important information for market participants, but it was released only with the meeting minutes about seven weeks later. By then, the information was stale. After much discussion, the Committee in December 1998 agreed to include significant changes in the bias in its post-meeting statement.

The "bias" in turn evolved. In February 2000 the Committee switched to language built around the concept of a "balance of risks" to the economy. If the economy appeared to be weakening, the statement would say that the risks were "weighted mainly toward conditions that may generate economic weakness." If the economy looked like it might be overheating, then risks "were weighted mainly toward conditions that may generate heightened inflation pressures." The balance of risks formulation implicitly embedded Phillips-curve thinking, in which inflation and economic growth were traded off. The possibility that, say, economic activity might be too cold and inflation simultaneously too hot—as was the case with stagflation in the 1970s—was hard to capture in balance-of-risks language.

The second messaging issue was who owned the statement. The early statements came from Greenspan personally, with no Committee input. But it soon became evident that the statements themselves, by shaping market expectations for future rates, were a form of policy. Over time, Greenspan faced pressure to allow the Committee to influence the statement. In early 1995, Al Broaddus, president of the Richmond Fed, had suggested that the staff prepare alternative statements, perhaps with different biases, and that the FOMC formally vote on the language. Greenspan acknowledged that the bias was an element of policy but argued that editing the statement during the meeting was impractical and the matter went no further. For some time, Greenspan, or his staff lieutenant, Don Kohn, would read the statement only at the very end of the meeting, after the Committee had voted on the policy action.

As the statement's ability to influence policy expectations became increasingly evident, Greenspan shifted. The FOMC in May 1999 first announced a change in its bias (toward tightening) without a rate change. Markets reacted strongly, as if it were an announcement of a rate increase rather than merely the possibility of one. At the December 1999 meeting Greenspan distributed alternative statements for consideration and, starting with the February 2000 meeting, the Committee's vote included approval of the statement as well as of the policy action.

In March 2002, in another step toward transparency, the FOMC began to immediately release the votes on the policy action and statement, including dissents. Although driven in part by legal concerns—it seemed possible that the Freedom of Information Act would compel the prompt release of votes—the opportunity to register dissent in the meeting statement would become a vehicle for opponents of a policy move to gain greater attention for their views.

Despite changes since 1994, as of 2002, Fed transparency under Greenspan remained limited, compared with many other central banks. But shifts in the underlying economic and policy environment would soon lead to changes in communication as well.

ENTER THE MAESTRO

The soft landing of 1994–96 prolonged the expansion into its sixth year. Could the Fed keep the winning streak—solid growth, low unemployment, stable inflation—alive? It did, and contemporary observers gave

Greenspan much of the credit. In 2000, the *Washington Post*'s Bob Woodward, of Watergate fame, published a book about Greenspan's leadership of the Fed, titled *Maestro: Greenspan's Fed and the American Boom*.[23] The moniker would stick, signaling Greenspan's ascendance to rock-star status. Greenspan did handle the post-soft-landing period successfully, but the story is more complicated than portrayed in hagiographic accounts.

In mid-1996 the Fed had faced a situation reminiscent of 1994. The economy was growing at a solid pace—about 3 percent in the first half—and unemployment, at 5.5 percent, had fallen modestly below the staff's estimate of the natural rate. By the usual Phillips-curve logic, inflation should soon become a problem, and the pre-emptive-strike strategy espoused by Greenspan in 1994 argued for beginning rate hikes soon. Several FOMC members favored exactly that strategy.

Greenspan, however, was not so sure, and was inclined toward caution. He knew, from 1994, that initiating a sequence of rate increases after a period of flat or declining rates could shock markets, especially the bond market. Also, the situation in 1996 differed somewhat from the situation two years earlier. For one, monetary conditions in 1996 were not evidently all that easy. The federal funds rate stood at 5½ percent, a relatively normal level for the time, not the 3 percent of 1994. More important, as of mid-1996 there was little hint of inflation. As measured by the core consumer price index, inflation was stable at 2.7 percent, and Reserve Bank presidents reported at the July meeting that their business contacts were unable to increase prices without losing sales. Wage inflation also seemed tame, with only scattered indications that wages were rising more quickly. Pre-emption of inflation was one thing; shooting at shadows was another.

The absence of evident inflation pressures justified a cautious approach by the FOMC, but it also raised a question: With a strong economy and falling unemployment, why wasn't inflation higher, as standard Phillips-curve reasoning would imply?

Greenspan had developed a view of why wages and prices were rising only modestly, despite the expanding economy and tightening labor market. It turned on what he saw as an acceleration in the pace of technological change. By the late 1990s, the internet revolution was sparking talk of a New Economy, and Greenspan was becoming a convert.* He believed that New Economy gains in *productivity*—that is, increases in the quantity of output that could be produced by any given combination of capital and labor—were slowing inflation in two ways. First, technological changes like the use of robots in factories or advanced software in offices made workers feel less secure in their jobs, since they knew that they could more easily be replaced. According to Greenspan's *worker insecurity hypothesis*, these developments made workers less willing to push for wage increases, despite low unemployment. Second, gains in productivity helped offset the effects of wage increases on the costs of producing goods and services, which in turn moderated inflation pressures. Thus, Greenspan concluded, notwithstanding the strong economy, rapid improvements in technology and thus in productivity would help keep inflation at bay, reducing the need for pre-emptive Fed action.

The Federal Reserve's influential professional staff disagreed with both of Greenspan's arguments, at least initially. The staff had raised the worker insecurity hypothesis at the September 1995 FOMC meeting, before Greenspan had focused on it. At that meeting, research director Mike Prell told the Committee that the staff had used polling data and measures of job-loss risk to explore the hypothesis and had not come up with anything persuasive. Nevertheless, anecdotes and media reports led many on the FOMC to accept Greenspan's views about a shifting balance of power in the labor market.[24] The Committee held its fire over the summer of 1996, leaving rates unchanged.

The data between the July and September 1996 meetings were "foggy,"

---

* I attended a Greenspan talk about this time in which he extolled the fact that the physical weight of U.S. gross domestic product was much less than in the past. I was puzzled at first but then understood that he was contrasting an old-fashioned, manufacturing-based economy, which produces heavy material outputs, with the internet-based economy, in which value is embodied in light or weightless forms like software or advanced design. Greenspan did not consider weight-based measures to be entirely a metaphor; the Fed staff were asked to come up with estimates of the weight of production in various sectors.

as Greenspan put it. The labor market had tightened further, with the unemployment rate declining to 5.1 percent. Workers also evidently felt a bit less insecure, as some measures showed wage growth picking up. But consumer price inflation nevertheless remained low.

Greenspan, still hesitant to raise rates, retreated to the second part of his argument: that, even if wages were to rise modestly, increased productivity would prevent those wage gains from passing into inflation. Here again, Greenspan was at odds with the staff, who had the official data on their side. Output per hour of work in the second quarter of 1996—a simple indicator of productivity—had grown only 0.9 percent from the same quarter a year earlier, according to data available at the time, not a particularly impressive rate and lower than when the Fed had begun raising rates in 1994. However, Greenspan (along with many on the FOMC) was once again influenced by anecdotes from their business contacts about improved efficiency, and Greenspan instructed the staff to dig further. He argued that the available data might be understating actual productivity gains, for two reasons: First, corporate profits had been high, despite wage increases, suggesting that increased efficiency was holding down costs. Second, productivity growth in manufacturing—where productivity is easiest to measure—had been quite strong, while productivity growth in service sectors—less well measured, in Greenspan's view—seemed implausibly low.[*]

A substantial minority of the Committee had been pushing to tighten but Greenspan's arguments, and personal influence, convinced them to hold off to get more information. Rather than beginning a cycle of rate increases in September 1996, the FOMC held rates steady for the rest of the year. And, indeed, the economy continued to perform well, without a pickup in inflation. Greenspan's forecast had been right, the staff and the more-hawkish FOMC participants had been wrong.

---

[*] Measuring productivity requires accurate measurements of output, which may be easier to obtain for manufacturing than services. For example, it's easier to measure how many tons of steel a mill produces than to determine the quantity of financial services produced by a bank.

However, the delay in beginning tightening was, in the end, not so long. By early 1997, despite little evident change in the economy, Greenspan's views began to shift. At the February 1997 meeting, he announced that he thought the time to move was fast approaching. "We are getting to the point—March may be the appropriate time—when we will have to move unless very clear evidence emerges that the expansion is easing significantly."[25] The Committee did raise rates in March, but it would put rate increases on hold when another international financial crisis, this time in Asia, created economic headwinds.

Did Greenspan's performance in 1996 and 1997 justify the adulation he received in Woodward's book and elsewhere? In many ways, yes. Most important, the economic results were good. Solid growth and low inflation continued. And without doubt, the episode showcased Greenspan's strengths, including his skill at managing the Committee and his ability to see beyond standard economic data. His insights about productivity were particularly impressive. Revised data later showed that productivity growth in 1996 and 1997 was indeed notably higher than first measured, as Greenspan had predicted.[26]

On some other counts, Greenspan's analysis was less on point. His worker insecurity hypothesis, which he in any case had abandoned when wages started to rise, has not held up well in retrospect. Subsequent studies documented that most workers considered the risk of job loss to be lower than normal during that period, not higher; and that actual job security in the 1990s was higher, if anything, than it had been in previous decades.[27] Moreover, the productivity gains that Greenspan presciently identified probably only partially explained the failure of inflation to pick up. Alan Blinder and Janet Yellen—both prominent economists as well as members of the Fed Board at the time—later cowrote a book about the Fed and the 1990s economy that downplayed the role of productivity growth in suppressing inflation.[28] They argued that, in retrospect, much of the unexpected weakness of inflation during this period can be accounted for by other, short-term factors, including a strengthening dollar, a fall in oil prices, and methodological changes in how inflation was measured.

Much evidence also now suggests that the underlying behavior of inflation was changing in a favorable direction at about that time. Although estimates of the natural rate of unemployment are not precise, it appears that the natural rate fell by about a percentage point between about 1980 and the mid-1990s.[29] In a 1999 paper, labor economists Larry Katz and Alan Krueger attributed this apparent decline to several factors. First, with the aging of baby boomers, the labor force had become more experienced and better educated than in 1980—and better-educated workers generally experience less unemployment. Second, changes in the structure of the labor market, such as the advent of a temporary-help industry, provided an alternative means for the unemployed to find work.[30] A lower natural rate of unemployment allowed the economy to achieve more growth and a lower unemployment rate, without inflation pressure.

Another key factor dampening inflation pressures was the restoration (mostly under Volcker, but continued under Greenspan) of the Fed's credibility as an inflation fighter. With households and businesses more confident in the Fed's commitment to price stability, wage-price spirals driven by rising inflation expectations were no longer a serious concern. Consequently, upward pressures on inflation—arising from rapid growth in demand or from supply shocks—were likely to have only transient effects on the rate of price increase, rather than persistent effects as in the 1970s. In pinning his inflation forecast on his admittedly prescient views on productivity, rather than other factors, Greenspan might have been somewhat lucky—although, as the baseball executive Branch Rickey often said, luck is the residue of design.[31]

Finally, Greenspan's insight on productivity delayed tightening for only about six months—perhaps not enough to have made a major difference—and productivity (we now know) was actually accelerating when the Fed tightened in March 1997. Perhaps, then, too much has been made of this one episode. Nevertheless, it further enhanced Greenspan's reputation, giving him still greater influence, not only at the Fed but in economic policy more generally.

THE ASIAN FINANCIAL CRISIS:
MANAGING THE RISKS

Helped by Greenspan's skillful policy management, the U.S. economy performed well in the late 1990s, until once again it confronted foreign financial stresses. In this case, the epicenter was southeast Asia, especially Indonesia, South Korea, Malaysia, the Philippines, and Thailand. These countries had been growing robustly for several decades, with rapidly rising incomes, high investment rates, and climbing asset prices. It wasn't surprising that return-seeking foreign money had poured in.[32]

Then, in July 1997, in an unexpected development, the Thai government exhausted its foreign exchange reserves and was forced to devalue its currency, the baht. Over the next months, the currencies of other southeast Asian economies followed the baht down. As when Mexico devalued in 1994, investor sentiment changed abruptly, and lenders pulled their funds from developing Asian economies. A panic—dubbed the Asian financial crisis—hit global markets, and the affected countries suffered significant slowdowns or recessions.

What caused the reversal? As usual, political and economic factors combined, and the vulnerabilities are easier to see in retrospect. First, local banks, which in many cases were neither well managed nor well regulated, intermediated much of the foreign lending to East Asia. And, in the heady atmosphere of the time, the banks took excessive risks. Often, politicians directed lending to favored firms—so-called crony capitalism. Thus, even though the economic prospects of East Asia as a whole appeared strong, much of the capital flowing in from abroad was poorly invested.

The form of the capital inflows also mattered. Local Asian banks relied heavily on short-term financing, which is cheaper and easier to obtain than long-term financing but is also more prone to runs. As in the Mexican case, local banks borrowed from abroad in dollar-linked securities while lending in local currency. This currency mismatch was not necessarily a problem so long as the exchange rate between the dollar and the local currency remained fixed, as the East Asian governments had promised. But once the foreign investors began to withdraw their money, governments with limited dollar reserves found it impossible to keep their exchange rates stable. The devaluation of Asian currencies severely hurt the profitability and capital of the local banks, whose loans to local businesses and other assets (mostly in local currencies) fell in value compared with their liabilities (in dollars). In a vicious circle, the threat of bank failures led to further withdrawals of dollars by foreign investors and further devaluation.

Greenspan and the Fed regarded these developments calmly, at least initially. The U.S. economy seemed solid in 1997. Indeed, the FOMC had cited strong demand and growing inflation risks when it raised the funds rate by a quarter percentage point in March. That increase, and indications that more might be coming, attracted capital to the United States and strengthened the dollar, probably contributing to the emergence of the Asian crisis a few months later. For a time, though, financial volatility in Asia appeared to have little relevance to the United States. When U.S. stock prices finally reacted to the growing Asian turmoil—most notably in a 7 percent decline on October 27—Greenspan remained optimistic. He noted that, by helping both to limit emerging inflation risks and cool what he saw as an overheated stock market, Asia's troubles had done some of the FOMC's tightening work for it.[33]

As with Mexico three years earlier, Greenspan and the Fed worked closely with Treasury Secretary Rubin and his deputy, Summers. As usual in international debt crises, they needed to persuade lenders to cooperate rather than to withdraw their funds and debtor countries to forge agreements with the IMF. The IMF would provide loans to the troubled countries on the condition that they implement reforms. Since many of the IMF's demands, such as cutting government budget deficits or running tighter monetary policies, involved significant short-term pain in the hope of longer-term gain, the negotiations were tense.

A particularly tricky moment came in November 1997, when it became known that South Korea had considerably fewer dollar reserves than had been widely believed. South Korea was by this time a country of significant economic weight, a major U.S. trading partner, and the fear was that, following a large and uncontrolled devaluation of its currency, it would default on many of its dollar-denominated debts. That, in turn, could have caused bank failures (U.S. banks were among the major creditors) and stock-market crashes in other countries, spreading the panic. South Korea was also strategically important to the United States, owing to its border with North Korea and a large American military presence. Working with the Treasury and the Fed, who persuaded U.S. banks to renew their short-term loans to South Korea, the IMF defused the crisis with a $55 billion rescue package. *Time* magazine featured Summers, Rubin, and Greenspan on its cover with the caption, "The Committee to Save the World." The cover, which showed Greenspan in the center, flanked by Rubin and Summers, captured the close relationship that Greenspan had developed with the Clinton administration and his central role in a range of issues outside of domestic monetary policy.

The U.S. economy remained strong in the first half of 1998, despite the Asian problems. But then, in August, Russia unexpectedly defaulted on its debt, a reflection of the slowing global economy and the associated drop in the price of oil (a principal Russian export) to a low $11 per barrel. The default came after the IMF halted its lending to Russia because it would not accept reform conditions. Russia's default shocked global markets, to the point that it also shook Greenspan's confidence that foreign financial disturbances did not threaten the U.S. economy.

Speaking at the University of California at Berkeley, Greenspan told his audience that the Russian default had prompted a "major rethinking at the Fed."[34] "It is not credible," he said, "that the United States can remain an oasis of prosperity unaffected by a world that is experiencing greatly increased stress." In other words, to fulfill its domestic mandate, the Fed had to consider developments in the rest of the world, especially financial developments that could be transmitted instantaneously from country to country. This was a very different attitude from the relative unconcern Greenspan had projected early in the Asian crisis.

In the United States, a large hedge fund, Long-Term Capital Management (LTCM), became a high-profile victim of post-Russia financial volatility. Founded in 1994 by famed Salomon Brothers bond trader John Meriwether, LTCM's board members included two economics Nobelists, Myron Scholes and Robert Merton. Former Fed Board Vice Chair David Mullins, who had served under Greenspan, was also a principal. The firm used sophisticated, quantitative strategies and was initially extraordinarily profitable. It was also highly leveraged. At the end of 1997, LTCM owed about $30 in debt for every dollar in capital.[35] The company's strategy involved exploiting temporary deviations of specific asset prices from what were thought to be their normal levels. It bet that over time those deviations would disappear as more-normal relationships reasserted themselves. However, Russia's surprise default sideswiped that strategy by creating a surge in market volatility, which caused prices to move in unexpected directions, imposing large losses on LTCM. It became clear that the thinly capitalized firm was unlikely to survive.

Because LTCM had borrowed heavily from most major Wall Street firms, the Fed became concerned that its uncontrolled failure could severely disrupt the markets, particularly if it were forced to dump its assets at fire sale prices. Greenspan agreed to try to find a solution. On September 23, 1998, top officials of sixteen major Wall Street firms met at the Federal Reserve Bank of New York, under the eye of New York Fed President William McDonough. The Fed itself provided only the venue (and sandwiches and coffee, as Fed lore had it). Prodded by McDonough, fourteen of the sixteen firms agreed to a $3.6 billion infusion that avoided LTCM's immediate collapse, allowing for a more orderly wind-down. (One of the two firms that refused to participate was Bear Stearns; LTCM was its customer and Bear's margin calls helped precipitate the crisis. Bear Stearns itself would need government assistance a decade later.) In 2000 LTCM was finally liquidated.

The Fed was criticized at the time for creating moral hazard with its intervention, incentivizing other firms to take reckless risks, much as the government had been criticized for its interventions in the Mexican and Asian crises. In an interview years later, Greenspan expressed some discomfort about the Fed's involvement.[36] However, although bailouts are rarely popular, it appears that the LTCM rescue was reasonable and justified. First, it was based on policymakers' judgment that LTCM's uncontrolled failure would pose serious risks to the broader financial system and, ultimately, to the economy. In contrast, in 1990 the Fed had determined that the system could handle the failure of the investment bank, Drexel Burnham Lambert, and chose therefore not to intervene when it collapsed. Second, the moral hazard from the intervention was likely minimal. All of the funds used to prevent LTCM's collapse came from its creditors, none from public sources. And the owners of LTCM ultimately lost most of their investments and suffered damaged reputations—hardly a path that others would want to emulate. A more legitimate criticism was that the rescue was *ad hoc*, creating market uncertainty and raising concerns about fairness. In this respect, LTCM was like previous (and future) financial rescues by the U.S. government, which were hampered by the lack of a clear legal framework for dealing with the potential failure of a systemically critical financial organization.

Leading up to and during the LTCM episode, Greenspan became increasingly worried about the compound effects of the Asian and Russian crises (which had spread to Latin America) on the U.S. economy. On a conference call with the FOMC on September 21, 1998, he said that the "economy has been holding up, but it is now showing clear signs of deterioration."[37] The FOMC followed through with three quarter-percentage-point rate cuts in the fall of 1998. After the last, in November, the FOMC strongly signaled in its statement that it had done enough, despite continuing volatility in financial markets. The FOMC stayed on hold until it raised rates in June 1999, judging that, with financial conditions having become more stable, some of the 1998 easing could be safely removed.

Greenspan's three rate cuts in 1998 signaled a subtle shift in monetary policy strategy to take greater account of not only the most likely scenario for the economy, but also the range of possible outcomes. The best guess in September 1998 was that the fallout from the Asian crisis would slow economic growth in the United States. On an October 1998 conference call, Greenspan told the Committee, "it would be an extremely rare event for this type of financial environment to emerge and eventually to recede without having any impact on the economy."[38] So the easing of policy was certainly aimed at improving the economy's most likely trajectory. At the same time, Greenspan was thinking probabilistically. In arguing for the first of the rate cuts, he observed that the projected slowing was likely but not certain. "It is conceivable that we may end up viewing this action [the rate cut] not as the first in a series of moves but as an insurance premium," he said.[39] In other words, the proposed cuts were perhaps a little larger than justified by the most likely forecast, with the extra easing intended to provide protection against less likely but more severe outcomes.

The 1998 "insurance cuts" fit nicely with what Greenspan would come to think of as his risk-management approach, which attempted to incorporate the Committee's inevitable uncertainty about the various risks at play. In practice, Greenspan's risk-management strategy involved tilting policy as needed to counter the most worrisome, but relatively less likely, risks to the economy, with the intention of taking back the policy insurance if the feared risks did not occur. Greenspan would look back on the Asian crisis and its fallout as the genesis of this approach. In his memoir he wrote that the Fed's response to the developments in Asia and Russia "reflected a gradually evolving departure from the policymaking textbook. Instead of putting all our energy into achieving the single best forecast and then betting everything on that, we based our policy response on a range of possible scenarios."[40] Greenspan was not the first Fed chair to incorporate the balance of risks into policy analysis, but since his tenure policymakers have become more explicit in considering how the central forecast for the economy might prove wrong and how policy can best prepare for alternative scenarios.

IRRATIONAL EXUBERANCE: GREENSPAN AND THE STOCK MARKET

The 1987 stock-market crash had been Greenspan's first test as chair. The Fed responded swiftly, helping to limit the crash's effect on the broader economy. But the stock market would remain at the center of economic developments during the 1990s.

Stock prices more than tripled over the decade as the economy grew year after year and inflation remained low. Economists at the time disagreed about whether the rise in stocks portended trouble. The efficient markets doctrine, associated most closely with the University of Chicago, dismisses the notion that the stock market can be predictably overvalued or undervalued. Instead, it holds that the prices of stocks and other financial assets, which aggregate the views of millions of investors, appropriately reflect all available information about the economy—as imperfect as that information must inevitably be—at any point in time. According to this doctrine, a stock-market boom is a rational response to greater optimism about the economy, lower interest rates (which make stocks relatively more attractive compared to bonds), or other fundamental factors. If markets are efficient, then—although markets can certainly sometimes get things wrong—policymakers should not try to supersede the market's judgments.

Despite his libertarian roots and strong faith in markets in general, Greenspan was not an efficient-markets fundamentalist. In FOMC meetings he often expressed views about the appropriateness of stock-market values. Moreover, he was, at least in his early years at the Fed, prepared to use monetary policy to lean against what he saw as unjustified swings in market sentiment, on the grounds that such swings, or their inevitable reversal, could endanger the economy.

His decision to begin what ultimately became a 3-percentage-point tightening in February 1994 offers a key example. The principal goals of the rate increases were getting ahead of inflation and guiding the economy toward a soft landing. But Greenspan was also thinking about the stock market. "I think it may be very helpful to have anticipations in the market now that we are going to move rates higher," he told the FOMC at the February 4 meeting, "because it will subdue speculation in the stock market. . . . . If we have the capability of having a Sword of Damocles over the market we can prevent it from running away."[41] A bit over two weeks later, in a conference call, Greenspan rated the early effort a success: "Let me say that looking back at our action, it strikes me that we had a far greater impact than we anticipated. I think we partially broke the back of an emerging speculation in equities." He also observed, regarding bonds, "We pricked that bubble as well." [42]

Greenspan's declaration of victory was premature, however. Whether an unsustainable bond bubble had been pricked by the rate increase or instead whether bond traders were simply shifting their views about the economic fundamentals and the outlook for policy is not clear. In any case, if there was a bond bubble, it deflated not gently but violently, in a bond "massacre" that had financial-stability side effects. Moreover, the rise in bond yields would reverse once the policy tightening ended. As for the stock market, the Dow Jones average rose only 2 percent in 1994, consistent with the restraining effects of policy tightening and the resulting sharp increases in longer-term interest rates. But the slowdown was temporary. The stock market surged anew in 1995 as policy eased modestly, rising more than 33 percent. The monetary policies that had seemed so successful in guiding inflation and growth had proved a much-less-precise tool for managing the caprices of longer-term bond yields and stock prices.

The 1996 Maestro episode illustrates a different approach to the market. Greenspan delayed tightening on the grounds that stronger productivity growth would reduce inflation pressures. Logically, stronger productivity growth would also justify solid stock gains, but FOMC members who favored an earlier start to rate increases cited not only inflation risks but the risk that stock prices would overshoot their fundamental values. Persuaded that raising rates too soon to cool the market would unnecessarily slow the economy, Greenspan tried a new tactic for limiting stock gains: jawboning. Could he talk stock prices down?

In December 1996 Greenspan and the Board heard a presentation from two well-known financial economists, Robert Shiller (a future Nobelist) and John Campbell, who argued that the high ratio of stock prices to dividends indicated that the stock market was seriously overvalued. [43] Shortly thereafter, in a speech at the American Enterprise Institute, a conservative think tank, Greenspan made his concerns about the market public by asking: "How do we know when irrational exuberance has unduly escalated asset values, which then become subject to unexpected and prolonged contractions, as they have in Japan over the past decade?" He told his audience that, for central bankers, asset bubbles matter only if they threaten to damage the economy, but, nevertheless, "we should not underestimate, or become complacent about, the complexity of the interactions of asset markets and the economy."[44] The Dow dropped more than 2 percent in the first 30 minutes of trading the next morning, perhaps because traders thought Greenspan was signaling an imminent rate increase. But the effect was transitory, and the market resumed its rise.

With the benefit of hindsight, at the time of Greenspan's speech stock prices probably were not seriously overvalued. Some conventional metrics—such as the equity risk premium, the difference in expected returns between stocks and safe government bonds—were within normal historical ranges. Indeed, if you had purchased a representative basket of stocks at the end of 1996, at the time Greenspan was worrying about "irrational exuberance," and sold it at the end of 2002, the year in which the stock market hit its post-internet-bubble bottom, you would still have enjoyed a total nominal gain of 32 percent, including reinvested dividends.[45] Only near the end of the decade, with the advent of the internet boom, would clearer indications of bubbly behavior become apparent.[46]

Greenspan made one more gesture toward reining in the stock market. The FOMC's rate increase in March 1997, which signaled the end of the Maestro episode, was aimed primarily at forestalling any inflationary pressures. But Greenspan wrote later that the tightening in March was also motivated by his worry "that a stock-market bubble might cause inflationary instability."[47] He recalled that at the February 1997 meeting, he "told the Committee we might need an interest rate increase to try to rein in the bull [market]." But neither the rate increase nor the subsequent crises in Asia and Russia dented stock prices much.

The gains in the market continued over the next three years, increasingly driven by internet fever. The Dow closed above 10,000 for the first time on March 29, 1999. As Greenspan would write in his memoir, "The boom rose to a crescendo late in the year. . . . Most people who'd invested in stocks were feeling flush, and with good reason. This presented the Fed with a fascinating puzzle: How do you draw the line between a healthy, exciting economic boom and a wanton, speculative stock-market bubble driven by the less savory aspects of human nature? As I pointed out drily to the House Banking Committee, the question was all the more complicated because the two can coexist."[48]

Far from subscribing to the view that financial markets are efficient and rational, Greenspan had strong views during the 1990s about whether stocks were properly valued. He made several efforts to slow what he saw as unsustainable gains, using both interest-rate increases and jawboning. However, he was at best temporarily successful, and as time passed, he became both less confident in his ability to separate "good" from "bad" stock-market booms or to predict how stock prices would respond to Fed interventions. Whatever the theoretical case for such interventions, these uncertainties create substantial difficulties in practice.

Despite worries about the market expressed by some Reserve Bank presidents, the FOMC did not raise rates in early 1999. However, concerned about rising inflation, the Fed did begin a significant monetary tightening later in the year. Ironically, since it was not a stated goal of the tightening, the rate increases doubtless contributed to what would become a sharp downturn in stock prices, beginning in the spring of 2000.

PART II

21ST CENTURY MONETARY POLICY

■

The Global Financial Crisis and the Great Recession

4

NEW CENTURY,
NEW CHALLENGES

As the new millennium approached, Federal Reserve officials (and others) worried that the world's computers would not adjust to the year-2000 (Y2K) date change, plunging the new digitalized global economy into chaos. It was a false alarm. Whether because of good preparation, or good luck, Y2K came and went with barely a hiccup.

But 2000 did herald major changes: The economy seemed to have lost the buoyancy of the 1990s, and in stark contrast to much of the post–World War II era, too-low inflation and ultralow interest rates were becoming major concerns for central bankers. The constraints on monetary policy posed by low interest rates would become salient when a global financial crisis, the worst at least since the 1930s and perhaps ever, pushed the economy into a deep recession.

THE DOT-COM BUBBLE AND THE 2001 RECESSION

The real Y2K shock was in the stock market. Greenspan and many on the FOMC had worried about "irrational exuberance" throughout much of the 1990s as the market shrugged off multiple international financial crises, pre-emptive monetary policy strikes against inflation, and Greenspan's jawboning. But, in retrospect, stock prices for most of the decade—a decade of sustained growth, low inflation, and comparatively low interest rates—had probably been less irrational than Greenspan and some of his FOMC colleagues feared. The economy was strong; inflation was low; and, given the alarming frequency of international financial crises in the 1990s, U.S. stocks promised a safer return than investing abroad.

Clearer signs of unhealthy speculative fever emerged in the last years of the decade. The internet was creating a vision of a "new economy" that at times enamored even Greenspan himself. Seemingly every dot-com company was hot, no matter how tenuous the underlying business proposition. People gave up their jobs to become day traders, using their home computers to buy and sell stocks. For a while it seemed impossible to lose money. As Robert Shiller, an expert on the psychology of financial bubbles, has observed, popular narratives can have tremendous power, in markets and in the economy generally.[1] The surest sign of a bubble is when everyone is confident that outsized price gains will continue with no end in sight. The tech-dominated Nasdaq stock index tripled between the end of 1997 and early 2000.

As Greenspan had pointed out, a stock-market boom can be simultaneously rational and irrational. The late-90s enthusiasm about the economic potential of the internet was not wrong—just early. Tech firms are among the largest and most dynamic firms in our economy today, and the imprint of the internet and other new technologies is evident in many industries, from retail to communications to finance. But, as in the 1920s boom, also fueled by expectations of a "new economy" built on technologies such as the automobile and radio, the market overreached. By the turn of the century, it was becoming evident that many dot-com companies would not earn a profit for a long time, if ever. In March 2000 a *Barron's* magazine cover article warned that, with revenues well below their optimistic forecasts, many internet companies were running out of cash.[2] Meanwhile, concerned that a boisterous economy would stoke inflation, the Fed had begun raising interest rates. In the second half of 1999 it took back the three quarter-percentage-point "insurance" cuts made after the Russian default, then raised rates an additional percentage point—to 6½ percent—in three moves in the first half of 2000. It was the highest setting of the funds rate in nearly a decade.

Combined with the shifting narrative about the prospects of dot-com companies, the monetary tightening of 1999–2000 helped trigger what policy maneuvers and Greenspan's jawboning in the previous decade had never achieved—a decisive break in the market. After peaking in March 2000, the Nasdaq index fell 47 percent by the end of the year. It bottomed in October 2002, down 72 percent from its peak. Broader stock indexes fell by less but were hardly immune. Over the same two and a half years, for example, the S&P 500 index—which reflects the values of 500 of America's largest companies—dropped by nearly half.

The October 1987 crash had demonstrated that even large stock-market declines may only modestly affect the economy, so long as they are not accompanied by high leverage and broader disruptions in credit markets. Generally speaking, that lesson was reaffirmed in 2001. Even as stock prices fell sharply, and despite the extraordinary shock of the terrorist attacks on September 11, the economy experienced only a moderate, eight-month recession, from March to November 2001.* Consumer spending cooled as stock-price gains evaporated and sentiment soured.[3] Investment in the tech sector dropped sharply, as did investment in supporting activities like office construction in Silicon Valley and fiber-optic network installations.

It helped that the FOMC quickly reversed its earlier tightening. After a January 3, 2001, conference call, the Committee started with a half-percentage-point intermeeting cut, from 6½ percent to 6 percent. Further rate cuts followed, to 3½ percent before the 9/11 attacks, and then to 1¾ percent by the end of 2001. The economy contracted in the third quarter of 2001, which included the terror attacks, and then resumed growing. The immediate economic impact of the burst bubble was thus limited. But

---

* An academic at the time, I was on the National Bureau of Economic Research committee that made the recession call.

something had changed, and the national mood in the early 2000s felt very different from the optimism of the 1990s. Although the 2001 recession was not particularly deep or long, the recovery, like the recovery from the 1990–91 recession, was sluggish.

Some of the change in mood reflected the events of 9/11, which shocked the country and convinced many that more attacks, and perhaps full-fledged war in the Middle East, were inevitable. The attacks tested the Fed in an unprecedented way, and it met the challenge. With billowing smoke from the strike on the Pentagon visible from his office window, Vice Chair Roger Ferguson—the only Fed Board member in Washington that day—worked with staff at the Board and at the New York Fed (only blocks from the World Trade Center) to help restore the functioning of the U.S. financial system.[4] (Greenspan and New York Fed President Bill McDonough were returning from a meeting in Switzerland on September 11.) One of Ferguson's first steps was to issue a statement, reminiscent of the Fed's statement after the 1987 crash: "The Federal Reserve is open and operating. The discount window is available to meet liquidity needs." With the Fed's help, most critical financial operations continued, despite the tragic human toll at the World Trade Center and extensive damage to infrastructure, including telecommunications networks. The stock market reopened in less than a week.

Besides stock declines and the new terrorist threat, which affected industries from air travel to insurance, several other factors increased uncertainty and depressed business confidence in the early 2000s. These included a spate of corporate scandals (Enron, WorldCom, Arthur Andersen); the Sarbanes-Oxley law, which in response to the scandals toughened accounting and auditing requirements on companies listed on public stock exchanges; and the growing possibility that the United States would invade Iraq, which it did in March 2003. (In its March 2003 statement, the FOMC made the unusual admission that, given the degree of geopolitical uncertainty, it could not usefully characterize the balance of risks to the economy.) In an environment of high uncertainty and slow growth, business investment was tepid. Particularly concerning, the job market remained soft even as output growth resumed. Once again, the phrase "jobless recovery" came in vogue. The unemployment rate, at 5.5 percent when the recession ended in November 2001, continued to rise, reaching 6.3 percent in June 2003.

Fiscal policy can bolster a sluggish economy and Greenspan—as he had during the George H. W. Bush and Clinton administrations—got involved in the policies of the incoming president, George W. Bush. The strong economic growth in the 1990s and capital gains in the stock market had raised tax revenues and generated a rare federal budget surplus. Fed staff had even considered how to conduct monetary policy if, as a consequence of ongoing surpluses, the federal government paid off its debt. (With no government debt outstanding, the Fed would no longer be able to buy and sell Treasury securities to adjust bank reserves and, thus, interest rates in its accustomed fashion.) During the campaign, Bush had promised a $1.6 trillion tax cut, which, given the prospect of budget surpluses, Greenspan, despite his fiscal conservatism, was inclined to support. Greenspan hedged in congressional testimony. Concerned as always about the federal government's long-run fiscal prospects, he proposed adding "triggers" to the tax bill that would rescind the cuts if the surplus fell by too much—but his generally favorable comments were interpreted as an unconditional endorsement of the Bush plan and, for years, were resented by many Democrats.* Bush signed a $1.35 trillion tax cut (over ten years) into law in June 2001.

As it turned out, the projected federal surplus proved ephemeral. The combination of the recession, the fall in stock prices (which reduced revenues from taxes on capital gains), and the tax cut pushed the budget back into deficit. Greenspan opposed Bush's next tax cut ($350 billion over ten years), which was passed in 2003. He nevertheless maintained a close relationship with the administration. In April 2003, more than a year before Greenspan's term as chair was to expire, Bush said he would reappoint him to a fifth term.

---

* Early in my time as chair, Senate Democratic Leader Harry Reid cited Greenspan's support of the Bush tax cuts in warning me not to meddle in fiscal policy.

Greenspan's main focus, of course, was monetary policy, and the slow recovery and post-2001 developments more generally were raising new concerns. Many economists and investors had begun to worry that the unexpectedly low levels of both interest rates and inflation that had persisted even after the economy had begun to grow again might be part of a new normal, rather than a temporary aberration. The Fed had cut the federal funds rate quickly in 2001 to fight the recession and, in response to the slow recovery and declining inflation, it would reduce the funds rate further—to 1 percent in 2003. Moreover, the Phillips curve, which had seemed dormant during the 1990s, was showing signs of working again—this time in the downward direction, with persistent slack in the labor market slowing price and wage increases.

For technical reasons, for monitoring inflation the Federal Reserve by this time was focusing less on the consumer price index and more on an alternative measure based on the price index for personal consumption expenditures (PCE).* By mid-2003, core PCE inflation (excluding food and energy prices) was running at about 1 percent and the Board staff projected it to fall further over the next year, with a one-in-four chance, according to the staff models, of outright deflation (falling prices). For central bankers whose formative years had been the 1970s and 1980s—basically all of the policymakers, at that point—the combination of very low interest rates and low inflation was disorienting. Could inflation, the bane of central bankers from Martin to Burns to Volcker, really be too low? The answer would become clear in the years to come: Yes, it could.

---

* The price index for PCE is produced by the Bureau of Economic Analysis as part of its calculation of GDP. One reason for the switch was that PCE inflation makes better allowance for ongoing change in the mix of goods and services purchased by consumers, whereas the CPI assumes the shares of spending on major categories of goods and services are fixed (with weights adjusted only periodically). Historically, inflation as measured by the PCE index has usually been a few tenths of a percentage point lower than CPI inflation, although the two indexes generally move closely together.

THE LONG-TERM DECLINE IN INTEREST
RATES AND INFLATION

In the short run, central banks exert considerable control over interest rates, especially short-term rates like the federal funds rate. However, over longer periods, other, structural economic factors determine the general, or "normal," level of interest rates. Following the ideas of the late-19th century Swedish economist Knut Wicksell, economists have defined the *neutral rate of interest*—R* (pronounced R-star) for short—as the rate of interest that prevails when the economy is at full employment with stable inflation.*5 Like the natural rate of unemployment, u*, the neutral rate of interest can change over time. Indeed, since the early 1980s—even as the Fed has gone through multiple sequences of tightening and easing, raising and lowering short-term rates—the overall tendency of interest rates has been consistently downward, both in the United States and in other developed economies. For example, as can be seen in Figure 4.1, the yield on ten-year Treasury securities peaked above 15 percent early in Volcker's term but has declined fairly steadily since then, to less than 2 percent in the period before the 2020 pandemic. This long-term decline in interest rates, continuing through both recessions and economic expansions, strongly suggests that the neutral interest rate is much lower today than it was a few decades ago.

Why has R* fallen so much on average over the past forty years, and why does it matter? The conquest of inflation under Volcker and Greenspan is one big reason for the decline in the neutral interest rate. As the early-20th century economist Irving Fisher observed, savers care about the buying power of their investment returns, not the number of dollars they receive.6 To preserve the purchasing power of their returns, they will demand, roughly speaking, an extra percentage point of interest for each additional percentage point in expected inflation, a rule of thumb

---

* I use (uppercase) R* to stand for the neutral rate in market, or nominal, terms. The real neutral rate, which is the nominal neutral rate less inflation, is often designated by (lowercase) r*. In this book I usually use R* to refer to the short-run neutral interest rate, but short-run and long-run neutral rates generally move closely together.

FIGURE 4.1.   TEN-YEAR TREASURY YIELDS, 1980–2021

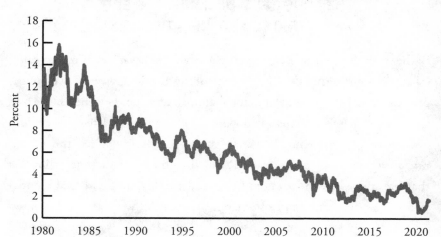

Even as the Federal Reserve has raised and lowered the federal funds rate to meet its macroeconomic goals, since the early 1980s the longer-term trend in market interest rates has been downward. Source: FRED database, Federal Reserve Bank of St. Louis.

known as the *Fisher principle*. Because of the Fisher principle, the decline in inflation in the past forty years—core PCE inflation averaged nearly 7 percent from 1975 to 1980 and a bit more than 1.5 percent from 2015 to 2020—can explain a substantial portion of the downward trend in the neutral interest rate.

However, declining inflation is only part of the story, as interest rates over the past four decades have fallen by even more than inflation. Put another way, the real, or inflation-adjusted, interest rates on Treasury securities and other investments—the interest rate less the rate of inflation—have also fallen, and by quite a lot in many cases.[*7] What else has been going on?

---

* According to a methodology developed in 2003 by Federal Reserve economists Thomas Laubach and John Williams (now president of the New York Fed), the real neutral interest rate in the United States fell from more than 3.5 percent in 1985 to less than 0.5 percent today, with a particularly sharp drop around the 2007–2009 financial crisis. A subsequent 2017 paper by the same authors, with Kathryn Holston, found similar results for other advanced economies.

Two related and complementary theses have sought to explain the long-term decline in real interest rates. Larry Summers, an economist whose role in fighting the international financial crises of the 1990s was discussed in the previous chapter, and who later served as Treasury secretary under President Clinton, has popularized what he calls the *secular stagnation* hypothesis.[8] The phrase was coined in 1938 by Alvin Hansen, a prominent Harvard economist.[9] Hansen feared that factors such as slower population growth and a declining pace of technological innovation would leave the economy stagnant even after the end of the Great Depression. Of course, that didn't happen—the Depression and World War II were followed by an economic boom—but Summers sees new relevance in Hansen's ideas.

In Summers's updating of Hansen's hypothesis, the modern U.S. economy suffers from persistent drags, including slowing labor force growth as the population ages, a dearth of major technological advances compared with earlier periods, and the fact that the most rapidly growing industries do not require as much physical capital (think of Facebook's relatively modest needs for equipment and buildings versus those of, say, General Motors in the 1950s). According to Summers's variant of the secular stagnation hypothesis, these factors add up to a weak demand for new capital goods as well as slower economic growth overall. Slow growth and limited opportunities for productive capital investments in turn depress the demand for investable funds, lowering the neutral rate of interest. Importantly, secular stagnation implies that the sluggish economic recoveries of recent decades did not result primarily from one-off factors, such as the bursting of the tech bubble, 9/11, or corporate scandals. Rather, slow growth and low interest rates are the results of fundamental forces that likely will persist.

Are there solutions to secular stagnation? Public policy can affect trends in demographics and productivity growth, but generally only over a long time. In principle, public investment—construction of new highways, airports, and bridges, for example—could substitute for lagging private investment, and Summers has argued forcefully for aggressive fiscal policies to help offset secular stagnation. Fiscal deficits around the world have in fact been quite large for some time, even before ballooning during the pandemic. However, Summers, in work with Łukasz Rachel, concluded that, without sustained fiscal deficits, real neutral interest rates would have been even lower, probably quite negative.[10]

The second, complementary explanation for declining real interest rates is a hypothesis known as the *global savings glut*. As a Fed governor, I introduced the concept in a 2005 speech.[11] The basic idea is that, at the level of real interest rates that has prevailed over much of the post–World War II period, global saving today significantly exceeds the global demand for new capital investment—which, along with government deficits, is the main use of savings. Because the supply of savings exceeds the demand for investable funds, savings earn lower returns than in the past. Where are the extra savings coming from? In my 2005 speech, I focused on the high saving propensity of people in China and other rapidly growing East Asian countries, as well as saving by high-earning oil producers like Saudi Arabia. More recently, the largest sources of global savings have included Europe, especially Germany.

More fundamentally, though, the rise in global savings has been driven by worldwide income growth and demographics. The incomes of billions of people around the world have increased significantly in recent decades, giving them greater capacity to build wealth. At the same time, people in both emerging-market economies and most developed economies are living longer, leading to longer expected retirements, which in turn require people to save more. With both the capacity and the need to save greatly increased, and with investment opportunities limited by slow growth in working-age populations and in productivity, real (inflation-adjusted) rates of return have fallen, not just in the United States but globally.

The secular stagnation and global savings glut stories differ somewhat in emphasis. Secular stagnation arguments, at least initially, focused on the United States, whereas the global savings glut thesis drew attention to the worldwide nature of saving and investment flows and the increasing integration of global capital markets that facilitate those flows. Secular stagnation has emphasized the demand for investable funds (to finance business capital formation or government deficits), while the global savings glut hypothesis has focused more on the supply of funds. Nevertheless, the two theses are mutually reinforcing. Both argue that, for a variety of demographic, economic, and technological reasons, the global supply of savings has increasingly outstripped the demand for those funds. That imbalance is persistently holding down real interest rates, even when the economy is at full employment and monetary policy is not expansionary.

Other theories have been advanced to explain the long-term decline in R*. Some economists have argued that, in recent decades, there has been a chronic global shortage of safe assets—securities that hold their value during economic crises.[12] A general shortage of safe assets can help explain why yields on securities like U.S. Treasuries, which tend to be in especially high demand during periods of economic uncertainty, have trended downward particularly sharply.* Recently, it has also been suggested that increased wealth inequality can help explain the falling neutral rate, since the wealthiest tend to save more of their income.[13] (However, although inequality has increased in the United States and some other advanced economies, it has not increased globally in recent decades.) While economists do not fully agree on the reasons for the long-term decline in the neutral rate, that it has declined significantly over the past forty years or so is beyond dispute.

Why does the long-term decline in R*, the neutral rate of interest, matter? It obviously concerns savers and investors, who earn lower returns. On the other hand, borrowers—including governments, homeowners, and corporate bond issuers—benefit from lower interest rates, all else equal.

The lower level of the neutral interest rate matters to the Fed (and to other central banks) because it potentially limits the scope for monetary policy. In the 1980s and 1990s, substantial monetary easing could be achieved simply by reducing the federal funds rate. Before the global financial crisis, in a typical recession, the Fed stimulated the economy by cutting the funds rate between 5 and 6 percentage points. However, when the neutral interest rate—the rate that prevails at full employment—is already very

---

* Pandemic-era federal deficits, which add to the supply of Treasury securities, should—according to this theory—help ease the shortage of safe assets and push up Treasury yields over time.

low, say only 2 or 3 percent, then monetary policymakers have less room to cut when a recession hits and thereby less power to stimulate growth.

The lowest level at which monetary policymakers are willing (or able) to set their short-term policy rate is called the *effective lower bound*. Before the financial crisis of 2007–2009, the effective lower bound in most countries was assumed to be zero, or perhaps slightly positive, out of policymakers' concern that zero rates would interfere with the functioning of the financial system.* After the crisis, some central banks revised down their estimates of the lower bound, setting their policy rates at zero or, as we'll see, even modestly negative values. (Negative policy rates can be enforced by requiring banks to pay a fee on the reserves they hold at the central bank.) The key point is that when the neutral rate of interest is low, an effective floor on the policy rate—usually in the vicinity of zero—limits the scope for central bankers to rely on traditional short-term rate cuts.

The possibility that, because of the lower bound, monetary policy cannot provide enough stimulus is concerning enough. But a vicious circle can make the problem worse. If the effective lower bound prevents monetary policy from providing adequate stimulus, then over time unemployment will be higher and (because of the increased slack) inflation lower than monetary policymakers would like. Declining inflation, working through the Fisher principle, in turn tends to lower the neutral interest rate. But a lower neutral interest rate further reduces the scope for monetary policy to stimulate the economy, completing the vicious circle. This situation has been called a *Japan trap*, because it describes that country's experience in recent decades, during which inflation and interest rates have hovered around zero and monetary policy has had limited effect.

---

* For example, banks and money market mutual funds, which promise their retail depositors and investors at least a zero return, would find it difficult to make a profit if their short-term investments also paid zero.

THE 2003 DEFLATION SCARE: FORWARD
GUIDANCE TO THE FOREFRONT

Low interest rates and declining inflation after the 2001 recession raised the possibility that the United States might fall into a Japan trap. Given the difficulties of exiting very low inflation or deflation, most FOMC participants agreed that situation must be avoided at all costs. As Greenspan would later write, by mid-2003 deflation was "Topic A" in the Committee discussions.[14]

What might be done to avoid the combination of persistently low inflation and low interest rates in the United States? In 2003, with the funds rate already very low, the question became whether tools other than further short-term rate cuts could help a flagging economy. Economists had studied possible alternatives, often in connection with Japan's long-standing battle with deflation.[15] In October 1999 the Federal Reserve held a research conference on policy at the effective lower bound in Woodstock, Vermont, which I attended when still a professor. In November 2002, having recently joined the Board as a governor, I gave a speech titled "Deflation—Making Sure 'It' Doesn't Happen Here," which discussed alternative monetary tools, and I published research on the topic with Fed staff.[16] However, before 2003, the FOMC had never systematically examined how it might respond if the economy needed monetary stimulus but further cuts to the funds rate were infeasible or undesirable.

Greenspan directed the staff to present options to the Committee for dealing with the lower bound. The staff's extensive work would come in handy a few years later when the problems posed by the lower bound were no longer quite so hypothetical. Some of the options the staff reviewed, such as purchasing large quantities of Treasury securities to push down longer-term interest rates, looked pretty exotic and seemed neither necessary nor desirable in 2003. (This did not prevent some speculation in bond markets that such purchases might occur, however.) The Committee instead opted to rely on public communication to achieve its goals.

Why communication? How can simply talking about policy help? The evolution of the post-meeting statement under Greenspan, which showed that markets responded not only to current policy actions but to the Committee's hints about future policy, pointed the way. The interest rate that the Fed most directly controls, the federal funds rate, is not in itself very significant. It applies only at a very short maturity (overnight or over the weekend) and to a relatively small market (loans of reserves between banks). Changes in the funds rate affect the economy primarily through their influence on other asset prices and yields, including longer-term interest rates, like mortgage rates and corporate bond rates.

The link to these more important rates arises because, in part, longer-term interest rates depend on market expectations of future short-term interest rates. For example, if investors come to believe the Fed is going to keep short rates higher than previously thought, longer-term rates will tend to move higher as well. If longer-term rates did not rise, investors would earn more by investing in short-term securities, rolling them over when they mature, than by holding longer-term bonds. Likewise, if investors come to believe that the Fed plans to keep short-term rates low for a while, then longer-term rates should also move down. In short, by shaping market expectations about where the funds rate will be set in the future, the FOMC may be able to influence current longer-term rates, which most affect the economy. By similar logic, market expectations about the funds rate affect other important asset prices, such as stock prices and the dollar exchange rate, each of which also has economic effects.

Although the chair and other FOMC participants communicate policy intentions in many ways, by this time the post-meeting statement best reflected the FOMC's collective view and was closely watched by markets. The Committee decided to exploit this fact. At the May 2003 meeting, the FOMC for the first time indicated its concern that inflation might fall too low. The Committee's statement included the (admittedly convoluted) phrase: "the probability, though minor, of an unwelcome substantial fall in inflation exceeds that of a pickup of inflation from its already low level." If policymakers were worried about inflation falling too low, the implication was that policy would remain easy. Indeed, in June the Committee followed through by cutting the funds rate to 1 percent, its lowest level since 1958.

However, the hint was not strong enough. By the August meeting, markets had shrugged off the Fed's subtle message and had begun to anticipate near-term tightening. Committee participants focused again on how they might better align the market's expectations for the funds rate with their own. Greenspan suggested including more-explicit guidance about the future course of policy in the statement, and the FOMC concurred. The August post-meeting statement reiterated the Committee's concerns about an "unwelcome substantial fall in inflation . . . from its already low level," but then added, "In these circumstances, the Committee believes that policy accommodation can be maintained for a considerable period."

The changes in language in May and August 2003 were important in several respects. The reference, beginning in May, to an "unwelcome" fall in inflation contrasted starkly with Fed policy of previous decades, in which low or declining inflation had always been treated as desirable. Effectively, the Fed had publicly acknowledged that it had an inflation target, and that the target was greater than zero, even if it was not yet willing to give a precise number. Moreover, according to the May statement, low inflation would likely be the Committee's "predominant concern for the foreseeable future."

The August statement also explained what the Committee intended to do about the "unwelcome" decline in inflation: It planned to keep policy easy "for a considerable period." This language was not very specific, but it did indicate that market expectations for near-term tightening were unfounded. This time the signal came through loud and clear; long-term rates fell sharply over the ensuing weeks. "It's very evident that our effort to communicate that message [of policy ease] has succeeded," Greenspan said at the December meeting.[17] The August 2003 statement is an example of what we now call *forward guidance*, or communication by monetary policymakers about the likely course of policy. Forward guidance to manage policy expectations, and thus to affect broader financial conditions, would become increasingly important, particularly when the funds rate approached its lower bound.

The Committee retained the "considerable period" language until January 2004, when it executed a gentle pivot by stating that it could "be patient in removing its policy accommodation." In this way the FOMC signaled that it was now looking to tighten policy, but cautiously. Following a period of strong growth and labor market improvement—the unemployment rate had been moving steadily down for about a year—tightening began with a rate hike in June 2004, along with the guidance that policy accommodation was expected to be taken back "at a pace that is likely to be measured." The rate hikes that followed were indeed measured. They never exceeded a quarter of a percentage point at a time. But they occurred at seventeen consecutive meetings, through June 2006. When the hikes ended, the funds rate target was back to a historically normal-looking 5¼ percent, the unemployment rate had fallen to less than 5 percent, and core inflation was close to 2 percent. By those metrics, at least, the Fed's policies appeared successful.

In August 2005 the Federal Reserve System held its annual meetings in Jackson Hole, Wyoming. The conference, hosted since 1982 in the majestic setting of the Grand Tetons by the Federal Reserve Bank of Kansas City, drew, as always, a distinguished list of participants from around the world, from central banks, the media, and academia. Greenspan—then in his final months as chair—was feted, hailed by his former vice chair and occasional critic Alan Blinder as having "a legitimate claim to being the greatest central banker who ever lived." [18]

THE HOUSING BUBBLE

Notwithstanding the lavish praise for Greenspan, danger was brewing. House prices had been rising briskly since the late 1990s. They rose especially rapidly toward the end of Greenspan's tenure, by more than 13 percent in both 2004 and 2005. [19] Together with the weakening mortgage lending standards that helped to fuel it, what proved to be an enormous bubble in house prices would provide the tinder for the worst financial crisis since the Great Depression.

What caused the bubble? Some have argued that easy monetary policy stimulated house prices, but the evidence for that view is slim and it has little support among economists.*[20] Like other interest rates, thirty-year mortgage rates had trended slowly down since the 1980s, but in 2004 and 2005 they remained around 6 percent, or 4 to 5 percent in inflation-adjusted terms, not levels associated before or since with exceptional house price gains. A retrospective study found that changes in real interest rates (which themselves were not entirely due to monetary policy) can explain only about one-fifth of the increase in house prices between 1996 and 2006.[21] Another study confirmed that, although low interest rates do of course tend to raise house prices, the historical relationship between the two is consistent with interest-rate movements making at most a moderate contribution to the early-2000s bubble.[22] In addition, sharp increases in house prices occurred at about the same time in other countries, like the United Kingdom, that ran more-restrictive monetary policies than the United States.[23]

If not interest rates or monetary policy, then what? Most research on the origins of the bubble has focused on three factors: mass psychology; financial innovations that reduced the incentive for careful lending; and inadequate regulation of lending practices and risk-taking generally.

Mass psychology supported widespread and growing optimism about housing as an investment. Rapid house price increases in the late 1990s and early 2000s, especially in a few major cities, led many to believe that house prices would inevitably continue to rise, a belief reinforced through social interactions ("My brother-in-law made a fortune flipping houses!")

---

* In 2017, the Initiative on Global Markets surveyed economic experts in the United States and Europe on what they saw as the main factors contributing to the 2008 global financial crisis, offering twelve alternatives. Flawed financial regulation and supervision was ranked first, followed by underestimation of the risks of new financial instruments and bad mortgage lending. Loose monetary policy was ranked next to last.

and by the media. Robert Shiller's theory of popular narratives—simple stories that structure people's thinking about economic events and that "go viral" in the public consciousness—seems to fit the case well.[24] Shiller noted that house prices began to accelerate in the United States around 1998 and attributed the boom to the same overoptimistic thinking that helped generate the tech bubble in stocks.

Financial innovation, combined with the global savings glut and the perceived shortage of safe assets, also helped to inflate the housing bubble. Global savers in the early part of the 2000s—including in high-saving China, which was at about that time being increasingly integrated into global trade and capital markets—were scrambling to find investments that, on the one hand, paid at least a moderate return but, on the other hand, appeared reasonably safe and liquid. Such assets were in increasingly short supply as the savings glut took hold. In particular, the shift toward smaller deficits or even surpluses by the federal government limited the supply of the most coveted of safe assets, U.S. Treasury securities.

Wall Street financial engineers aimed to meet the powerful demand for (putatively) safe assets by constructing and selling complex securities that packaged together a wide range of mortgages (and often other types of private credit). Because combining many different credit assets was assumed, through diversification, to reduce the overall risk of the security, and because the resulting security could be carved into riskier and less risky components, this process created new, apparently safe assets that could be sold to global investors. The enormous demand for raw material for these credit-backed securities in turn encouraged mortgage originators to drastically lower standards to generate more loans. After all, if the mortgage went bad it was not the originator's problem, but the problem of the ultimate purchaser of the mortgage-backed security. Looser credit standards in turn increased the effective demand for housing, fueling the bubble.

Finally, regulators failed to prevent a proliferation of gimmicky and deceptive mortgage loans. In some cases, borrowers were allowed to pay so little each month that their principal balance rose rather than fell over time. Regulators also did not insist that mortgage lenders require sufficient documentation to ensure creditworthiness. One result was the infamous NINJA loan—no income, no job, no assets; lenders verified only a borrower's credit rating.

The regulatory failures in turn flowed from several factors, beyond regulators' lack of diligence and imagination. Most important, for historical and political reasons, U.S. financial regulation was poorly designed and did not adequately reflect the evolving nature of the modern financial system. The regulatory structure had both large gaps—for example, many nonbank mortgage lenders and mortgage investors were subject to very limited oversight—and overlaps, where multiple regulators clashed and sometimes competed for "clients." In March 2007 the subprime lender Countrywide, by changing the charter of the depository institution it owned, replaced the Fed as its primary supervisor with the Treasury Department's Office of Thrift Supervision, which Countrywide expected to be more easygoing.[25] Regulatory gaps—particularly severe outside the traditional banking system—reduced regulators' ability to monitor and respond to mortgage trends. In 2005, for example, only about 20 percent of subprime loans (mortgages to borrowers with weak credit records) were made by lenders under direct federal supervision, while about 50 percent were made by institutions chartered and supervised by state regulators, whose resources and effectiveness varied greatly.[*][26]

It mattered also that, in the run-up to the crisis, the political winds favored easier, rather than tougher, mortgage standards. Many legislators and regulators were loath to be seen as standing in the way of an overdue expansion of home ownership to minorities and other groups that had traditionally been shut out. If nontraditional lending arrangements that accommodated weaker credit records were needed to get lower-income people into their own homes, then—in the widely held view of the time—the

---

* The other 30 percent were nonbank lenders owned by bank holding companies, which in turn were supervised by the Federal Reserve. However, in what became known as the "Fed lite" provision, the 1999 Gramm-Leach-Bliley financial regulatory overhaul law presumed that the Fed as the holding company overseer would defer to the primary supervisors (usually at the state level) of holding company subsidiaries.

risk might be worth it.* Unfortunately, it was these financially weak home buyers who would take the biggest hit when the mortgage crisis arrived.

In arguing that psychology, Wall Street financial innovation, and a flawed regulatory system drove America's housing bubble, I don't absolve the Federal Reserve from its share of blame—and, after August 2002, that includes me personally. Fragmented financial regulation—in particular, the absence of any agency responsible for the stability of the financial system as a whole—and the political support for expanded homeownership would have hindered any effort by the Fed or other regulators to slow or reverse the building risks in housing and mortgage markets. Nevertheless, in retrospect at least, we can identify steps that the Fed and other regulators might have taken. For example, Greenspan and other agency heads could have more aggressively used their bully pulpits to point out the growing risks or the deficiencies of the regulatory system. This likely would not have led to dramatic changes—for years, Greenspan actively criticized the federal mortgage agencies, Fannie Mae and Freddie Mac, over their inadequate capital and risky practices, with essentially no effect—but jawboning would at least have raised the consciousness of Congress and the public. The Fed also might have pushed banks to hold more loss-absorbing capital and to better measure and manage the risks they were taking. And it could have made greater use of its authority to outlaw lending practices deemed "unfair or deceptive"; more often used its contingent authority to examine nonbank firms owned by bank holding companies; and more systematically assessed risks to the financial system.[27]

Should Greenspan have understood in real time that tougher regulation was needed? As someone who was at the Fed during part of this period and did not anticipate the crisis, it's difficult for me to judge. For what it's worth, I believe Greenspan's blind spot was *not* inattention to possible risks. In his final years as chair he expressed concerns about "froth" in the

---

* Regulators and politicians of the time drew a strong distinction between subprime lending, which aimed to help people with lower credit scores become homeowners and was desirable, and predatory lending, which involved unfair or deceptive practices intended to take advantage of less sophisticated borrowers and should be prohibited.

housing market (although he saw it confined mostly to certain geographic areas) and the general increase in risk-taking in financial markets.[28] His libertarian roots notwithstanding, he was also not opposed to financial regulation in principle. His error was that he trusted too much in market forces, including the self-interest of bank executives and boards, to limit bad lending and excessive risk-taking. Moreover, he was pessimistic about the ability of the government's bank examiners to usefully second-guess banks' decisions in most cases. He saw examiners, good intentions notwithstanding, as vastly outnumbered and outgunned by the thousands of highly compensated and specialized employees of international banks. Thus, in retrospect, he was too passive about intervening in even the parts of the financial system under the Fed's authority. Greenspan would acknowledge as much. In congressional testimony in October 2008, he expressed his "shocked disbelief" that market forces and bankers' self-interest had not been more effective in preventing the bad lending that led to the crisis.[29]

This "flaw" in Greenspan's thinking, as he called it, was shared by many economists and policymakers of the precrisis era. The 1980s and 1990s were a period of substantial deregulation in many industries, as policymakers became increasingly amenable to free-market arguments. The savings and loan crisis in particular, which was seen as having been caused in part by excessive regulation of the S&L's deposit rates and lending activities, helped spur financial deregulation and innovation, which in turn created greater scope for risk-taking. The more general lesson may be that Fed chairs, and other leaders, should be careful of conventional wisdom. Like others, I have criticized Arthur Burns for letting inflation get out of the control in the 1970s, but Burns's monetary policies conformed with the views of many economists and politicians of the time. In his single-minded attack on inflation, Volcker was the maverick. The need to hear a range of views is another argument for central banks to be transparent about their thinking and open to exchanges with outsiders.

Whatever the source of the housing bubble, once it took shape monetary policymakers faced a difficult call. If the house price increases were unsustainable, as some suspected (including Greenspan), then the question was what to do about it. A sharp tightening of monetary policy to slow house price gains relatively early on, say in 2002 or 2003, seemed a non-starter. The near-term imperatives of supporting the sluggish economic recovery and avoiding deflation argued for easier, not tighter, policy in the years following the 2001 recession. Moreover, in 2002 or 2003, the view that house prices were in an unsustainable bubble was by no means universally accepted.

The FOMC's solution was to keep rates low for a relatively short time—the funds rate remained at its nadir of 1 percent for only about a year, from mid-2003 to mid-2004—and, once signs of recovery became well established, to begin a gradual but extended policy tightening. If the air could be let slowly out of the housing bubble, perhaps the economy as a whole could glide to a soft landing. That approach looked promising in 2006 and early 2007, as the economy continued to grow despite falling house prices and rising subprime mortgage defaults. However, that strategy did not sufficiently recognize the serious financial vulnerabilities created by a decade of bad lending.

5

THE GLOBAL FINANCIAL CRISIS

I BECAME FED CHAIR IN FEBRUARY 2006, with the unenviable assignment of following the legendary Greenspan. Before joining the Fed as a Board member in 2002, I had spent more than twenty years in academia, starting at Stanford's Graduate School of Business in 1979 and then, in 1985, moving to Princeton, where my wife Anna and I raised our two children. I had a rewarding career as a researcher and teacher, focusing on monetary policy, financial markets, and economic history. My work on the Great Depression supported the evolving consensus that the economic collapse of the 1930s resulted from the malfunctioning of the international gold standard and a global financial crisis that the authorities failed to contain.[1]

In early 2002 I was invited to interview with President George W. Bush for a position on the Fed's Board of Governors. It seemed an ideal opportunity to put what I had learned in my research and writing to practical use. I agreed to be nominated, the Senate confirmed me without controversy, and I started my policymaking career in August 2002. I found the environment at the Fed stimulating and collegial (some of my former graduate students were on the staff). I joined in the debates about deflation risk and supported the rate cuts and the use of forward guidance in 2003. I also spoke publicly about issues important to me, including advocating that the Fed introduce a numerical target for inflation as a step toward more effective and transparent policymaking.

In June 2005 I moved, for seven months, to the White House to chair President Bush's Council of Economic Advisers. Heading the council was fascinating but high-pressure work. My colleagues and I had to develop instant expertise in a wide range of issues, from health care to immigration. When Hurricane Katrina hit New Orleans, we worked on problems like how to reroute gasoline shipments to supply the stricken area. I frequently briefed the president and vice president on the economy, building personal relationships that would prove useful during the financial crisis.

Doubtless my existing relationship with the president was an important reason why Bush nominated me to succeed Greenspan. The Senate again approved me without opposition. I promised continuity with the Maestro's policies. And my goal, at least initially, was to follow through on that promise. I worked with the FOMC to continue the long sequence of quarter-point rate hikes begun under Greenspan in 2004, ending them in June 2006. By then the economy seemed to have finally recovered fully from the 2001 recession and the ensuing jobless recovery, with the unemployment rate fluctuating narrowly around 4.5 percent from the fall of 2006 through the spring of 2007. With a modest rise in core inflation having ended deflation concerns, it seemed possible that another soft landing had been achieved.

The greatest uncertainties as I settled into my new position were in the housing and mortgage markets. The extended rise in the Fed's policy rate likely contributed to the decline in housing prices that began in the summer of 2006, shortly after I became chair, although mortgage rates rose by surprisingly little even as the FOMC tightened.[2] As dramatized by Michael Lewis's book *The Big Short* and the subsequent film, by this time some financial market players had become increasingly skeptical about the housing and mortgage boom, and newly developed derivative financial instruments tied to the values of subprime mortgages made it easier for the skeptics to monitor and bet against the subprime market.[3] In any case, the FOMC was watching housing and mortgage developments closely. We were particularly concerned about growing delinquency rates among lower-income mortgage borrowers and the associated increase in foreclosures.

We hoped for a relatively benign outcome if—and these turned out to be important "ifs"—housing price declines continued at a moderate rate and the rising delinquency and default rates on subprime mortgages (which constituted a relatively small share of mortgages and credit generally) did not infect broader financial markets. In March 2007, in congressional testimony, I said that, based on what we had seen so far, the subprime problems were "likely to be contained."[4] It was as much an expression of hope as a prediction, but it seemed a reasonable assessment at the time. I believed that by stopping rate increases in mid-2006—despite objections by some hawks on the Committee—we had avoided over-tightening. If inflation remained moderate, as expected, then the end of tightening should give the economy the breathing room it needed to absorb the effects of the cooling housing market. And indeed, despite the continuing fall in housing prices, the economy continued a steady expansion, growing about 2.5 percent at an annual rate over the remaining three quarters of 2007.

Our guarded optimism about the economy did not imply that we intended to ignore housing and mortgage developments. In public forums, I advocated a targeted approach: With the encouragement of their supervisors, banks and other lenders should clean up problems already apparent in the mortgage market. I argued that in many cases banks and other mortgage holders, rather than foreclosing on delinquent borrowers, would be better off renegotiating with the borrowers to lower monthly payments while keeping the borrowers in their homes. Loan modifications were obviously good for the borrowers. But lenders, and the broader economy, should also benefit, I argued, because foreclosed homes often sat empty, and empty homes, frequently neglected, lost value while depressing housing prices in their neighborhood.

The Fed encouraged the banks it supervised to cooperate with a voluntary loan modification program—Hope Now—led by President Bush's Treasury secretary, Hank Paulson, and Housing and Urban Development Secretary Alphonso Jackson. The Federal Reserve Banks organized local events to promote and facilitate loan modifications. But the program's benefits would be limited. Bankers talked a good game but remained skeptical of the argument that renegotiating troubled mortgages would be profitable, especially if doing so encouraged some nondelinquent borrowers to engage in "strategic default"—failing to pay in the hope of getting better terms. Moreover, many mortgages, wrapped as they were into complex securities, could not legally be renegotiated without the permission of investors scattered around the world. And mortgage servicers—the firms or bank divisions that would have to execute loan modifications—were grossly unprepared to handle a surge of modifications or delinquencies, a problem that would dog all subsequent efforts to clean up the mortgage mess.

THE GREAT FINANCIAL PANIC

The Fed was thus working on two tracks in 2006 and 2007: using monetary policy to try to keep the economy healthy and deploying regulatory tools (including moral suasion) to tackle the deteriorating mortgage situation. But in the summer of 2007 we were seeing early evidence that subprime problems threatened the broader financial system.

In August 2007 the French bank BNP Paribas made the surprising announcement that it had stopped investor redemptions from three of its funds holding securities backed by U.S. subprime mortgages. The bank said that, under current market conditions, it could no longer value those securities. In other words, by the summer of 2007 investors had begun to distrust subprime mortgage securities so much that they were unwilling to buy them at any price. The announcement, seen by many as a wake-up call, set off a wave of panicky selling around the world.

Why were investors suddenly so afraid? During the years when housing prices only went up, both borrowers and lenders had seen subprime lending as relatively low risk. If borrowers could not make their monthly payment, the reasoning went, they could sell their house and pay off the mortgage (making the lender whole) while still enjoying a profit from capital gains on the home. Win-win. That strategy no longer worked when housing prices started to fall. When prices began to slide, subprime borrowers who couldn't pay faced default and eviction, and subprime lenders and investors held mortgages that might well prove worthless.

Still, at the time, less than 8 percent of outstanding U.S. mortgages were subprime loans with adjustable interest rates, the category most exposed to the Fed's rate increases from 2004 to 2006.[5] Indeed, in early 2007 the Fed staff calculated that the immediate default of every subprime mortgage (with both adjustable and fixed rates; 13 percent of all mortgages) would impose aggregate losses on lenders and investors smaller than the losses from a single bad day in global stock markets. Most other mortgages, including the prime mortgages issued to borrowers with good credit and the so-called Alt-A mortgages issued to borrowers with medium-quality credit, were still performing well in 2007. Moreover, banks appeared to be in good financial shape, with only one federally insured bank having failed in the previous two and a half years and with banks having little trouble attracting deposits and other short-term funding.[*] With what looked to be adequate levels of capital, at least as measured by the regulatory standards at the time, banks appeared able to absorb the expected mortgage losses.

These considerations had helped to motivate my "likely to be contained" comment in March, but they were false comfort. Although actual and prospective losses on subprime mortgages were not themselves extraordinarily large, the subprime debacle proved massively damaging because it triggered an old-fashioned financial panic—albeit, in an unfamiliar guise. The panic began with subprime mortgages but ultimately mushroomed into a loss of confidence in virtually all forms of household and business credit, nearly bringing down the financial system and, with it, the economy.

As an economic historian, I knew something about financial panics, which date back centuries if not millennia (the Roman emperor Tiberius stopped a crisis in 33 CE by offering interest-free loans).[6] Most panics follow

---

* The one failure in a two-and-a-half-year period contrasts, for example, with the more than 100 depository institution failures each year from 1984 through 1992, during the savings and loan crisis and credit crunch.

a similar sequence. Typically, they occur after a period in which banks or other financial institutions have greatly expanded their speculative loans or investments, financed largely by issuing debt, especially short-term debt. Things go well for a while as borrower and lender optimism fuels a credit boom. There may even be talk of a "new era" in which the old rules don't apply. Sometimes the optimism proves justified, but sometimes bad news about some of the investments—possibly true, though false rumors have also started panics—suddenly changes investor attitudes. Those who can get out, do. Providers of short-term money to financial institutions, who can easily pull their funding and have little to lose by doing so, are the most prone to run. Like the proverbial patrons in a crowded theater when someone shouts "FIRE!" (true or not), it's in everyone's individual interest to be among the first out the door, even though an orderly exit best serves the collective good.

A run on the short-term debt of key financial institutions in turn leaves them unable to fund their investments, which are typically longer-term and *illiquid*—not easy to sell quickly at full value. If they cannot replace the lost funding, lenders may have little choice but to sell their assets—the good and the not-so-good ones—at whatever price they can get. A general rush to sell—a *fire sale*—results in plunging asset prices, pushing institutions toward insolvency and magnifying the panic. Needless to say, no one makes new loans during a panic—why do so when old loans can be bought at bargain-basement prices?—and the lack of new credit, falling asset prices, and plummeting confidence drag down the broader economy.

As we've seen, disruptive financial panics throughout the 19th century had motivated Congress to create the Federal Reserve to serve as lender of last resort, and waves of bank failures had greatly worsened the Great Depression. But in the summer of 2007, financial panics seemed like ancient history, at least in the United States.* The creation of federal

---

* The crises in Mexico, southeast Asia, and Russia during the 1990s were essentially panics, driven by investors' withdrawal of short-term funding—but many economists rationalized that those were emerging-market countries with underdeveloped and underregulated financial systems. Crises in the 1980s and 1990s in Japan and the Nordic countries were likewise often dismissed as the result of factors specific to those countries.

deposit insurance by Congress in 1933 had largely ended runs on banks by ordinary depositors, who knew they would be protected even if their bank failed. The seven or so decades that followed that and other New Deal reforms—dubbed the "quiet period" in American finance by financial historian Gary Gorton—saw numerous financial disruptions, including foreign financial crises and the blowup of the savings and loans, but no major panics and no domestic crises that seriously threatened the overall economy.[7] However, over this long period, complex new vulnerabilities were developing that would lay the groundwork for a global financial crisis of unprecedented scale. Among the most important of these were the rapid growth of shadow banking, wholesale funding, and securitization.

Shadow Banking and Wholesale Funding

Shadow banking refers to a network of nonbank financial institutions and markets that developed in the United States alongside the traditional commercial banking system; it collectively provides many of the same services as banks—including business and household lending and the creation of liquid, short-term assets for investors. In the years prior to the crisis, the shadow banking system comprised a diverse group of lightly regulated firms, like mortgage companies and consumer finance companies that lent primarily to households, as well as institutions such as investment banks and hedge funds that operated primarily in securities markets. Another key component of the shadow banking system, *money market mutual funds*, invested in relatively safe, short-term assets and promised on-demand liquidity to their shareholders, providing a close substitute for bank deposits. Shadow banks competed with the traditional banking system but also complemented it. For example, major banks often owned shadow banking firms, such as mortgage brokers or securities dealers, or sponsored shadow banking activities such as various off-balance-sheet investment vehicles.

All credit providers need sources of funding, and shadow banks are no exception. Federally insured deposits are available only to commercial banks and savings associations, so shadow banking firms typically relied instead on various types of uninsured short-term funding, known collectively as *wholesale funding*, to distinguish it from *retail funding*, like individuals' deposits in commercial banks. Important examples of wholesale funding include commercial paper and repurchase agreements, or repos for short.

Commercial paper, a very old form of business financing, is a type of short-term debt, traditionally used by nonfinancial companies to finance inventories or for other short-term needs. Historically, commercial paper was usually unsecured—meaning that it was a general obligation of the borrowing firm, not backed by specific collateral, and subject to loss if the borrower went bankrupt. However, in the years before the crisis, some financial institutions began to repurpose commercial paper, using it to finance so-called *special-purpose vehicles*, legal structures set up only for the purpose of holding a variety of loans and securities. Special-purpose vehicles, which were legally separate from the banks or other financial institutions that created them, became an important means of holding and funding assets in the shadow banking system. Under the rules that governed special-purpose vehicles, in case of default, the funders of the vehicle had no claim on the institution that set up the vehicle, but instead received a share of the vehicle's assets. Commercial paper issued to fund special-purpose vehicles thus became known as *asset-backed commercial paper*. Reflecting the growth in special-purpose vehicles, asset-backed commercial paper grew rapidly before the crisis, reaching about $1.2 trillion by the summer of 2007.[8]

Repos, the second major type of wholesale funding, are effectively short-term—often overnight—collateralized loans.* Each repo loan is protected by specific collateral, in the form of a financial asset put up by the borrower. If the borrower fails to repay, the lender gets the collateral, without having to go through a formal bankruptcy process. The amount of collateral a repo lender requires depends on the riskiness and marketability of the collateral

---

* In practice, repos are not legally structured as loans. In a typical repo transaction, an institution that needs funds—say a hedge fund or a broker-dealer—sells a security (a Treasury bond, for example) to a supplier of funds—a money market mutual fund, for example. By contract, the security seller buys it back at a slightly higher price the next day—hence the name "repurchase agreement," or repo. Economically, this arrangement is equivalent to an overnight, collateralized loan.

asset. For example, for each dollar of (highly safe and liquid) U.S. Treasury securities put up as collateral, a borrower might be able to get a loan of 99 cents, whereas a dollar's worth of subprime mortgages might have collateralized a loan of only 60 cents. In this example, the *haircut* on Treasury securities (the difference between its market value and what can be borrowed against it) is 1 percent, while the haircut on subprime mortgages is 40 percent. Haircuts varied with market conditions—in volatile conditions, risky or illiquid collateral would be accepted by lenders only with a large haircut, if at all.

Using wholesale funding, as well as longer-term sources of funding such as corporate debt and equity, the shadow banking system was able to perform standard banking functions like making new loans, holding existing loans and securities, and packaging loans and securities for sale to other investors. Indeed, by the time of the financial crisis, the shadow banking sector provided more credit to U.S. firms and households than the traditional banking sector.[9]

Why did shadow banks expand and prosper in the decades before the crisis, despite their inability to use federally insured deposits? One important advantage was that, given U.S. regulatory arrangements, the institutions that made up the shadow banking system could avoid many of the regulations applied to traditional commercial banks, such as minimum capital requirements and restrictions on their activities. Light regulation allowed shadow banks to be more flexible and innovative, for example in offering new products, but it also implied few restraints on their borrowing or risk-taking. Investments that were too risky for traditional banks thus often migrated to the shadow banking sector, out of the purview of bank regulators.[*]

---

[*] Most shadow banks, if federally regulated at all, are overseen by the Securities and Exchange Commission, which historically has seen its role as protecting investors against misinformation or fraud and ensuring market integrity—by preventing insider trading, for example—rather than monitoring the leverage or risk-taking of regulated firms. In contrast, bank regulators (including the Fed) are more focused on companies' "safety and soundness," for example, by requiring that banks hold capital commensurate with the risks they take.

Moreover, notwithstanding the absence of government insurance, reliance on wholesale funding arguably promoted the shadow banking sector's rapid growth, rather than constraining it. Providers of wholesale funding, such as money market mutual funds, pension funds, insurance companies, and corporate treasurers, liked the potentially higher returns and lower transactions costs of putting their money to work in the wholesale markets. Government insurance in any case only covered deposits up to comparatively low limits per account, while much wholesale funding (such as repo lending) was backed in full by specific collateral. Wholesale lenders did not expect to lose money even if they lent to a shadow bank (say, an investment bank or a hedge fund) that failed—if they were not repaid, they could claim the collateral. Indeed, many commercial banks also began to rely on wholesale funding, along with retail deposits. At the end of 2006, on the eve of the crisis, government-insured bank deposits in the United States totaled $4.1 trillion, while financial institutions' uninsured wholesale funding totaled $5.6 trillion. The use of wholesale funding allowed financial firms to expand their lending and investments but also made them more vulnerable to runs.[10]

In short, the rapidly growing shadow banking system collectively functioned much like any banking system—attracting short-term funds from investors, lending those funds to households and firms, and either selling those loans to investors or holding them in their own portfolios. Many shadow banks also actively hedged or speculated in financial markets. Exemption from the traditional bank regulatory regime, including oversight by the Federal Reserve and other banking agencies, gave the shadow banking sector wide scope, including the ability to take greater risks and hold less capital. Critically, shadow banks played a large role in the development and marketing of the exotic mortgage loans that helped fuel the financial crisis, and a disproportionate share of losses and financial distress would occur in that sector. In theory, being a shadow bank came with disadvantages, primarily the inability to use insured deposits but also the lack of access to short-term loans from the Fed's discount window, which under normal circumstances are only available to traditional commercial banks. However, when the financial crisis threatened the entire system, shadow banks would find themselves protected by the government safety net after all.

Securitization

Securitization—the bundling of diverse types of loans into complex securities—is conceptually separate from shadow banking but closely related to it in practice because, like shadow banking, it provides an alternative to traditional banking. We have already seen how the development of financially engineered securities undercut mortgage lending standards and contributed to the housing bubble. The rapid growth of this practice would do further damage by intensifying the financial panic, so we will look at it more closely here.

The mortgage industry itself illustrates the motivations for securitization. At one time, mortgage lending was largely a retail business. The mortgage officer at the local bank or savings and loan knew many potential borrowers personally, or at least did careful homework on each applicant. The mortgage, if extended, was financed by the bank's deposits, and the bank kept the mortgage on its own books. This system had some decided advantages: It made use of local knowledge and, since banks held the mortgages they made and suffered any losses that might occur, they were motivated to vet their potential borrowers carefully.

The system had disadvantages as well. Loan decisions could be slow, inefficient, and subject to the personal biases of the lending officer. Lack of diversification was also a problem because local lenders were vulnerable to declines in real estate prices in their area. And the ability of a bank to make loans often depended on the availability of deposits. When S&Ls saw an outflow of deposits in the 1980s, for example, their ability to make new mortgage loans declined.

Over the years, technological changes and financial innovations addressed some of the weaknesses of traditional lending. Computerized credit records and standardized credit scores made mortgage lending more efficient, more competitive, and less subjective. National lenders, with technological advantages and economies of scale, supplanted many local banks.* Importantly, banks and other mortgage lenders were no longer restricted by the quantity of deposits they could raise. Instead, lenders could sell the mortgages they made to third parties, including the GSEs Fannie Mae and Freddie Mac.† These third parties in turn packaged the mortgages together—securitized them—and either held the newly created securities on their own books or sold them to global investors. Securitization allowed mortgage lenders—even a storefront lender with no deposit base or ability to raise wholesale funding—access to an enormous pool of savings from around the world.

Mortgage borrowers and lenders liked the new system. So did investors. The new mortgage-backed securities could be structured to reduce risk—by combining mortgages from different regions of the country, for example, thereby offering protection against regional declines in house prices. The securities could also be sliced into segments, called *tranches*, with each tranche sold separately, allowing investors, in principle at least, to choose their preferred level of risk. As the popularity of securitization grew, the mix of assets included in the securities expanded to include many types of private and public credit, not just mortgages, with increasingly complex combinations of assets and mixes of funding. Very often, those tranches were pooled and resecuritized into yet another layer of complex securities. Shadow banks, such as investment banks, often took the lead in creating and marketing these so-called *asset-backed securities*, or ABS, and held them in their own portfolios as well.

In theory, the securities were designed to match the risk and liquidity preferences of different investors, but ultimately securitized assets became

---

* The 1994 Riegle-Neal Act allowed unrestricted branching of commercial banks across state lines, opening the door for the creation of truly national banking institutions.
† Fannie Mae and Freddie Mac are the nicknames of the Federal National Mortgage Association and the Federal Home Loan Mortgage Corporation, respectively. Although they are government-sponsored enterprises, with special rights and responsibilities legislated by Congress, both firms were publicly traded prior to the financial crisis. In their efforts to establish a national mortgage market, the GSEs helped create the practice of securitization.

so complex and opaque that even sophisticated investors could not reliably evaluate them. Instead, they relied on the grades that credit rating agencies, such as Moody's and Standard and Poor's, assigned to each security and its tranches. Relying on rating agencies had its own problems, however, as the agencies were paid by issuers and thus had potential conflicts of interest; and, in retrospect, the agencies would prove too credulous about the ability of financial engineers to make good securities out of bad credit. Despite these drawbacks, the growing supply of global savings generated an enormous hunger for standardized, liquid, and high-return assets. Securitizations filled that need, or so it was thought. One consequence of securitization was that U.S. subprime mortgages became, effectively, a global asset, held by entities as varied as German savings banks and Japanese pension funds, as well as by American investors.

The Stages of the Panic

The puzzle that confronted the Fed and other regulators in the summer and fall of 2007 was why relatively small quantities of troubled mortgages were linked to so much havoc in the financial system. The answer was that the damage from subprime mortgages and other dicey credit products was amplified by their securitization and resecuritization into asset-backed securities. When subprime mortgages started to perform poorly, what were investors in complex asset-backed securities supposed to do? In an ideal world, they would assess the fundamental values of the assets that made up those securities and accept that they were now worth less. But the complexity of the securities made it difficult and costly to determine their fundamental values, and the rating agencies had lost their credibility. The simplest option was to dump the securities on the market—including not only the subprime mortgages lurking within but also all the other credit instruments entangled in the security. The result was, effectively, a fire sale of all private credit assets, from credit card debt to auto loans, along with subprime mortgages.

Wholesale funding providers were even less inclined to give securitized assets the benefit of the doubt. Just as pre-FDIC bank depositors rushed to withdraw their money from banks that had made doubtful loans, investors providing short-term funding panicked and ran from special-purpose vehicles, investment banks, and other institutions holding securitized credit. For example, outstanding asset-backed commercial paper began to decline sharply after the BNP Paribas announcement, as funding providers became increasingly hesitant to renew their loans. Between August 2007 and August 2008, the amount of asset-backed commercial paper outstanding fell by a third, squeezing the special-purpose vehicles they funded.[11]

Remarkably, even providers of repo loans—which, remember, are fully collateralized and typically of very short maturity—showed signs of panic after August 2007. As documented by the economists Gary Gorton and Andrew Metrick, the run on the repo market did not necessarily take the form of investors refusing to make repo loans entirely.[12] Rather, lenders instead required much more collateral (a larger haircut) as backing for their loans. For example, if prior to the crisis one dollar's worth of a given security might have been sufficient collateral for 95 cents of credit, as the run on repo worsened, lenders might offer only 70 cents of funding for the same collateral. With larger haircuts—and with some types of assets no longer accepted as collateral at any price—adequate funding in repo markets became harder and harder to obtain.

Once begun, the panic spread beyond securitized assets to put pressure on large financial institutions. These institutions were directly exposed to losses on subprime mortgages and asset-backed securities that they held in their own portfolios, but they were also exposed indirectly in ways that neither they nor their regulators had fully appreciated. For example, a bank might not only hold subprime loans directly, it might also own derivative instruments whose values depended in complex ways on mortgage performance. The special-purpose vehicles that some institutions sponsored to hold a mix of mortgages and other assets were, as we have noted, legally separate. But the sponsoring institutions might still be exposed to the vehicles indirectly, for example, through prearranged commitments to replace lost funding, or through reputational incentives to prop up the vehicles or make

good on investors' losses. Asset markdowns, followed by increased difficulty in finding adequate funding, forced major financial institutions—
especially the besieged investment banks—to dump riskier and less-liquid
assets on the market for whatever they would bring. With no one eager to
hold even loans that were performing reasonably well, like auto and credit
card loans, the prices of credit-related assets collapsed, pushing many financial institutions close to or into insolvency.

The panic waxed and waned as policymakers responded and as investors assessed and reassessed the risks. In March 2008, the Fed and the Treasury collaborated to avoid the failure of the investment bank Bear Stearns
by arranging its acquisition by a large commercial bank, JPMorgan Chase.
That action seemed to calm the fever for a while, and the economy and
markets showed signs of improvement over the next few months. But the
long-simmering crisis boiled over in September 2008. The month began
with the government's takeover of the two huge GSEs, Fannie Mae and
Freddie Mac, which were brought down by losses on the trillions of dollars of mortgages the companies held or guaranteed, including securities
backed by subprime or other low-quality mortgages that they had acquired.
Then came the fateful week of September 14. The investment bank Lehman
Brothers declared bankruptcy. The Federal Reserve, using its emergency
lending powers, bailed out AIG, the world's largest insurance company,
also brought down by mortgage exposures. Bank of America purchased
the investment bank Merrill Lynch, staving off another likely bankruptcy.
And a run began on money market mutual funds, which had previously
been viewed as safe, though they were uninsured. These blows, and more to
come, convinced investors that there were no safe havens other than Treasury securities. The panic became white-hot, bringing the financial system
close to collapse.

In broad outline, then, the crisis followed the usual sequence of a classic financial panic: a buildup in risky lending, followed by a loss of investor
confidence in the soundness of those loans; runs on the lending institutions by short-term funding providers; forced fire sales of troubled assets,
contributing to sharp asset price declines; and insolvencies of lenders and

borrowers, extending the downward spiral. But in real time, the complexity and opacity of the global financial system obscured, at least at first, the analogies between the 2007–2009 crisis and past financial panics. Regulators at the Fed and elsewhere particularly underestimated the potential for a run on wholesale funding, since they thought that the collateralization of much of that funding would reassure investors. But wholesale funding providers were not eager to receive collateral in lieu of repayment because they were not sure they could quickly sell the collateral assets in disrupted and volatile markets. They just wanted their money back.

Critically, from the perspective of policymakers at the Fed, the shocks of the panic were felt well beyond Wall Street. Economic activity decelerated sharply as credit became unavailable, asset prices fell precipitously, and fear-stricken businesses and households stopped spending, hoarding cash when they could. The magnitude and speed of the collapse was stunning. To be sure, the decline in housing prices and construction that began in 2006 had slowed the economy to some degree, as had the growing pressure on struggling mortgage borrowers, whose efforts to avoid default and foreclosure led them to cut other spending. The National Bureau of Economic Research would date the beginning of the recession as December 2007, four months after the fateful announcement by BNP Paribas. But the escalation of the panic in September 2008 and the months that followed signaled a new phase in the downturn.

To cite just one key indicator, payroll employment in the United States grew in 2006 and early 2007, was roughly stable from the first tremors of the subprime turmoil in August 2007 until the rescue of Bear Stearns in March 2008, and then declined relatively modestly until Lehman's failure, even as house prices declined and mortgage markets deteriorated throughout the entire period. In contrast, in the last four months of 2008, as the system descended into the worst stage of the panic, 2.4 million jobs disappeared, with an additional 3.8 million jobs lost in the first half of 2009. Inflation-adjusted consumer spending fell at a 4.2 percent annual rate between August and December of 2008, and firms' capital investment fell even more sharply. The intensification of the financial crisis—by pushing banks, households, and firms into a defensive crouch, afraid to act because of fear of financial collapse—made the ensuing Great Recession great.[13]

THE FEDERAL RESERVE'S RESPONSE: LENDER OF LAST RESORT

The Federal Reserve responded to the financial crisis along two conceptually separate—though, in practice, sometimes overlapping—tracks. First, beginning in the summer of 2007, in our role as lender of last resort and crisis fighter, we worked to stabilize the financial system and restore the normal flow of credit. Second, we tried to cushion the economic effects of the crisis through monetary policy—first, through standard rate cuts, then subsequently through increasingly novel policies.

Our attempts to calm the panic and restore financial stability, the first track, were of a scale and scope unprecedented at the time, reflecting the magnitude of the crisis gripping the system and the size, complexity, and global interconnectedness characteristic of modern finance. Fundamentally, though, central bankers of 150 years earlier would have recognized our strategy. In 1873 British journalist and economist Walter Bagehot, in his short book *Lombard Street: A Description of the Money Market*, provided the classic prescription for central banks facing a panic.[14] To end a panic, Bagehot advised central banks to lend early and freely, to solvent firms with good collateral, at a "penalty [interest] rate," a principle now known as *Bagehot's dictum.** Greenspan's Fed had invoked the central bank's lender-of-last resort role in its terse statement in the wake of the October 1987 stock-market crash, which made clear its willingness to provide short-term loans to banks facing liquidity strains. Roger Ferguson issued a similar statement after the 9/11 attacks. In the spirit of Bagehot, beginning after the BNP Paribas announcement we searched for ways to serve as

---

* Bagehot advocated that the bank lend at a high ("penalty") rate to protect its gold reserves, not a consideration in 2007–2009. We did however follow this advice in usually setting lending rates above normal (noncrisis) rates, which encouraged financial firms and markets to return to private sources of funding when conditions calmed.

an effective lender of last resort to financial firms and markets, providing liquidity to replace lost funding and reduce the need for destabilizing fire sales. More generally, we used whatever authorities were available and worked with lawmakers, financial executives, and others to try to restore confidence in the financial system.[15]

Since its founding, the Federal Reserve's basic lender-of-last-resort tool has been the discount window, through which the Fed provides short-term funding to banks, taking their loans and other assets as collateral. Although after the BNP Paribas announcement we substantially eased the terms of discount-window loans and encouraged banks to borrow, it quickly became clear that it wouldn't be enough. During the years before the crisis, with plenty of alternatives for banks who needed liquidity, and with Fed lending officers having traditionally frowned on routine discount-window borrowing, the window had fallen into disuse.* Banks became afraid that borrowing through the window—should that become public—would signal they were in financial trouble. The *stigma* of borrowing through the discount window meant that even the banks most desperate for cash were reluctant to use it.

Our first effort to overcome the stigma barrier was to persuade a few large banks to borrow at the discount window, hoping that would set an example for other banks. However, that effort collapsed when the banks in question, though using the window, went out of their way to publicize that they really didn't need the money and that their borrowing was strictly symbolic. We ultimately solved the stigma problem by creating a new

---

* Reserve Bank discount-window officers discouraged routine borrowing from the window because, until 2003, the discount rate was set below market (below the federal funds rate) and they did not want banks to exploit the window as a regular source of cheap funding. Thus, to borrow from the window, a bank had to show it could not borrow in the market. The discount rate fell below the federal funds rate in the mid-1960s because, according to Federal Reserve staff lore, it was politically easier for the FOMC to tighten monetary policy by raising the federal funds rate, which was done without public announcement until 1994, than it was to raise the discount rate, which of necessity must be announced to banks. Effective in January 2003, following a review of lending procedures, the primary discount rate (for banks in sound financial condition) was raised above the federal funds rate and the Federal Reserve and other banking supervisors began encouraging banks to use the discount window if needed.

facility, the Term Auction Facility, which distributed discount-window credit in regular auctions, with the interest rate on the Fed's loans set by banks' competitive bidding. Because the auction resulted in a low cost for this credit, and because the credit was distributed with a two-day delay (signaling that participating firms did not need the cash immediately), the Term Auction Facility did not inherit the stigma of the discount window, and banks used it freely.

Besides stigma, another significant shortcoming of the discount window was that—because the Fed was established when banks dominated the financial landscape—only banks, among all financial institutions, were legally eligible to use it. But the 2007–2009 crisis was centered in the shadow banking system, which by definition comprised only nonbank institutions. To control the panic, we needed to serve as lender of last resort to this broader set of firms and markets. To do that, we invoked Section 13(3) of the Federal Reserve Act, which allows the Fed—under "unusual and exigent circumstances," when normal credit channels are blocked—to lend outside the banking system. The Fed had not made 13(3) loans since the Great Depression, when the authority was created, but starting in 2008 we used it actively, lending to shadow banks (such as investment banks), supporting the wholesale funding market, and providing liquidity as part of government efforts to prevent the collapse of systemically critical firms.

Because financial markets are international, because securitizations including U.S. assets were widely held outside our borders, and because a number of countries suffered their own real estate booms and busts, the financial crisis was global. Major central banks like the European Central Bank and the Bank of England joined the Fed as lenders of last resort, providing euros or pounds as needed to financial institutions in their jurisdictions. What the foreign central banks could not easily do however was provide U.S. dollars—the global reserve currency, used in much international banking business—to their local financial institutions. The international shortage of dollars in turn forced foreign banks to try to acquire dollars in U.S. markets, adding further pressure on available funding for American firms. To address this problem, we established agreements,

known as currency swap lines, with fourteen foreign central banks, including the central banks of four major emerging-market economies.* Under
these arrangements, we temporarily swapped dollars with our central bank
partners in exchange for foreign currencies. The foreign central banks could
then lend these dollars to financial institutions in their own jurisdictions,
easing the strains on dollar markets globally. In effect, through the swap
lines we were serving as lender of last resort to the world, although our
motivation was to defend the stability of the dollar and our own economy.
At their peak the swap lines involved many hundreds of billions of dollars.
However, the U.S. taxpayer was never at risk. All the credit risk on loans to
foreign institutions was borne by foreign central banks.

Traditional last-resort lending was aimed at counteracting runs and
ensuring that financial institutions had enough liquidity to avoid fire sales
and continue operating. But the crisis led to breakdowns in key credit markets, as well as in financial institutions. That development, and the risks it
posed for the economy, led us to lend directly to nonfinancial firms and to
take actions to support credit flows more broadly—that is, we became the
lender of last resort for nonfinancial borrowers as well. For example, when
the commercial paper market froze, preventing even highly rated corporations from obtaining needed short-term financing, we set up a Commercial
Paper Funding Facility to make short-term loans to those corporations. We
also lent (through a program called the Term Asset-Backed Securities Loan
Facility, or TALF) to investors buying credit-backed securitizations, helping to restore liquidity to critical credit markets. Both of these programs
required us to invoke our 13(3) authority.

Most of the many studies of the Federal Reserve's lending programs
during the crisis conclude that they were effective in getting cash where
it was needed and helping calm the targeted markets, or at least preventing greater damage.[16] Yet our lending did not end the crisis. In retrospect,

---

* Currency swap lines are within the normal powers of the Fed—we had had small lines with Canada
and Mexico since the North American Free Trade Agreement went into effect in 1994—and do not
require 13(3) authority.

despite the unprecedented size and scope of the Fed's programs, they were evidently not early enough or large enough to entirely prevent funding shortages and fire sales. Our insufficient understanding of the risks prior to the BNP Paribas announcement, our desire not to be seen as overreacting or bailing out improvident investors, and our hesitation in invoking our little-used emergency lending authorities—whose use was in any case legally restricted to extreme conditions that were not evident early on—delayed sufficiently forceful action in the early months of the crisis. Even when the Fed made adequate funding available, some institutions were slow to accept the loans, for fear that doing so would identify them as being in financial trouble—the stigma problem again. Some holders of troubled assets, such as special-purpose vehicles, were not set up to use even the Fed's expanded facilities. On net, our lending replaced much but not all the lost funding, slowing but not ending the panic.

In addition, for last-resort lending to work, borrowers must be solvent. If they are not—if their assets are worth less than their liabilities—then central-bank lending can delay, but cannot prevent, failure. (Indeed, the law requires that the firms receiving Fed loans be able to secure their loans with adequate collateral.) Policymakers could not do much about investors' sudden revulsion for mortgages and asset-backed securities. As a consequence, financial firms with heavy exposures to low-quality mortgages and other risky assets, and with low capital cushions, were quickly pushed to the brink—or over the brink—of insolvency.

As illiquidity progressed toward insolvency, we worked with the Treasury, the FDIC, Congress, and the financial industry itself to try to restore confidence. Our tools included moral suasion, our supervisory powers, and, in some cases, our 13(3) authority. Like the Volcker Fed during the Latin American debt crisis, or the Greenspan Fed during the 1987 stock-market crash, our goal was to help the relevant parties work together to avoid collective disaster.

Because major financial firms are so interconnected, with wide webs of customers, creditors, and counterparties, we recognized early on that the uncontrolled failure of a large firm would magnify uncertainty and panic.

It was that concern that led the Fed and the Treasury to mediate JPMorgan Chase's acquisition of Bear Stearns in March 2008. Bear's near collapse occurred after investors refused to provide it with short-term (repo) funding, even when collateralized by the highest-quality Treasury and GSE-issued securities. To persuade JPMorgan Chase CEO Jaime Dimon to go ahead with the deal, in a controversial step, the Fed agreed to provide funding (and thus take responsibility for potential losses) for a portfolio made up of about $30 billion of Bear's risky loans and securities. We judged that these assets would ultimately have sufficient value to pay off the Fed's loan, which in fact they did (and even provided a profit). The Fed was further protected in this unorthodox transaction by JPMorgan's agreement to bear the first losses on the Bear portfolio, up to $1 billion. We also supported the Treasury as it lobbied Congress during the summer of 2008 for the authority to take over Fannie Mae and Freddie Mac—a power Treasury had hoped not to need, but would have to use in September. To preserve the functioning of the mortgage market, Fannie and Freddie were allowed to keep operating, but under strict government control.

However, our *ad hoc* efforts with the Treasury and other regulators finally failed with Lehman Brothers. An investment bank, like Bear Stearns only larger, Lehman—whose extreme risk-taking had exposed it to crippling losses—also suffered a run on its funding and a rapid exit by customers and counterparties that put it hours away from bankruptcy. As with Bear Stearns, the Treasury's and the Fed's strategy was to arrange for a stronger company to buy the firm, guarantee its liabilities, and stabilize its business. A fateful meeting at the Federal Reserve Bank of New York brought together two potential buyers—Bank of America and Barclays, a British bank—as well as leaders of other major Wall Street firms. Treasury Secretary Hank Paulson and New York Fed President Tim Geithner ran the meeting. After careful review of Lehman's balance sheet, the Wall Street experts present judged it to be deeply insolvent, well beyond the point of viability unless a solvent firm acquired it. Bank of America ultimately declined to buy Lehman without a large injection of government capital, which at that stage the Treasury had no authority to provide. Meanwhile,

British regulators, fearful of becoming responsible for Lehman's bad assets, effectively forbade Barclays from buying the firm.

Unable to stand on its own, even with Fed loans, and with no savior company to guarantee its liabilities, Lehman declared bankruptcy on September 15, 2008. However, the next day, the Fed and the Treasury were able to save AIG, the world's largest insurance company, which had large payments coming due on bad bets it had made on subprime loans. The difference from Lehman was that, based on what we could discern at the time, AIG appeared to be fundamentally viable; and it had enough collateral, in the form of profitable subsidiary insurance companies, to justify a loan from the Fed large enough to meet the company's immediate obligations.

After Lehman's failure, the panic intensified, and many financial markets almost ceased to function entirely. Although Lehman was only about a third the size of the largest commercial banks, its many interconnections with other financial institutions soon became painfully evident. Importantly, a prominent money market mutual fund, the Reserve Primary Fund, suffered losses on its holdings of Lehman commercial paper, which meant it could no longer honor its implicit promise to honor investor withdrawals, dollar for dollar. In the lingo of Wall Street, the Reserve Primary Fund "broke the buck." Fear that other funds might break the buck led to a widespread run on money funds. Since many investors in money market mutual funds were ordinary Americans, the run brought the crisis home to Main Street. Working quickly and using money from the Exchange Stabilization Fund (the same fund used to make loans to Mexico in 1994), the Treasury created an insurance program (analogous to FDIC deposit insurance) that protected investors in the money funds. The Fed also provided liquidity to money funds indirectly, through a program that incentivized banks to buy money fund assets. The government's response ended the runs, but not before the infliction of much damage to confidence—and, more specifically, to the wholesale funding market, of which the money funds were an important part.

The fact that the panic greatly worsened after Lehman's collapse raises two questions.[17] First, could Lehman have been saved? Second, would saving Lehman, if that had somehow been possible, have ultimately avoided the acceleration of the crisis in the fall of 2008? The answers, I believe, are no and no.

All the experts who examined Lehman's books on that September weekend testified to its deep insolvency (and that was before accounting irregularities came to light, which made clear the firm's condition was even worse than anyone thought). Thus, the Fed could not provide the cash that Lehman needed to meet its obligations while satisfying the requirement that its lending be secured by adequate collateral. But, even if Lehman had been borderline solvent, against all the evidence available at the time, its business simply was not viable without a stronger firm to buy it and guarantee its liabilities. Financial firms, especially those as highly leveraged and opaque as Lehman was, cannot operate profitably without the confidence of those with whom they do business. In the days leading up to Lehman's collapse, its customary lenders declined to fund it overnight, even against the best collateral it could offer, including Treasury securities. Meanwhile, customers pulled their assets from the company's custody and creditors (counterparties in derivatives transactions, for example) sought to collect what was owed to them as quickly as possible. With so little trust from funders, customers, and counterparties, Lehman could not conceivably have operated for long as a stand-alone firm, even if a Fed loan had delayed its technical failure for a few days. At that point, moreover, neither the Fed nor the Treasury had any authority to provide Lehman with new capital, nor would any private investors do so, despite the government's efforts to persuade them. The only plausible option for saving Lehman—as with Bear Stearns the previous March—was for one or more solvent financial firms to acquire it. But that proved impossible.

On the question of whether saving Lehman—if that had been feasible—would have stopped the panic: In mid-September 2008, many firms, not just Lehman, were close to failure. Fannie and Freddie had just been taken over by the government. The AIG situation loomed large on our radar screens during the negotiations over Lehman and our intervention

there occurred the day after Lehman failed. Only Bank of America's acquisition of Merrill Lynch (which it later tried to reverse) prevented Merrill's
collapse that week. Other big financial firms soon required interventions of
one sort or another, including Morgan Stanley, Goldman Sachs, Wacho-
via, Washington Mutual, Citibank, and then Bank of America itself. All
of these firms suffered large losses on their holding of mortgages and other
forms of private credit. The Fed alone could not have restored stability
under those conditions. Lender-of-last-resort actions can help only firms
that are temporarily illiquid but fundamentally solvent. What was needed,
and eventually obtained, was a major fiscal commitment by the U.S. government to recapitalize the financial system.

However, Congress would not agree to such a politically distasteful
step until it was convinced that no viable alternative existed.* Indeed, the
first attempt to approve the $700 billion recapitalization bill, known as the
Troubled Asset Relief Program (TARP), failed despite the chaotic aftermath of Lehman's failure. We faced a catch-22: Without evidence of the
urgent need for intervention, Congress would not act. If the Fed and Treasury had somehow saved Lehman, presumably by arranging an acquisition
by a stronger firm, there would have been no TARP until some other, possibly larger and more interconnected, firm had failed. Congress's delay, given
the wide unpopularity of Wall Street bailouts, was politically understandable but economically very costly. Some other major countries' political systems were nimbler than ours, however. For example, the United Kingdom,
under Prime Minister Gordon Brown, moved proactively to ensure that
none of several troubled British financial firms failed in chaotic fashion,
although several had to be propped up by the government.

With the sharp deterioration of economic and financial conditions
that followed Lehman's collapse in September, Congress finally took strong
measures to fight the crisis. Most importantly, Treasury Secretary Paulson

---

* During the previous summer Secretary Paulson and I had broached the possibility of Congress
making capital available for such contingencies. We were told that getting this type of authorization,
if possible at all, would have been a laborious and extended process.

proposed, and (on the second try) Congress approved, the $700 billion TARP legislation. Initially, the TARP was billed as a fund to buy troubled assets from banks. But it soon became evident that that approach would be too complex and take too long. And it would be underpowered, given the huge quantities of troubled assets in the system. Paulson thus redirected the program to injecting capital directly into U.S. banks and other financial institutions, a step that would help restore solvency to the financial system and prove essential in controlling the panic. Funds from the TARP were also used to bail out auto companies and to provide relief to homeowners who were "underwater"; that is, who owed more on their mortgages than the reduced value of their homes.

THE FEDERAL RESERVE'S RESPONSE:
MONETARY POLICY

As we worked to stabilize the financial system, we also used monetary policy to try to counter the economic effects of the crisis.[18] Initially, to better explain our actions to Congress and the public, we tried to maintain a conceptual distinction between our crisis-fighting policies, such as lender-of-last-resort activities, and ordinary monetary policy. In practice, the division between monetary policy and crisis-fighting tools was often blurry. Monetary easing helped markets, directly by lowering the cost of funding and indirectly by promoting a better economic outlook. In turn, crisis-fighting measures helped the economy, for example, by improving credit availability, raising asset prices, and boosting confidence.

After the initial signs of crisis appeared in the summer of 2007, we focused on market-calming measures, such as our emergency lending programs and swap lines with foreign central banks. At first, because the economy continued to grow reasonably well despite the financial stresses, aggressive interest rate cuts didn't seem necessary. Moreover, with labor markets relatively tight and energy prices rising rapidly, we could not entirely ignore inflation pressures. Nevertheless, as financial volatility persisted and Committee members became more worried about its effects on the broader economy, the FOMC cut the federal funds rate by a percentage point, to 4¼ percent, by the end of 2007.

Despite the Fed's efforts, both financial and economic conditions worsened in early 2008. The stock market fell by about 10 percent during the first three weeks of the year and the economy felt increasingly shaky. We worried that the reluctance of banks and other financial institutions to lend was negating the benefits of our rate cuts, and that a feedback loop between the financial system and the economy might be developing, in which worsening financial conditions slowed the economy and a deteriorating economic outlook in turn dragged down market sentiment. Concerned that the situation might be spiraling out of control, at an unscheduled meeting (via conference call) on Martin Luther King Jr. Day in January, the Committee at my urging cut the funds rate by three-quarters of a percentage point. A week later, at the regular January meeting, I proposed and the Committee approved an additional half-point cut. More cuts would follow. Even though the Bear Stearns acquisition in March calmed markets somewhat, we nevertheless cut rates by three-quarters of a point at the end of March and a quarter point in April, bringing the funds rate to 2 percent. Other major central banks were now also cutting rates, although the Fed's response was the most rapid.

After that, we watched and waited, taking no further action through the spring and summer. With financial conditions showing some improvement after the Bear Stearns rescue, the economy seemed to be doing better than feared. Contemporaneous data, as reflected in the staff briefing materials for the August 2008 FOMC meeting, showed the economy growing at a pace near 2 percent in the first half of the year. Another worrisome pickup in inflation also raised concerns. A surge in oil prices—the price of a barrel of oil reached an all-time high of $135 in June—had increased overall inflation to nearly 4 percent over the summer, while core inflation measures exceeded 2 percent. We expected these inflation pressures ultimately to recede, but we acknowledged our uncertainty about inflation prospects in our post-meeting statements.

About this time, we began to experience problems controlling the federal funds rate. Following its traditional approach, the Fed managed the funds rate indirectly by varying the supply of bank reserves. However, in our lender-of-last-resort role, we had been pumping hundreds of billions of dollars into the financial system. As the borrowers deposited the proceeds of the loans with their banks and the banks redeposited the funds in their Fed accounts, bank reserves swelled. With plenty of reserves available, the funds rate—the rate banks charge each other to borrow reserves—regularly fell below the FOMC's 2 percent policy target. In short, our provision of liquidity, in our role as lender of last resort, was interfering with our ability to conduct monetary policy.

To help regain control of the policy rate, we sold Treasury securities and took other measures to sop up some of the extra reserves, a procedure called sterilization. More importantly, Congress gave us a new tool.[19] Two years earlier, Congress had approved a measure giving the Fed the ability to pay interest on reserves held by banks. That authority was not scheduled to become effective until October 2011, but we successfully lobbied to move the effective date to October 2008. Paying interest on reserves gave us a new way to try to put a floor under the federal funds rate. Presumably, we believed, banks would not lend to each other at a rate lower than they could earn by holding reserves at the Fed, so by varying the interest rate paid on reserves we should be able to control the funds rate as well. The power to pay interest on reserves would become an essential tool in the longer term, but as of late 2008, the question of how to keep the funds rate from falling would soon become moot.

While we worked closely with the Treasury and other agencies to bring the panic under control, managing monetary policy—in what were rapidly becoming unprecedented circumstances—was solely our responsibility, consistent with the Fed's policy independence. In retrospect, we initially underestimated the economic damage that would result from the acceleration of the panic, in part because the forecasting models that guided our analyses did not adequately incorporate the possibility of a widespread breakdown in credit markets.[20] At the September 2008 FOMC meeting, the day after Lehman's failure, the Fed staff still expected the economy to eke out a bit of growth over the rest of the year. And, focused on the AIG rescue and uncertain about the economic impact of the latest events, we did not cut our target rate at the meeting—clearly a mistake, in retrospect. But as the weeks passed and credit markets continued to deteriorate, it became evident that more easing would be needed.

Although our greatest concern was the trajectory of the U.S. economy, we kept a close eye on global developments. The most intense financial stresses were in the United States and western Europe. But, given the financial and economic importance of those two regions, the effects of the crisis spread rapidly through Latin America and Asia, including Japan and China. I spoke regularly, on the phone and in international meetings, with central bankers from around the world. In October 2008, looking for a way to show markets that the world's central banks were working together, I advocated a joint rate cut to be announced simultaneously by the Fed, the Bank of England, the European Central Bank (ECB), and other major central banks. The joint rate cut would also provide cover for the ECB to reverse course from an ill-advised rate increase over the summer, in reaction to a sharp rise in oil prices that had temporarily raised inflation above the ECB's objective. After discussions with Mervyn King (governor of the Bank of England) and Jean-Claude Trichet (president of the ECB), we proceeded with this unprecedented step.

The simultaneous rate cut was a complicated piece of theater. Monetary policy committees with different meeting schedules in different time zones had to agree, all the while avoiding leaks. Finally, on October 8, at 7:00 a.m. in New York and Washington, the Fed, the ECB, the Bank of England, the Bank of Canada, the Swiss National Bank, and Sweden's Riksbank each announced rate cuts of half a percentage point. The Bank of Japan (BOJ), with rates already near zero, expressed strong support. We had not consulted with the People's Bank of China, but it too cut rates that morning.

Although the joint rate cut was a logistical success, it did not prove particularly effective. Markets jumped on the announcement but ended down for the day. Perhaps market participants saw the action as inadequate, or perhaps they inferred from its unusual nature that prospects were even worse than they feared. A lesson of the episode is that the context and the communication surrounding any policy action can be as important as the action itself.

The October rate cut brought the federal funds rate to 1½ percent, but we did not see much evidence that our monetary easing was helping the economy. The Fed's staff economists were now predicting a recession lasting through the middle of 2009. Their timing proved accurate but neither the staff nor the FOMC appreciated how deep the downturn would be. We know now that the U.S. economy shrank at a sharp 8.5 percent annual rate in the fourth quarter of 2008, and at a slower but still quite severe 4.6 percent rate in the first quarter of 2009. Meanwhile, inflation fell rapidly, reflecting a steep drop in oil prices and plummeting demand by consumers and businesses.

At our meeting at the end of October, three weeks after the coordinated rate cut, the FOMC voted unanimously to reduce the federal funds rate another half percentage point to 1 percent, equaling the low reached in 2003. As in 2003, the funds rate was descending toward its effective lower bound, leaving us with little conventional monetary policy ammunition to fight the still-out-of-control crisis. The Committee remained divided on whether to cut the funds rate further, with some participants worrying that even lower rates might be destabilizing—for example, by increasing the risk of a money market fund earning such low returns that it could "break the buck" and touch off a new run. But standing pat was not a viable alternative. The damage to the economy was mounting by the day, with more people losing their jobs and their homes. As the economic outlook darkened further, it became clear we would need to get creative.

6

A NEW MONETARY REGIME

From QE1 to QE2

EVENTS MOVED QUICKLY AFTER LEHMAN'S failure as the ensuing financial chaos threatened economic collapse. The Fed flooded the system with liquidity through its various lending programs and currency swap agreements, the FOMC continued the series of rate cuts begun in 2007, and the passage of the TARP legislation set in motion the recapitalization of the teetering U.S. financial system. But clearly, given the size of the shock and the economic damage already sustained, more support would be needed to restore stability and ensure recovery. Accordingly, beginning in late 2008, the Fed turned to new and experimental monetary policy tools.

In my time as chair of the Princeton economics department, I had led with a deliberative, consensus-building style, and I had tried to bring that approach to the Fed. But, with markets in disarray and every economic indicator pointing down, that approach fell by the wayside, at least for a time. On November 25, 2008—in between regularly scheduled FOMC meetings and without the formal approval of the Committee—the Federal Reserve, at my direction, announced a new tool—large-scale purchases of longer-term securities, in this case, government-guaranteed mortgage-backed securities, or MBS. In various forms, this tool would become the centerpiece of our monetary strategy over the next few years. Inside the Fed we would call it "LSAPs," short for large-scale asset purchases. Everyone else called it "QE," short for quantitative easing.

The immediate goal of the new program was to stabilize the rapidly deteriorating housing and mortgage markets. The GSEs Fannie Mae and Freddie Mac had become wards of the federal government a week and a half before Lehman's failure. Investors in their securities, including the trillions of dollars of MBS issued by the two companies, had long assumed that the U.S. government would protect them if the companies ran into trouble, notwithstanding the absence of any formal guarantee. With Treasury's takeover, the GSEs were now fully backed by the government—the implicit guarantee had become explicit. But many traditional buyers of GSE-issued securities, notably including foreign governments, were shaken by the extent of the companies' deterioration and the government's unexpected intervention. Uncertain about the companies' future, GSE securities owners now worried that their investments were less rock-solid than they had believed. They dumped GSE-issued MBS on the market, driving down their prices and pushing up their yields. Interest rates on new mortgage credit—even where it was available—rose in sympathy, threatening to kill what was left of the housing market.

I hoped that large-scale Fed purchases of GSE securities—we committed to buying $500 billion of MBS and $100 billion of other GSE-issued debt over the next few quarters—would backstop investors' demand for mortgages, add liquidity to a stressed market, and send yet a stronger signal about the government's commitment to protecting the GSEs and the mortgage market more generally. Now, in addition to serving as a lender of last resort to financial and nonfinancial companies, the Fed would act as a *buyer of last resort* for mortgage-backed securities. We were moving well beyond Bagehot's dictum.

The program achieved its goals, helping to calm roiled mortgage markets and providing early evidence that Fed securities purchases could ease broader financial conditions. Even though we would not begin the purchases for some time, the announcement of the program itself had a powerful effect. The spread between the yield on Fannie's and Freddie's MBS and that on longer-term Treasury securities, a sensitive indicator of the risk that investors perceived in the GSE securities, fell by a significant 0.65 percentage points within a few minutes of our press release. Rates on thirty-year mortgages in turn fell by about a percentage point in December. That promised a bit of relief for the reeling housing market, as well as for individual and institutional investors in MBS. Encouraged, I said in a speech on December 1 in Austin, Texas, that the FOMC could consider wider use of securities purchases as a policy tool, including purchases of Treasury securities.[1]

Although the announcement of the MBS program had the desired effects, it also raised the consequential question: Who decides? As chair, I had approved the purchases of the GSE securities—not the Committee. I had discussed the initiative with many FOMC members in a series of calls but had not followed the usual practice of extended discussion, consensus-building, and formal approval. Instead, in response to what I saw as an emergency, I relied on an FOMC rule that allowed the chair, based on economic or financial developments during the intermeeting period, to independently order purchases of securities, with the goal of adding reserves to the banking system and adjusting the federal funds rate. But, even if it conformed to the letter of the law, my unilateral decision to buy mortgage-related securities at large scale went beyond what the FOMC's rule contemplated. Instead, it set a precedent for what might become a critical new dimension of U.S. monetary policy.

After hearing from unhappy Reserve Bank presidents, I realized that their concern was not about the substance of the purchase program—most were comfortable with it—or even the legalisms, but about process and legitimacy. As the FOMC evaluated policy options, it became increasingly clear that, with the funds rate near the effective lower bound, other measures—including large-scale securities purchases—might well become integral to monetary policy. If so, it made sense for the FOMC, the official overseer of monetary policy, to exercise authority over them. I asked the FOMC to formally approve the program, which it did at the December 2008 meeting, before any MBS purchases took place. And at the January

2009 meeting I said that I would henceforth hew to the principle that, when in doubt about whether an action was part of monetary policy, I would fully engage the Committee.

MONETARY POLICY AT THE
EFFECTIVE LOWER BOUND

Despite the hiccup over the GSE securities purchase program, by the December 2008 meeting we all recognized the situation we were in. The staff had revised up its unemployment forecast, projecting the rate to exceed 8 percent by the end of 2009. It seemed like a dire forecast but would turn out to be too optimistic. Based on their analysis of how the FOMC had responded to past recessions, the staff also predicted that the Committee's target for the funds rate would hit zero soon and remain there through 2013—for five more years—a stark indication of how severe they expected the downturn to be.

Everyone agreed that, even though the federal funds rate was now near its effective lower bound, limiting the scope of traditional rate cuts, we needed to provide more stimulus. The staff prepared or updated twenty-one memos on nonstandard policy options for the meeting. Collectively, the memos—many built on staff work from the 2003 deflation scare—provided an exhaustive review of the potential costs and benefits of alternative strategies. By the end of the meeting, the Committee had agreed on several points. First, it cut the federal funds rate target from 1 percent to a range of zero to ¼ percent. Second, having already endorsed the GSE securities purchase program I announced in November, it went further and said it stood ready to expand those purchases "as conditions warrant." Third, consistent with my December 1 speech in Austin, the Committee hinted strongly at future action by saying it was also "evaluating the potential benefits of purchasing longer-term Treasury securities." And, finally, it said it expected the near-zero target range for the fed funds rate to persist "for some time."

Cutting the funds rate target close to zero was justified by the economic outlook, but it was also an acknowledgment that our emergency lending, by flooding the system with bank reserves, had already forced the funds rate close to zero. We had expected that the new authority to pay interest on bank reserves would help us keep the funds rate at our target, but so far it had not. In principle, banks' ability to earn interest on their reserves at the Fed should have set a floor on the funds rate, since they have no incentive to lend to other banks at a rate lower than they can earn at the Fed. But, at least initially, the floor proved porous, with the funds rate often slipping well below the interest rate on reserves. The problem was that our authority to pay interest on reserves excluded the few nonbank participants in the federal funds market, most importantly the GSEs, who consequently had an incentive to lend any extra cash they held at a lower rate.*

Our cut in the target rate in December, then, only validated what we were already seeing in the market. Likewise, our switch from a point target for the funds rate to a target range acknowledged the difficulty we were having in tightly controlling the rate. Regaining firmer control of the funds rate would be a task for later, but at the end of 2008 the economy needed a policy rate near zero.

Beyond the rate cut, the steps we took at the December 2008 meeting foreshadowed what would become the FOMC's two main approaches to easing policy when short-term rates could go no lower: forward guidance and large-scale securities purchases.

The FOMC under Greenspan had used forward rate guidance with generally positive results. In response to the 2003 deflation scare, the Greenspan Fed shaped market expectations by announcing that it saw rates remaining low "for a considerable period." Other central banks had gone even further. The Bank of Japan, which had been battling deflation since the mid-1990s and had confronted the lower bound earlier than any

---

* In principle, banks should have had an incentive to solve this problem for us, by borrowing from the GSEs at a rate just below the funds rate and then depositing the proceeds at the Fed to earn the interest rate on reserves, which was set at the top of the funds rate target range, pocketing the difference. But, in the chaotic financial conditions of the time, banks were not interested in using their limited balance-sheet space to earn the small returns available from that activity.

other central bank, had pioneered a "zero-interest-rate policy," known as the ZIRP. Specifically, in April 1999, the BOJ promised to hold short-term rates at zero until "until deflationary concern was dispelled." Tying forward rate guidance to economic conditions—in the case of Japan, to inflation—was an innovative·step that the Fed would adopt later.*

In late 2008 we were not yet ready to make a long-term commitment to zero or near-zero rates, but we were concerned that some market forecasts saw the funds rate increasing in the next couple of quarters. Internally, in line with the staff's pessimistic forecast, most FOMC participants saw rates as likely to remain very low for longer than that. We agreed to use the phrase "for some time" in the statement to try to persuade the markets that we were in no hurry to start tightening.

The most significant phrases in the December post-meeting statement, though, were the Committee's official embrace of large-scale securities purchases as a policy tool. How would that work, and how would such purchases help the Committee achieve its objectives?

Mechanically, the process was straightforward. If, on the FOMC's order, the New York Fed bought, say, a billion dollars' worth of Treasury securities from dealers in those securities, the Fed's assets would rise, of course, by a billion dollars. To pay for the purchased securities, the Fed would credit the bank accounts of the sellers, payments that would ultimately appear as reserves held by commercial banks at the Fed. Since bank reserves are liabilities of the Fed, the liability side of the Fed's balance sheet would also expand by a billion dollars, leaving the central bank's net worth unchanged but both sides of its balance sheet larger by a billion dollars. In short, our plan was to buy longer-term securities from the private sector, paying for them by creating an equal amount of reserves in commercial banks. Incidentally, although central-bank asset purchases are sometimes

---

* However, in a move widely regarded as a mistake in retrospect, the Bank of Japan raised its policy rate in August 2000, despite ongoing deflation and its earlier commitment. The Japanese economy subsequently fell back into recession. Perhaps worse, because it failed to follow through on its commitment, the Bank of Japan had damaged its credibility and, thus, its ability to use forward guidance in the future.

referred to as "printing money," such purchases actually have no direct effect on the amount of currency in circulation.*

Although the mechanics were clear, and the New York Fed had long experience in buying and selling securities on the open market, we disagreed about how our large-scale purchases would affect financial markets and the economy. A few FOMC participants, such as Richmond Fed President Jeff Lacker, argued that the expansion of bank reserves would, itself, be the purchases' main benefit. Bank reserves, used by banks to settle obligations with each other, are included in the narrowest measure of the national money supply (the so-called monetary base). And, if banks chose to lend out their reserves, putting their extra liquidity into circulation, broader measures of the money supply could ultimately increase as well. Following monetarist ideas like those that influenced Paul Volcker, these participants believed that the expansion in the money supply would itself ultimately lead directly to higher output and inflation.

Indeed, the monetarist perspective had helped define the one recent example of central-bank large-scale asset purchases—Japan's. In 2001, with short-term rates near zero and the country in mild deflation, the Bank of Japan began buying a range of financial assets to try to stimulate the economy. And, it had measured and evaluated its program primarily by its effect on bank reserves. Because its focus was on increasing the quantity of money (including bank reserves), the Bank of Japan called its program "quantitative easing"—the name that subsequently would be applied to other central-bank purchase programs, including ours.

However, most of us on the FOMC, including me, were skeptical of Japanese-style, reserves-focused quantitative easing. "I think that the verdict . . . is fairly negative," I said at the December meeting.[2] For reserves-based QE to work, banks would have to lend large amounts of their new reserves to finance profitable projects and new spending. But, in a depressed

---

* Currency in circulation is determined by the public's choices, not Fed policy. For example, when people withdraw cash from their checking accounts to do Christmas shopping, the amount of currency in circulation automatically rises.

economy, with the risks of lending high, banks would have little incentive to lend more and would be just as happy leaving their reserves at the Fed. Counting on the expansion of reserves alone to stimulate the economy would be like the proverbial pushing on a string, most of us believed. In short, although securities purchases would increase bank reserves, unless the banks put those reserves to work, that increase by itself would not automatically translate into growth in lending and economic activity. Consequently, Fed securities purchases would likely have only minimal effects through the reserves channel.[3]

This logic would not dissuade some external critics, who warned that the massive expansion of bank reserves resulting from large-scale Fed purchases threatened hyperinflation, the collapse of the dollar, and other disasters. This critique had roots in an extreme form of monetarist theory, which held that the money stock and the price level are not just related, as some Committee members had indeed argued, but are strictly proportional in the long run. In this view, a tenfold rise (say) in bank reserves must ultimately translate into similar increases in the broader money supply (that includes, for instance, checking accounts and savings deposits) and, subsequently, in the prices of goods and services. Since our quantitative easing policies would multiply bank reserves by many times, the extreme monetarist position forecast out-of-control inflation.

Milton Friedman, the creator of monetarism, who had died in 2006 at the age of 94, would have disavowed these arguments. (He had, in fact, advocated quantitative easing in Japan.) In his writings Friedman recognized that many factors influence the relationship between the money supply and prices and appreciated that, in particular, when interest rates are very low and lending opportunities scarce, banks may simply hold on to most of the extra reserves, negating most of the effect of reserves creation on the broader money supply and inflation. I explained this reasoning in a January 2009 lecture at the London School of Economics.[4] Using Phillips-curve logic, I said that in an economy awash with unemployed workers and unused capital, and absent major supply shocks, inflation pressures were unlikely to be strong. I could have added that, in the thirty years since Paul

Volcker was appointed to lead the Fed, the institution had gained great credibility, anchoring inflation expectations and ending the tendency for higher inflation to generate 1970s-style wage-price spirals. But the charge that our asset purchases would ignite hyperinflation or otherwise "debase" the dollar persisted, particularly on the political right. As it happened, though, inflation was generally too low, not too high, during the quantitative easing period, much as most of the Committee (and the staff) expected.

If our purchases would not influence the economy by increasing bank reserves, then how could we create the desired stimulative effect? What would become the majority view of the Committee started with the observation that the effective lower bound was constraining short-term interest rates but not longer-term rates, which in late 2008 remained well above zero. (The yield on ten-year Treasury securities was as high as 4 percent at the end of October and was still about 2.25 percent at the end of the year.) Buying long-maturity Treasuries could conceivably help stimulate the economy by pushing down the yields on those securities. As we removed longer-term Treasuries from the market, investors, such as pension funds and insurance companies, with a strong preference for longer-term Treasuries, would compete for the remaining supply, pushing up their prices and (equivalently) pushing down their yields. Just as we had been able to lower mortgage rates by purchasing large quantities of MBS, we reasoned we could reduce longer-term Treasury rates by buying and holding long-maturity Treasuries.

Our ultimate goal was to influence private-sector decisions, which don't usually depend directly on Treasury yields. But we expected that lower yields in the Treasury market would result in lower yields elsewhere—for example, on residential and commercial mortgages and corporate bonds. Treasury yields are used as a benchmark for yields in other markets, and investors who sold longer-term Treasuries to the Fed would presumably use the proceeds to buy other types of longer-term assets, driving down those yields as well. Lower long-term, private-sector interest rates should stimulate business investment and consumer spending on new cars and houses. Lower long-term interest rates would also increase the prices of other financial assets, such as stocks, and weaken the dollar, easing financial conditions more broadly. If ordinary monetary policy was about changing short-term interest rates, indirectly influencing longer-term rates and other asset prices, this new approach would aim to directly affect longer-term interest rates, which had not yet been constrained by a lower bound. From that perspective, this alternative means of conducting monetary policy would not be such a radical change after all.

Since the Bank of Japan had dubbed their reserves-focused purchase program "quantitative easing," or QE, I tried to distinguish our approach by referring to it as "credit easing," reflecting our emphasis on lowering the longer-term interest rates paid by households and businesses. But, like the staff's "LSAPs," that name never caught on. QE it would be.

Although we were skeptical of the Japanese approach in general, one aspect of their program was particularly instructive. As I had pointed out in a 2004 paper with two Fed economists, Vincent Reinhart and Brian Sack, and as staff presentations explained, the start of the Bank of Japan's quantitative easing in 2001 seemed to strengthen the market's belief that the Bank would keep its short-term policy rate at zero for a long time.[5] In other words, the adoption of quantitative easing, a relatively novel and dramatic step, served as a *signal* of the Bank of Japan's broader policy intentions. By conveying policymakers' commitment to keep policy easy, QE in Japan seemed to have worked, at least for a time, as a form of forward guidance. Unfortunately, Japanese central bankers sometimes stepped on their message, by expressing skepticism about the effectiveness of QE or hinting that it and other extraordinary measures would be as short lived as possible. The lesson for us was that how we talked about the new policy tools could matter a great deal.

We had a theory of how QE might work, but there was a lot we didn't know. We didn't really know precisely how big our purchases needed to be to achieve a given reduction in longer-term interest rates. The staff estimated that purchasing $50 billion of Treasury securities (equal to a bit less than 1 percent of Treasury debt held by the public at the time) would lower longer-term rates by between 0.02 and 0.10 percentage points. This rather wide range of estimates came mostly from studies (including my paper with Reinhart and Sack) that observed how rates on Treasury securities changed when the Treasury Department changed the relative supplies of different maturities of bonds. One striking example: After the Treasury announced in October 2001 that it would stop issuing thirty-year Treasury bonds, yields on existing thirty-year bonds fell as investors competed for the suddenly reduced supply.

This experience and others like it provided an indication that our basic approach was sound, but it was difficult to gauge precisely how powerful it would be. Our purchases would be larger than the issuance changes typically made by the Treasury, they would be taking place in highly disrupted markets, and they might signal information about our future intentions. Our main conclusion was that, to have a palpable effect on financial conditions and the economy, our purchases would have to be big. It would also be important that the Treasury Department not offset our purchases of longer-term Treasury securities by increasing its issuance of new longer-term debt to take advantage of the lower rates. (Tim Geithner, who would be named Treasury secretary by President Obama, later assured me that the Treasury would follow its previously announced issuance plans, which it did.)

Our uncertainty about the effectiveness of our purchases was matched by our uncertainty about possible side effects. Would Fed purchases, by inserting a new, big buyer, crowd out private buyers and thereby hurt rather than help the functioning of Treasury and mortgage-backed markets? (We tried to avoid this by limiting the percentage of each bond issue that we bought.) Would the flood of liquidity, as reflected in the expansion of bank reserves, stimulate new risks to financial stability? Would the Fed, by expanding its balance sheet several times over, expose itself to future capital losses if interest rates unexpectedly rose, leading the value of the securities we had purchased to fall below what we had paid? How would we stop purchasing securities, when the time came, and return to more-normal monetary procedures? We would discuss these and many related issues at length in FOMC meetings to come. Most of us, though, were not concerned that large-scale securities purchases might ignite excessive inflation or collapse the dollar. To the contrary, we mainly worried that our purchases would have only modest effects, not nearly enough to counteract the tsunami of bad news hitting the U.S. and global economies.

QE1 SAILS

Barack Obama was inaugurated in January 2009. My wife and I attended the inauguration on a freezing day in Washington. At the Fed, we continued to work with President Bush, Treasury Secretary Hank Paulson, and their team in their last weeks in office, with Obama remaining judiciously offstage. But we would tackle severe challenges, like the rescues of Citibank and Bank of America, without the benefit of Tim Geithner's knowledge and experience. After Obama announced that he would nominate Tim to lead his Treasury, Tim had to recuse himself from his duties at the New York Fed.

As Treasury secretary, Geithner took over the management of the TARP rescue funds, which Paulson had begun using to recapitalize the teetering U.S. banking system. (Famously, Paulson had summoned the CEOs of nine large banks to his conference room on Columbus Day, 2008, where he got them to agree to accept a total of $125 billion in government capital.) Geithner continued Paulson's work and, in cooperation with the Fed, devised an important innovation: comprehensive *stress tests* of the nineteen largest banks, administered by the Fed and other bank regulators. The stress tests (which have since become a centerpiece of routine bank supervision, both in the United States and abroad) were designed to estimate how much capital the tested banks would need to survive a hypothetical recession—one even deeper than what the country was experiencing—and significant further deterioration in financial markets. Under the Geithner plan, banks without enough capital to withstand the worst hypothetical scenarios and continue to lend would have six months to raise capital in the private markets. If they could not, they would be required to accept TARP capital on tough terms. Either way, we hoped, the tests would prove the banks to be viable and restore confidence in them.

The new administration also quickly assembled a fiscal package to support households and businesses. On February 17, 2009, less than a month into his term, President Obama signed the American Recovery and Reinvestment Act of 2009. The $787 billion program included tax cuts—notably, a temporary reduction in Social Security payroll taxes—and aid to state and local governments. The rest was spread among federal spending programs, including extended unemployment benefits and infrastructure investment. Additional fiscal measures over the next few years, such as the extension of the payroll tax cut and unemployment benefits, supplemented the initial package.[6]

Although the banking and fiscal initiatives were promising, their success was far from ensured when the FOMC gathered on March 18, 2009. The completion of the bank stress tests was still two months off, and we worried that the results would either appear too optimistic to be credible or, conversely, that they would show losses too large to be filled by the remaining TARP funds. There also were doubts at the Fed about whether the administration's fiscal program was big enough, relative to the size of the problem, or could be implemented quickly enough.

Accordingly, as the FOMC met, a turning point in the crisis remained elusive. The economy had shrunk rapidly for two quarters, the unemployment rate exceeded 8 percent and was rising, the stability of the banking system remained in considerable doubt, and the stock market had dropped by half in the past eighteen months. Payrolls were reported as having fallen by 651,000 jobs in February (later revised to a loss of 743,000). Conditions abroad, both in advanced economies and emerging markets, were also deteriorating rapidly.

Fed staff economists had revised up their projection of peak unemployment to 9.5 percent (closer, but still short of what would be the actual peak of 10 percent) and predicted that, with so many out of work, core inflation would fall to near zero. They estimated that, in a hypothetical world with no lower bound on interest rates, the FOMC would have to lower the federal funds rate to *minus* 6½ percent to revive the economy.[7] Of course, the lower bound did exist, and so significant additional stimulus would have to be found some other way.

The discussion at the meeting that March was the darkest I ever heard as a central banker, before or since. Reserve Bank presidents, relaying anecdotes and conversations with contacts in their districts, conveyed a sense of increasing and pervasive fear. Richard Fisher of the Dallas Fed reported that one of his contacts asked him if he wanted to hear some good news. When Fisher said yes, the contact said, "Call somebody else." That was one of the few laughs at the meeting.[8] Charlie Evans, president of the Chicago Fed, summed up the sense of the Committee: "I think it's important that we do something big."[9]

Most FOMC participants supported significantly expanding our securities purchases, a step that would have once been viewed as radical. But, by that time, more evidence suggested that the purchases could work. A staff memo looked at market responses to several recent events, including the announcement of the mortgage securities purchase program in November; my December 1 speech, when I said we would consider buying Treasuries; the FOMC statement after the December meeting, which affirmed that possibility of Treasury purchases; and the statement after the January meeting, which disappointed markets because it did not announce new purchases. The direction and size of interest-rate moves on each of those days, as market participants reassessed the probability and size of new purchases, suggested that a large program might substantially lower longer-term yields and thus boost the economy.

We also now had a new international example. On March 5 the Bank of England had cut its policy rate to 0.5 percent and announced that it would buy £75 billion of (primarily) longer-term British government securities, known as gilts, over the next three months, about 10 percent of the government debt held by the public. It also promised to purchase smaller amounts of private-sector liabilities, including corporate bonds and commercial paper. Over the next two days, the yield on ten-year British government debt fell by more than half a percentage point, with yields on other types of debt following the government yields down. The Bank of England would extend its purchase program three times over the next year.

The Board staff had presented alternative policy options for the FOMC to consider—one focused on purchases of mortgage-backed securities and another emphasizing purchases of longer-term Treasuries. The Committee decided to do both. We supplemented the already-promised $500 billion in MBS purchases with an additional $750 billion of planned purchases, and we raised the commitment to purchase GSE-issued debt from $100 billion to $200 billion, bringing our total planned purchases of GSE securities to $1.45 trillion. And, for the first time, we also said we would buy Treasury securities, up to $300 billion in the next six months, raising the total asset-purchase commitment to $1.75 trillion. In one meeting, we had decided to almost double the size of the Federal Reserve's balance sheet.

We also strengthened our forward guidance. We said we saw the federal funds rate at "exceptionally low levels" for "an extended period" rather than "for some time." And we announced the Term Asset-Backed Securities Loan Facility (TALF), aimed at improving the market for securities backed by loans to households and businesses. At that stage, we were highly uncertain about how our new tools would work, but we felt at least that we were throwing everything we had at the problem—as the statement noted, the FOMC was prepared to use "all available tools." The Committee vote was unanimous. And, encouragingly, the market effect was dramatic. Ten-year Treasury yields dropped by about half a percentage point on that day, similar to the effect in the United Kingdom. It looked like securities purchases might be effective, after all. But it was still early.

Conditions brightened a bit over the next few months. The stock market bottomed in March and began what would become a long bull market. The Dow would rise by more than 40 percent between the March meeting and the end of the year.

Our QE initiative had shown that we were not out of ammunition. But, long-term yields, after their initial decline following announcements, began to rise. Skeptics argued that meant that the effects of our purchases were only temporary or even counterproductive. But, as I told the Committee in a June conference call, the higher yields, which were accompanied by higher stock prices and better conditions in credit markets, more likely reflected increased optimism about global economic growth, slightly higher inflation expectations, and reduced demand for U.S. Treasury debt as a safe haven. In another good sign, demand for the Fed's emergency lending waned as private-sector credit became more available. And, most importantly, we saw tentative signs of improvement, or at least stabilization, in economic data. We talked at the April FOMC meeting about "green shoots" in markets and the economy, which sprouted many garden-related analogies. "In the realm of green shoots," the director of the Board's International Finance division, Nathan Sheets, said, "our forecast is more like a small potted plant or a vulnerable asparagus garden than a large leafy tree."[10] But over the next few months at least a few more green shoots would appear.

The results of the bank stress tests announced in May also helped restore confidence.[11] The Fed's Board and the other bank regulators had decided to make detailed results public, despite some reluctance on the part of the Treasury and even some of our supervisory staff, who worried that the unprecedented publication of banks' internal data would make it more difficult to get them to share confidential information in the future. Our hope was that full transparency would make the results more credible to the markets. It was a gamble since the disclosure of unexpected weakness could have further eroded confidence and perhaps even triggered new pressures on banks' short-term funding. Fortunately, the gamble paid off. Outside analysts agreed that the stress tests were rigorous and credible and that the results were consistent with independent estimates. It was also evident that, in part because of the improvement in economic and financial conditions, the estimated capital needs of the large banks were manageable and could be covered by the remaining TARP funds if necessary. As it turned out, most banks were able to raise additional capital in private markets, without government assistance. Only one, GMAC, the financing arm of General Motors, needed TARP money as a result of the stress tests. With fears of large failures or government takeovers allayed, the banking system looked to be turning the corner. The stock prices of the major banks rose sharply in 2009, and lending began to recover.

The administration's tax cuts and spending increases were also beginning to help. As some economists including many at the Fed as well as Obama's CEA chair, Christina Romer, had worried, the package was smaller than the economy needed. The severity of the downturn had not been fully appreciated at the time of its passage and Congress, citing deficit concerns, had resisted a bigger program. Another problem was that states and localities, almost all of them subject to balanced-budget requirements, raised taxes and cut spending as their budgets came under severe pressure from the economic slump. Contractionary policies at the state and local level meant that, overall, fiscal stimulus was less powerful than it otherwise could have been. Nevertheless, the combination of new monetary firepower, the success of the stress tests, and the federal fiscal program helped stabilize shaky financial markets and restart growth. The National Bureau of Economic Research would eventually declare June 2009 as the end of the recession. Unemployment remained high and output far below potential, but at least the economy was growing again.

Meanwhile, as financial conditions improved, use of our emergency lending programs slowed to a trickle and we began to phase them out. The repayment of emergency loans meant that the asset side of the Fed's balance sheet was now dominated by our holdings of Treasury and GSE securities, which we continued to buy on the promised schedule, ending QE1 purchases in March 2010.

MONETARY POLICY AFTER MARCH 2009: A QUIET PERIOD

After our dramatic announcements in November 2008 and March 2009 of what would eventually come to be known as QE1, we began carrying out our promised purchases, kept the funds rate in the 0-to-¼ percent range, and continued to predict an "exceptionally low" funds rate "for an extended period." However, with the new fiscal steps, calmer markets, and evidence that the banking system had turned the corner, we took no new monetary actions over the next year and a half. The Committee was pulled in two directions: On the one hand, the economy had improved enough that aggressive (and controversial) new policy measures seemed unwarranted, at least for the moment. But, on the other hand, the outlook remained sufficiently weak that pulling back from what had already been done was not an option either.

Within the broad consensus to watch and wait, views varied. Some on the FOMC were more hawkish—concerned about longer-term inflation risks, worried about the potential side effects of the new policies, and hence more inclined to signal tighter policies ahead. And some were more dovish—focused on the very high level of unemployment, worried about headwinds to the recovery, and thus more inclined to keep policy easy or to make it even easier.

The internal debate dragged on. The hawks—represented, for example, by Reserve Bank Presidents Charles Plosser (Philadelphia), Jeff Lacker (Richmond), Thomas Hoenig (Kansas City), and Richard Fisher (Dallas)—drew attention to the economic and financial improvement since the nadir of the crisis. By the September 2009 meeting, the staff had revised up its forecasts for GDP growth significantly, predicting a 2.75 percent growth rate in the second half of 2009 and 3.5 percent growth in 2010. Futures market traders expected the funds rate to reach 2 percent by the end of 2010, suggesting that they thought policy tightening would soon be justified. Several hawks raised the question of when the "extended period" forward guidance could be scaled back or dropped.

The doves on the FOMC—represented by, among others, Reserve Bank Presidents Janet Yellen (San Francisco), Eric Rosengren (Boston), Charles Evans (Chicago), and Board member Daniel Tarullo—acknowledged the economy had improved but emphasized that it remained in a very deep hole, with unemployment—including, increasingly, long-term unemployment—expected to remain exceptionally high. The same staff forecast that saw above-trend growth in 2010 also predicted that unemployment would decline only to 9.6 percent by the fourth quarter of that year.

The doves also argued that the staff forecasts, despite projecting a recovery too slow to put many unemployed people back to work, might nevertheless prove too optimistic. Those forecasts, they pointed out, were based on historical experience with economic recoveries, which did not include financial crises of the magnitude of the one we had endured. It was possible that the crisis would have lingering effects on economic behavior that would create further drags on growth, including tightened credit standards by lenders and increased saving by households trying to rebuild lost wealth and protect against new shocks. This more-pessimistic view was supported by an influential (and perfectly timed) book by Carmen Reinhart and Kenneth Rogoff.[12] They argued, based on historical case studies, that recessions that follow financial crises—particularly crises associated with a collapse in housing prices—are deeper and have slower recoveries than other recessions.

Although the doves argued for keeping policy easy, for the most part they did not push very hard for new securities purchases or other new measures during 2009 or early 2010. Most Committee members, including me, remained torn. We had no definite answers to many questions. Had QE1 been effective primarily because it helped calm highly volatile financial conditions? If so, would purchases still be useful now that financial conditions were more normal and longer-term interest rates were already quite low? And given powerful headwinds, like tight credit and a glut in the housing market left over from the precrisis boom, would modestly lower interest rates do much to stimulate new economic activity and hiring?

And if the benefits of new purchases were uncertain, so were the risks. Although most of us on the Committee did not believe the large expansion of bank reserves would spark serious inflation, others—in the media, Congress, and the markets—did. Might inflation concerns, even if not well justified, work against the confidence-increasing benefits of aggressive monetary action? The possibility was not purely hypothetical. In 2009, Fed staff highlighted signs of inflation jitters in financial markets at many meetings, including increased inflows into mutual funds that invested in inflation-protected securities, higher gold prices, and a falling dollar. Rising federal budget deficits also seemed to be adding to inflation worries. None of the market inflation indicators reached disturbing levels and some reversed later in the year, but the FOMC hawks thought the confidence-reducing effects of new purchases would outweigh the benefits. Others cited risks to financial stability. With uncertainty about both the economic outlook and our tools so prevalent, the FOMC—despite significant philosophical differences among us—agreed without dissent to keep policy largely unchanged from March 2009 through the end of the year, except for modest fine-tuning of the timing of our purchases.

As chair, I helped shape that consensus. Like the doves on the Committee, I was dissatisfied with the economy's progress. I worried particularly about the job market's slow recovery and the hardships it was creating for many people. Based on my academic work on the Great Depression, which had highlighted the damage wrought by bank failures, I agreed with the doves that the credit-market disruptions could have lasting economic effects. But I also expressed uncertainty about the effectiveness of additional securities purchases and worried about whether any negative side effects would overwhelm the uncertain benefits. Accordingly, I agreed to wait.

Given what we know today about the benefits and risks of asset purchases, I was too timid. The recovery turned out to be quite slow, consistently below our forecasts. Some of this weakness reflected factors mostly outside the control of monetary policy, including unexpectedly lackluster productivity in the years after the crisis and a turn to less expansionary fiscal policies after the passage of the initial package in February 2009. In retrospect, we likely could have provided more help in the early stages of the recovery through additional securities purchases to further reduce longer-term interest rates. Our forward guidance could also have pushed back harder against markets' belief that rates would begin increasing within a year or so.

However, instead of pressing the FOMC to implement new measures as QE1 wound down, in the face of increasing disagreement among FOMC participants I sought instead to ensure we preserved our flexibility to act.

In particular, I wanted to be sure that we kept the option of ramping up securities purchases if the recovery faltered. And I avoided giving any public signal that we planned to tighten in the near term. A bit paradoxically, one of the ways I tried to maintain the option of new securities purchases was by asking the staff and the Committee to plan for the eventual exit from our novel policies.

I certainly did not think an exit was imminent, nor did most of my colleagues. But we had launched the large-scale securities purchases with only general ideas about how they could be reversed when the time came. Planning for the eventual exit was only prudent, and indeed members of Congress, market participants, the media, and others asked us to explain how we would reverse our unusual policies. Most importantly, though, I knew that, if more purchases did become necessary, Committee members would be more likely to approve them if they were confident in our exit plan.

We knew that the ultimate exit would pose challenges. Tightening monetary policy, at some point, would include raising the funds rate from near zero. But assuming the balance sheet remained large, and the banking system remained flooded with reserves, precrisis methods of raising the funds rate—modest open-market securities sales to reduce the quantity of reserves—would not work. Our authority to pay banks interest on reserves seemed likely to provide a floor for the funds rate in more-normal financial conditions even though it had not worked that well following Lehman's failure. But in 2009 and early 2010 we considered other options for raising rates as well. One possibility, which would ultimately be put into practice, was to finance part of our securities holdings by means other than creating bank reserves. We could do that by borrowing short-term from institutional investors other than banks—money market mutual funds, for example—in what would become known as "reverse repo" operations. Financing part of our holdings by borrowing from nonbank investors would reduce the necessary buildup in bank reserves, making it easier to raise the funds rate when the time came to do so.

Of course, one clearly available way to tighten policy would be to begin reducing bank reserves by reversing QE, selling the securities we had purchased. If reserves were lowered to more historically normal levels, then the funds rate could be raised by the standard precrisis method of managing the supply of bank reserves. However, most of us, including me, were uncomfortable with that approach. If experience was a guide, the eventual tightening of monetary policy would have to be more gradual and finely calibrated than the easing had been. (Think of the long sequence of quarter-point moves that began in 2004, in contrast to the sharp cuts in 2001.) We were unsure that we would be able to precisely manage the withdrawal of policy stimulus by selling securities and could not predict how markets would respond if we announced sales.

Most FOMC members therefore agreed to delay securities sales. We would begin the eventual exit instead by stopping new purchases and taking other measures (short of selling securities) to reduce bank reserves, including not replacing securities on our balance sheet as they matured. We would then begin raising the federal funds rate, using the interest rate on excess reserves and possibly other tools, like reverse repos. Once the funds rate had moved decisively above zero, we would then try to, orderly and predictably, unwind the remaining QE purchases, selling securities only if necessary.[13]

In August 2009 President Obama had told me that he would reappoint me to a second four-year term as chair beginning in February 2010. The Senate voted 70–30 to confirm me, quite a comedown from the unanimous voice vote in favor of my first appointment as chair. Republican opposition to our aggressive monetary policy and dislike in both parties of the bailouts during the financial crisis explained most "no" votes. President Obama consistently supported the Fed and its independence. However, our relations with Congress were often rocky and would remain difficult.

A CHANGE IN THE OUTLOOK

The economic recovery showed more signs of picking up steam in late 2009 and early 2010, even though the labor market, following what was becoming an established pattern of jobless recovery, continued to lag.

Inflation was lower than we liked, but fears of both very low and very high inflation were beginning to dissipate (although the Fed's outside critics continued to harp on inflation risks). As planned, QE1 purchases gradually slowed and ended in March 2010, although—as our holdings continued to reduce the net supply of longer-term securities available to investors—we expected our expanded balance sheet, then at about $2.3 trillion, to continue to put downward pressure on longer-term rates, supporting economic growth. With the tentative signs of improvement, the FOMC hawks had begun talking more about preparing the markets for an exit. In January 2010, President Hoenig of the Kansas City Fed dissented on the grounds that the "extended period" language was no longer appropriate. But my preference was to keep our policies where they were and to monitor the developing recovery.

However, after this period of relative calm, the summer of 2010 brought new financial volatility, emanating primarily from western Europe. Europe's sovereign debt crisis, a kind of aftershock of the 2007–2009 crisis, threatened not only Europe's own slow recovery but the American and global recoveries as well.

In 1999, as part of a push toward greater political and economic integration, eleven of the twenty-eight European Union countries, including Germany, France, Spain, and Italy (but, prominently, not the United Kingdom), had agreed to adopt a common currency, the euro, to be managed by the newly created European Central Bank. With the elimination of national currencies like the mark, franc, peseta, and lira, the central banks of the member countries could no longer run independent monetary policies. Instead, they became part of the euro system, playing roles analogous to the Fed's regional Reserve Banks.* Together with rules to promote the free movement of capital, goods, and labor, the adoption of the euro was intended to create a massive new free-trade area in Europe, similar in size

---

* For example, the governors of the national central banks, like the presidents of U.S. Reserve Banks, monitored local conditions and joined the committee that made monetary policy for the euro area. Like Reserve Banks, European national central banks also retained some bank supervisory responsibilities.

to the United States. With a single currency, doing business across national borders would become easier. For countries like Italy or Greece, with histories of inflation and currency devaluation, the new currency had the potential added benefit of creating instant anti-inflation credibility—so long as the ECB, modeled after the German central bank, the Bundesbank, was credibly committed to low inflation, as its designers intended. And, beyond the economic benefits, the euro (it was hoped) would foster political cooperation on a continent that had been the center of two devastating world wars during the previous century.

However, in 2010 the euro area was a project still under construction, with vulnerabilities that the global financial crisis would lay bare.[14] First, with a single currency, the euro area could have only a single, common monetary policy, creating a problem when different countries needed different degrees of monetary easing or tightening. Second, although monetary policy was unified by the adoption of the euro, fiscal policy was not. Each country retained control of its own government budget. Absent a common budget, any collective fiscal action in the euro area required complex and politically fraught negotiations among the member countries, each of whom worried that its taxpayers would end up paying for the mistakes or profligacy of other countries. Finally, Europe's banking system and bank regulation were not integrated. There was no euro-area-wide system of deposit insurance, analogous to the FDIC in the United States, for example, nor centralized policies and resources for dealing with troubled banks, which remained a national responsibility. That lack of coordination worsened the European crisis and complicated efforts to respond to it.

The crisis of 2007–2009 had hit Europe hard, in part because many European financial institutions had binged on the same questionable securities as their American counterparts. Many countries suffered serious banking problems, and the output and employment losses that followed were comparable to those in the United States. Also, Europe's monetary and fiscal responses were less effective than those of the United States or United Kingdom. Much of the blame for that lay with the conservative doctrines of Germany and like-minded countries in northern Europe. Perhaps because of a cultural memory of the disastrous hyperinflation of the 1920s, the Germans favored tight government budgets and opposed quantitative easing, which they viewed as illicit central-bank financing of governments. Because of concerns about the legal and political barriers to buying government debt in large quantities, the ECB would not start a U.S.-style QE program until 2015. Interventions by national governments avoided the uncontrolled collapse of any major financial firm—there was no European equivalent of Lehman Brothers—but several large firms, such as ABN Amro in the Netherlands, Commerzbank in Germany, and UBS in Switzerland, had to be placed under temporary government control. Importantly, the lack of integrated fiscal and banking policies—and, in some cases, a lack of political will—prevented the eurozone from recapitalizing its damaged banking system to the extent that the United States did, leaving it in weakened and vulnerable to any subsequent crisis, as well as less able to lend.

To make matters worse, in the years leading up to the global crisis several euro-area countries had allowed their private and public debt to reach levels that would prove unsustainable when a worldwide recession shook Europe's economy and banking system. In October 2009, the new prime minister of Greece, George Papandreou, made the shocking announcement that his government's budget deficit was close to 13 percent of national output, much higher than the ceiling of 3 percent that eurozone members were supposed to meet. Investors, for the first time, considered the possibility that Greece would default on its debts and even abandon the euro. And if Greece defaulted, would investors lose confidence in other heavily indebted countries—Portugal? Spain? Italy? Ireland? And if public and private defaults exploded, what would happen to the European banking system? It was an existential crisis for the euro.

As European leaders debated what to do, the consequences of not having a single fiscal authority became apparent. Proposed bailouts for Greece and possibly other countries needed not only to be robust enough to calm market fears, but they had to be perceived as sharing the burdens among the member countries, or else voters would rebel. The IMF, headed by Christine Lagarde, the former French finance minister and future president of the ECB, also became involved. Discussions dragged on for months. A bailout for Greece was announced May 2, 2010, but it was widely seen as inadequate and market volatility surged, as did the interest rates on the debt of other troubled European countries. Only a year and a half after Lehman's failure had helped spark a global panic, fundamental questions about the stability of the global financial system were rising again. Could the effects of defaults by whole countries be contained? Were the fractious Europeans capable of assembling coherent responses to what might prove to be a sequence of crises, as investors lost confidence in one country after another? Europe had navigated one financial crisis only to enter a new one.

At least at first, the second-wave European crisis appeared to have little effect on the United States. The fourth quarter of 2009 was strong, and the U.S. recovery continued at what the FOMC characterized as a moderate pace through the first half of 2010. Private spending—household consumption and business investment—was picking up. Unemployment was too high, still close to 10 percent, and inflation too low, but in early 2010 the staff and FOMC participants continued to project that both would move in the right directions. The unwinding of our emergency lending programs continued, and monetary policy remained on hold, with the funds rate target still near zero but no new securities purchases planned.

By the summer of 2010, however, the failure of the Europeans to resolve their debt crisis was beginning to take a toll on U.S. markets and business confidence. A staff memo at the June FOMC meeting warned that the financial shocks from Europe could push the United States into a new recession.[15] In August 2010, the staff, noting a slowdown in payrolls and production, significantly revised their growth forecast down and their unemployment projection up. And—as an object lesson of the difficulties of making policy with incomplete and preliminary data—we learned from newly revised figures that the recession had been deeper and the recovery weaker than initial estimates had suggested. With the outlook deteriorating and downside risks mounting, the Fed's quiet period was coming to an end.

A NEW PUSH: QE2

As our worries about the recovery grew, the FOMC took a technical action that was also an important policy signal. In August 2010, we announced that we would replace maturing (paid-down) securities on our balance sheet by purchasing new ones, avoiding any net reduction in our holdings and thus any passive policy tightening. In taking this step, we hoped to underline our commitment to continued stimulus.

I sent another, more straightforward signal soon afterward. At the Federal Reserve's annual symposium in Jackson Hole, Wyoming, in late August, I spoke about the "painfully slow recovery in the labor market" and said that the Committee was "prepared to provide additional monetary accommodation through unconventional measures [meaning quantitative easing and forward guidance] if it proves necessary."[16] Echoing my language, in the statement following its September 2010 meeting the FOMC said it was "prepared to provide additional accommodation if needed." In Fedspeak, the word "prepared" suggested imminent action, barring a major near-term improvement in the outlook. Internally, I had worked to gain support for new securities purchases and was confident the Committee would support them. However, opponents, although in the minority, raised serious concerns—mostly, that the purchases would not be effective, would create future risks to inflation or financial stability, or would create political problems for us.

Nevertheless, the case for new action was strong and, on November 3, 2010, the FOMC approved a new round of purchases, dubbed QE2 by markets and the media. Specifically, we said we would buy $600 billion of longer-term Treasury securities, at a pace of $75 billion a month through June 2011, raising the size of the balance sheet to about $2.9 trillion. There was only one dissenting vote, by Tom Hoenig of Kansas City. In the Fed's tradition of consensus, a formal dissent is a strong statement of disapproval, and the other QE skeptics were not ready to take that step, so long as they thought their views would receive consideration at future meetings.

Unlike QE1, market participants almost perfectly anticipated QE2, so our announcement did not move markets. Instead, the effects had been felt over the previous weeks and months as the Committee's signals and the weakening outlook had raised the likelihood of new purchases from a possibility to a near-certainty.* Indeed, our regular survey of primary dealers showed that, between June and November 2010, the percentage of dealers expecting new purchases rose from 40 percent to close to 100 percent. Their expected date of the first increase in the federal funds rate moved from June 2011 to October 2012. The episode showed once again the power of central-bank communication.

POLITICAL BLOWBACK

The new round of QE did prompt a political backlash, as some hawks had warned. I was particularly troubled by an unprecedented letter on November 17, two weeks after the QE2 announcement, from the top four Republicans in Congress. John Boehner and Eric Cantor in the House and Mitch McConnell and Jon Kyl in the Senate wrote that our purchases could "result in . . . hard-to-control, long-term inflation and potentially generate artificial asset bubbles."[17] An open letter from conservative economists, commentators, and asset managers, published on November 15 in the *Wall Street Journal*, had expressed similar concerns. It argued that our purchases "should be reconsidered and discontinued."[18] A second letter from the four Republican leaders in 2011 called on us to "resist further extraordinary intervention in the economy."[19] Representative (and future Vice President) Mike Pence of Indiana and Senator Bob Corker of Tennessee, both Republicans, introduced legislation to remove full employment from the Fed's dual mandate. It would have required us to focus only on inflation— although, with inflation quite low at the time, the switch to a single mandate might not have changed our policies much in the near term.

---

* The Dow Jones Industrial Average rose by 12 percent between my Jackson Hole speech and the announcement of QE2, for example.

Foreign governments also pushed back. Policymakers in emerging-market countries were concerned that our securities purchases would further decrease long-term interest rates in the United States (as was our intention), which in turn might generate excessive capital flows into their economies as investors searched for higher returns. And, by weakening the dollar, lower U.S. rates could amount to a form of "currency war" (in the words of Brazilian finance minister Guido Mantega) that favored U.S. exports.[20] These arguments, typically aimed by politicians at domestic audiences, ignored the likelihood that a stronger U.S. economy would benefit our trading partners by increasing our demand for their exports and by improving global financial conditions. Foreign central bankers, in a spirit of collegiality, were generally less inclined than finance ministers to publicly speak against QE2, but in October I fielded many challenging questions in Korea at a closed-door session of central bankers from the G20 (Group of Twenty) countries.[21] President Obama, attending a G20 summit in Seoul in November, also heard criticism of our policies and had to explain to a skeptical audience that the Fed operated independently from the administration.

The political backlash to QE2 was part of a much broader wave of anti-Fed feeling that had been building since the crisis. Only 30 percent of respondents in a July 2009 Gallup poll thought the Fed was doing a good job. The Fed ranked last among nine federal agencies, behind even the IRS (40 percent) and Congress (32 percent). Both ends of the political spectrum were angry—on the right, the Tea Party, which became prominent in 2009, and, on the left, Code Pink and later Occupy Wall Street. Many on the right saw the Fed's monetary experimentation as dangerous and inflationary, while many on both the left and the right had not forgiven actions we took to prop up failing Wall Street firms in the crisis. Demonstrators gathered in front of Reserve Banks, disrupted testimonies, and even came to my home. The protests, reminiscent of those during Volcker's war on inflation, focused even greater attention on the Fed and its policies.

The Fed aims to make policy decisions independently of short-term political pressures, and we had done so, but we did worry the anti-Fed wave could have longer-term consequences. During 2010 Congress and the administration focused on financial regulatory reform, under the leadership of Treasury Secretary Geithner, Senate Banking Committee Chair Christopher Dodd (D-Connecticut), and House Financial Services Committee Chair Barney Frank (D-Massachusetts). The reforms that ultimately emerged, together with a series of international agreements, addressed many—though certainly not all—of the weaknesses that had led to the financial crisis.[22] What became the Dodd-Frank Wall Street Reform and Consumer Protection Act, Dodd-Frank for short, strengthened capital and liquidity requirements for banks (including requiring regular stress tests), improved the transparency of financial derivatives markets, created a new consumer protection agency, and—importantly, given the experience with Lehman and other firms—established procedures for unwinding financial firms whose imminent failure posed serious risks to financial stability.

However, while Congress considered these reforms, the Fed spent a lot of time in the legislative crosshairs. Senator Dodd, in particular, recognized the broad-based anger and, as a means of building a bipartisan consensus for his bill, proposed stripping the Fed of virtually all its supervisory and regulatory authority, confining it to monetary policy. Congress also seriously considered "Audit the Fed" proposals championed by Senator Bernie Sanders (D-Vermont) on the left and Representative Ron Paul (R-Kentucky) on the right, which would have subjected the Fed's day-to-day monetary policy decisions to direct political oversight. The Sanders-Paul Audit the Fed proposals, like those that would later be advanced by Paul's son, Senator Rand Paul (R-Kentucky), had nothing to do with financial auditing (the Fed's books are regularly and publicly audited). Rather, these proposals would have allowed the Government Accountability Office (GAO) to report to Congress about each monetary policy decision, providing a new vehicle for legislators to second-guess and apply pressure on the FOMC. In its early incarnations, the financial reform legislation was a nightmare for the Fed.

My substantive reasons for resisting these proposals were the same as Alan Greenspan's in 1991 when he opposed efforts to consolidate banking oversight in a new agency. The Fed's authority to regulate and supervise the banking system was essential to our serving as an effective lender of last resort and to our monitoring the financial system and the economy. And monetary policy insulated from short-term political pressures would better serve the longer-term interests of the economy.

In the end an array of political forces turned the tide. Reserve Bank presidents, with their many local connections, including their boards of prominent local citizens, were an important factor. The presidents were highly motivated since bank supervision was one of the Reserve Banks' main roles. Critical support for our position also came from Treasury Secretary Geithner, community banks, and a few key Republican senators, including Kay Bailey Hutchison of Texas and Judd Gregg of New Hampshire. The Dodd-Frank bill somewhat limited the emergency powers that the Fed, Treasury, and FDIC had used to stabilize the financial system during the crisis. But the Fed kept its regulatory and supervisory authorities—except for consumer protection regulation, which went to the new Consumer Financial Protection Bureau. And it did not lose its monetary independence; "Audit the Fed" failed. I believe these outcomes were the right ones for the country, but the episode vividly illustrated that the Fed cannot ignore politics.

Why was anti-Fed rhetoric in Congress so heated? An explanation that resonates with me is the "scapegoat" theory, advanced by Sarah Binder and Mark Spindel.[23] In their view, Congress gives the Fed a degree of independence so that the central bank can take necessary but unpopular actions that Congress, for political reasons, does not want to take itself. This dynamic was evident during the financial crisis, when, among its many actions to stabilize the system, the Fed helped prevent the failures of several major financial institutions. I believe these bailouts were necessary to protect both the financial system and the economy, but they were highly unpopular—understandably. They were seen as benefiting people who had helped create the crisis in the first place, at the same time that many ordinary people were left unshielded.* Consistent with the Binder-Spindel theory, I knew from private conversations that many members of Congress saw the bailouts as distasteful but necessary to protect the economy. Nevertheless, in public, many echoed the popular anger, letting the Fed and the Bush and Obama administrations take the political heat.

The political opposition to our monetary policy, especially the domestic opposition, I find more difficult to explain. In substance, the arguments against securities purchases, as reflected for example in the letters to the FOMC from Republican congressional leaders, were quackery. For example, the risk that the purchases would lead to runaway inflation or a collapsing dollar was very low and not supported by either mainstream analysis or by the initial experience with QE in the United States and the United Kingdom. The economy was deeply depressed, implying little upward pressure on wages and prices.† And, indeed, market indicators of inflation expectations showed that, when forced to put their money where their mouths were, investors fully expected inflation to remain low, even too low. We paid attention to the risk that low rates could promote financial instability, but in 2010 investors were taking too little rather than too much risk for the health of the economy.

Rather than being based on principled concerns, much of the opposition to nontraditional monetary measures appears to have been scorched-earth right-wing partisanship—opposition to policies that might improve the economy with a Democrat in the White House. The anti-Fed rhetoric of the financial crisis era would spill over into the early campaigning for the Republican presidential nomination. Texas Governor Rick Perry called our efforts to support the economy "almost treasonous." Former House Speaker

---

* A particular source of popular anger was the fact that no CEO of a bailed-out company went to jail. Criminal prosecutions are the responsibility of the Department of Justice (DOJ), not the Federal Reserve. For the most part, the DOJ determined that it could not build winning cases against individuals—taking excessive risks is not illegal in most cases—and focused instead on imposing large fines on firms that had employed questionable practices.

† It is possible to have high inflation in a depressed economy if the government's finances are collapsing. But the U.S. government, enjoying tremendous global demand for its securities, was not remotely near that point in 2010.

Newt Gingrich said he would fire me if elected and called me "the most inflationary, dangerous, and power-centered chairman . . . in the history of the Fed."[24]

The political furor did prompt a change in our communication strategy. In the dozen or so years before the crisis, the Fed had become decidedly more open, but continued to largely focus its communication narrowly on influencing the policy expectations of financial market participants. But with the Fed now in the media and political spotlight, we needed to make our case to the broader public. I took the lead on that, beginning with an appearance (then rare for a Fed chair) on CBS-TV's *60 Minutes* program in March 2009.[25] I followed that interview with other media appearances, town halls, and, in spring 2012, a series of lectures at George Washington University that became the basis of a short book.[26]

In April 2011, after much discussion and planning, and with the support of the FOMC, I started conducting quarterly post-meeting press conferences. Although press conferences were common at many other central banks, Fed chairs had only rarely held them. They would become central to the Fed's efforts to inform the public and guide markets. More generally, the shift in communication strategy toward a broader audience proved to be an enduring and constructive change that, among other things, allowed the Fed to better appreciate the effects (as well as the public perceptions) of its actions on average Americans.

7

MONETARY EVOLUTION

QE3 and the Taper Tantrum

MY FIRST POST-MEETING PRESS CONFERENCE, on April 27, 2011, came eight months after I had first hinted at QE2 at Jackson Hole. Financial conditions had eased considerably in the interim, with a 25 percent increase in stock prices suggesting growing optimism. Longer-term Treasury yields had fallen in the run-up to QE2 as the likelihood of new purchases rose, but subsequently rebounded as investors became more confident about future growth and less worried about falling inflation. That pattern was similar to what we had seen after the introduction of QE1 in 2009.

Easier financial conditions in turn appeared to be helping the economy. The unemployment rate fell from 9.8 percent in November 2010, when QE2 was announced, to 9.0 percent by March 2011—better, though still much too high. I told the reporters at the press conference that we expected the recovery to continue at a moderate pace, with unemployment falling slowly. But I cautioned that some developments—notably, the disastrous earthquake and tsunami that hit Japan on March 11—could temporarily slow growth (for instance, by disrupting shipments of Japanese-made auto parts to U.S. assembly plants). Inflation had also recently picked up, due largely to global increases in oil and food prices. However, with both core inflation and inflation expectations stable, we were confident that the jump in overall inflation would prove temporary.

We were right about inflation, which quickly receded, but, despite the positive signs early in the year, 2011 would again disappoint. After its initial drop, the unemployment rate stalled for most of the year, falling only to 8.5 percent by December. Output growth fluctuated around 2 percent, probably close to the economy's long-run potential pace of growth. But that was not fast enough. For unemployment to fall meaningfully, with underutilized resources being put back to work, output growth needed to exceed, not simply equal, its normal long-run rate. At FOMC meetings we debated the reasons for the apparent inability of the economy to reach "escape velocity," a self-sustaining path of healthy growth. The discussion focused on putative "headwinds"—factors that were slowing the recovery more than we had expected.

The ongoing European crisis was the most prominent headwind. Reacting to the ongoing risk that one or more euro-area countries might default or leave the euro, financial markets remained volatile, and a premature turn to fiscal austerity—prioritizing fiscal balance over economic recovery—further slowed growth in Europe. American fiscal policy was becoming a headwind as well. The effects of the big 2009 federal stimulus package were fading, and state and local governments were cutting spending and jobs in response to falling tax revenues.

A gratuitous and self-inflicted blow to the recovery came in August 2011, when Congress refused until the very last moment to raise the national debt limit. Without the increase, the federal government could not have paid its bills, including, in some scenarios, even the interest on the national debt. At the Fed, which is responsible for processing many payments made by the government, including interest payments, we wargamed how we would deal with a government default, even as I and others at the Fed pleaded with Congress to avoid an unnecessary disaster. The unthinkable near-default on U.S. government securities added to financial market jitters and led the Standard & Poor's rating agency to downgrade the United States' credit rating. Reacting to global slowing and fiscal malfeasance, the Dow fell by about 16 percent between late July and the beginning of October.

Other headwinds appeared to be aftereffects of the crisis itself, consistent with Carmen Reinhart and Kenneth Rogoff's observation that deep recessions and slow recoveries often follow financial crises.[1] Despite the recapitalization of the banking system that followed the stress tests, credit remained relatively tight, especially for mortgage borrowers, as both lenders and regulators imposed stricter standards. Better-off households focused on paying down debt and rebuilding wealth rather than on new borrowing and spending, while the less-fortunate struggled just to hang on. And the housing bust had left a massive hangover in the form of unsold and foreclosed-upon houses. Builders started construction on only about 600,000 new homes in 2011, compared with more than 2 million in 2005.

The crisis may have also contributed to unexpectedly weak productivity gains, which—combined with a more slowly growing workforce, as baby boomers retired and immigration slowed—further dragged on economic growth. Some research has found that the productivity slowdown may have begun around 2005, before the crisis hit, and that it resulted largely from the normal ebb and flow of technological advances and their commercial application, rather than from the crisis itself.[2] That may be, but, intuitively, it made sense that the financial crisis would depress productivity growth as well. The crisis slowed research and development, the pace of new start-ups, and business investment in new capital equipment, as well as crimping consumer demand. All of that would be expected to slow the introduction of new products and new, more-efficient methods of production.

With the outlook distinctly mediocre and with no new initiatives from Congress, monetary policy became "the only game in town" for battling unemployment, to use the phrase that Paul Volcker coined in connection with fighting inflation. But the effective lower bound on short-term interest rates remained a problem. Near-zero short-term rates, several trillion dollars' worth of securities purchases, and forward guidance had helped the economy return to growth but had not restored it to full health. Once again, it was time for something new. From 2011 to 2013, we reconsidered our policy tools, our approach to communication, and even our overarching policy framework. Not all these initiatives proceeded smoothly, as would be exemplified by a bond market "tantrum" in 2013. Ultimately, however, the changes helped improve the economy and labor market and, in the longer run, left a lasting imprint on the conduct of monetary policy.

AMPING UP FORWARD GUIDANCE

Under Greenspan and during my time as chair, the FOMC had become increasingly ambitious about using forward guidance as a policy tool. In March 2009, when it announced QE1, the Committee tried to guide market expectations by saying that it anticipated "exceptionally low levels of the federal funds rate for an extended period." More than two years later, that phrase remained in the post-meeting statement.

It was strong language by traditional Fed standards, but not as strong as it might have been. First, it was vague. It was not specific about how long "an extended period" might be nor did it provide guidance about the conditions under which rates would be raised. Second, the guidance was not a full-throated promise. It said only that the Committee *anticipated* that rates would stay low. Indeed, some critics, notably my former Princeton colleague Michael Woodford, would point out that the "extended period" language could be interpreted as the FOMC saying only that it was pessimistic about the outlook, not making any clear commitment about future policy.[3] If read that way, our forward guidance, by depressing household and business sentiment, could have been counterproductive.

I thought our guidance, even though not phrased as a firm commitment, did create a presumption that we would be patient and keep rates near zero for a while. Moreover, ongoing securities purchases and other communication—including speeches and congressional testimony—reinforced our signal that we planned to keep policy easy. Still, I agree with Woodford's argument that more-specific and forceful guidance would have been even better.

As time passed, it became increasingly clear that the "extended period" guidance was not strong enough. In 2009 and 2010, even as staff analyses—and many, though not all, FOMC participants—had concluded that the federal funds rate would likely need to stay near zero for years, futures markets (in which investors bet on the course of the funds rate) anticipated the first rate increase no more than a few quarters away. The "extended period" was thus not as extended in the minds of many market participants as most on the Committee would have preferred. Very likely, markets were using as their reference point earlier Fed policy cycles, in which the typical period from easing to tightening had been shorter. We needed to do more to convince markets that we would not raise our target rate for a while.

We took the next step at our August 9, 2011, meeting. After noting that economic growth so far that year had been disappointing, our statement offered more explicit forward guidance. It said that we anticipated "exceptionally low levels of the federal funds rate *at least through mid-2013* [italics added]," that is, for almost two more years. The statement added that the Committee was discussing a "range of policy tools," signaling that further policy innovations might be coming soon. Three Reserve Bank presidents dissented—Richard Fisher of Dallas, Charles Plosser of Philadelphia, and Narayana Kocherlakota of Minneapolis. All three believed that new monetary stimulus was unnecessary and preferred to leave the guidance in the statement unchanged. Three "no" votes are a lot for a Fed policy decision; it suggests considerable discomfort with the outcome.

Plosser and several others also argued that, if we were going to make a new commitment on rates, we should tie it to a specific set of economic conditions, not to a fixed date. The FOMC's August 2011 statement made a *time-dependent* commitment, linking the future course of the federal funds rate only to the calendar. If we were going to make a commitment, Plosser argued, it should be *state-contingent*, specifying the economic conditions that would lead to an increase in the funds rate.

A state-contingent commitment is, in principle at least, more flexible and responsive to incoming economic news. Plosser and those sympathetic to his view worried that, if economic conditions improved more quickly than we expected, our time-dependent commitment would force us to keep the funds rate low for longer than, ideally, we should. In contrast, a state-contingent commitment—one that tied the rate liftoff to the unemployment rate, say—would give us the flexibility to tighten more quickly. Of course, state-contingent guidance could work in the other direction as well, effectively lengthening the duration of our commitment if the economy worsened unexpectedly. Time-dependent commitments don't have this nice self-adjusting aspect. In fact, reflecting continuing disappointments in the outlook, in January 2012 we agreed to extend our commitment by a year and a half to "at least through late 2014" and then once again, in September 2012, "to mid-2015." Notably, both of these latter promises extended past the likely end of my term as chair, so it was encouraging that there was only one dissenter—Richmond Fed President Lacker—in each case.

Plosser had made a valid conceptual point—even if his economic forecast proved too optimistic. And, indeed, the FOMC would later use state-contingent guidance to convey its plans about both short-term interest rates and securities purchases. However, in August 2011, I believed that time-dependent guidance was our best option. Given the divergence between market expectations of policy and our own, we needed to do something dramatic to get the markets' attention. State-contingent guidance involves ambiguity and risk of misunderstanding because policymakers can never fully specify the conditions that would trigger a policy change. A date, by contrast, is simple and direct. At the time, the direct approach seemed best.

Experience suggests that the right form of guidance depends on circumstances, and, indeed, both approaches—time-dependent and state-contingent—remain in use. For example, the Bank of Japan promised in 2016 to continue its highly expansionary policies as long as needed to raise inflation above its 2 percent target "in a stable manner" (a form of state-contingent guidance), while the European Central Bank has on several occasions in recent years promised to keep its policy rate low until at least a certain date (time-dependent guidance). In any case, our August 2011 guidance appeared effective. Interest rates fell, and our surveys found that, as a result of the guidance, financial market participants expected us to exercise greater patience in raising rates.[4]

Although the new guidance added stimulus, we did not expect it by itself to be a game changer. The next few FOMC meetings involved intensive discussion of additional options, including the possibility of changing our underlying monetary policy framework.

THE MATURITY EXPANSION PROGRAM

In the fall of 2011 many of my colleagues and I believed monetary policy not only had to do more, but that we also had to find new ways to do more. Exploring the options and developing a consensus would take time. The economy, however, needed additional support as soon as possible. As an interim measure, in September 2011 we therefore decided to purchase $400 billion of Treasury securities of longer maturities (six to thirty years) by the end of June 2012.

We expected this new round of securities purchases would, as with previous rounds, increase the demand for, and thus depress the yield on, longer-term securities, and ease financial conditions more generally. But, instead of funding the purchases by creating new bank reserves, as was the case with QE1 and QE2, we decided to pay for these purchases by selling an equal amount of short-term Treasury securities, with maturities of three years or less. As a result, although the purchases significantly increased the average maturity of the securities held by the Fed, the overall size of the balance sheet did not change.

This program was consistent with the view that our purchases worked primarily by reducing the net supply of longer-term securities, thereby raising their prices and lowering their yields, rather than by increasing bank reserves or the money supply. We hoped it would be at least as effective as earlier securities purchases, while perhaps soothing internal and external critics who worried that creating more bank reserves could cause higher inflation or financial instability.

Our new approach also had shortcomings. First, its size was limited by the quantity of securities we owned with maturities of three years or less. Once we sold them, we would have to go back to financing purchases by creating bank reserves. Second, shifting toward longer-term securities would make the exit from our large balance sheet more difficult when the time came, since our holdings would on average take a longer time to mature. Still, it seemed a useful interim step. The staff estimated it would provide meaningful additional stimulus while giving the Committee time to debate a more comprehensive strategy.

We called the new program the Maturity Extension Program (MEP). Markets and the media, as usual, ignored its official name and dubbed it Operation Twist, after a Fed program in the 1960s. In the original Operation Twist, under Chair Martin, the Fed bought longer-term securities and sold shorter-term securities in an attempt to "twist" the yield curve, that is, to lower longer-term rates (to stimulate spending in the economy) while raising shorter-term rates (with the goal of protecting the exchange value of the dollar). Subsequent analysts judged that earlier operation had only modest effects, perhaps because it was small and temporary.[5] The MEP was larger and longer lasting than its 1960s precursor. Like the original Operation Twist, it aimed to lower longer-term rates, but we did not expect shorter-term rates would rise because the high level of bank reserves already in the system kept them near zero.

INCREASING TRANSPARENCY: THE INFLATION TARGET AND THE SUMMARY OF ECONOMIC PROJECTIONS

Our debates about how to make monetary policy more effective, despite the lower bound, led to broader discussions about our policy framework. If we were going to offer useful guidance and give coherent explanations of our policy plans, it could only help to be more specific about our objectives, our outlook, and our views on appropriate policy. For me, and for most FOMC participants, that meant being clearer about the framework that guided our actions. The Committee spent many hours considering a range of possibilities.

Following these deliberations, the Committee in January 2012 approved a statement of monetary policy principles, the first such document in Fed history. In it, we announced a formal inflation target—2 percent a year as measured by the personal consumption expenditures (PCE) price index. Our statement emphasized that the adoption of the target did not mean that we were no longer interested in promoting full employment. Instead, it said we would take a "balanced approach" that gave roughly equal weight to both of our congressionally mandated objectives of price stability and maximum employment.

The idea of an inflation target was hardly new. Indeed, by 2012, it was increasingly becoming the international norm. Beginning with the Reserve Bank of New Zealand in 1990, many central banks had announced targets (or sometimes target ranges) for inflation. In advanced economies, these included the Bank of England, the European Central Bank, Sweden's Riksbank, the Reserve Bank of Australia, and the Bank of Canada. Inflation-targeting middle-income countries included Brazil, Mexico, Chile, Israel, and South Africa.

Why have an inflation target? The rationale was *not* that inflation was or should be the only objective of monetary policy. In practice, all inflation-targeting central banks practice "flexible" inflation targeting, meaning that they retain scope to pursue multiple goals, including employment and economic growth, so long as doing so is consistent with achieving the inflation target over time. It is out of concern for employment and other goals that no central bank has chosen an inflation target of zero—that is, literal price stability. Targeting an average inflation rate of zero, by lowering the inflation expectations of bond traders, would translate into very low nominal interest rates. A low neutral interest rate in turn would increase the risk that the lower bound would prevent monetary policymakers from responding forcefully to recessions. Our 2 percent target thus aimed to balance the two parts of our dual mandate—inflation low enough to be consistent with price stability, but high enough to preserve our ability to pursue full employment by providing some space to reduce rates without hitting the lower bound.

As an academic, I had contributed to the research on inflation targeting—mostly in work with Frederic (Rick) Mishkin of Columbia

University, who served as a Board member during the financial crisis.[6] I saw an inflation target as a key element of a more transparent and systematic framework that would make policy easier for markets and the public to understand and predict. To reap the full benefit of inflation targeting, as Mishkin's and my research documented, central banks were going well beyond simply announcing a target. They were also providing much more information about their forecasts, their assessment of risks, and their expected policy responses, including—in some cases—forecasts of their policy interest rate. This transparency made forward guidance more effective and reduced uncertainty, Mishkin and I argued, since outsiders could gain more insight into the considerations that were driving policy. Transparency also supported central-bank independence by helping politicians and the public better understand the rationale for policy decisions, thereby reducing the tension between democratic oversight and the delegation of those powers to unelected central bankers.

Debate about an inflation target overlaps with another long-standing debate—whether monetary policy should be run by *rules* or by *discretion*. Advocates of policy rules, like the canonical rule proposed by the economist John Taylor in 1993, hold that policymakers should set short-term interest rates according to a simple numerical formula, which in Taylor's rule includes only the current levels of unemployment and inflation.[7] A policy rule, if closely followed, would indeed make policy changes easy to predict and would prevent policymakers from deviating too far from established norms, for example, by responding to an increase in inflation very differently than in past episodes. The problem is that strict policy rules leave no room for judgment based on information not included in the rule and so cannot easily accommodate special circumstances—such as the 2008 financial panic or the coronavirus pandemic in 2020. Ongoing changes in the structure of the economy, such as in the relationship between unemployment and inflation or in the influence of interest rates on spending, likewise pose a problem for fixed rules.

Under policy discretion, by contrast, interest-rate decisions are made judgmentally meeting by meeting, using all available information. The discretionary approach is better at taking special factors or structural change into account, and policymakers who place a high value on flexibility prefer it. But purely discretionary policies are harder for market participants to understand or forecast, provide fewer safeguards against risky or untried policies, and offer less accountability overall. By preventing policymakers from committing to future actions, a discretionary approach also limits the use of forward guidance as a policy tool.

Mishkin and I argued that inflation targeting is a reasonable compromise between strict policy rules and unfettered discretion, allowing policymakers what we called *constrained discretion*. With constrained discretion, policymakers can use their judgment to account for special circumstances and to weigh the goals of policy against each other. On the other hand, they are constrained by the requirements: first, to achieve the targeted level of inflation over time and, second, to publicly explain their decisions. These requirements enhance predictability and accountability. Additionally, a credible inflation-targeting regime tends to stabilize people's inflation expectations around the target. Arthur Burns's attempts to control inflation in the 1970s had been plagued by poorly anchored inflation expectations, which contributed to destructive wage-price spirals. Announcing and, more importantly, consistently hitting an inflation target can help avoid this dynamic. If the inflation target is credible, people should look through temporary changes in inflation, such as shocks to food and energy prices, without incorporating them into their longer-term expectations and wage- and price-setting behavior.

Given the international trend toward inflation targets, it's not surprising that the subject had been discussed by the FOMC. As early as 1989, Lee Hoskins, president of the Cleveland Fed, had suggested that an inflation target would increase the coherence of FOMC policymaking.[8] Greenspan allowed several extended discussions of the idea at FOMC meetings, including a staged debate in 1995 between Janet Yellen, then a governor, and Richmond Fed President Al Broaddus. In that debate, Yellen argued against policies aimed solely at targeting inflation, but she subsequently became a strong supporter of inflation targeting that was flexible enough to incorporate the Fed's employment goals along with inflation goals. In July 1996, the Committee supported conducting policy based on an informal inflation target of 2 percent. Greenspan agreed—but only if there were no public discussion of or commitment to the target, a proviso that eliminated many of the benefits of having a target.[9]

The FOMC's acknowledgment in 2003 that inflation could be too low as well as too high—which revealed that the Fed had an implicit target—raised the issue yet again. In February 2005 Greenspan allowed another extensive discussion of inflation targeting by the FOMC. But he continued to oppose a formal, public target and the idea went no further. Greenspan prized discretion, and he worried that an inflation target might unnecessarily constrain monetary policy. He also had political concerns. If the Fed were to unilaterally announce an inflation target, would Congress believe that its prerogative to set the goals of monetary policy had been usurped and respond by limiting the Fed's operational independence?

When I was appointed to the Board in 2002, the media speculated that Greenspan and I would clash over inflation targeting. I did speak publicly about it. I noted in a speech that the American media treated inflation targeting like the metric system: as something "foreign, impenetrable, and slightly subversive"—and I continued to push the idea.[10] Greenspan never objected overtly. We had a few friendly discussions, but I had no illusions about overcoming his resistance.

When I became chair in 2006, I moved only gingerly toward instituting a target. I still thought it was the right approach, but I recognized that I needed to do substantial spadework with the Committee. In my new position, I also better appreciated the political issue Greenspan had raised. In some countries, including Canada and the United Kingdom, the monetary policy regime, including the inflation target, is determined jointly by the government and the central bank. In other jurisdictions, including the eurozone, the central bank determines the numerical inflation goals it sees as consistent with its mandate, along with the supporting elements such as the release of forecasts. I thought that the Fed was best equipped to determine the target and develop the framework to implement its price stability mandate from Congress. But consultation and building support with the administration and Congress seemed wise.

Rather than trying to introduce a formal target right away, I expanded the information we provided about our outlook for the economy and policy, steps that would support the eventual adoption of a formal inflation-targeting framework. Since 1979, the FOMC had released economic projections twice a year, as part of its *Monetary Policy Report to Congress*, but they received little attention. At its September 2007 meeting, in my second year as chair, the FOMC approved my plan to release projections quarterly, rather than semiannually, with a horizon of three years rather than two. Projections were made by FOMC participants individually—not by the Committee collectively—and the resulting document was called the *Summary of Economic Projections* (SEP). We submitted projections for four variables: output growth, unemployment, overall inflation, and core inflation, which were then released without attribution to individuals. The idea was to show more explicitly how the Committee saw the economic outlook evolving.

We expanded the SEP over time. In January 2009 we added projections, under the assumption of "appropriate monetary policy," for inflation, unemployment, and economic growth "over the longer run," defined as roughly three to five years. These long-run estimates provided important insights into the Committee's thinking. In particular, the long-run inflation projection, under appropriate monetary policy, was an indirect way of giving the FOMC's effective target range for inflation. Most participants favored a target of around 2 percent or a bit below. And the long-run projection of unemployment could be interpreted as revealing the Committee's estimates of the natural rate of unemployment, u^*.

Meanwhile, I continued consulting, inside and outside the Fed, about formally adopting an inflation target. Most FOMC participants had become receptive (or maybe they had just become tired of discussing the subject in our meetings, as Fed Governor Betsy Duke commented). I met with Obama's advisers and then with Obama himself, who told me that the administration did not object. However, Barney Frank, the Massachusetts

Democrat who chaired the House Financial Services Committee, was nervous. Employment and production were collapsing—the wrong psychological moment, he believed, to give the impression, even if mistaken, that the Fed cared primarily about inflation. To some extent, then, the addition of longer-run inflation projections in January 2009 was an end run around Frank's objections. It was a much lower-profile step than announcing a target, yet it implicitly defined at least a target range. And, since we also gave long-run projections for unemployment, I believed we would not be seen as prioritizing inflation over employment.

When the FOMC returned to the consideration of its framework in 2011, I asked Janet Yellen, who had recently succeeded Don Kohn as Board vice chair, to lead a subcommittee to study the issue. Janet's subcommittee recommended that we formally adopt a 2 percent inflation target, but that we also emphasize a balanced approach to pursuing price stability and maximum employment. The term "balanced approach" reflected the reality (implied by the Phillips curve) that monetary policy may at times face a short-run trade-off between its inflation and unemployment goals— although not in 2011, when both high unemployment and low inflation were reasons for more stimulus. Under a balanced approach, when the goals conflicted, policymakers would choose an intermediate path that reflected the importance of both goals but also favored the goal that was furthest from its desired level.

The policy principles raised an obvious question: Why didn't we have a numerical goal for the unemployment rate as well as for the inflation rate? The difference is that, in the long run, monetary policy is the primary determinant of the inflation rate but not the unemployment rate. Monetary policymakers can set a target for inflation and—barring complications like the effective lower bound—expect to be able to hit it, at least over several years. Notably, there is no "natural" rate of inflation toward which the inflation rate tends. In the long run, inflation reflects the actions of monetary (and fiscal) policymakers.

In contrast, while monetary policy affects unemployment in the short run, in the longer term, in a healthy economy, unemployment tends toward its natural rate, which is determined by factors largely outside the control of monetary policy. These factors include demographics, workforce skills, businesses' needs and strategies (for example, reliance on automation), and the efficiency of the labor market at matching employers and workers. Moreover, the natural rate can't be observed directly nor is it likely to be stable over time. Monetary policymakers thus can't be expected to hold unemployment indefinitely at an arbitrary long-run target. Although it would not be feasible to set and expect to meet a fixed target for unemployment, the FOMC's estimate of the long-run, sustainable level of unemployment (as shown in the quarterly SEP) could be thought of as a provisional target for the unemployment rate—even if one subject to significant uncertainty and change. In that interpretation, the symmetry of the underlying, balanced approach becomes more apparent.

By the time we had adopted and announced the new policy principles, in January 2012, I had brought Barney Frank around. We had developed mutual trust during the financial crisis and its aftermath. More importantly, he now understood the balanced nature of our approach. And it didn't hurt that, with inflation below target, the new policy framework was fully consistent with continuing the easy money policies that Barney favored. The announcement of the policy principles, including the inflation target, went smoothly, with no objections from Congress or the administration.

The SEP also continued to evolve. The January 2012 SEP, released at the same time as our statement of principles, was the first to contain projections (made individually by FOMC participants) of the future path of the federal funds rate. Fed-watchers called the figure displaying the rate projections the *dot plot*. The Committee also began releasing a bar chart summarizing participants' projections for the year when the funds rate would first increase.

The inflation target and the SEP economic projections have become widely accepted as essential elements of the Fed's communication. The dot plot has been more controversial. Understood simply as a compilation of the current views of individual FOMC participants, it supplies useful information about how those participants would like to see policy evolve, but in a more systematic way than provided by individual speeches and interviews. In many cases, the dot plot provides clues to the likely direction of policy, at least given current information, and markets react accordingly to significant changes. During my time as chair, for example, the rate projections reinforced the message of continued ease—in contrast to 2009–2010, when markets mistakenly saw the Fed "normalizing" rates in the near future. On the other hand, the dot plot is a collection of individual views of appropriate policy, based on each person's assumptions about outside factors like oil prices or fiscal policy, not the collective view or the official forward guidance of the Committee as a whole.* Being anonymous, the dot plot projections also do not reflect the greater influence of Committee leadership, especially the chair, in policy decisions. The SEP rate projections published each quarter thus do not always align exactly with the rate guidance in the Committee's post-meeting statement. These discrepancies risk muddying the policy message and put a burden on the chair to clarify the Committee's collective intentions in the press conference. Nevertheless, taken together, the inflation target, the SEP (including the dot plot), the press conferences, and the use of more-explicit forward guidance have made monetary policy significantly more transparent.

QE3: OPEN-ENDED ASSET PURCHASES

Although the economy grew in 2012, the pace of recovery, particularly in the job market, remained disappointing—by now a familiar, and frustrating refrain. By the time we gathered for the annual Jackson Hole symposium at the end the summer, the unemployment rate was still at 8.2 percent, with about 40 percent of the unemployed having been out of work for six months or more. The FOMC projections released in June reflected

---

* We tried to develop economic and interest rate projections that would be owned by the whole Committee, as some other central banks do (the Bank of England, for example), but our experiments persuaded us that the FOMC was too large, diverse, and geographically dispersed for this to be practical.

growing pessimism. They saw unemployment remaining above 7 percent through the end of 2014, more than two years later and more than five years since the beginning of the recovery. They also significantly marked down expected economic growth for 2012 and 2013. Inflation was expected to remain below our newly established target as well.

Federal fiscal policy, which boosted the economy during the first few years after the crisis, was now dragging down growth. The federal government was heading toward a "fiscal cliff"—the confluence of three fiscal deadlines at the end of 2012. Barring congressional action, on December 31 the federal government would reach its borrowing limit, the Bush-era tax cuts would expire, and sequestration—deep automatic spending cuts—would begin. Fortunately, Congress averted the worst outcomes, but tax increases (including the end of a temporary 2 percentage point reduction in payroll taxes) and spending cuts were poised to deliver a blow to the economy at a time when the recovery remained tepid. The nonpartisan Congressional Budget Office estimated a 1.5 percentage point hit to growth in 2013 from fiscal tightening.[11] Worried about Fed independence, I had generally avoided Greenspan's practice of getting involved in fiscal policy deliberations, but I made an exception when I believed that the direction of fiscal policy would endanger the Fed's achievement of its mandated goals. I supported fiscal stimulus in 2009 and, in 2012, pushed back in testimony and speeches against what I saw as counterproductive austerity. In an increasingly partisan and ideological Congress, my comments had little noticeable effect.

Europe also remained a concern. In November 2011 Mario Draghi replaced Jean-Claude Trichet as president of the European Central Bank. Draghi had previously served as chief of the Italian central bank and head of the influential Financial Stability Board, an international body of regulators. He had earned a PhD in economics from MIT, where, like me, he studied under Stan Fischer. Draghi promptly took the ECB in a dovish direction, reversing two 2011 rate hikes. Even more importantly, Draghi's promise, in a London speech in July 2012, to "do whatever it takes to preserve the euro" had helped calm a spiraling crisis in the markets for the debt of Italy, Spain, and other countries.[12] But, facing opposition from Germany and its allies, Draghi's ECB lagged other major central banks in undertaking large-scale securities purchases, while European fiscal support was also limited. Governments with heavy debt burdens were forced into austerity (budget cuts and tax increases) and governments with space to spend generally chose not to. As a result, the European economy remained weak, with increasing risks of outright deflation. Eurozone weakness spilled over to its trading partners, including the United States.

The economic outlook as of mid-2012 supported a strong case for yet more monetary stimulus—assuming we had the tools to deliver it. We had already moved the expiration date of the Maturity Extension Program from June 2012 to the end of the year. That committed us to purchases of $45 billion of longer-term Treasury securities per month for six more months, financed by sales of our remaining short-term securities. That seemed unlikely to be sufficient. In the same statement that announced the extension of the MEP, the FOMC said it was "prepared to take further action as appropriate." At Jackson Hole on August 31, I reinforced that signal by calling the weak job numbers "a grave concern" and saying that we would "provide additional policy accommodation as needed to promote . . . sustained improvement in labor market conditions."[13]

After my foreshadowing, there was little doubt that the FOMC would follow through. In September, the Committee approved a new program of securities purchases that would become known, naturally enough, as QE3. With the goal of providing more help to the housing market, we first added $40 billion per month of purchases of GSE-guaranteed mortgage-backed securities to the ongoing $45 billion in monthly purchases of longer-term Treasury securities under the extended MEP, bringing our total purchases to $85 billion per month. At the same meeting we also extended our forward guidance to promise low rates "at least through mid-2015," almost three years away. In December, to replace the expiring MEP, the Committee agreed to continue purchasing $45 billion per month of Treasuries (financed by creating bank reserves), keeping the overall flow of purchases at $85 billion per month—$45 billion in Treasuries and $40 billion in

MBS. At that pace (close to a trillion dollars a year), QE3 would soon dwarf QE2.

Crucially, unlike our previous securities-purchase programs, QE3 was *open ended*, with no total purchase amount or end date given. The FOMC said instead that "if the outlook for the labor market does not improve substantially," then purchases would continue until it did. In other words, the duration and magnitude of purchases were not predetermined but depended on our assessment of the labor market. It was a state-contingent rather than a time-dependent commitment. My hope was that the open-ended commitment would provide assurance that, in the spirit of Draghi's "do whatever it takes" promise, the Fed would be there as long as needed—no more start and stop.

Despite only one dissenting vote against QE3—from Jeff Lacker of the Richmond Fed, a regular opponent of policy ease—it was nevertheless controversial within the Committee, and it became increasingly so over time. Unfortunately, this disagreement would complicate our communication and create uncertainty, both within the FOMC and in markets, about how long we would continue buying securities and under what conditions purchases would end.

The qualms within the Committee were similar to the concerns about earlier rounds of QE, but sharper because of QE3's open-ended nature. Broadly speaking, the reservations fell into two categories: doubts about QE3's likely effectiveness and concerns about its potential costs and risks. On effectiveness, staff economists presented analyses suggesting that new securities purchases would help quicken the recovery by pressing down on long-term interest rates, but several FOMC participants were skeptical and argued that the projected benefits were unrealistically large. They noted, correctly, that the recovery had remained disappointing despite previous rounds of purchases and that estimates of the effects of this comparatively untested tool were, at best, highly uncertain. If purchases were not in fact very effective, then an open-ended promise to keep buying until things got better might lead only to a swollen Fed balance sheet, complicating the ultimate exit from the program without much gain in terms of jobs or growth. (Board member Jeremy Stein called this the Groundhog Day scenario: continued purchases, with disappointing results, forcing yet more purchases, and so on.) Indeed, the skeptics argued, undertaking an ineffective program could be worse than doing nothing, since it would sap public confidence and damage the Fed's credibility in the financial markets.

Regarding costs and risks, some FOMC participants argued that protracted low interest rates might lead to financial instability, if not immediately then later. For example, persistently low yields might lead investors to take unreasonable risks to get higher returns ("reaching for yield") or to borrow too much, making them vulnerable to future shocks. Yet another concern was that, if long-term interest rates were to rise unexpectedly, the market value of the bonds held by the Fed could fall sharply, resulting in large paper losses on our portfolio.* Relatedly, our plan for raising short-term rates, when the time came, was to pay interest to banks on their reserves at the Fed. New securities purchases, financed by increasing bank reserves, would increase the aggregate interest payments we would have to make to banks in the future, reducing the profits we sent to the Treasury. As St. Louis Fed President Jim Bullard and others pointed out, the combination of losses on our portfolio and a reduction or cessation of our regular payments to the Treasury (with the money going to banks instead) could provide powerful ammunition to our numerous critics on Capitol Hill.

FOMC participants, in an internal survey before the December 2012 meeting when we announced that QE3 would be open ended, had identified financial instability and the possibility of losses on our portfolio as the two risks that most concerned them. Besides possible exit difficulties from a historically large balance sheet, other concerns included the risk of impairing the functioning of securities markets and, for a few hawkish members, the possibility that the barrage of monetary stimulus would at some point create a surge in inflation. Reflecting the general sense of uncertainty, several respondents also cited the possibility of "unanticipated" or "unknown"

---

* It was only modest consolation that, under the Fed's accounting procedures, any losses would be formally recognized only if the securities were sold.

side effects. I took as good news that FOMC participants rated none of these risks as more than "moderate," suggesting that most saw the potential downsides of new purchases as tolerable.

Personally, I had become increasingly convinced that new securities purchases would help an economy that still very much needed it, and that an open-ended approach might prove more powerful and confidence-inducing than the earlier fixed-size programs. I also told the Committee in December that, based on our experience thus far, most of the concerns about costs and risks were not worrisome enough to prevent us from moving ahead, although I acknowledged that we did not understand very well the links between monetary policy and financial stability in particular. But—as Janet Yellen argued at the meeting—given our pessimistic outlook for the economy, doing nothing also involved significant risks.

Nevertheless, reading the Committee's concerns, I agreed that we still had more to learn about the efficacy and costs of large-scale securities purchases, and that what we learned might affect our views about continuing them. As a result, although believing that it was time to try an open-ended, state-dependent approach, I did not push the Committee to tie the termination of the purchases to a specific indicator, such as the level of the unemployment rate. Instead, to maintain some flexibility, I supported the more-qualitative language about requiring substantial improvement in the labor market outlook before ending QE3.

I also proposed, with broad concurrence, that we should say that, in determining the future pace of purchases, we would "take appropriate account of [their] likely efficacy and costs. . . ." This language was an escape clause. It left open the possibility that securities purchases could end, not because our economic objectives had been fully met, but because we had determined that the program was not working or had excessive costs. We hoped not to have to invoke the escape clause. It would be an admission of failure. Also, it would be difficult to determine, and then communicate, that the costs of the program had begun to exceed the benefits. But the language comforted FOMC participants who worried that we could end up trapped in Groundhog Day.

Besides announcing the extension of QE3, with the goal of reaffirming our commitment to keeping rates low, in December 2012 we also changed our forward guidance on the federal funds rate. As with the QE3 purchases, we made our rate guidance contingent on economic outcomes, although—in light of our greater understanding of and experience with policy rate changes—in this case we were comfortable quantifying the contingencies. Adopting a formulation advocated by Charles Evans, the president of the Chicago Fed, and replacing the promise of low rates through mid-2015, we said we expected the federal funds rate to stay low at least as long as (1) the unemployment rate remained above 6½ percent and (2) our projections for inflation during the next one to two years remained at or less than 2½ percent. That is, consistent with the "balanced approach" we had announced at the start of that year, we were willing to countenance a modest over-shoot of our new inflation target, if the trade-off was lower unemployment.* Importantly, these new, more-explicit conditions were thresholds, not triggers, a distinction that sometimes seemed lost on investors and outside commentators. We were not saying we would certainly raise rates when unemployment hit 6½ percent. We were saying that we would not even *consider* a rate increase until unemployment sank to 6½ percent. In fact, as it transpired, the FOMC would not raise the federal funds target until the unemployment rate had fallen to 5 percent, suggesting in retrospect that our guidance could have been even more forceful.

Overall, we had eased monetary policy considerably between August 2011, when we introduced the stronger, time-dependent guidance, to December 2012, when we confirmed the $85 billion pace of open-ended purchases under QE3, along with forward-looking, state-contingent guidance. The new measures reflected our continued disappointment in the progress of the economy. Personally, I also saw our improved, though still

---

* The SEP released at that meeting showed unemployment reaching 6½ percent near the end of 2015, so, as the Committee noted in its statement, the new guidance was consistent with the time-dependent guidance it replaced.

imperfect, understanding of our new policy tools, gained through four years of experience, as tipping the cost-benefit balance in favor of action.

THE TAPER TANTRUM

Unfortunately, from my perspective, the patience of many FOMC participants for QE3 proved thinner than I expected, even though the continuation of QE3 was supported by a series of 11–1 votes through most of 2013, with only Kansas City Fed President Esther George dissenting. (The roster of voting members changed at the start of the year and Jeff Lacker did not vote.) But the reservations that other FOMC participants had tentatively expressed when QE3 was introduced seemed to grow with the size of our balance sheet.

At the March 2013 meeting the staff presented new research and again argued that securities purchases would lower longer-term interest rates and aid the economy, and that the potential costs remained moderate and manageable. But, only a few months into QE3, many on the Committee seemed to be having second thoughts. The minutes of the March meeting, released on April 10, revealed that many participants thought a slower pace of purchases could be justified "beginning at some point over the next several meetings."[14]

As an academic, I had criticized the Bank of Japan for a half-hearted commitment to its otherwise innovative monetary policies in the late 1990s, arguing that the Bank's ambivalence had limited those policies' effects on market participants' expectations and thus on the economy.[15] I feared that the continuing disagreements within the FOMC would have the same effect. Instead, a different problem emerged. Even as influential members of the FOMC were publicly arguing for a limited program, and our March meeting minutes reported that some participants supported slowing QE3 purchases by late 2013 or even earlier, our market contacts and surveys suggested that many investors saw QE3 continuing much longer at its current pace, perhaps well into 2014. I worried about this disconnect.

As chair, I had the increasingly delicate task of conveying the

Committee's decisions and plans to the outside world. On the one hand, I wanted to communicate the Fed's ongoing commitment to supporting the recovery and job creation, especially now that fiscal policy was becoming more hindrance than help. On the other hand, some signs of economic improvement were beginning to appear. The unemployment rate had fallen from 8.1 percent from just before the announcement of the first QE3 purchases in September 2012 to 7.5 percent in April 2013. And, with the increased anxiety on the Committee about possible side effects of purchases, I needed to explain that some slowing in the pace of purchases might occur sooner than some in the markets were apparently expecting. Because the conditions laid out for continuing QE3 were qualitative and subjective, there was plenty of room for misunderstanding.

My first attempt to wrest some flexibility on purchases was in testimony before Congress's Joint Economic Committee on May 22, 2013. I noted that, in general, the pace of our securities purchases would depend on the economy's progress. I also reiterated guidance that had been added to the May FOMC statement, which emphasized that, even after the purchases stopped, the FOMC would be in no hurry to raise its target for the funds rate.

In the question-and-answer session, legislators tried to pin me down on when we might wind down QE3. When pressed, I focused on the goal of the program—substantial improvement in the outlook for the labor market—and said, "If we see continued improvement and we have confidence that that is going to be sustained, then we could, in the next few meetings, take a step down in our pace of purchases." And I offered a qualification: ". . . if we do that, it would not mean that we are automatically aiming towards a complete wind down. Rather, we would be looking beyond that to seeing how the economy evolves, and we could either raise or lower our pace of purchases going forward."[16]

News coverage seized on my comment about possibly taking "a step down" in the pace of purchases "in the next few meetings." Later the same day, the minutes of the FOMC's April meeting were released, and showed emerging tensions inside the Committee. On the one hand, according to the minutes, although "most" FOMC participants saw progress in the labor market since the introduction of QE3, "many" of those participants wanted to see yet more progress before slowing the pace of purchases. On the other hand, "a number of" participants, according to the new minutes, expressed willingness to adjust the flow of purchases downward "as early as the June meeting"—the very next month—if the evidence of improvement was sufficiently strong.[17] Overall, the day's Fed communications had signaled that purchases could begin to slow later in the year, but the conditions under which that might happen remained muddled. Markets interpreted the communication as hawkish. The S&P 500 stock index fell moderately—about 3.5 percent between May 22 and June 5. The ten-year Treasury yield moved a more-significant amount, by about a half percentage point between the April 30–May 1 meeting and the June meeting.

The June FOMC meeting, which included the release of new economic projections and was followed by my press conference, was pivotal. The economic news had been mildly encouraging, and, in the SEP, FOMC participants had marked down their predictions of the unemployment rate for the next two years. The general view of the Committee was that the unemployment rate would be down to 7 percent by mid-2014 and by early 2015 should reach the 6.5 percent level that the Committee had indicated would be the threshold for considering rate increases. At the meeting, the Committee began to focus on 7 percent unemployment as a level that might reasonably be seen as representing substantial improvement in the labor market, relative to where it had been when QE3 had begun. The staff also reported that its survey of the primary dealers suggested that the apparent disconnect between market expectations and our own about the duration of QE3 seemed to have diminished, perhaps reflecting both my public comments and some improvement in the outlook. The dealers told us they expected "tapering"—the slowing of purchases—to begin in December 2013 (although September 2013 was also a possibility), with purchases ending entirely sometime in 2014. Given our economic projections, those results lined up reasonably well with a plan to stop securities purchases sometime in mid-2014, when the unemployment rate was expected to reach 7 percent.

After a contentious and inconclusive discussion, the FOMC decided to leave its statement unchanged and asked me to explain our plans at the post-meeting press conference. My assignment was to outline a scenario for slowing purchases conditional on the economy improving as we expected. Committee members agreed that the 7 percent unemployment rate could be mentioned as one indicator of the degree of labor market improvement we would need to see, but since factors other than the unemployment rate were relevant for assessing labor market progress, the end date for our purchases would not be formally tied to hitting 7 percent.

At the press conference, I reviewed the FOMC's quarterly projections and then explained our plan, emphasizing that it was contingent and depended on the evolution of the economy:

"If the incoming data are broadly consistent with this forecast," I said, "the Committee currently anticipates that it would be appropriate to moderate the monthly pace of purchases later this year. And if the subsequent data remain broadly aligned with our current expectations for the economy, we would continue to reduce the pace of purchases in measured steps through the first half of next year, ending purchases around midyear. In this scenario, when asset purchases ultimately come to an end, the unemployment rate would likely be in the vicinity of 7 percent . . . a substantial improvement from the 8.1 percent unemployment rate that prevailed when the Committee announced this program." I emphasized again that "any need to consider applying the brakes by raising short-term rates is still far in the future."[18]

As I returned to my office, I thought that the press conference had accomplished our main goals. I had laid out a plan for slowing and then ending QE3 that, based on our surveys, aligned closely with what we believed were market expectations. Indeed, in contrast to Committee views revealed in recent FOMC minutes, which showed that many favored stopping purchases by the end of the year, I had indicated that purchases were likely to continue well into 2014. And I had reiterated that slowing purchases did not mean that we planned to raise the funds rate soon—quite the contrary.

Nevertheless, the market reacted negatively. The ten-year Treasury yield rose between one- and two-tenths of a percentage point and stocks fell about 2 percent on the day. The longer-term move was more worrisome: From my May testimony to the Joint Economic Committee until September, the ten-year yield rose a full percentage point, from about 2 percent to 3 percent. It added up to a significant tightening in monetary conditions. The episode, reminiscent of the bond "massacre" of 1994, would be dubbed the "taper tantrum." The response puzzled me: I had anticipated that talking about slowing purchases would induce some reaction, but I had also thought that the plan I laid out was close to market expectations, which should have limited the response.

It appears in retrospect that the primary dealers survey did not capture the full range of bondholders' views. Some traders apparently saw purchases continuing for much longer—the catchphrase was "QE infinity." When those traders woke up to the reality that QE3 was finite, they scrambled to dump their longer-term Treasuries. The unexpected selling sent shock waves through the markets. Another sign that our message had not gotten through was that, after my press conference, markets started to price in relatively near-term increases in the funds rate, inferring that if the Fed was tightening on securities purchases it would soon raise short-term rates as well—despite the conditions we had laid down for even considering a rate rise.

Over the next month, FOMC colleagues and I fanned out to fix the misconceptions. Our message was that monetary policy was, and would remain, highly accommodative; that the reduction in the pace of purchases would be drawn out and would be delayed if the economy slowed; and that the Fed's large securities holdings would continue to depress long-term interest rates even after new purchases stopped. And, critically, repeating my message from my May testimony and June press conference, short-term rates would be kept low for a long time after the end of QE3. The message ultimately got through, and financial markets began to calm down.

By September, markets widely expected the FOMC to announce a step down in the pace of purchases. Delivering a dovish surprise, though, we delayed our announcement, to be sure that policy remained sufficiently easy to support continued labor market progress. We also were concerned about a possible federal government shutdown, which in fact began October 1. Finally, in December 2013, we announced the first step toward winding down QE3, reducing monthly purchases from $85 billion to $75 billion. As I had indicated in June, the gradual reduction in purchases continued well into 2014, finally ending in October. Meanwhile, aiming to keep our interest-rate policy separate from our securities purchases, we strengthened the December 2012 forward guidance by promising that we would keep rates low "well past the time" the unemployment rate declined below 6½ percent, especially if inflation continued to run below the 2 percent target.

Fortunately, the taper tantrum did little apparent damage to the U.S. recovery. We had expected unemployment to fall to 7 percent by the time QE3 ended, in mid-2014. But the news was better than that. Unemployment was already down to 6.7 percent in December 2013, when we announced we would slow purchases. And by the time that purchases ended, in October 2014, the unemployment rate had reached 5.7 percent, about two and a half percentage points below where it had been when QE3 was announced. Also, the economy grew at a relatively strong pace of 2.5 percent during 2013, despite the fiscal headwinds of tax increases and spending cuts. By any standard, substantial improvement in the outlook for the labor market, and in the economy overall, had been achieved. Communication bumps notwithstanding, monetary policy had almost certainly contributed to the improvement.

The taper tantrum had considerably more negative effects on some emerging-market economies. When the Fed pushes U.S. interest rates lower, some investors are drawn to the higher yields typically available in emerging-market countries. The inflows strengthen emerging-market countries' currencies, raise the prices of their stocks and other assets, and increase bank lending, sometimes resulting in a boom. Conversely, when the Fed raises U.S. rates—or is expected to, as in the taper tantrum—the process reverses. As we had seen during the Mexican and Asian financial crises of the 1990s, which followed U.S. tightening, "hot money"—short-term investments—flows out of emerging markets, causing sharp drops in their currencies (which raise domestic inflation), stock-price declines, and reduced bank lending. Countries that rely on foreign money to finance large trade or budget deficits or have undeveloped financial regulatory regimes are particularly vulnerable. Among the countries hit hardest by the tantrum in 2013 were the so-called Fragile Five: Brazil, India, Indonesia, South Africa, and Turkey.

In the case of India, conditions calmed when former University of Chicago professor and IMF Chief Economist Raghuram Rajan became governor of the central bank. He added credibility to India's monetary policy and instituted financial reforms. Rajan became a frequent and eloquent critic of advanced-economy (especially U.S.) monetary policy, which he argued paid insufficient attention to financial spillovers to emerging markets. Rajan did not deny that the Fed sometimes needed to take strong measures in the interest of the U.S. economy, but he advocated a cautious and predictable approach to minimize spillovers. For me, the potential spillover effects of U.S. policies were another powerful argument for increased transparency at the Federal Reserve.

I took several lessons from the taper tantrum. Ideally, in retrospect, we would have provided more precise criteria from the beginning for slowing and stopping securities purchases, as well as more information about how we would sequence changes in securities purchases and changes in short-term interest rates. Unfortunately, our uncertainty and internal disagreement about the benefits and costs of more QE had made it difficult to agree on more-specific guidance. Also, in 2013, inadequate market intelligence misled us into thinking that market expectations and our own expectations were aligned. Since then, the Fed has expanded its surveys and other information-gathering to reduce the risk of this kind of misunderstanding.

The fundamental source of the taper tantrum, though, was the inconsistency between what the economy needed from the Fed in 2012 and what the majority of the FOMC was willing to give it. I believe that open-ended QE was the right policy, and despite the communication problems it helped the economy and the labor market. However, to be most effective, the program required a "do whatever it takes" mentality, which I was unable to convince Committee participants to adopt. The taper tantrum was the result of the disconnect between the "whatever it takes" logic that motivated open-ended asset purchases under QE3, which market participants broadly understood, and our hesitancy in following through on that logic.

We have considerably more evidence now for the effectiveness of securities purchases and more confidence that the costs, though not zero, are generally manageable. As the response of the Fed and other central banks to the 2020 pandemic crisis would demonstrate, monetary policymakers today are consequently more willing to "do whatever it takes" to respond to major economic risks, reducing (though not eliminating) the danger of a disconnect between policymakers and markets.

A CHANGING INSTITUTION

My last meeting as chair was in January 2014. Of course, the crisis and its aftermath dominated my eight years leading the Fed. But, as I discussed in a speech to the American Economic Association near the end of my term, a substantial part of my legacy was changes to the Federal Reserve as an institution, in three areas in particular.[19]

First, transparency and communication. During my tenure, the Fed provided much more public information about its goals, outlook, and policy plans. The key changes were the introduction of the inflation target; the formal statement of policy principles; the substantial expansion of the *Summary of Economic Projections*, including longer-run projections of economic variables and of the policy rate itself; and post-meeting press conferences. More generally, the Fed now works harder to explain its actions to Americans broadly, not just financial market participants.

Second, more systematic attention to threats to financial stability. The 2007–2009 crisis made clear that dealing with financial-stability risks, rather than an occasional concern to be handled case by case, is central to the mission of the Fed and other central banks. The Fed now monitors the financial system in a much more structured way than before the crisis.

In 2010, I created an Office of Financial Stability at the Fed, charged with overseeing this monitoring and coordinating within the Fed and with other agencies. A senior staff economist, Nellie Liang, was the office's first director. The office is now a division, meaning that it has a status on par with the divisions responsible for monetary policy analysis, economic research and forecasting, and banking supervision. The division briefs the Board and the FOMC and, under Chair Jay Powell, the Board began issuing regular public reports assessing financial-stability risks.

Third, mostly out of necessity, during my time at the Fed we developed or expanded a new suite of policy tools, including the Fed's first use of large-scale purchases of securities and more-explicit forward guidance. In addition, during the crisis we introduced or expanded our lending tools, some based on our emergency 13(3) powers, which had last been used during the Great Depression. These tools allow the Fed to lend not only to banks, but to other types of financial institutions and even to nonfinancial corporations. Although the ultimate effects of these tools on the Fed's role in the economy, and on its independence, are still debated, the contemporary Fed wields—for better or worse—an arsenal much larger than in the past.

PART III

21st CENTURY MONETARY POLICY

■

From Liftoff to the
COVID-19 Pandemic

8

LIFTOFF

Janet Yellen, President Obama's choice to succeed me as chair, took the oath of office on February 3, 2014, becoming the first woman to lead the Fed. A Fed veteran, Janet had worked closely with me throughout the crisis and its aftermath. I was delighted that she was chosen.

Yellen came to the job with more relevant experience than any of her predecessors—an indicator, perhaps, of the extra hurdles facing women seeking leadership roles in economic policymaking. Her first professional exposure to the Fed came as a visiting economist at the Board in the summer of 1974. She returned to the Board as a staff economist in 1977–78, which proved life-changing in another way: She met George Akerlof, her future husband and frequent coauthor, in the Board's cafeteria.* Like me, though, she spent most of her early career as an economics professor, starting at Harvard, moving to the London School of Economics, and then to the University of California at Berkeley.

Yellen served as a governor on the Fed Board (from 1994 to 1997), moving on to become chair of the president's Council of Economic Advisers—under President Clinton, from 1997 to 1999. She also served as president of the Federal Reserve Bank of San Francisco (from 2004 to 2010), which

---

* Akerlof went on to win the Nobel Prize in Economics in 2001 for his work on how incomplete information can prevent markets from working well.

gave her a seat on the Federal Open Market Committee throughout that critical period. And in 2010 she became vice chair of the Board. In that capacity she helped shape policy and led efforts to improve our communications, including the adoption of the formal inflation target in 2012. Yellen would later serve as President Biden's Treasury secretary, adding to her unprecedented résumé.

Yellen's promotion left the vice-chair position vacant. Wanting a strong number two with international experience and reputation, Yellen encouraged the president to appoint my old mentor, Stanley Fischer. Fischer had, like Yellen, been a major academic contributor to the modernization of Keynesian economics. Unusually for a Fed appointee, his policy experience was outside the United States; he had served as the governor of the central bank of Israel from 2005 to 2013.

Based on her life experience, academic research, and policy record, Fed-watchers had reason to expect Yellen to take a dovish approach as chair, prioritizing the maximum employment half of the Fed's dual mandate. Born in August 1946, she grew up in the working-class Bay Ridge neighborhood in Brooklyn, where her physician father treated longshoremen and other blue-collar workers and their families. Her graduate school mentor at Yale, James Tobin, was a prominent liberal economist (and, in 1981, a Nobel Prize winner) who had been part of the brain trust that persuaded President Kennedy to adopt pro-employment Keynesian policies. In the spirit of Tobin, Yellen's academic work supported the view that the government should vigorously counter recessions. And, during and after the financial crisis, Yellen was among the most consistent and persuasive proponents at the Fed of sustained monetary ease, with the goal of restoring a healthy labor market as quickly as possible.

The perception that Yellen cared deeply about reducing unemployment was certainly correct, but as chair she faced a complex balancing act. She found herself in a position roughly analogous to Alan Greenspan's. The necessary direction of policy under Greenspan's predecessor, Paul Volcker, had been clear: tighter money, to bring inflation under control. With inflation successfully contained, albeit at the cost of a deep recession, Greenspan's subtler but still demanding task had been to consolidate the Volcker-era gains—to keep inflation low while promoting economic growth and stability. Like Volcker, during most of my term as chair, the required direction of policy had been evident—toward ease, using all available tools to reduce unemployment and boost too-low inflation. Much like Greenspan, Yellen's primary task was to preserve and extend the progress that had been made, while preparing for an ultimate return to more-normal economic and monetary conditions—with unemployment low, inflation around 2 percent, and short-term interest rates above zero.

Achieving that economic nirvana would require delicate judgments about when and how quickly to exit from the extraordinary postcrisis monetary policies. Many central banks had pushed short rates to zero (or below), but at the time that Yellen took office, none had succeeded in reversing zero-rate policies. A lot depended on getting it right: A too-early or too-rapid liftoff could snuff the recovery and force rates back down to their effective lower bound whereas a liftoff that came too late might generate inflation or financial-stability risks.

The initial exit from the crisis-era regime began in December 2013, near the end of my term, when we decided to begin slowing QE3 purchases, pending continued improvement in the labor market. The last purchases were made, under Yellen, in October 2014. They marked the end, at least for a time, of the rapid postcrisis growth of the Fed's balance sheet. At that point, the balance sheet stood at $4.5 trillion, compared with $875 billion in August 2007. With the Fed continuing to replace maturing securities with new ones, for the time being the balance sheet stayed roughly at October 2014 levels.

The tasks ahead were ultimately to reduce the Fed's securities holdings and begin raising the federal funds rate, without disrupting the recovery. Both aspects of the policy tightening would proceed more slowly than expected. The delay, in part, reflected global developments that clouded U.S. prospects. But it also reflected the Fed's ongoing reassessment of the U.S. economy, including policymakers' recognition that the neutral interest rate had continued its long decline; that the economy had become better able to sustain very low levels of unemployment without spurring inflation; and, indeed, that the behavior of inflation was itself fundamentally changing. As Yellen and her colleagues came to grips with the "new normal," they found that existing monetary policy was not as expansionary, and labor markets not as tight, as they had thought.

PREPARING FOR LIFTOFF

The relatively straightforward part of the new chair's task was overseeing the continued slowing in QE3 purchases. Updating of the Committee's forward guidance about the likely future path of the federal funds rate required more careful attention. As of my last FOMC meeting, the guidance—originally issued in December 2012, along with the announcement of QE3 Treasury purchases—still set a 6½ percent unemployment rate as the threshold for when the Committee might consider a rate increase, although we had added the proviso that the first rate rise would likely come "well past the time" that the unemployment threshold had been met. By early 2014, it looked like the 6½ percent threshold might be reached soon, raising the possibility of near-term tightening. Indeed, as of Yellen's first regular meeting as chair in March 2014, the unemployment rate already stood at 6.7 percent and most FOMC participants projected that, by year-end, it would fall to a range of 6.1 to 6.3 percent, below the rate in the guidance.

As I've noted, we had always intended the 6½ percent unemployment rate to be a threshold, not a trigger. In other words, attaining 6½ percent unemployment would not necessarily lead to a rate increase; the actual decision about whether to tighten would depend on the FOMC's assessment of the durability of the recovery and the prospects for inflation at the time. Yellen worried that the distinction between threshold and trigger might be misunderstood. It was possible that the existing guidance could lead markets to price in an earlier tightening than was appropriate. She knew that lifting off from zero would likely be tricky in any case, with uncertain effects on markets and on a still-vulnerable economy. On an FOMC call in March, before the regularly scheduled meeting, she emphasized the need for patience: "I would urge everyone to remain mindful . . . of the numerous 'false dawns' the economy has presented."[1]

The March 2014 post-meeting statement, as expected, announced another reduction in the pace of securities purchases and reiterated that purchases would likely continue to decline in "measured steps." More important was the Yellen Fed's change in the forward guidance on the federal funds rate target. The Committee dropped the 6½ percent unemployment threshold and indicated that it planned to keep rates near zero "for a considerable time after the asset purchase program ends, especially if projected inflation continues to run below the Committee's 2 percent longer-run goal." With securities purchases seen as likely to conclude in the fall of 2014, the intent of the guidance was to push expectations of the first rate hike well into 2015. The statement also suggested, for the first time, that the pace of rate increases, once they began, would be slow, with the funds rate remaining "for some time" below the neutral rate of interest, the benchmark for a normal policy rate.

At her press conference after the meeting, Yellen defined the phrase "considerable time" as "on the order of around six months, or that type of thing."[2] That would have put the first rate hike in early 2015, evidently earlier than many in the markets were expecting. The ad-lib response to a reporter's question would prove a rare misstep for Yellen, a meticulous and careful communicator. The markets sold off, though only temporarily. Yet the idea now circulated that 2015 could be the first year since 2006 in which the Federal Reserve might increase its policy rate.

Since the start of near-zero rates and QE securities purchases in 2008, we had regularly debated our exit strategy, with the goal of reassuring the markets—and ourselves—that we could in time return to a more normal policy stance. In the minutes of the June 2011 meeting, the Committee had published a set of principles to guide the eventual exit. Yellen's Fed refined and clarified the plan. In September 2014, with an announcement confirming that QE3 purchases were about to end and with possible rate hikes coming into view, the FOMC released a document titled "Policy Normalization Principles and Plans."[3]

The document affirmed that, as monetary policy returned to normal, the federal funds rate would reassume its role as the principal policy tool, with balance sheet changes playing at most a supporting role. The Fed had decades of experience using the funds rate, and market participants knew how to interpret FOMC signals about rates. In 2008, when the funds rate had hit the effective lower bound, we had had little choice but to turn to quantitative easing. But QE was a blunt tool—its effectiveness and potential side effects remained under debate even in 2014. The FOMC was eager to return to managing policy through the funds rate rather than the balance sheet.

Consistent with the basic approach laid out in 2011, the Committee agreed to raise the funds rate first—by increasing the interest rate paid to banks on their reserves held at the Fed. Once the funds rate had risen enough to create some space for rate cuts if they were needed, then the balance sheet could decline. This would be done, the principles explained, by ending the practice of replacing maturing securities with new ones. As maturing securities ran off, the balance sheet would shrink without the Fed having to conduct outright sales of securities.

The new exit principles did not specify the final size of the balance sheet. But in a nod to QE critics, both internal and external, the principles said that, in the long run, the Fed would hold no more securities than those needed to implement monetary policy "efficiently and effectively." Exactly what that phrase meant would be debated by the Committee for some time. The FOMC also said that, ultimately, the Fed's securities holdings would comprise mostly Treasuries. Holdings of mortgage-backed securities would be minimized, at least in normal times, to avoid overly favoring housing construction and sales at the expense of other sectors.

LIFTOFF DELAYED, LIFTOFF ACHIEVED

The economy continued to recover through 2014. When the Committee met in March 2015, the unemployment rate had fallen to 5.4 percent, not far above most FOMC participants' 5–5.2 percent estimate of the natural rate of unemployment at the time. Full employment seemed in sight. Because monetary policy works with a lag, and because the near-zero funds rate remained far from its neutral level—estimated by most FOMC participants in March 2015 as between 3.5 and 3.75 percent—most on the Committee believed rate increases would need to begin soon. As John Williams, then president of the San Francisco Federal Reserve, would later put it, "When you're docking a boat . . . you don't run it in fast towards shore and hope you can reverse the engine hard later on. . . . Instead, the cardinal rule of docking is: Never approach a dock any faster than you're willing to hit it."[4] The argument, reminiscent of the pre-emptive strikes against inflation embraced by Chairs Martin, Volcker, and Greenspan, resonated with most Committee members. The March 2015 dot plot had, at the median, two quarter-point rate increases expected in 2015 and four more in 2016.

In its March 2015 statement, the FOMC accordingly signaled that the long-awaited liftoff of the funds rate, while not imminent, could be coming soon. As it turned out, rather than raising the target for the funds rate twice in 2015 and four times in 2016, the Committee would increase its target range only once in 2015 and once more in 2016. Rates were no longer grazing zero, but more historically normal conditions seemed further off than had been anticipated.

What happened? Yellen's "false dawns" warning had proved prescient. First, international developments reverberated in the United States and delayed liftoff. But even as the international headwinds died down, Fed policymakers found themselves reassessing some of their basic assumptions about what constituted normal in the postcrisis U.S. economy.

China's Devaluation

The first shock from abroad came from an unexpected source: China. China had emerged from the global financial crisis relatively unscathed. Its economic growth remained impressive through the global recession, boosted by a large fiscal package and a government-directed surge in bank lending. More fundamentally, over the prior three decades, China had benefited from a development strategy that combined government central planning and decentralized markets. Like the centrally planned Soviet Union decades earlier, China had pumped investment into heavy industry and public infrastructure and given a primary role to favored state-owned enterprises. It suppressed private consumption, leading to a very high national saving rate, and encouraged millions of rural workers to migrate to cities to take jobs in manufacturing and construction. Unlike the Soviet Union, though, China's model included a role for market forces. Over time it had increasingly allowed prices to be determined by supply and demand, and it allowed domestic private firms and (with restrictions) foreign companies to compete with state-owned firms for China's huge domestic market.

China also used market discipline indirectly by orienting key industries toward exporting, particularly following its admission to the World Trade Organization in 2002. Like other Asian countries before it, such as Japan and South Korea, China began by exporting cheap manufactured goods. But as its companies learned from competing in global markets and became increasingly integrated into global supply chains, China began exporting a wider range of higher-value goods and became an increasingly dominant player in world trade.

China's export strategy was bolstered by a controversial exchange-rate policy. It had tightly controlled the value of its currency, the renminbi—first by fixing it against the dollar and then, after July 2005, by allowing only gradual adjustments. Importantly, during most of China's rapid growth, the renminbi was kept cheap relative to other currencies, giving Chinese exports a price advantage. That changed after the financial crisis, when China gradually allowed the renminbi to strengthen. Reasons for the shift included diplomatic pressure from China's trading partners, China's desire to make the renminbi a major global currency (which required that its value respond to market forces), and its decision to drive growth less through exports and more through expanding domestic demand.[5] By 2015 some economists thought that the renminbi had strengthened too much, to the point that it was hurting China's exports. Meanwhile, the Fed's intention to push U.S. interest rates higher attracted capital and strengthened the dollar. That made China's overvaluation problem worse. Though the renminbi was no longer rigidly fixed to the dollar it remained linked to it, so when the dollar strengthened against the euro and the yen, the renminbi did as well.

Xi Jinping took office as China's president in March 2013. He promised extensive reforms and set ambitious economic targets. But, after years of superheated economic growth, Xi also inherited serious imbalances. Borrowing by companies and consumers, long encouraged by the government to promote domestic spending and investment, had surged since 2008 and contributed to excess capacity in heavy industry and an overbuilt real estate sector. Subsequent attempts to cool the economy and rein in the credit boom succeeded all too well. The Chinese stock market began to slide in June 2015, with the Shanghai Composite Index plunging 30 percent in three weeks. As economic growth slipped from 7.8 percent in 2013 to (a still-high) 6.9 percent in 2015, foreign and Chinese investors began moving money out of China, putting downward pressure on its currency.

On August 11, 2015, in a two-sentence statement, the People's Bank of China, the Chinese central bank, announced a change in the system for setting the exchange rate and a 1.9 percent devaluation of the renminbi. The renminbi depreciated an additional 1 percent the next day. The decline—though small in absolute terms—raised fears that a more substantial devaluation was coming. More seriously, the devaluation—and the absence of official explanation—led investors to worry that the slowdown in China might be more severe than previously thought and that it would hurt the rest of the global economy. Stock prices fell sharply around the world.

The implications for the U.S. economy, and for Fed policy, were uncertain. Until the surprise devaluation, the FOMC had been widely expected to raise the near-zero funds rate in September 2015. Now it was not so clear. An unusual public rift opened among the Fed's leaders. On August 26, New York Fed President Bill Dudley said at a press briefing that "the decision to begin the normalization process at the September FOMC meeting seems less compelling to me than it was a few weeks ago."[6] His comments came after the Dow had fallen more than 10 percent in the prior five trading days. Following Dudley's remarks, stocks rebounded more than 6 percent over the next two days. But then in an interview with Steve Liesman of CNBC from Jackson Hole, Board Vice Chair Stan Fischer said, "I wouldn't want to go ahead and decide right now what the case is—more compelling, less compelling, et cetera." He added that "there was a pretty strong case" for a September rate hike, although that had not yet been finally decided.[7] Since the New York Fed president and the Board vice chair are generally viewed as the FOMC's most influential members after the chair, their public comments revealed that the Committee was wrestling with its decision.

As it turned out, the Committee left the funds rate unchanged at its September meeting. In its statement, it noted that it was "monitoring developments abroad," a reference to China. However, 13 of 17 participants continued to project a rate increase by year's end. In her press conference, Yellen explained the Committee's inaction by noting that the tightening of financial conditions following China's devaluation—including the drop in stock prices and the further appreciation of the dollar—could slow the U.S. economy. But clearly the Committee, like market participants, was wondering whether the devaluation signaled deeper weakness in China, with consequences for developing economies and other countries that relied on selling their products to China. Since few expected U.S. monetary policy to tighten rapidly in any case, it seemed worthwhile to wait a bit.

By the December meeting, greater clarity had materialized. Fears about China had calmed, the economic outlook in the United States had improved, and financial markets had rebounded. The FOMC, for the first time in nearly a decade, raised its target for the federal funds rate—to a range of ¼ to ½ percent. In her press conference, Yellen noted that the criteria that the Committee had set out for liftoff—considerable improvement in the labor market and reasonable confidence that inflation was moving back toward 2 percent—had been met. The unemployment rate, at 5 percent in November 2015, was half its peak after the Great Recession. She conceded that many participants did not see inflation hitting the Fed's target until 2018, more than two years later. But, in an explanation that echoed Greenspan's pre-emptive-strike strategy, she said: "Were the FOMC to delay the start of policy normalization for too long, we would likely end up having to tighten policy relatively abruptly at some point to keep the economy from overheating and inflation from significantly overshooting our objective. Such an abrupt tightening could increase the risk of pushing the economy into recession."[8] In other words, the best way to achieve and sustain full employment was to be sure that inflation stayed in check.

Consistent with that logic, FOMC participants continued to project slow but steady rate increases—four quarter-point rises in 2016 and four more in 2017. If those increases occurred, the funds rate would breach 2 percent— still quite low, but at least on track to escape the gravitational pull of the zero lower bound. The projection would once again prove too ambitious.

The Mini-Recession and Brexit

Several developments stayed the Fed's hand after the first increase. First, although the funds rate remained very low, the FOMC, through speeches and rate projections, had communicated that at least two more years of tightening lay ahead. Demonstrating once again that in monetary policy words can be as consequential as actions, both the markets and the economy reacted badly. The Fed's tightening plans appeared to be too much for a still-recovering economy.

In a September 2018 column in the *New York Times*, Neil Irwin considered the aftermath of the December 2015 rate increase, dubbing it the "mini-recession of 2015–16." Within weeks of the Fed's action, Irwin would write, "global markets were sending a message: Not so fast. The dollar kept strengthening, the price of commodities kept falling, and the S&P 500 dropped about 9 percent over three weeks in late January and early February. Bond yields plummeted, suggesting that the United States was at risk of recession."[9] Even though the economy continued to grow in early 2016, and unemployment kept falling, the mini-recession manifested in slowdowns in business investment, in energy and agriculture (as the prices of oil and commodities dropped), and in manufacturing (where a strengthening dollar discouraged exports). The FOMC, noting tighter financial conditions and some slowing of growth, left the funds rate unchanged at its January 2016 meeting.

The mini-recession and the financial jitters that accompanied it would prove brief, largely because of two subsequent developments. First, two days after a late-February meeting in Shanghai of the G20 finance ministers and central-bank governors, China took steps to support its economy. It encouraged lending by lowering the share of assets that its banks were required to hold in cash and liquid reserves. It also calmed concerns about further devaluation of the renminbi by clarifying how it would manage its currency in the future. Second, in March, the FOMC not only left the funds rate unchanged, as it had in January, but recalibrated to a more dovish stance. Policymakers reduced the number of expected rate increases in 2016 from four to two. Markets were relieved by the Fed's more cautious approach and by the reduced prospect that a stronger dollar would further slow U.S. exports.

In 1985, then-chair Paul Volcker had helped negotiate the Plaza Accord, which was aimed at weakening what was seen as an overvalued dollar. While that agreement was formal and public, market watchers began speculating in 2016 that an informal, secret deal, dubbed "the Shanghai Accord," had been struck at the G20 meeting. The supposed goal—as in the Plaza Accord—was reducing the dollar's exchange value. A weaker dollar, the theory went, would serve China by reducing the overvaluation of the dollar-linked renminbi; the United States, in turn, would get help for its sluggish manufacturing sector and, as commodity prices increased, for its farmers and energy producers. As the speculation went, the Fed had agreed to an easier policy stance in exchange for China clarifying that it would not further devalue the renminbi. Japan and Europe were also supposedly party to the deal, agreeing not to weaken their own currencies against the dollar.

In an interview with Irwin, Yellen acknowledged that U.S. and Chinese officials extensively discussed the global economy in Shanghai, as is standard at international meetings. But she said no secret deal—no promises, no explicit agreements—had been made. Having attended many similar meetings, I am certain that is true. No Fed chair would make such a deal because it would improperly pre-empt the FOMC and the oversight responsibilities of Congress. Yellen could not have guaranteed that the FOMC would go along with a deal or that individual participants' rate projections would align with it. In any case, conspiracy theorizing aside, policy in both China and the United States did shift in an expansionary direction in early 2016.

Brexit—Great Britain's proposed exit from the European Union—further delayed U.S. monetary policy normalization in the spring of 2016. A referendum, scheduled for June 23, appeared likely to be close, and concerns about what a "yes" vote would mean for financial markets and the global economy gave the FOMC reason to hold rates steady. As it turned out, financial turbulence following a yes vote in the referendum led Yellen to cancel a trip to the European Central Bank's annual forum in Portugal (the ECB's Jackson Hole equivalent). Uncertainty about Brexit—when and in what form it would occur, and what the economic implications would be—would remain a concern for years.

ASSESSING THE "NEW NORMAL"

By mid-2016, after two and a half years as chair, Yellen had presided over only one increase in the federal funds rate, well short of what many on the FOMC, including Yellen herself, had expected. The slow pace could be explained as the result of reasonable caution and unexpected foreign developments. However, the mini-recession had hinted at another explanation—that the plans for tightening policy were too ambitious from the start, and that structural changes in the U.S. economy required a more measured approach. FOMC participants would gradually shift toward this view under Yellen and her successor, Jay Powell.

Ylan Mui, of the *Washington Post*, highlighted some of the Fed's evolving views in a July 2016 article, "Why the Federal Reserve Is Rethinking Everything."[10] As Mui described, during my term and early in Yellen's term, the Fed often rationalized the relatively slow pace of the recovery from the Great Recession as the result of "headwinds," including restrictive fiscal policy, still-tight credit, and an overhang of unsold homes following the housing bust. Implicit in this diagnosis was the idea that growth would pick up when the headwinds abated. However, as time passed and growth remained slow, Fed officials came to put more weight on the possibility—consistent with Larry Summers's secular stagnation hypothesis—that the economy's long-term growth potential had in fact declined.

Two factors determine an economy's production potential in the long run: the size of the labor force and the quantity of goods and services that each worker can produce (labor productivity). The growth rates of both had slowed during the recovery from the Great Recession. Slower workforce growth was largely the result of demographic factors, such as the aging of the baby boom generation, and had been anticipated. The productivity slowdown, in contrast, was unexpected. Many on the FOMC, including me, had viewed some piece of the weakness in productivity as an after-effect of the crisis. We hoped that productivity growth would recover as the crisis receded. But others began to see the slowdown as more enduring. For example, an influential 2016 book by Robert J. Gordon, *The Rise and Fall of American Growth*, argued that the rapid U.S. productivity growth during the decades immediately after World War II was historically excep-tional, the result of the commercial application of an unusual number of new technologies, from jet aircraft to television, whose civilian use had been slowed by depression and war.[11] Consequently, Gordon argued, the slower growth of productivity in recent years was not an aberration but sim-ply a return to a more historically normal rate. Gordon is certainly correct that—internet hype notwithstanding—the new technologies of the past few decades have not been as transformative of our daily lives as those of the mid-20th century. Whether that will remain true a decade or two from now, given promising innovations in artificial intelligence, the biological sciences, and elsewhere, is much less clear.

In any case, whatever its source, slower potential growth in the decade after the crisis implied lower returns to new capital investments, which—together with other factors, including increased global saving and mod-est inflation—can explain the apparent decline in the neutral interest rate, R*. Of course, Fed officials recognized that the neutral interest rate had fallen significantly since the 1980s. That was why the effective lower bound on rates had become a challenge. What was new was a growing appreciation that the neutral interest rate might have declined further after the financial crisis.

From the FOMC's perspective, a lower estimate of the neutral interest rate supported a slower pace of policy tightening. Since the neutral rate is, by definition, the endpoint of the process of returning rates to more-normal levels, a lower R* means that less tightening would be needed to achieve the Fed's targeted levels of employment and inflation. In addition, the effects of a given policy rate can be measured by how far that rate is below its neutral level. With a lower neutral rate, the near-zero setting of the federal funds rate—though low in absolute terms—might not have been as stimulative as the FOMC had assumed. Thus, as Yellen began to note in speeches and press conferences, a low neutral interest rate was another reason to tighten policy only gradually. The idea that the economy faced a "new normal" of low interest rates, in which the return of policy to a neutral level might look very different than in the past, became a recurring theme of Fed communication.

Reassessment of the natural rate of unemployment, u*, would prove equally important for policy. Like the neutral interest rate, the natural unemployment rate is a critical input to policymaking. Every FOMC member knew the history of the Great Inflation and the role played by policymakers' attempts to push unemployment down to 4 percent or below, well below what economists now believe to have been the natural rate at the time. That experience warned that pushing unemployment down to very low levels too quickly might end up stoking inflation and destabilizing the economy.

Where did the natural rate stand in 2016? On the one hand, some economists worried that the severity of the Great Recession, by exacerbating mismatches between workers' skills and firms' needs and by increasing economic uncertainty, might have raised the natural rate of unemployment, at least temporarily.[12] On the other hand, factors such as the aging labor force (older, more experienced workers tend to have lower unemployment rates) and improved matching of firms and workers (through job-finding web sites, for example) should have pushed the natural rate down. Because the natural rate of unemployment cannot be directly observed and is influenced by so many factors, economists have recognized for some time that available estimates of u* are inevitably quite imprecise.[13]

Drawing on her experience as a labor economist, Yellen had often argued that the unemployment rate should not be the only gauge of slack in the labor market, particularly during periods of severe stress or structural change. In public remarks she provided a list of alternative labor market indicators, such as the labor force participation rate, the number of people working part-time who would prefer full-time work, and the voluntary quit rate (an indicator of workers' confidence in their ability to find new work).[14] Fed-watchers began to regularly update Yellen's labor market "dashboard" to try to better understand the Fed's view of labor market conditions.[15]

By mid-2016 the unemployment rate had fallen below 5 percent and was heading still lower. As inflation remained tame—indeed, too low, relative to target—despite continuing unemployment declines, the Board staff and FOMC participants began to revise down their estimates of the natural unemployment rate. A lower natural rate meant that the economy could run hotter without stoking inflation and so—like a lower neutral interest rate—it implied less need for tightening as the economy recovered. Instead, the FOMC could be patient, allowing the labor market to strengthen without worrying about inflation.

The FOMC's reassessment of these two key variables can be seen in the quarterly *Summary of Economic Projections*, which includes participants' estimates of the long-run federal funds rate (a measure of the neutral interest rate) and the long-run sustainable unemployment rate, which can be interpreted as an estimate of the natural rate of unemployment. The table shows the evolution of these estimates from 2012 to 2021.[16]

FOMC estimates of both the natural unemployment rate and the neutral interest rate declined throughout this period. Given these reassessments, the slow pace of rate increases in the first three years of Yellen's term becomes easier to understand. The Committee was learning in real time how much tightening the economy needed and could tolerate.[17]

	TABLE 8.1. FOMC ESTIMATES OF LONG-RUN UNEMPLOYMENT AND INTEREST RATES	
YEAR	NATURAL UNEMPLOYMENT RATE	NEUTRAL INTEREST RATE
2012	5.2–6.0	4.25
2013	5.2–6.0	4.0
2014	5.2–5.5	3.75
2015	5.0–5.2	3.75
2016	4.7–5.0	3.0
2017	4.5–4.8	3.0
2018	4.3–4.6	2.9
2019	4.0–4.4	2.5
2020	4.0–4.3	2.5
2021	3.8–4.3	2.5

Source: *Summary of Economic Projections*, June of each year. The natural unemployment rate is the projected long-run unemployment rate (central tendency, with top three and bottom three projections dropped). The neutral interest rate is the projected long-run federal funds rate (median value).

THE DEATH OF THE PHILLIPS CURVE?

Policy thinking during the Yellen era went beyond the neutral interest rate and the natural unemployment rate to investigate a broader question: Was the Phillips curve, the Fed's basic model of inflation since the 1960s, still valid? Or, as many commentators phrased the question: Was the Phillips curve dead?

The Phillips curve, recall, describes the relationship between inflation (in terms of either wages or consumer prices) and measures of slack, such as the unemployment rate. It captures the intuition that when labor and product markets are tight, wages and prices tend to rise more quickly, implying a trade-off between unemployment and inflation.

The traditional Phillips curve seemed to explain the rise of inflation in the United States in the late 1960s. However, as Chapter 1 detailed, the still-higher inflation of the 1970s led economists to make two amendments to the original curve: First, the traditional Phillips curve is based, implicitly, on the assumption that the economy is buffeted primarily by demand shocks, which move prices and employment in the same direction. But supply shocks, such as large increases in oil prices, also occur. Supply shocks may send prices up but employment lower, leading to stagflation (the combination of high inflation and high unemployment). Second, the traditional Phillips curve also ignores changes in inflation expectations. But if through experience people come to expect high inflation, as they did in the 1970s, those expectations can become self-confirming, as workers press for higher wages to maintain their purchasing power and firms raise prices to cover their higher costs.

The traditional Phillips curve relationship strongly reasserted itself during the early 1980s, when the Volcker Fed's tightening to bring down high inflation generated dramatic increases in unemployment. Economists agree, however, that somewhere around 1990, or perhaps a bit earlier, there was a significant break in the behavior of inflation and in the nature of the Phillips curve itself. Like the 1960s, the 1990s saw strong growth and low unemployment, yet—unlike in the 1960s—inflation remained both low and stable. Some of this may have been the result of Alan Greenspan's adroit management, and some due to declines in the natural rate of unemployment that were not fully appreciated at the time. But, at least in retrospect, the evidence strongly suggests that the behavior of inflation was itself changing, in at least two distinct ways.

First, after 1990 or so inflation began to respond less than before to short-run changes in unemployment (or other measures of economic slack). In graphical terms, the Phillips curve—the short-run relationship between inflation and unemployment—appeared to have "flattened."[18] The weak response of inflation to labor market slack persisted through the Great Recession and the ensuing recovery—and, if anything, became weaker after 2008. During my time as chair, despite being well aware of the changes in the behavior of inflation over the previous two decades, staff forecasters and FOMC participants were nevertheless surprised by how modestly inflation declined following the financial crisis, despite the rise in the unemployment rate to 10 percent.[19] During Yellen's term, as the Fed prepared to tighten policy, the inflation puzzle resurfaced, but in the other direction. Inflation remained *below* target, and below the Fed's forecasts, despite the improvement in the labor market. Downward revisions in the estimated natural unemployment rate, together with various special factors—such as one-off changes in Medicare reimbursement rates or the cost of cellular phone plans—helped explain some of the forecast misses, but to many it looked like the traditional Phillips curve relationship had gone AWOL.

The second important change in the behavior of inflation was that, again after about 1990, inflation appeared to have become much more stable from year to year. Although economic shocks, like large changes in oil prices, could still drive overall inflation up or down temporarily, it tended to quickly revert to its preestablished level—rather than spiraling to a new level, as had happened during the 1970s.[20] Since "normalizing" policy required raising inflation back to the 2 percent target, the Yellen Fed—and economics researchers generally—focused on trying to understand how and why the dynamics of inflation had changed.[21]

Empirically, recent studies of the short-run relationship between inflation and unemployment have concluded that the Phillips curve is still breathing. For example, analyses of data from many countries, and from U.S. states and metropolitan areas, show that inflation continues to respond to measures of slack, although less strongly than in the past.[22] There is less agreement, however, on why the unemployment-inflation relationship appears to have weakened. Some studies have tied the flattening of the Phillips curve to changes in the structure of the economy. For example, some economists have argued that increased globalization has flattened the Phillips curve, since firms that sell their products in many countries and face competition from foreign firms even at home are less likely to raise prices based only on domestic economic conditions.[23] Another plausible argument holds that inflation responds less to slack today because consumers spend more now on goods and services that are little influenced by market forces—such as health care, where prices are now often determined largely by government policies.[24] Yet another possibility is that, because of long-term changes in the labor market, such as more jobs with flexible hours, and less rigid social expectations for the division of labor within the family, people today move more freely in and out of the labor force when economic conditions change. That is, labor supply is more elastic, so that changes in demand induce smaller changes in wages than in the past.

Although a full explanation of the weaker short-run response of inflation to unemployment remains elusive, we have a better understanding of the other important change in the behavior of inflation: namely, its tendency, in the absence of major supply shocks, to remain stable over time. The most compelling explanation for this change is the conduct of monetary policy itself—specifically, the restoration of the Fed's credibility after the Volcker disinflation of the 1980s. Volcker's costly victory over inflation, followed by three decades in which the Fed kept inflation low and stable, helped to anchor the public's inflation expectations at low levels. When monetary policy is credible, people tend to react less to short-run changes in inflation, which—in self-confirming fashion—they expect ultimately will reverse.[25]

What implications do these changes in inflation dynamics—the flatter Phillips curve and better-anchored inflation expectations—have for monetary policy and the economy? On the positive side, with inflation more stable and less likely to react to changes in unemployment, monetary policymakers have more scope to ease policy in response to recessions. By the same token, recessions, when they do occur, are less likely to reduce inflation to undesirably low levels. Well-anchored inflation expectations also give monetary policymakers more scope to "look through" temporary supply shocks, such as oil price increases, without concern that, by raising inflation expectations, those shocks will lead to long-lasting increases in overall inflation, as they did in the 1970s. (Pervasive and extended supply shocks, as would accompany the reopening of the economy from the 2020–21 pandemic, pose a tougher challenge.) Overall, the changes in recent decades in the behavior of inflation should allow policymakers to achieve on average more-stable inflation and a healthier labor market. These outcomes are the most important payoff of Volcker's restoration of the Fed's anti-inflation credibility in the 1980s.

There are downsides, however. A flat Phillips curve means that inflation is a less reliable indicator of economic overheating. Should inflation get too high, the costs, in terms of unemployment, of bringing inflation back down to target could be higher than in the past. And although the Fed's anti-inflation credibility gives it greater leeway to ease policy in the short run, over the longer term that credibility is like a capital asset that will depreciate if it is not maintained. The Fed must still ensure that inflation does not stray from target by too much or for too long, and that it reliably returns to target over time after being displaced by some shock. Setting a formal inflation target; establishing a policy framework that clarifies how the inflation target will be met over time; carefully monitoring inflation expectations; and, most importantly, following through on commitments to maintaining price stability, all help the Fed maintain its inflation credibility.

RATE HIKES RESUME

By mid-2016, with unemployment continuing to decline and the mini-recession over, pressure to move was building within the Committee. The FOMC vote to remain on hold in June, just before the Brexit vote, had been unanimous. But, at the July meeting, Esther George of Kansas City dissented from the decision to hold steady. At the September meeting she was joined by Loretta Mester of Cleveland and Eric Rosengren of Boston. The 7–3 vote (with two Board seats vacant) to leave rates unchanged was close by FOMC standards.

Although the Committee left rates unchanged in September, its statement noted an improving labor market and more-rapid growth, and it dropped a strong hint that a second postcrisis rate hike was not far off: "The Committee judges that the case for an increase in the federal funds rate has strengthened but decided, for the time being, to wait for further evidence of continued progress toward its objectives." Indeed, fourteen of the seventeen FOMC participants projected at least a quarter-point rate increase by the end of the year.

If another rate increase was so likely, why didn't the FOMC hike in September? Yellen had earlier channeled Alan Greenspan's concept of pre-emptive strikes on inflation. She now shifted subtly toward Greenspan's risk-management approach, with a twist created by the proximity of the effective lower bound. With the funds rate near zero, the risks were asymmetrical, she argued at her press conference. If the economy proved stronger than expected, creating incipient upward pressure on inflation, the Fed could always compensate by hiking rates a bit more. But if it proved weaker than anticipated, the fact that the funds rate was already near the lower bound would make it difficult for the Fed to respond, at least by traditional methods. That asymmetry strengthened the case for caution, she argued. Implicit in her argument was the assumption that inflation, if it came at all, would emerge slowly and that a rapid series of rate increases would not be required to bring it under control. That assumption proved correct, as core inflation continued to fluctuate below the 2 percent target.

When the Committee finally did move, on December 14, the unemployment rate had fallen to 4.7 percent, close to FOMC estimates of the natural unemployment rate at the time (4.8 percent, according to the median participant). The vote to increase the funds rate by a quarter percentage point—to a range of ½ to ¾ percent—was unanimous. The tone of the post-meeting statement remained dovish, however. It indicated that further rate increases would likely be gradual and reiterated that "the federal funds rate is likely to remain, for some time, below levels that are expected to prevail in the longer run," that is, below the neutral rate.

The median federal funds rate projection was less dovish, though, with the *Summary of Economic Projections* showing three rate increases anticipated for 2017. This time the dot plot would prove correct. The Committee increased the funds rate by a quarter point each in March, June, and December, ending the year with a target range of 1¼ to 1½ percent. The economy weathered the tightening, with unemployment falling to 4.1 percent by December 2017.

In 2017, the Fed's balance sheet at last began to shrink. In June, expanding on its earlier statement of principles, the FOMC released more details about how it would proceed. Beginning in October—exactly three years after QE3 had ended—it would reinvest only a portion of the proceeds from maturing securities in new securities. The monthly reduction in the balance sheet would be capped, but the allowed reduction would gradually increase over time. As previously announced, the Fed would not sell nonmaturing securities. This passive, predictable approach—as exciting as "watching paint dry," as Philadelphia Fed President Patrick Harker put it—was intended to minimize market uncertainty.[26] Policymakers hoped market participants would resist making unwarranted inferences about the likely course of the funds rate, as they had during the taper tantrum. But the plan was still missing any explicit guidance about when the balance sheet would stop shrinking. That would depend on several unknowns. Most importantly, the Committee had technical decisions to make about how best to control short-term interest rates—decisions that had implications for how big the balance sheet needed to be.

The FOMC's "paint drying" approach meant the process would be slow—in practice, most of the reduction in the balance sheet did not occur until the first two years of Jay Powell's term, which began in 2018.

POLITICS: CONGRESSIONAL RELATIONS AND TRUMP'S REAPPOINTMENT DECISION

During my tenure as chair, the Fed had come under sustained political fire, especially from Congress, for its regulatory failures before the crisis, for the bailouts of failing financial firms and other extraordinary actions during the crisis, and for its use of quantitative easing and other new monetary tools. The rocky relations with Congress extended into Yellen's term.

As had been true in my case, congressional Republicans remained the most fervid critics, although Democrats often sharply criticized the Fed's regulatory policies as too bank friendly. Yellen got a taste of what was in store on February 11, 2014, eight days after her swearing in. The event was the semiannual *Monetary Policy Report* testimony that the chair presents to the Fed's House and Senate oversight committees. Testimony by the Fed chair is usually limited to three hours or so. However, in what felt like a hazing ritual, Republican Jeb Hensarling of Texas, chair of the House

Financial Services Committee, subjected Yellen to a grueling six-hour hearing, marked by mostly hostile questioning.

Many of the fights with Congress during Yellen's term were over tangential issues, at least relative to the Fed's critical decisions about how and when to tighten monetary policy. For example, House Republicans lambasted Yellen for a speech on income inequality in October 2014, which the Republicans saw as supporting liberal policies. (Yellen replied that her speech contained no policy recommendations.) Hensarling also pressured Yellen by generating negative news about the Fed with frequent and public demands for information about a leak of confidential FOMC information in October 2012—during my term as chair. An investor newsletter, published by Medley Global Advisors, had included nonpublic information about FOMC deliberations on QE3. I ordered an internal investigation, which did not find the source of the leak. But the Commodity Futures Trading Commission opened an insider trading case, ultimately referring the matter to the U.S. Attorney's office, which began a criminal investigation but brought no charges. On April 4, 2017, Richmond Fed President Jeffrey Lacker resigned abruptly, acknowledging that he had spoken to the author of the newsletter report about confidential deliberations.[27]

The testy relationship with Congress notwithstanding, the Fed was spared major legislative changes during Yellen's term. Senator Rand Paul (R-Kentucky) continued to push Audit the Fed legislation, which would have subjected the Fed's monetary policy decisions to congressional review. Two senators—Elizabeth Warren (D-Massachusetts) and David Vitter (R-Louisiana)—in 2015 proposed further limiting the Fed's ability to serve as lender of last resort in a financial crisis.[28] (They viewed Fed lending as an unfair bailout of financial interests at the expense of Main Street; they did not consider, however, that the health of Main Street depends on a functioning financial system.) Neither proposal advanced.

In September 2016, Hensarling introduced the Financial CHOICE Act. A revised version of the bill passed the Republican-majority House in June 2017. Its main goal was to roll back certain 2010 Dodd-Frank reforms. It also incorporated Paul's Audit the Fed legislation. Most radically, the bill would have required the FOMC to declare a mathematical policy rule to justify its interest rate choices and to report to the Fed's House and Senate oversight committees and the GAO after each meeting. The default policy rule would be the simple rule developed by John Taylor, which links changes in the federal funds rate only to the current levels of inflation and unemployment. The FOMC would be required to set rates according to the rule or justify any deviation.

Hensarling's proposal revived the issue of whether monetary policy should be run by rules or discretion. As I've noted, proponents of policy rules argue that they would increase the predictability and accountability of the Fed's interest-rate decisions. Opponents counter that the use of a rule would allow policymakers little or no room for dealing with unusual circumstances—such as a financial panic—or changes in the structure of the economy. Yellen made the case against rules forcefully at a conference at Stanford in January 2017, with the leading advocate of rules, John Taylor, present.[29] She acknowledged that simple policy rules "can be helpful in providing broad guidance" but that following them mechanically could produce very bad results. She showed that, given the unemployment and inflation rates at the time, the standard Taylor rule would prescribe a much higher funds rate than the FOMC thought reasonable, and she explained why the FOMC had made different choices. Also, the Taylor rule only implied a value for the federal funds rate. It did not account for the effective lower bound on the short-term rate nor the potential use of alternative tools like quantitative easing.

The CHOICE Act did not become law. However, Yellen and Hensarling had a rapprochement of sorts on the issue of rules. The Fed began regularly publishing a box in its semiannual *Monetary Policy Report* that discussed the role of simple rules in the Fed's policy process (essentially, they are used as a benchmark and frame of reference) and compared the FOMC's policy decisions with the predictions of five alternative rules. At a hearing in July 2017 Hensarling pronounced himself "very heartened" by the new material, though he urged the Fed to give more complete explanations of why it deviated from the rules it described.[30]

As in 2012, when Republican presidential candidates had trashed the Fed and me personally, the 2016 presidential campaign brought attacks on Yellen. Candidate Donald Trump criticized Yellen for being "a very political person," said she was keeping interest rates low to please President Obama, and that she should be "ashamed of herself" for "creating a false stock market."[31] And days before the election, he narrated a television ad widely perceived to be anti-Semitic. It featured the Federal Reserve's seal and vilified, in addition to Trump's opponent Hillary Clinton, three people (all Jewish) associated with finance: Lloyd Blankfein of Goldman Sachs, the Hungarian-American investor George Soros, and Yellen. Ominous music played and Trump intoned the words "global special interests" as Yellen's picture flashed on the screen.[32]

After his election, Trump left the Fed alone—for a while. Eighteen days after he took the oath of office, on February 7, 2017, he met briefly with Yellen in the Oval Office. In the meeting, according to a *Wall Street Journal* account based on an anonymous source, he told Yellen she was doing a good job and that she was a "low-interest-rate person," like himself.[33] And, likely under the influence of Gary Cohn, the first director of Trump's National Economic Council, Trump did not tweet about the Fed or monetary policy during the first part of his term. In an interview after leaving office, Yellen said that Trump did not try to influence the Fed's decisions during her tenure, either publicly or privately.[34]

Yellen's four-year term ran through January 2018. Despite Trump's harsh criticism during the campaign, it seemed possible he would reappoint her, a "low-interest-rate person." There was plenty of precedent. Paul Volcker, Alan Greenspan, and I had been reappointed by presidents of the opposite party from the president who first named us. Trump's choice for chair reportedly came down to four candidates: Yellen, John Taylor, former Board member Kevin Warsh, and current Board member Jerome (Jay) Powell. Each had supporters in the administration, but Treasury Secretary Steven Mnuchin pushed hard for Powell.

True to his campaign statements that he likely would replace Yellen with a Republican, Trump on November 2, 2017, announced he would nominate Powell to become Fed chair in February 2018. Breaking with tradition, Yellen was not invited to the Rose Garden nomination ceremony. According to press reports, Powell was perceived by the administration as in sync with Yellen's (and Trump's) dovish monetary policy inclinations but potentially more sympathetic to the administration's deregulatory philosophy. In contrast, Yellen had delivered a speech, at Jackson Hole in August 2017, in which she lauded postcrisis financial reforms and called for keeping the lessons of the crisis "fresh in our memories."[35]

9

POWELL AND TRUMP

FOLLOWING THREE CHAIRS WITH PhDs IN ECONOMICS, Jay Powell brought a different background to the job. Born in Washington, DC, Powell graduated from Princeton University and Georgetown Law School, where he was the editor of the law review. He then went to work for the investment firm Dillon, Read & Company, where he became a protégé of the company's chair, Nicholas Brady. When Brady was named Treasury secretary by President George H. W. Bush, Powell followed him to Washington, serving in senior positions. At Treasury, Powell oversaw the investigation and sanctioning of Salomon Brothers after one of its traders submitted false bids in an auction of new Treasury debt. From 1997 through 2005, Powell was a partner at The Carlyle Group, a private equity firm based in Washington. After Carlyle, Powell became a visiting scholar at the Bipartisan Policy Center in Washington, where, during the 2011 congressional squabble over the government debt ceiling, he worked behind the scenes to educate legislators about the risks of defaulting on the national debt.

President Obama appointed Powell to be a member of the Fed's Board in May 2012. Obama paired the nomination of the Republican Powell with the nomination of Harvard professor Jeremy Stein, a Democrat, to increase Stein's odds of confirmation. Still chair at the time, I was pleased with the appointments. Both new Board members were highly capable and eager to contribute. I often met with them in my office—we had a semi-regular Saturday morning session—to discuss monetary policy and the economy.

I had persuaded Stein and Powell to support QE3 when it was announced in 2012, though they each had reservations. Along with Board member Betsy Duke and several of the Reserve Bank presidents, Stein and Powell were concerned about QE3's effectiveness and potential financial-stability risks. The disagreements on the FOMC contributed to what proved to be a less-than-full commitment to open-ended QE, which muddied our communication and helped spark the 2013 taper tantrum. Powell was no ideologue, though, and as the recovery continued without a new financial crisis or other serious side effects, he changed his view. In a speech in February 2015, when he was still a Board member, Powell said: "I too expressed doubts about the efficacy and risks of further asset purchases. But let's let the data speak: The evidence so far is clear that the benefits of these policies have been substantial, and that the risks have not materialized."[1]

During his more than five years as a Board member, Powell proved effective and committed. He immersed himself in monetary policy, but also in the less glamorous and highly technical issues of financial regulation and financial "plumbing," the critical infrastructure through which trades are executed and recorded. He was thus well-equipped for his new job. Following his nomination by President Trump, Powell was confirmed in the Senate by a wide bipartisan margin, 84 to 13. At his swearing-in ceremony on February 5, 2018, Powell noted the importance of Fed independence—its "long-standing, nonpartisan tradition to make decisions objectively, based only on the best available evidence."[2]

Powell would not be the only new member of the Fed's leadership. Trump in July 2017 nominated veteran policymaker and investor Randal (Randy) Quarles to be vice chair for supervision (a new position created by the Dodd-Frank Act). In April 2018 Trump nominated the prominent Columbia University economist Richard Clarida to be Board vice chair. Bill Dudley retired as president of the New York Fed and was succeeded in June 2018 by San Francisco Fed President John Williams, a longtime monetary economist at the Board and the San Francisco Fed.

As noted in the previous chapter, from the administration's point of view, much of the case for Powell over Yellen had been Powell's supposed openness to the president's deregulatory agenda. On regulatory matters, however, Powell would mostly stick to the middle of the road. Working with Quarles, he would look for ways to ease regulatory burdens and rationalize the Fed's rules and oversight, including simplifying capital and stress-testing requirements for all but the largest banks. Lael Brainard, the last remaining Obama appointee on the Board, opposed many of the proposed regulatory changes during Powell's tenure, arguing that they went too far in weakening necessary protections. Clearly, Powell was of a more deregulatory bent than Yellen (or Brainard), and there would be no major regulatory initiatives on his watch. However, on the other hand, neither was Powell interested in dismantling the strengthened regulatory framework created by Dodd-Frank and international agreements since the crisis. "The whole idea is to preserve . . . the important core reforms," he said.[3]

NEW EFFORTS AT "NORMALIZATION"

On monetary policy, Powell soon made clear that, the president's preferences notwithstanding, he planned to continue gradually moving toward a more neutral, or "normal," policy stance. At his first meeting as chair, in March 2018, the FOMC voted unanimously to increase the target range for the federal funds rate by another quarter percentage point, to 1½–1¾ percent. Twelve of the fifteen meeting participants projected either two or three more quarter-point increases in 2018, and more in 2019. In his press conference, Powell said "the process of gradually scaling back monetary policy accommodation . . . has served—and should continue to serve—the economy well."[4] He noted that the balance sheet reductions begun in October under Yellen would also continue.

FOMC participants projected continuing above-trend growth and low unemployment, partly reflecting a potential boost from the corporate and personal tax cuts signed by Trump the previous December, as justification for continued tightening. Some early salvos in Trump's trade war had created risks—tariffs on imported washing machines and solar panels in January 2018, and on steel and aluminum imports in March—but Powell indicated that the tariffs had, so far, not affected the broader economic outlook. In June, the Committee raised the target range for the funds rate by another quarter percentage point, to 1¾–2 percent.

President Trump had praised Powell at the announcement of his nomination: "He's strong. He's committed. He's smart." And he remained silent on monetary policy through Powell's first five and a half months. The honeymoon ended on July 19, 2018, when Trump, in a CNBC interview, said "I'm not thrilled" about the Fed's interest-rate increases. A day later, in a tweet, Trump lamented that "the U.S. is raising rates while the dollars [sic] gets stronger and stronger with each passing day—taking away our big competitive edge" with China and the European Union.[5] His public criticism of the Fed's policy decisions would continue—a sharp break from the norm that, with few exceptions, had governed presidents after Nixon. Trump's complaints also reversed his campaign-trail rhetoric that easy-money policies had created a "false" stock market.

Powell's strategy for dealing with Trump was multipronged. As he had at his swearing-in ceremony and, earlier, at the announcement of his nomination, he regularly and publicly emphasized that independence allows the Fed to make decisions in the public interest based on objective data and analysis and free of short-term political considerations. To help people better understand what the Fed was doing and why, he aimed to explain Fed policy decisions "in plain English." He also announced that, starting in January 2019, he would hold a press conference after every FOMC meeting, or eight times a year rather than quarterly, as Yellen and I had done. He also steadfastly refrained from commenting on policies outside of the Fed's jurisdiction—even the president's trade war, which created risks for the economy and was widely panned by economists. He consistently declined to respond directly to the criticisms made by Trump or other politicians. And finally, and crucially, Powell worked to balance the president's attacks by developing relationships and cultivating support for Fed policies in Congress. "I'm going to wear the carpets of Capitol Hill out by walking those halls and meeting with members," he said in an interview.[6] Yellen and I also spent considerable time with legislators, on the phone and in one-on-one meetings, explaining our strategy and answering questions. But Powell took these efforts to a new level. They paid off in a much-improved relationship with Congress, on both sides of the aisle.

Powell defined his monetary policy approach in a speech at his first Jackson Hole meeting as chair, in August 2018, in which he stressed that policymakers must always remain mindful of our pervasive uncertainty about the structure of the economy.[7] The FOMC's changing estimates of the neutral policy rate (R^*) and the natural rate of unemployment (u^*) were one manifestation of that uncertainty. Given the state of our knowledge, he argued, good policymakers must be humble and flexible. He thus took the Fed's revisionism under Yellen a step further—from reassessing estimates of critical variables like R^* and u^* to emphasizing that policymakers must always be open to adjusting policy in response to incoming data, even when (or especially when) that data seemed inconsistent with their economic models.

In his speech, Powell discussed R^* and u^* ("R-star" and "u-star") by playing on the theme of celestial navigation. "Navigating by the stars can sound straightforward," he said. "Guiding policy by the stars in practice, however, has been quite challenging of late because our best assessments of the location of the stars have been changing significantly. . . . The stars are sometimes far from where we perceive them to be." As an example of the pitfalls of taking estimated "stars" too seriously, Powell cited 1970s-era policymakers whose overconfidence in their estimate of the natural rate of unemployment had contributed to the Great Inflation. In contrast, he argued, Alan Greenspan's data-driven, risk-management approach, which put policymakers' uncertainty about the economy front and center, helped the Fed promote strong growth without inflation during the 1990s. My sense of the speech at the time was that Powell was signaling a step back from model-driven forecasts and policy analyses in favor of a more agnostic approach, with greater reliance on Greenspanian deep dives into the economic data and anecdotal information from business contacts and others "on the ground."*

What did all that mean for near-term policy decisions? Given that inflation had for several years been undershooting the predictions of the Fed's Phillips curve models, despite many attempts to patch them up, Powell might have seen uncertainty about models and the locations of the "stars" as a reason to stop or slow monetary tightening. As he made clear in his speech, though, he did not draw that inference. Instead, he argued that, given unavoidable uncertainties, both tightening too quickly and tightening too slowly involved risks. Consequently, the best policy, he concluded, was to continue Yellen's policy of gradual rate increases, with close attention to economic developments and a willingness to adjust nimbly. As foreshadowed in Powell's speech, the FOMC raised the target range for the funds rate again in September, bringing it to 2–2¼ percent.

The September 2018 meeting was the first for the new Board vice chair, Richard Clarida. His swearing-in marked the end of nearly nine months with only three of the Board's seven seats filled—by Powell, Quarles, and Brainard. Michelle Bowman joined the Board in November, bringing the membership to five. Bowman, who had been state banking commissioner in Kansas and vice president of her family's community bank, fulfilled a requirement of the Dodd-Frank law that one member have experience working in or supervising community banks.

Besides Quarles, Clarida, and Bowman, Trump nominated two more prospective Board members with conventional qualifications: Carnegie Mellon economics professor and former Richmond Fed economist Marvin Goodfriend and economist Nellie Liang, former director of the Federal Reserve's Division of Financial Stability. Goodfriend's nomination lapsed after opposition from Senate Democrats and Republican Rand Paul. (Goodfriend died of cancer in December 2019.) Liang withdrew

---

* The FOMC has long taken account of anecdotal information gleaned from personal contacts, and a summary of such information is released before each meeting in a publication known as the *Beige Book*. Powell's greater emphasis on qualitative information was thus building on an existing strategy, not setting an entirely new direction.

from consideration in January 2019 in the face of opposition from banking lobbyists and Senate Republicans. She would later become undersecretary for domestic finance to Treasury Secretary Yellen in the Biden administration.

On December 19, 2018, near the end of Powell's first year as chair, the FOMC increased the federal funds rate target to 2¼–2½ percent. It was the ninth quarter-point increase since the tightening of policy had begun three years earlier under Yellen, and the fourth under Powell's chairmanship. The vote was again unanimous. As it turned out, it would also prove to be a high-water mark for the funds rate, even though the Committee did not change its previous guidance that "some further gradual increases in the target range for the federal funds rate will be consistent" with its employment and inflation objectives.

Markets had been volatile that fall, with the Dow falling 8.3 percent in the two weeks before the December announcement. Doubtless with the market action in mind, Powell at his press conference sought to cast a dovish light on the FOMC's rate increase and projections of further hikes. "We have seen developments that may signal some softening relative to what we were expecting a few months ago," he said. He noted that "some crosscurrents have emerged" since the September meeting, including a moderation in global economic growth, increased financial market volatility, diminishing stimulus from Trump's tax cuts, and overall tighter financial conditions. And, he strongly hinted the Committee had a low bar for pulling back from its plan for further rate increases. He noted that the latest increase had put the funds rate "at the lower end of the range of estimates of the longer-run normal rate provided by the Committee."[8] That contrasted with a comment in an early October interview with PBS's Judy Woodruff, a week after the previous rate increase, when he had roiled markets by saying, "We're a long way from neutral at this point, probably."[9] On the other hand, Powell signaled lack of flexibility on the Fed's balance sheet by suggesting that the planned drawdown was on "automatic pilot."[10]

Powell's efforts at softening the blow notwithstanding, markets—in a reaction reminiscent of the mini-recession episode under Yellen—clearly thought that the Fed's tightening was going too far and too fast. Four rate hikes in 2018, the promise of more in 2019, and the ongoing reduction in the balance sheet—which traders had dubbed "quantitative tightening"—added up to a significant prospective tightening, which seemed hard to justify when set against the agnostic stance that Powell had taken in Jackson Hole or the economic crosscurrents he cited at the press conference. The Dow Jones index dropped an additional 1.5 percent on the day of the announcement and press conference. Markets continued to slump after the December meeting, reacting not only to developments at the Fed but to concerns about slowing global growth, U.S.-China trade tensions, lackluster corporate earnings, and a budget standoff between Trump and congressional Democrats over funding for a wall along the border with Mexico. On December 22, as both Trump and the Democrats refused to concede, what would become the longest shutdown of the federal government (thirty-five days) began.

Bloomberg News reported on December 21 that Trump had discussed firing Powell—a step of doubtful legality, since Board members can be removed only "for cause," that is, for violations of the law, not policy differences. Trump's staff scrambled to walk back that report. But the president's displeasure was clear. On December 24, amid an ongoing stock-market rout, he tweeted, "The Fed is like a powerful golfer who can't score because he has no touch—he can't putt."

PIVOT

The end-of-the-year stock-market decline—it was the worst December for the market since 1931—helped convince Powell and his colleagues that four rate hikes in 2018, with more promised, had been too much for an economy confronting slowing growth and worsening trade tensions. He needed to signal a policy shift. Conveniently, he was scheduled to appear—jointly with Janet Yellen and me—on January 4, 2019, at the American Economic Association's annual meeting in Atlanta. As incoming president of the professional association for economists, I had arranged for Neil Irwin of the *New York Times* to interview the three of us together on stage.

Irwin's first question to Powell was, "What is your outlook for 2019 and beyond?" Reading from handwritten notes, Powell acknowledged recent improvement in the labor market, but observed that "financial markets have been sending different signals, signals of concern about downside risks, about slowing global growth, particularly related to China, about ongoing trade negotiations, about what maybe let's call general policy uncertainty coming out of Washington. . . ."[11]

Monetary policy "is very much about risk management," Powell said, echoing his remarks the previous August at the Jackson Hole symposium. Then he added, "particularly with the muted inflation readings that we've seen coming in, we will be patient as we watch to see how the economy evolves." He recalled 2016, when the Committee's median projection had been four rate increases but, in the face of the mini-recession, the Committee raised its target for the funds rate only once. "No one knows whether this year will be like 2016," he said, "but what I do know is that we will be prepared to adjust policy quickly and flexibly, and to use all of our tools to support the economy should that be appropriate. . . ."

The takeaway message was policy patience—no more rate hikes for the foreseeable future. Markets breathed a sigh of relief, with the Dow jumping 3.3 percent on the day. At its next meeting, on January 30, 2019, the FOMC left the funds rate target unchanged and repeated Powell's message in its statement: "the Committee will be patient as it determines what future adjustments to the target range for the federal funds rate may be appropriate. . . ." The Committee did not release economic projections at that meeting, but at its next, in March, the median rate projection was for no increases in 2019 and only one in 2020. The Committee also made clear, in a separate statement, that the balance sheet runoff—the "quantitative tightening" that had been worrying markets—was not on "automatic pilot," as Powell had suggested in December. Rather, the FOMC was prepared to stop shrinking the balance sheet if economic or financial circumstances warranted. The policy pivot, in response to market signals and a shifting outlook, was a sharp one but it was also consistent with Powell's emphasis on flexible and data-responsive policymaking.

The political environment made all policy decisions fraught, however. At the January press conference, Jim Puzzanghera of the *Los Angeles Times* asked whether the Fed, in its shift to easier policy, had "just caved to the president's demand." Powell replied, "[W]e're always going to do what we think is the right thing. We're never going to take political considerations into account or discuss them as part of our work. You know, we're human. We make mistakes. But we're not going to make mistakes of character or integrity." [12]

TRUMP, THE TRADE WAR, AND THE INSURANCE CUTS

In 2019, Powell and the rest of the FOMC navigated continued pressure from the president. They had to avoid "caving" to Trump's demands but also not allow a desire to demonstrate independence to distort their decisions.

Following the rumors in December that the president was considering firing Powell, the president's advisers began arranging a meeting between the two. Trump and Powell had not had a substantive discussion since November 2017 when Powell's nomination was announced. On February 4, 2019, at the president's invitation, Powell and Vice Chair Clarida dined with Trump and Treasury Secretary Mnuchin at the White House.

Ever since the Nixon-Burns fiasco, Fed leaders have generally tried to maintain a discreet distance from the White House. Communication with the administration flows primarily through the Treasury secretary and other senior economic officials. However, informal meetings between the Fed chair and the president do occur. As chair, I lunched a few times a year with President Bush, for whom I had worked in the White House. I also met occasionally with President Obama, usually to discuss the economic outlook or regulatory issues. But given President Trump's ongoing public criticism, and markets' suspicion that he had influenced the Fed's pivot, the dinner risked giving the impression of undue influence.

To forestall misinterpretation—and any misleading tweets from the president—the Fed issued a press release immediately after the dinner. It said, "Chair Powell's comments [at the dinner] . . . were consistent with his remarks at his press conference of last week. He did not discuss his expectations for monetary policy, except to stress that the path of policy will depend entirely on incoming economic information and what that means for the outlook." The press release reiterated that the FOMC would make its decisions "based solely on careful, objective and non-political analysis." [13]

Ironically, the president's evident dissatisfaction with the Fed lent credence to Powell's repeated assertions that the Fed's decision-making was independent and nonpolitical—notwithstanding the dovish pivot. Trump's comments, in interviews and tweets, grew more strident and more specific. Administration officials occasionally joined in. On March 29, National Economic Council Chair Larry Kudlow called on the Fed to immediately cut interest rates by a half percentage point. On April 5, the president told reporters that the Fed should cut rates, and on April 30 he tweeted that the economy would "soar like a rocket" if the Fed lowered its benchmark rate by a full percentage point. "They [Fed officials] don't have a clue," he tweeted on June 11. Powell received phone calls from Trump on March 8 and April 11. He would meet again with Trump and Mnuchin at the White House (without Clarida) in November, with the Fed once again releasing a pre-emptive statement immediately after.

It is hard to overstate how jarring Trump's tactics were, particularly compared with his predecessors' assiduous respect for Fed independence. Understanding the importance of not taking the bait, Fed officials responded to the inevitable press questions about the president's tweets and comments through gritted teeth. For decades, presidential jawboning has not been an effective way to influence Fed policy, and it was not this time. The more direct channel of influence, used by all presidents, is through appointments to the Federal Reserve Board. Despite his irritation with the Fed, Trump's early appointments, including Powell, Clarida,

and Quarles, had been conventional, well-qualified choices, widely praised
and easily confirmed by the Senate. His subsequent nominations of Marvin Goodfriend and Nellie Liang, neither of which advanced, were also
solid choices. In the spring of 2019, however, the president switched his
approach, proposing vocal loyalists, without conventional qualifications,
for the two empty Board seats. He floated the names of Stephen Moore
(a television commentator and a former member of the *Wall Street Journal*
editorial board, who had worked for the conservative Heritage Foundation)
and Herman Cain (former chief executive of the Godfather's Pizza chain
and a Republican presidential candidate in 2012). Both were Trump supporters who had echoed the president's calls to cut rates sharply. However,
neither was formally nominated after key Senate Republicans expressed
concerns—concerns which, in a bad omen for future Fed independence,
had more to do with the personal histories of the two men than with their
qualifications or policy views. [14] (Cain died in July 2020 after testing positive for the COVID-19 virus.)

In January 2020 Trump would make another unconventional nomination for the Board—conservative writer Judy Shelton. Shelton, a longtime
advocate of returning to the gold standard (and of other extreme positions,
such as abolishing deposit insurance) had conveniently reversed her lifelong
hawkish, hard-money views in favor of Trump's easy-money stance. Shelton was paired with a conventional nominee, Christopher Waller, research
director of the Federal Reserve Bank of St. Louis and a former economics
professor at Notre Dame. However, Shelton, too, lacked Senate support, in
this case because of her outré and inconsistent views, and she was not confirmed. (Waller would be confirmed in December 2020.) There were certainly candidates for the Board who would have supported Trump's policy
preferences and would have been confirmable, but the president's propensity for fringe nominations cost him an opportunity to indirectly steer the
Fed's monetary and regulatory policies.

Beyond his kibitzing on monetary policy, Trump added more economic
uncertainty by summarily rejecting the generally internationalist perspective of prior administrations of both parties. He pursued a multifront trade

war, imposing or raising tariffs (taxes on imports) on diverse products and trading partners, which in turn triggered retaliatory tariff increases. Projecting the effects of the trade war was a challenge for the Fed's economists. Standard economic theory holds that trade among nations is mutually beneficial because it allows countries to specialize in the goods and services they are relatively more efficient at producing.* Instead, the president had a zero-sum view of trade, arguing that if country A exported more to country B than it imported, then A was winning and B was losing. More broadly, he saw trade restrictions as tools for achieving political goals, such as the isolation of unfriendly regimes. Congress has given the president considerable discretion over trade rules, so Trump was able to impose—or threaten to impose—tariffs more or less at will.

The president's trade skirmishes had waxed and waned throughout 2018 and into early 2019. On May 5, 2019, Trump announced the United States would increase a previously announced 10 percent tariff on $200 billion of Chinese goods to a punitive 25 percent. On May 30, Trump threatened to put tariffs of up to 25 percent on all Mexican goods unless Mexico did more to stem the flow of Central American migrants through its territory and into the United States. Over the same period in May, the Dow fell 6.4 percent.

In a tit-for-tat trade war, like the one sparked by Trump, consumers face higher prices on imported goods subject to tariffs, and, because of retaliation, exporters (such as U.S. farmers) find it harder to sell their products abroad. Some domestic producers may benefit if tariffs raise the prices of competing imported goods. These direct effects are relatively easy to measure, by looking at changes in the prices and quantities of traded goods after trade restrictions. Contrary to the administration's claims, studies

---

* This view of trade, known as the theory of comparative advantage, was laid out by British economist David Ricardo in the early 19th century. The theory of comparative advantage does not imply that free trade makes everyone better off, only that it creates enough surplus that, in principle, the winners from trade could compensate the losers. In practice, such compensation rarely happens, so that free trade can make some people—like workers in industries that compete with imports—worse off.

found that the costs imposed by the tariffs were borne primarily by American consumers and firms.[15] Trump implicitly recognized that point by directing subsidies to farmers who had suffered losses in the trade war, as when China had embargoed American soybeans. By 2020, subsidies topped $50 billion, accounting for more than a third of farm income.[16] Although the tariffs amounted to a tax increase on Americans, the direct effects of that increase were not large or broad-based enough to significantly affect aggregate U.S. employment or inflation.

The greater, if more indirect, cost of the trade wars was the uncertainty they generated about globalization and U.S. relationships with other countries, especially China.[17] The global economy had become increasingly integrated, and not only through increased trade in the goods and services ultimately purchased by consumers. With the development of global supply chains, production processes increasingly spanned national borders, with producers relying on inputs from many countries. The longer-run implications of Trump's trade policy for this intricate system of mutual dependence were impossible to know. Perhaps the trade wars would be quickly resolved, with modest changes to global trade and even some beneficial concessions from U.S. trading partners. But perhaps they would lead to a reversal of the trend toward more open trade—in the extreme, to a "decoupling" of the U.S. economy from China and other trading partners—that would increase production costs in many industries and slow gains in output and average living standards.

Markets react badly to uncertainty, as the stock market demonstrated. Uncertainty can also be bad for the economy as a whole if, for example, firms delay capital investment or hiring until they have more information about their access to foreign suppliers and markets. Indeed, the FOMC noted at its May 2019 meeting that business investment had slowed in the first quarter and, at its June and July meetings, that investment remained soft, despite the recent cut in U.S. corporate taxes. The European and Japanese economies—more open to trade than the United States—were also slowing, with trade uncertainty an important factor.

As FOMC participants tried to assess how much the trade wars, diminishing fiscal stimulus, and a weaker global economy were holding back U.S. growth in the spring of 2019, they also noted a phenomenon in the bond markets: an inverted yield curve. The yield curve is inverted when longer-term interest rates (say, on ten-year Treasury notes) are lower than short-term rates (on three-month Treasury bills, for example). After a brief inversion in March, the yield curve inverted more decisively in May and remained inverted over the summer, with ten-year yields falling by half a percentage point below three-month yields by the end of August.

Policymakers and market participants paid attention because an inverted yield curve has often predicted recessions. Why? One explanation is that an inverted yield curve is a signal of tight monetary policy. The short-term interest rate can be thought of as a measure of the current stance of monetary policy, while the long-term rate—which reflects the expected average level of short-term interest rates in the future—can be seen as a proxy for the neutral interest rate, R*. When the yield curve is inverted, by this logic, monetary policy is restrictive—the short-term interest rate is above neutral—which may presage a recession. Put another way, an inverted yield curve indicates that bond traders expect the Fed to cut short-term interest rates over the next few years, suggesting that they see an economic slowdown on the horizon.

Whether the inverted yield curve portended a recession in this case was widely debated. Other factors, such as ongoing quantitative easing in Europe and Japan and the still-large size of the Fed's own balance sheet, might help explain why longer-term rates around the world were unusually low. Another possible factor was that, with inflation low and expected to remain so, long-term bondholders were not demanding extra return to compensate them for inflation risk. Still, together with trade war uncertainties and some other indications of economic slowing, the inverted yield curve increased concerns at the Fed that policy remained too tight. On June 4, in a speech in Chicago, Powell offered the first hint that he was thinking about cutting rates. "We are closely monitoring the implications of these [trade] developments for the U.S. economic outlook and, as always, we will act as appropriate to sustain the expansion . . . ," he said.[18] In reaction, the Dow jumped 2.1 percent.

Nevertheless, Trump again escalated pressure. On June 18, Bloomberg News reported that the White House was exploring the legality of stripping Powell of the chairmanship and demoting him to being a Board member only. Asked by reporters the same day whether he wanted to demote Powell, Trump replied, "Well, let's see what he does."

On June 19, 2019, the Committee voted 9–1 to maintain the federal funds rate target at 2¼–2½ percent. St. Louis Fed President Bullard dissented (the first dissent of Powell's term) in favor of a quarter-point cut. The dot plot made clear, however, that sentiment on the Committee was shifting. Although a bare majority of participants projected no rate change by year-end 2019, seven of seventeen projected two rate cuts by the end of the year, and one participant projected a single rate cut. In his press conference, Powell said the Committee saw "no strong case" for an immediate easing of monetary policy.[19] But, while being careful not to opine on the merits of the president's trade policies, he noted that they were creating greater uncertainty for business and causing sentiment in financial markets to deteriorate. It was clear which way the FOMC was leaning.

At the press conference, Heather Long of the *Washington Post* asked Powell about Trump's threat to demote him. He replied, "I think the law is clear that I have a four-year term [as chair], and I fully intend to serve it."[20]

The foreshadowed rate cut, along with an early end to the runoff of the Fed's balance sheet, came at the next meeting, at the end of July. In his press conference, Powell explained the cut by saying it was "intended to insure against downside risks. . . ."[21] In other words, while a slowdown was not yet evident, the rate cut was intended to protect the U.S. economy from the risks posed by trade uncertainty, a slowing of the global economy, and other factors. The language sounded like Alan Greenspan's risk-management approach, which Powell had lauded in his Jackson Hole speech a year earlier—praise he would repeat in his second Jackson Hole remarks the following month. Two FOMC members dissented. In a statement included in the minutes of the meeting, Esther George of Kansas City rejected the insurance argument, saying that a cut would be justified only by evidence of a "materially weaker outlook." In his own dissenting statement, Eric Rosengren of Boston worried that lowering rates too far would increase risks to financial stability.

As usual, market participants and other Fed-watchers tried to guess whether this rate cut would be followed by others. At his press conference, Powell seemed to suggest the Fed's willingness to ease policy was limited. He referred to the cut as a "midcycle adjustment," as opposed to the start of a lengthy sequence of rate cuts.[22] The next day, August 1, Trump threatened more tariffs on Chinese goods, and China halted purchases of U.S. agricultural products on August 5. The trade belligerence, together with the perception that the Fed might not do much more, brought down the Dow by 6.3 percent from before the July 30–31 FOMC meeting until August 14.

Despite the rate cut, the Fed's first in a decade, Trump continued to assail the Fed chair. On August 14 he called Powell "clueless." On August 19 he criticized Powell's "horrendous lack of vision." On August 22 Trump claimed Germany's sale of negative-rate bonds gave it a competitive advantage over the United States. Of course, negative-rate government bonds were in fact more a sign of euro-area weakness than of strength. They reflected a lack of private investment opportunities, demand from European investors for a safe haven in the midst of economic uncertainty, and the European Central Bank's aggressive attempts to stimulate the eurozone economy.

On August 23, the same day Powell was speaking in Jackson Hole, Trump asked, ". . . Who is our bigger enemy?"—Powell or Chinese President Xi Jinping. The tweet came even though Powell, in his speech, was about to signal at least one more rate cut to come by repeating, "We will act as appropriate to sustain the expansion," after citing the new China tariffs, financial turbulence, and a litany of geopolitical risks, "including the growing possibility of a hard Brexit, rising tensions in Hong Kong, and the dissolution of the Italian government."[23] On August 28 Trump said the

Fed cannot "mentally" keep up with competitor countries. On September 11 he called on the Fed to "get our interest rates down to ZERO, or less," labeling the FOMC, in a second tweet, "Boneheads."

At its September meeting the FOMC, as expected, cut the target range for the funds rate another quarter point, to 1¾–2 percent. As it had at its July meeting, the Committee said in its statement that it would "act as appropriate to sustain the expansion," driving home that it was open to further reductions. At his press conference on September 18, Powell again cited the insurance rationale for easing. Asked about his use of the term "midcycle adjustment," he noted two past episodes—1995–96 and 1998, both under Greenspan. Each encompassed three quarter-point rate cuts. The logical inference, that a third rate cut was likely at an upcoming meeting, was undercut to some degree by the fact that a majority of FOMC participants did not project another rate cut in 2019. But the third rate cut did come, at the next meeting on October 30. This time, though, the Committee dropped the language that it would "act as appropriate," suggesting it was done easing, at least for the time being. In his press conference, Powell confirmed that impression, saying that monetary policy was now "in a good place" and that a change in policy would require "a material reassessment of our outlook."24

The three-cut sequence between July and October seemed to have worked. Before the cuts, financial markets were pricing in a significant probability of an economic slowdown. Those concerns had largely dissipated by October. Economic growth and job creation picked up and financial markets calmed. Notably, the yield curve was no longer inverted, suggesting that bond traders no longer saw a recession on the horizon. Overall, the monetary policy three-step in 2019—the pivot, the pause, and the insurance rate cuts—helped the economy weather the trade wars and other sources of uncertainty. It looked like the Powell Fed had pulled off a proverbial soft landing, as Alan Greenspan had in the mid-1990s.

However, if Powell's 2019 policies had a Greenspanian flavor, it is debatable whether the three rate cuts in the summer and fall were true insurance cuts, in Greenspan's sense. Greenspan's rate cuts during the Asian financial crisis in 1998, for example, helped protect against risks to growth and jobs, but like any insurance policy they involved a premium, namely, increased perceived risks of higher inflation. For this reason, when an economic slowdown did not materialize, the Greenspan Fed reversed the cuts and more, ultimately raising rates by a total of 1¾ percentage points from the 1998 low. In contrast, Powell's cuts could be justified on non-insurance grounds, both by the developing economic slowdown and by inflation that, except for short periods, had remained below target and shown little upward momentum. Thus, unlike true insurance cuts, the 2019 rate reductions did not involve paying a premium—unless you count Eric Rosengren's concerns about financial stability—nor were they expected to be reversed anytime soon. The terminology was, of course, less important than the results. Whatever the policy shift was called, as of late 2019 it looked to have been a nimble response to a complicated set of circumstances, avoiding what might have been a painful economic slowdown.

FED LISTENS: THE STRATEGY REVIEW

It is not uncommon for central banks to periodically review the intellectual frameworks or strategies that guide their policy choices. The Bank of Canada reviews its framework every five years, and the Bank of Japan's review in 2016 led to major changes in its policy approach, including a decision to directly target longer-term interest rates ("yield-curve control"). The Fed had done such reviews in a piecemeal way, most recently before we introduced the inflation target in 2012. However, the policy challenges after the financial crisis had absorbed the full attention of policymakers and Fed staff, precluding a more comprehensive self-examination.

By 2018, with the economy in relatively good shape and with the funds rate lifted off zero, it seemed an opportune moment to look back at the past decade and draw some lessons. In November Powell announced that the Fed would in the next year "review the strategies, tools, and communication practices" it used to pursue its mandate. The review, Powell said, would include "outreach to a broad range of interested stakeholders."[25]

Powell put Vice Chair Clarida in charge of the review. Clarida, in a February 2019 speech, said the review would take the Fed's statutory dual mandate as a given. He added that the Committee's existing 2 percent inflation target was "most consistent" with the mandate—thereby ruling out proposals by some economists to raise the target as a means of pushing the neutral policy interest rate (R*) further above its effective lower bound.[26] Clarida said that the review would focus on three questions. First, should the Fed stick with the inflation-targeting strategy adopted in 2012? In particular, could the policy framework be changed in a way that would help the Fed better cope with the constraint of the effective lower bound? Second, the new tools of forward guidance and quantitative easing had been effective after the crisis, but, with increased concerns about the lower bound, were they enough? To ensure that sufficient stimulus could be delivered when needed, should the Fed adopt additional tools, including several that were already in the toolkits of other major central banks? Finally, should the Fed modify its approaches to communicating about policy?

Powell's promised outreach was realized in fifteen public "Fed Listens" events at the Board in Washington and at Reserve Banks around the country. The lists of invited participants went well beyond the Fed's more-typical advisers—academic economists, market participants, bankers, and businesspeople—and included community development specialists, union officials, leaders of groups representing minorities and senior citizens, and average citizens. The events gave policymakers a chance to make the case that the Fed policies are intended to benefit the broad public, not special interest groups like Wall Street bankers. This message dovetailed with Powell's efforts, in press conferences and testimony, to explain monetary policy decisions "in plain English." Policymakers attending the Fed Listens events also learned more about public perceptions of the Fed and its policies. They were told repeatedly that tight labor markets had widespread benefits. With the demand for workers strong, more people were drawn into the labor force, especially people in lower-income and minority communities. With inflation also low, and showing few signs of reviving, this feedback strengthened the commitment of Powell and his FOMC colleagues to press for an even more robust labor market.

The review was on track to wrap up in mid-2020 but the COVID-19 pandemic delayed its completion for several months—even as the new recession induced by the pandemic would make the review's conclusions more relevant and urgent.

MONEY MARKET TURMOIL

A more technical but consequential issue also occupied the FOMC's attention—the methods that would be used to implement monetary policy in the future, also known as its operating framework (as opposed to the policy framework). The question was, once policymakers set policy by choosing a range for the federal funds rate, how would they ensure the funds rate remained in that range? Obviously, effective monetary policy requires that the Fed have reasonably tight control over short-term interest rates. Moreover, the choice of operating framework was closely related to the question of how big the Fed's balance sheet should be in the long run.

Before the financial crisis, the FOMC had implemented monetary policy through what was known as a "scarce reserves" regime. The Fed controlled the federal funds rate by varying the supply of reserves in the banking system, which it accomplished by either selling Treasury securities in the open market to drain reserves or buying them to add reserves. This approach required close monitoring of banks' demand for reserves. For instance, the demand for reserves typically increases along with consumer spending during the holiday season, and when quarterly tax payments are made. As banks' needs for reserves fluctuated, the New York Fed engaged in frequent (roughly daily) open-market operations to keep the funds rate at target.

With the advent of quantitative easing in 2008, the Fed effectively transitioned to a new operating framework, known as an "ample reserves" system. Because the Fed paid for its securities purchases by creating bank reserves, banks after the crisis collectively held far more reserves than in the past. With reserves far exceeding their typical daily needs, banks had little reason to borrow reserves from other banks, with the result that the funds rate—the rate paid on interbank borrowings—remained close to zero. Of course, from 2008 through 2015, a near-zero funds rate was consistent with the FOMC's efforts to encourage economic growth and bring inflation up to target.

When the time came to begin tightening monetary policy, the Fed had to ensure that it would be able to raise the funds rate when needed. Given the surfeit of reserves in the system, traditional open-market operations would not accomplish this. Instead, the Fed nudged the funds rate higher by raising the interest rate it paid to banks on their reserves, using the authority first granted by Congress in 2008. However, as in 2008, technical factors introduced some slippage between the interest rate on reserves and the funds rate. To improve its control of short-term rates, the Fed in September 2013 had created a facility that allowed certain eligible nonbank institutions, such as money market mutual funds and GSEs, to make what were effectively short-term deposits with the Fed. These deposits earned another, slightly lower, interest rate set by the Fed, known as the overnight reverse repurchase rate, or ONRRP rate. Through the management of its two administered rates, the interest rate on reserves and the ONRRP rate, the Fed successfully kept the funds rate near target during liftoff, despite the abundance of reserves held by the banking system.

As the tightening got underway, the FOMC had to decide whether to continue using its new ample reserves framework or, instead, return to its precrisis scarce reserves approach. In January 2019 the FOMC permanently adopted the ample reserves approach. This framework was more straightforward. It did not require continuous monitoring and adjustment of the supply of reserves to keep the policy rate at its target—one reason that the ample reserves approach had long been used by most major central banks. And it had at least two other important advantages: First, the Fed might at some point again have to resort to QE, expanding its balance sheet and the quantity of bank reserves. If so, the ample reserves approach would facilitate raising the funds rate when the time came to exit, as it had from 2015 through 2018. Second, the increased level of reserves in the banking system implied by the ample reserves approach would promote financial stability by making banks less vulnerable to the loss of short-term funding during a panic. Indeed, new regulations following the global financial crisis required banks to hold greatly increased quantities of liquid assets, including reserves.

The adoption of the ample reserves approach also meant the Fed's balance sheet would remain permanently much larger than in the past. The approach assumes that the supply of reserves fully meets banks' needs, and those needs (for both regulatory and precautionary reasons) had grown enormously since the financial crisis. On the other hand, in its June 2011 exit principles the FOMC had promised that the balance sheet would be no larger than necessary for the efficient implementation of monetary policy. Together, those conditions implied that the Fed would aim for a balance sheet large enough to ensure ample bank reserves under most or all conditions, but not much larger than that.

Because no one really knew the level of reserves that would satisfy banks' needs under most circumstances, the ideal level of the Fed's balance sheet would have to be determined by trial and error. At its next meeting, in March 2019, the FOMC announced that it would in May begin to slow the balance sheet shrinkage, keeping a close eye on bank reserves and the behavior of the federal funds market. The Fed halted the runoff in August, with total assets of about $3.75 trillion, down from $4.5 trillion at the start of rate increases in October 2017. Bank reserves fell by more, from a peak of $2.8 trillion in October 2014 to about $1.4 trillion by mid-September 2019. A Fed survey of banks found that the lowest comfortable level of reserves was about $900 billion. With ample reserves estimated to be $100 billion or so above the minimum comfort level, the supply of reserves seemed adequate.[27]

That conclusion proved incorrect. In September 2019, turmoil erupted in repo markets and the repo rate, which usually trades close to the federal funds rate, spiked as the FOMC was gathering. With the top of the funds rate target range at 2¼ percent, the repo rate jumped to as high as

10 percent. At Powell's regular post-meeting press conference on September 18, he attributed the repo rate spike to a sudden surge in the market demand for liquidity, driven by special factors, including securities dealers' need to finance an increased issuance of new debt from the Treasury. But the greater puzzle was why the spike in the repo rate had persisted. In principle, banks could have taken funds from their reserve accounts at the Fed, then paying just over 2 percent, to lend in the repo market, earning as much as 10 percent. That inflow of cash should in turn have reversed the rise in the repo rate. That banks did not do that suggested that the Fed had miscalculated. Perhaps because of concern about regulatory constraints, banks did *not* believe that they had sufficient reserves in September 2019, at least not enough to devote a portion to lending in the repo market. The Fed's balance sheet shrinkage, and the resulting decline in bank reserves, had gone too far.

The repo market, enormous and used widely by financial institutions, is a critical link in the transmission of the Fed's rate decisions to the broader economy. Fortunately, the Fed had the tools to restore its normal functioning. In the short term, taking the place of the reluctant banks, the Fed supplied funds to the repo market, taking Treasury securities as collateral. These operations were very similar to the traditional open-market operations under the scarce-reserves regime, but at a much larger scale; loans were also provided on a longer-term basis, as well as overnight. The operations worked, and the volatility in the repo market subsided.

In the longer term, the solution to the liquidity shortage was to expand the Fed's balance sheet again, thereby adding to bank reserves. In an inter-meeting announcement on October 11, the FOMC said that it would begin increasing reserves, and the balance sheet, by buying $60 billion of short-term Treasury securities a month, at least into the second quarter of 2020. Moreover, the New York Fed would continue to temporarily inject funds into the repo market. The FOMC's statement stressed that these actions were not a change in monetary policy—in particular, they were not QE because they did not involve purchases of longer-term securities—but were "purely technical measures." But the effect was significant. At the end of

January 2020, the balance sheet stood at nearly $4.2 trillion and bank reserves had risen to $1.6 trillion, an increase of $200 billion from mid-September. The Fed's interventions had restored stability to money markets, but the balance sheet reduction had ended decisively.* In the process of asserting control over short-term interest rates, the Fed also established a new normal for the size of its balance sheet.

---

* The FOMC in July 2021 announced a longer-term solution. It set up two standing repo facilities, one for primary dealers (and eventually other depository institutions) and one for foreign official institutions, such as other central banks. These facilities offer funds to borrowers in the repo market, with the goal of avoiding spikes in repo rates even if lenders in the market do not offer sufficient funds.

10

PANDEMIC

The flare-up in repo markets aside, the FOMC was upbeat as 2020 began. At his January 29 press conference, Powell noted that the economic expansion was in its record-breaking eleventh year, and that the unemployment rate (3.6 percent in December) remained at historic lows. Confident consumers were spending, uncertainty about trade seemed to have diminished, and global growth showed signs of stabilizing. FOMC participants' most recent projections of the funds rate (at the previous meeting in December) had shown a long policy pause and, by implication, an expected soft landing. At the median, participants projected no rate increases in 2020 and only one quarter-point rise in 2021 and one in 2022. Powell said no rate change should be expected "as long as incoming information about the economy remains broadly consistent" with the Committee's outlook.[1] In other words, monetary policy was on hold.

Then something changed. News of an outbreak of a novel coronavirus in Wuhan, China, had come at the start of the year. Powell noted that the outbreak posed some risk to the U.S. economy and that the Fed was "very carefully monitoring" the situation.[2] But the risks Powell seemed concerned about were indirect and limited. For example, illness and shutdowns in China might affect its trading partners, particularly nearby Asian countries. The Fed's assessment echoed most public health authorities, who through January and much of February largely downplayed the risks of infection spreading globally.

By late February, however, the situation was looking very different. On Sunday, February 23, Italy locked down eleven northern towns after a major outbreak of coronavirus cases, raising the specter of worldwide transmission. On February 25 the Centers for Disease Control and Prevention in Atlanta warned of the possibility of an outbreak in the United States. By Friday, February 28, "cases in 14 other countries . . . could be traced back to Italy,"[3] according to the *New York Times*, while California and Oregon identified cases whose sources were unknown. The virus was no longer somebody else's problem.

Financial markets plunged. In the last week of February, U.S. stocks registered their largest weekly decline since 2008, more than 12 percent. (By late March, the Dow would lose, cumulatively, more than a third of its value.) On February 28 the yield on ten-year Treasury notes slumped to its lowest level on record, 1.13 percent. It fell to 0.54 percent by March 9. The decline in Treasury yields suggested that, in a pattern often seen during crises, investors were flocking toward the perceived safe haven of U.S. government debt. On February 28 Powell released a four-sentence statement that cited the "evolving risks" of the coronavirus, and promised that the Fed would "use our tools and act as appropriate to support the economy."[4]

The unusual statement plus the phrase "act as appropriate" signaled that the FOMC might cut interest rates before its next scheduled meeting. And indeed, three days later, on the evening of March 2, the FOMC held an emergency intermeeting call and decided to cut the funds rate target by half a percentage point. In a rapidly scheduled press conference after the decision was announced the next morning, Powell said the fundamentals of the U.S. economy remained strong, but the risks to the outlook had changed enough to meet the standard set in October for a rate change. At that point, the reach of the epidemic and the amount of economic damage it might inflict remained unclear. Perhaps the effects would be confined to specific sectors, like tourism and travel. But perhaps it would force a much broader shutdown of the economy. In that case, lower interest rates could provide only indirect help, by supporting investor and business confidence and helping to maintain stable financial conditions. Nevertheless, with risks mounting and market signals flashing red, the FOMC did not want to wait.

In the weeks that followed, the virus's threat to the world economy became clearer. On March 11, the World Health Organization declared the COVID-19 outbreak a global pandemic, with 118,000 cases identified in 114 countries.[5] On the same day, President Trump announced that he would block travel to the United States from Europe. And Dr. Anthony Fauci, the long-serving director of the National Institute of Allergy and Infectious Diseases at the National Institutes of Health, told Congress, "It is going to get worse."[6] Several European countries instituted lockdowns—confining everyone except essential workers to their homes. Businesses and schools in the United States began to close, sending home employees and students until further notice. To slow transmission, U.S. public health officials recommended large-scale "social distancing"—staying home, avoiding large groups, keeping at least six feet away from other people. The hope was to "flatten the curve," that is, to slow the rate of new cases sufficiently to avoid overwhelming the health-care system. By late March, confirmed U.S. cases exceeded 100,000—up from about 1,000 a few weeks earlier—and states and cities began issuing formal "stay-at-home" orders. It would indeed get much worse, both in the United States and abroad.* A historic contraction in economic activity looked inevitable.

THE PANDEMIC PANIC

With economic risks surging, financial markets buckled, bringing back painful memories of the 2008 crisis. On March 9, and again on March 12, stock prices fell sharply enough to trigger circuit breakers (temporary

---

* According to the *New York Times*'s COVID-19 dashboard, worldwide cases early in 2022 would exceed 300 million and deaths would exceed 5 million. In the United States, cases exceeded 60 million and deaths exceeded 800,000.

emergency trading halts) on the New York Stock Exchange. Less visible to the public but perhaps even more dangerous were disruptions in the Treasury securities market. Investor demand for the perceived safety and liquidity of U.S. government debt had kept long-term Treasury yields low in February and early March, but, beginning March 9—a few days before the World Health Organization declared a global pandemic—conditions in the Treasury market suddenly deteriorated. Prices and yields swung wildly and liquidity evaporated, making it extremely difficult and costly to execute even modest-sized transactions. Measures of bond-market volatility reached their highest levels since the financial crisis, while the heavily used markets for derivatives linked to Treasuries nearly ceased functioning.

The near breakdown signaled an intensifying panic, triggered by grim news about the spread of the virus. Suddenly, everyone wanted to hold the shortest-term and safest assets—the "dash for cash," as Fed Vice Chair for Supervision Randy Quarles would call it—and the quickest way to get cash was to sell longer-term Treasuries, often held in reserve for that very purpose.[7] Banks needed cash to lend to worried businesses drawing down their prearranged credit lines. Financial-market traders and highly leveraged hedge funds needed cash to settle short-term debts or meet margin calls. Asset managers—including mutual funds that invest in relatively illiquid corporate bonds—needed cash to meet withdrawals by fearful investors. Insurance companies and other institutional investors wanted to hold more cash (instead of stocks and bonds) to reduce their overall exposure to risk. And foreign governments and central banks needed dollars to support their currencies in the foreign-exchange market or to lend to their own domestic banks.

Normally, when market participants sell Treasuries, market-making banks and dealers buy and hold the securities until other buyers can be found. But in March 2020 the market-making institutions were already struggling to manage large increases in new Treasury debt issued to finance the burgeoning budget deficit and were additionally constrained by capital regulations and their own self-imposed limits on risk-taking. They were overwhelmed by the flood of sell orders. With many sellers and almost no buyers, market conditions became chaotic.

The Treasury market disruptions reverberated throughout the financial system. Besides offering (under normal conditions) safety, liquidity, and a return, longer-term Treasuries play multiple roles in financial markets. They serve as the benchmark for yields on all types of securities, as collateral for raising cash or financing purchases of other assets, and as a tool to hedge financial risks. As panicked investors ran out of Treasuries to sell, they began to dump other longer-term securities, such as corporate debt, municipal bonds, and mortgage-backed securities. Rates jumped, liquidity dried up, and issuance collapsed in each of these critical markets. As they did after Lehman's failure in 2008, money market mutual funds began to experience runs, and the commercial paper market—on which many firms rely for short-term borrowing—showed signs of breaking down.

The market disruptions fueled fears about the ability of businesses, households, and local governments to access credit and repay their debts. The *Wall Street Journal* described the market turmoil of mid-March as even more intense than 2008 and wrote that "few realize how close to collapse the financial system came on March 16," a day on which the Dow fell nearly 13 percent. "The 2008 financial crisis was a car crash in slow motion. This was like, Boom!" Adam Lollos, the head of short-term credit at Citigroup, told the *Journal*.[8]

Heeding the lessons of 2008, the Fed quickly assumed its role of lender of last resort. It had been injecting funds into the markets since September, when turmoil hit the repo market, but had been in the process of scaling back before the pandemic hit. On March 12, the Fed reversed course, sharply increasing lending to inundated banks and dealers, taking Treasury securities as collateral. By March 16 the Open Market Desk at the New York Fed was offering $1 trillion in overnight loans each day, alongside another $1 trillion for longer terms. The day before, to further backstop the dealers and the Treasury market, the Fed had also begun to serve as a buyer of last resort, purchasing securities outright for its portfolio. In an action reminiscent of our purchases of MBS in 2008, the Fed announced it would buy at least $500 billion in Treasuries and $200 billion in MBS.

Foreign central banks and governments were major sellers of Treasuries in March, motivated in part by the need to alleviate dollar shortages in their own banking systems. (As in 2008, foreign banks still conducted much of their business in dollars.) And, as it had in the earlier crisis, the Fed became the world's dollar lender of last resort. Aiming to prevent strains overseas from exacerbating turmoil in U.S. markets, the Fed provided dollars to foreign central banks through swap lines, taking foreign currency as collateral. In the global financial crisis, the Fed had established swap lines with fourteen major foreign central banks. Five of those lines, with the most important foreign central banks, had been made permanent. On March 19, the Fed reestablished the nine additional lines it had used a dozen years earlier. By the end of April, foreign central banks had drawn more than $400 billion.[9] In addition, the Fed set up a special repo facility that allowed foreign authorities, including those without formal swap lines, to borrow dollars using Treasury securities as collateral, avoiding the need to sell the securities outright. The Fed made clear that all these operations—lending into repo markets and to dealers, direct purchases of Treasuries and MBS, and swap lines—would continue as long as necessary.

Meanwhile, the FOMC was trying to assess the economic effects of the pandemic. The shock was unprecedented, so uncertainty was high. The FOMC met (virtually) on Sunday, March 15, rather than waiting for its regularly scheduled meeting the following Tuesday and Wednesday. Instead of a single forecast, the staff provided two alternative scenarios.[10] Both saw the economy entering a recession in the second quarter as people socially distanced, stayed home from work, and cut back on spending. In the first scenario, the economy began a solid recovery in the third quarter—a so-called V-shaped recovery. In the second, the recession dragged on through the end of the year. Both scenarios saw a sharp increase in unemployment. Both also anticipated a near-term decline in inflation, resulting from weaker demand as people stayed home, lower oil prices, and a stronger dollar as investors sought a safe haven.

With the outlook continuing to deteriorate, the FOMC dropped the target range for the federal funds rate by a full percentage point (on top of the half a percentage point cut two weeks earlier) to 0–¼ percent, equal to its low point during the 2008 crisis. The Committee said rates would stay near zero until the Committee was "confident that the economy has weathered recent events and is on track to achieve its maximum employment and price stability goals." This guidance was qualitative and vague, reflecting the Committee's uncertainty about the likely depth and duration of the recession, but in his press conference Powell made clear that the FOMC expected to keep rates low for a long time. Powell also discussed the Fed's recently announced plans to purchase large quantities of Treasuries and MBS. The primary purpose, he explained, was to stabilize critical financial markets, not to signal a new round of quantitative easing. The new purchases were across a range of maturities, whereas the QE of the financial crisis era had focused on longer-term securities to put downward pressure on longer-term interest rates. But markets understood that the reinstitution of large-scale securities purchases, once market conditions improved, could set the foundation for a sustained QE program aimed at supporting economic recovery.

The Fed's response to the pandemic crisis was admirably swift and decisive, but the devastating effects of the virus would be by far the most important influence on the economy. Within a week of the March 15 meeting, economic activity was contracting at unprecedented speed. With more cities and states issuing stay-at-home orders, nonessential businesses were closing, sporting and entertainment events were suspended, and spending on travel and tourism was collapsing. The Labor Department would report that more than 3 million workers had filed new claims for unemployment insurance that week, nearly five times the highest weekly total during the Great Recession.

If the 2020 recession had a silver lining, it was that—in stark contrast to the Great Recession—the United States entered it with the banking system much better capitalized and more liquid than it had been in 2008. There would be no need for weekend interventions by the Fed and

Treasury to prop up failing institutions. Nevertheless, lenders faced enormous uncertainties in March 2020, including about the financial resilience not only of individual household and corporate borrowers but of entire industries. Would hotels, restaurants, shopping centers, and airlines return to more-or-less normal operations after the pandemic receded? Or would we enter a new world, in which residual fears of infection would forever change how we worked, shopped, and went to school? Evaluating credit risks in this environment seemed nearly impossible. In the shadow of this uncertainty, despite the banks' strong balance sheets, a freeze in new lending threatened to spread.

To promote credit and preserve confidence in the financial system, the Fed returned to its 2008 playbook, serving as a lender of last resort to both financial and nonfinancial firms. At its March 15 meeting, it had eased the terms at its discount window and encouraged banks to borrow. Within days, it announced it was reestablishing several more programs under the 13(3) emergency lending authority used in the financial crisis. Through the Commercial Paper Funding Facility, the Fed would again make short-term loans to businesses. The Primary Dealer Credit Facility would lend to securities dealers against a wide range of collateral. The Money Market Mutual Fund Liquidity Facility would help money funds raise the cash they needed to meet investor redemptions. (The facility provided credit to banks so they could purchase assets from the funds.) The following week, the Fed revived another emergency program, the Term Asset-Backed Securities Loan Facility, to support securitization of household and business credit. Because the legal and operational details of these programs did not need to be developed from scratch, the programs could be quickly implemented.

Perhaps most important for financial stability were the Fed's continued efforts to restore order in Treasury markets. On March 23 it announced that its purchases of Treasuries and GSE-issued MBS would become open ended, "in the amounts needed to support smooth market functioning and effective transmission of monetary policy." And it said, in addition to residential MBS, it would buy securities backed by mortgages on commercial real estate, which had come under heavy stress as shopping centers and offices closed during the lockdowns. Between the first week of March and late July, the Fed purchased almost $1.8 trillion in Treasuries and $600 billion in GSE-issued MBS, far exceeding all its other programs combined.

The Fed also used its regulatory powers to help calm markets. On April 1 it temporarily suspended a requirement that large banks hold a minimum level of capital against their holdings of Treasury securities and their reserves at the Fed. The change gave these banking organizations and their subsidiary dealer firms more capacity and incentive to make markets in Treasury securities, while avoiding the possibility that large increases in reserves—the result of the Fed's active securities purchases—would tie up bank capital that could otherwise be used to support lending or market-making.

Reflecting the pandemic's global impact, other major central banks also intervened forcefully. In March the Bank of England cut its policy rate to 0.1 percent, expanded its programs to encourage bank lending, and restarted its government bond purchases.[11] In addition, the Bank of England, in conjunction with the U.K. Treasury, established the Covid Corporate Financing Facility to provide direct short-term credit to businesses. The Bank of Japan also increased its asset purchases, including purchases of commercial paper and corporate bonds, and created a facility to encourage bank lending to businesses.[12]

The European Central Bank, under new president Christine Lagarde, was perhaps the most active foreign central bank.[13] The ECB did not reduce its policy rate, already at minus 0.50 percent, but it expanded its securities purchase programs dramatically. In March, it added a new pandemic emergency purchase program of 750 billion euros, increasing to 1.35 trillion euros in June, while also expanding its existing program.[14]

Importantly, the new emergency program was more flexible and aggressive than the ECB's earlier QE. During the European debt crisis, the ECB had sought to stabilize sovereign debt markets by purchasing, as early as 2010, the debt of troubled eurozone countries. But, as we've seen, it did not adopt full-bore U.S.-style QE, involving large-scale purchases of longer-term securities as a monetary policy tool, until January 2015. It had held off in response to political opposition from Germany and other northern European countries and because of concerns about potential legal challenges based on the European Union's founding treaty, which prohibited monetary financing of governments. When the ECB did begin QE, it had been careful to impose restrictions to reduce the political and legal risks, including ensuring that its purchases of government debt did not favor some eurozone countries over others. Under the pandemic-era program, in contrast, the timing and maturities of the ECB's securities purchases would be determined only by market and economic conditions, and without rigid requirements for which countries' debt could be purchased or in what proportions. In particular, in contrast to the ECB's regular QE programs, Greek debt would be eligible.

To stimulate private credit extension, the ECB also greatly expanded its bank lending subsidies in 2020, providing long-term funding at rates as low as minus 1 percent to banks that increased their loans to qualified borrowers.[15] The take-up by banks would be large. On the fiscal side, in a political breakthrough, European Union leaders in July agreed to collectively sponsor a 750-billion-euro rescue package to provide loans and grants to hard-hit member countries.[16] The pandemic had led the Europeans to adopt fiscal and monetary policy innovations that the global financial and sovereign debt crises had not.

THE CARES ACT

On March 27 President Trump signed a $2.2 trillion, bipartisan emergency fiscal package—the CARES Act (Coronavirus Aid, Relief, and Economic Security Act). Its premise was that, to beat the virus, much of the economy would have to be shut down for a while. The primary goals of the CARES Act were to help people and businesses survive the shutdown and to minimize unnecessary job losses and bankruptcies. It included about $500 billion in payments to individuals and families (reflecting both more-generous and inclusive unemployment insurance and direct payments of up to $1,200 per adult and $500 per child); $150 billion to state and local governments; $150 billion to support health-care systems; and $350 billion to fund the Paycheck Protection Program (PPP). The PPP, administered by the Small Business Administration, offered loans to businesses with 500 or fewer employees, loans that could be forgiven if the business maintained its payroll.

From the Fed's perspective the most relevant provision of the CARES Act was an allocation of $454 billion to backstop Fed emergency lending. During the financial crisis, the Fed had frequently used its lending authority under Section 13(3) of the Federal Reserve Act. The law restricted 13(3) lending to "unusual and exigent circumstances" and to borrowers that, due to market disruptions, could not obtain credit through normal channels. The 13(3) loans had to be sufficiently collateralized or secured so that the Fed could reasonably expect to be repaid. The 2010 Dodd-Frank Act, in reaction to our use of 13(3) authority in unpopular bailouts of AIG and other companies, had added further restrictions on the Fed's lending powers, including tougher collateral requirements and a prohibition on lending to a single borrower (facilities instead had to be designed to lend to a well-defined class that included at least five potential borrowers). The law also required the Fed to obtain the Treasury secretary's permission before opening a 13(3) program. At the time Dodd-Frank passed Congress, many veterans of the financial crisis, including me, had worried that the new constraints might hamper the Fed's lending powers in the next financial emergency.

However, in the CARES Act, Congress saw the Fed's lending authority as a way to help the economy weather the pandemic. Its $454 billion appropriation enabled the Treasury Department to offer what amounted to a backstop for new 13(3) programs established by the Fed. So long as the Treasury's contributions were large enough to absorb any expected losses, the Fed could lend to risky borrowers and remain in compliance with the 13(3) requirement that it expect to be fully repaid. From Congress's perspective, this had advantages. Since the appropriated Treasury backstop would cover only potential losses, not the total amount lent, going through the Fed had a multiplier effect. Based on the $454 billion Treasury allocation, the Fed estimated that it could provide at least $2.3 trillion in loans.

Additional advantages, from Congress's perspective, were the Fed's expertise in financial and credit markets and its reputation for nonpartisanship and political independence—an important consideration in light of Democrats' distrust of the Trump administration.

Congress's embrace gave the Fed powerful new tools to fight the pandemic crisis but also posed risks to the institution. If the programs failed, the Fed's reputation and political standing would suffer. If they succeeded, would Congress seek to erode the Fed's independence in the future by ordering it to lend to favored beneficiaries outside of emergencies? The Fed also faced difficult technical challenges in setting up brand-new lending programs on an expedited schedule. Still, the Fed had good reasons to go along—most importantly, because the pandemic posed a dire threat to its economic goals and to financial stability. Moreover, the bill left the Fed, in consultation with the Treasury, the final say on the design of its programs, including the terms of the loans and who would be eligible to borrow. And the legal requirements that 13(3) lending was permissible only under "unusual and exigent circumstances" and when credit markets were dysfunctional would give the Fed a strong basis for insisting that the programs end when the emergency ended. The Powell Fed accepted the assignment and plunged into developing lending facilities—including, significantly, programs for nonfinancial borrowers—whose scope went well beyond what the Fed did in the global financial crisis.

Broadly, three types of borrowers were eligible for Fed loans under the CARES Act programs: corporations, state and local (municipal) governments, and medium-sized businesses. The Fed both lent directly and supported corporate and municipal debt markets by buying existing bonds from investors. The corporate and municipal programs were remarkably successful, swiftly restoring those markets to normal functioning. Even before the Fed made a single loan or purchased a single bond, the mere announcement of the facilities reduced interest-rate spreads and increased issuance in corporate and municipal markets to close-to-normal levels. The assurance that the Fed would stand ready to lend if no one else did gave investors the confidence to return to the market.

The remarkable power of the Fed's announcements recalled European Central Bank President Mario Draghi's 2012 promise that the ECB would "do whatever it takes" to preserve the euro. To make good on Draghi's promise to buy the sovereign debt of troubled countries if needed, the ECB had announced a new program, called Outright Monetary Transactions. However, the ECB never had to purchase a single government bond under that program. The announcement alone restored confidence, sharply reducing the interest rates paid by troubled eurozone countries almost overnight. The Fed's corporate and municipal programs had similar effects, achieving their goals even though actual lending would ultimately be far below their capacity. More generally, the Fed's interventions from March on, including its purchases of Treasuries and MBS, helped persuade investors to take risks again. That included investors in the stock market, which by midsummer had fully recovered from its earlier plunge and continued to rise from there.

Lending to medium-sized firms—a varied group of businesses, most with no access to stock or bond markets—proved a much tougher challenge. The Fed announced its Main Street Lending Program on April 9, backed by $75 billion from the Treasury.* The Fed decided to rely on commercial banks to evaluate and make the loans, subject to terms the Fed set. The rationale was that banks have far more information than the Fed has about potential borrowers, as well as the staff and experience needed to make what was expected to be many relatively small loans. The Fed would then buy a 95 percent share of each loan, removing most of the lending banks' risk, while the banks' 5 percent remaining share would give them an incentive to make good loans. The goal was to give medium-sized firms, on reasonable terms, the credit they needed to survive the partial shutdown of the economy. Nonprofit organizations would later be eligible as well. Unlike the PPP for smaller businesses, Main Street loans were not

---

* "Main Street" was a bit of a misnomer, as firms employing up to 10,000 workers or with annual revenues of less than $2.5 billion—later increased to 15,000 workers and $5 billion in revenue—were eligible to borrow. Smaller businesses were covered by other programs, such as PPP. The Fed backstopped the latter program by lending to banks making PPP loans, accepting the loans—which were guaranteed by the Small Business Administration—at face value as collateral.

forgivable, although the allowed repayment periods were long—four years at first, later extended to five years.

Setting the terms of Main Street loans was tricky. They had to be generous enough to attract borrowers, who in many cases probably needed grants (that did not need to be repaid) rather than loans to survive. At the same time, the terms had to make lending attractive for banks—who bore the costs of making and servicing the loans, as well as holding 5 percent of the risk—while also being tough enough to limit expected losses to the Treasury, which generally took a conservative attitude toward risk. Meeting these conditions, while making the facility flexible enough to accommodate different types of businesses and nonprofit organizations with varied financial structures and banking relationships, was difficult. The rollout of the Main Street facility was slow; it did not open for lender registration until June 15. Just a week before the opening, the Fed liberalized the terms for borrowers by lowering the minimum loan amount, raising the maximum loan, increasing the length of loans, and delaying principal repayments for two years instead of one. On October 30 the Fed eased terms again, lowering the minimum loan amount to $100,000. However, participation by both banks and borrowers remained disappointing.

Congress's big fiscal program and the Fed's actions reduced the pandemic's economic damage by protecting Americans' incomes and access to credit. But a sharp recession was unavoidable. The National Bureau of Economic Research (NBER) dated the start of the pandemic recession to February 2020, ending a 128-month expansion, the longest in the history of U.S. business cycles dating to 1854. Real output in the second quarter would suffer the sharpest decline, by far, in U.S. history.*

The job market suffered dramatic losses. Even when not subject to official lockdowns, many people chose to stay at home for fear of catching the virus. About a third of workers were able to do their jobs remotely, but most

---

* As deep as the contraction was, it would prove short, with the economy growing again by April. The NBER would later declare that the recession (the period of contraction) lasted only two months. That too would set a record, as the shortest recession in U.S. history.

could not. Unemployment soared from a fifty-year low of 3.5 percent in February to 14.7 percent in April, the highest on record since the start of the collection of monthly data in 1948. Even this figure was an underestimate: Because of the difficulties of determining who was employed during the general shutdown, the "true" unemployment rate was probably much higher than the official rate, as the Bureau of Labor Statistics (BLS), which produces the unemployment statistics, conceded. In an alternative calculation that attempted to correct for undercounts of laid-off workers, the BLS found that "true" unemployment could have been as high as 19.7 percent in April. In that one month alone, payrolls declined by a staggering 20.7 million jobs, or more than 13 percent of the workers employed in March.

The pandemic recession was unusual in ways other than its source and its severity. Unlike a typical recession, which hits manufacturing and housing the hardest, this time service industries, which require personal contact—such as "brick-and-mortar" retail, travel and tourism, and bars and restaurants—were hurt most. Because those industries employ many women, minorities, and lower-paid workers, those groups were disproportionately affected, even more than in a typical recession. Some would describe the recession as "K-shaped," meaning that better-off people did unusually well while people with lower incomes bore the brunt.

Following its dramatic steps in March, the FOMC went into wait-and-see mode on monetary policy. The Committee discussed additional policy options but took no action, citing high uncertainty. Also, at that point it was not clear that monetary policy could do much more than it had already done—primarily, stabilizing financial and credit markets and ensuring easy financial conditions. With the virus raging, would small changes in interest rates encourage people to shop more, or businesses to invest or hire more? Given the health risks of engaging in normal economic activity such as clothes shopping and dining out, were those outcomes even desirable? In a speech on May 13, Powell repeated what would become a mantra of his, that "the Fed has lending powers, not spending powers."[17] He urged Congress and the administration to consider providing more fiscal support for humanitarian reasons and to avoid long-term economic damage, or "scarring," that can arise for example from the shutdowns of many small businesses, the severing of relationships between firms and their workers, and the loss of skills and labor market connections among the unemployed. President Trump, who had consistently emphasized a more optimistic economic outlook than Powell, spoke to reporters the same day. He did not weigh in on Powell's call for more federal spending but did grudgingly acknowledge the Fed's efforts that spring. "He has done a very good job over the last couple of months," Trump said. "I call him my 'M.I.P.'—most improved player." [18]

The economy looked somewhat better in late April and May, as state and city governments began phasing out stay-at-home orders. In May, 2.8 million jobs were regained with the official unemployment rate falling to 13.2 percent, or 16.3 percent on an adjusted basis. The recovery continued over the summer. The economy added 6.6 million more jobs in June and July and the official unemployment rate fell to 10.2 percent.

But total payrolls nevertheless remained far below, and the unemployment rate far above, the levels achieved before the pandemic. Over the summer and fall, new waves of infections slowed the recovery and kept many schools and businesses closed. Powell, in press conferences and testimony, continued to emphasize the longer-run risks of an incomplete and uneven recovery. Although careful to defer to Congress on the details, Powell also began to stress that the earlier strong fiscal support would fall short of what was needed.

As the November presidential election approached, Congress and the administration stalemated on fiscal action. Among other disagreements, Democrats pushed for, and the administration and many Republicans resisted, providing more aid to state and local governments, many of whose revenues were being severely hurt by the downturn's effect on sales and income taxes. State and local cutbacks had slowed the recovery from the Great Recession, and Fed policymakers worried that would happen again.

Despite the many concerns, the economy made up a good deal of lost ground in the third quarter. After the sharp declines in March and April, real output in the second quarter of 2020 fell about 9 percent below the corresponding quarter in 2019. By contrast, third-quarter output surged back to a level only about 3 percent below a year earlier. Unemployment also continued to decline, reaching an official rate of 6.7 percent in November. The Fed's easy monetary policy helped the recovery, by promoting a strong housing market (with mortgage rates at record lows) and increasing the demand for big-ticket consumer purchases, such as automobiles. Still, the economy remained far from normal. Through November it had only regained a little more than half of the 22 million jobs lost in March and April. Moreover, a resurgence of the virus and the waning of fiscal support slowed growth over the winter. Payrolls actually declined in December and grew only modestly in January.

A NEW POLICY FRAMEWORK

The advent of the pandemic had delayed the Fed's ongoing review of its monetary policy framework, tools, and communications. However, by late August 2020, at an online version of the Jackson Hole conference, Powell announced important changes to the framework that would have almost immediate effects on the Fed's monetary response to the crisis.[19]

The strategy review, launched in November 2018 under much more favorable conditions, had been motivated by longer-term changes to the economic and policy environment. A sustained decline in the neutral rate of interest, which had apparently continued after the global financial crisis, had reduced the scope for monetary policymakers to cut short-term interest rates in recessions. This limit on the monetary policy response to downturns risked more-frequent and more-extended periods of high unemployment and low inflation. More benignly, the downward drift in the natural rate of unemployment, a flatter Phillips curve, and well-anchored inflation expectations looked to have given the Fed more room to push for a "hot" labor market with less concern about too-high inflation. As Powell noted in his speech, participants in the Fed Listens events the Fed held around the country had emphasized the substantial and widespread benefits of a strong labor market, particularly for minorities, less experienced or lower-skilled workers, and people from low- and moderate-income communities. Maximum employment should therefore be thought of as a "broad-based and inclusive goal" for the Fed, Powell said.

As a result of its review, the FOMC approved two principal changes to its policy framework. First, in pursuing its inflation goal, the Committee would henceforth try to make up for past undershoots (though not overshoots) of the inflation target. If inflation ran below 2 percent for a time, as it had through most of the expansion following the Great Recession, the Committee would compensate by allowing inflation to run "moderately above 2 percent for some time." The goal of the new approach would be to keep inflation near target *on average*. In contrast, in the traditional inflation-targeting approach, policymakers ignored the size or duration of past misses and tried to reach the target over time—letting bygones be bygones.

Powell dubbed the new makeup strategy "flexible average inflation targeting," or FAIT.* It was flexible in several senses. In keeping with the dual mandate and the approach we adopted in 2012, it would require the Committee to take account of employment as well as inflation. It would also be flexible in that no precise formula would be given to describe the new overshooting policy. For example, the Committee did not specify the period over which the inflation rate would be averaged. Nor did it provide numerical definitions of "moderately above 2 percent" or "for some time." The definition of these terms would depend on the economic outlook and the Committee's judgment. As is often the case in central-bank communication, the lack of specificity simultaneously preserved policy flexibility

---

* Flexible average inflation targeting, as augmented by the FOMC's September 2020 guidance, is very close to a strategy that I proposed in 2017, called temporary price-level targeting (Bernanke, 2017a, b). Bernanke, Kiley, and Roberts (2019) showed that temporary price-level targeting can improve economic performance when the effective lower bound constrains policy, even if the strategy is only understood by and credible to financial market participants, and not the general public. Chicago Fed President Charles Evans had earlier made a similar proposal (Evans, 2012). This approach is discussed further in Chapter 13.

and scope for judgment while increasing the risk of miscommunication or misunderstanding by markets.

If understood and believed by the markets, Powell argued, flexible average inflation targeting should help monetary policymakers overcome the constraint imposed by the effective lower bound. In particular, the FOMC's commitment to allow inflation to overshoot the 2 percent target after a period below target amounts to a promise that interest rates will be kept "lower for longer" as the economy recovers from a period of low inflation and employment. The lower-for-longer commitment, if credible, should put downward pressure on longer-term interest rates, adding to economic stimulus even if short rates are at the lower bound. Moreover, by keeping inflation near 2 percent on average, the new approach should help keep the inflation expectations of households and businesses well anchored near the target. Well-anchored inflation expectations make controlling inflation easier and help keep interest rates from falling too low, preserving space for rate cuts in downturns. In contrast, under a traditional inflation-targeting approach—because of the constraint of the lower bound on monetary policy—frequent shortfalls of inflation below 2 percent could result in average inflation, and ultimately, inflation expectations, falling dangerously below the FOMC's target.

The second major change to the Fed's framework was a more proactive approach to ensuring full employment. In his speech, Powell said that monetary policy would henceforth respond only to *shortfalls* of employment from its maximum level, rather than to *deviations* (either shortfalls or overshoots) from that level. In other words, the FOMC would no longer tighten policy simply in response to low or falling unemployment—unless there also were "signs of unwanted increases in inflation" or other risks, to financial stability for example.

Since William McChesney Martin, Fed chairs had often opted for pre-emptive strikes on inflation, beginning policy tightening before the preconditions for higher inflation—including an overheated labor market—are in place. The rationale was that monetary policy works with a lag, and in waiting too long the Committee risked "falling behind the curve" on inflation, forcing it to play catch-up with rapid rate increases later. Under this second change to its framework, the FOMC would effectively end pre-emptive strikes. It would no longer tighten policy based solely on the presumption that low unemployment today must lead to high inflation tomorrow.

The new approach reflected the FOMC's increased focus on the high uncertainty surrounding estimates of the natural rate of unemployment, u*, cited by Powell in his "navigating by the stars" speech at Jackson Hole in 2018. For pre-emptive strikes on inflation to be well timed and effective, policymakers need a reasonably good estimate of the natural rate. Otherwise, the Phillips-curve models used to forecast inflation likely would not be accurate, as was apparent in the years before the pandemic. In its new strategy the FOMC agreed to take a more agnostic view about u*. It would push for lower unemployment until inflation or other signs of overheating provided tangible evidence that maximum employment had been reached. Undeniably, that strategy would carry some risk that inflation would rise too high, forcing a sharp policy response. But the FOMC saw that risk as limited by the flat Phillips curve and well-anchored inflation expectations. And it saw substantial benefits in both pushing for a stronger labor market and avoiding the too-low inflation that has plagued Europe and Japan.

To formalize its new strategy, the Committee unanimously voted to amend its Statement on Longer-Run Goals and Policy Strategy (first published in 2012 as part of the introduction of the inflation target) and said it would review its policy framework every five years.* In his August speech, Powell did not specify the policy actions that would follow in the near term. However, additional guidance came at the next FOMC meeting, in

---

* In July 2021, the European Central Bank also updated its monetary policy strategy, after a year-and-a-half review. But it did not go as far as the Fed. It jettisoned its previous description of its inflation objective as "below, but close to, 2 percent." Instead of viewing 2 percent as a ceiling, it said it would aim for 2 percent inflation over the medium term and would view undershoots and overshoots of its target as equally undesirable. It would also continue to use inflation forecasts in determining when to tighten policy. The new ECB strategy was influenced by the Fed's changes but more closely resembled the Fed's pre-2020 symmetric "bygones" strategy than its new approach.

September, when the Committee said it intended to keep rates near zero until three conditions had been met: that labor market conditions were consistent with the Committee's assessment of full employment, that inflation had risen to 2 percent, and that inflation "is on track to moderately exceed 2 percent for some time." The Committee's rate projections released at that meeting revealed that most FOMC participants did not expect all these conditions to be met for three years or more.

In December, the Committee also provided guidance about its plans for securities purchases, promising to increase its Treasury and MBS holdings by at least $120 billion per month "until substantial further progress has been made toward the Committee's maximum employment and price stability goals." "Substantial further progress" was not defined, a surprising omission given that very similar language had contributed to the 2013 taper tantrum, when missed signals between the Fed and the markets had led to sharp increases in yields and volatility. However, relative to 2013, the Committee seemed more united in its willingness to persist with QE, and it promised to give markets plenty of warning before slowing its purchases. Overall, by the end of 2020, the Fed's message was that monetary policy was likely to remain easy for quite a while.

The Fed's new framework, and the easier policies it implied, were not immediately matched by new fiscal action. However, Democrat Joe Biden was elected president in November, with effective control of both houses of Congress; and in December the lame-duck Congress passed a new fiscal aid package exceeding $900 billion. Even more important, the development of several effective vaccines raised hopes for controlling the pandemic.

The Fed's lending facilities authorized by the CARES Act came up for renewal on December 31, and Treasury Secretary Mnuchin opted to let them expire. Powell signaled his reluctance in a statement but agreed to return the Treasury's contributions and to stop making new loans and securities purchases from those facilities. Congress, as part of the December fiscal package, confirmed Mnuchin's decision but also specified that the Fed's 13(3) authorities would not be further constrained, relative to where they stood before the pandemic. The 13(3) facilities not supported by CARES Act funding, such as the commercial paper program, remained open for the time being. Likely believing that the facilities could be quickly restarted in a new emergency, market participants took the closings calmly. The market reaction was consistent with the conclusion that it was not the actual lending through CARES Act facilities that was important—the amounts lent were very small compared to the facilities' theoretical $2.3 trillion capacity—but the demonstration that the Fed and Treasury stood ready to provide a backstop to dysfunctional markets. In June 2021 the Fed would announce its intention to sell the corporate bonds it had acquired through its CARES Act facilities.

The Biden administration took office in January 2021—with Janet Yellen as Treasury secretary—and wasted little time in passing the $1.9 trillion American Rescue Plan in March to provide additional support for households, businesses, and state and local governments. This powerful new dose of fiscal relief, together with earlier fiscal actions and pent-up consumer demand—by some estimates Americans accumulated more than $2 trillion in extra savings during the pandemic—provided impetus for new spending and job creation in the early months of 2021. In addition, by early summer, a national vaccination program had reached most adults who wanted to get a shot, although vaccine skeptics and refusers remained a significant minority.

The stage seemed set for an economic boom. At their June 2021 meeting, FOMC participants projected that the unemployment rate would fall to 4.5 percent by the fourth quarter, with growth for the year at a robust 7 percent. Employment grew rapidly over the summer, with nearly a million jobs added in each of June and July. Following through on their new framework and policy guidance, the FOMC kept rates near zero and continued securities purchases.

Despite the powerful fiscal and monetary tailwinds, however, the recovery would not be as smooth as hoped. By the end of 2021, the unemployment rate had fallen to 3.9 percent, but only because many potential workers remained out of the labor force. Total employment, despite the summer gains, remained nearly 3.6 million jobs below its pre-pandemic peak. An uneven recovery, with some sectors reopening more quickly than others and many people slow to return to work, led to mismatches between employers' needs and the availability of workers, resulting in the odd juxtaposition of a shortfall of millions of jobs and widespread employer complaints of worker shortages. Factors depressing labor supply included closed schools and lack of childcare, which prevented some parents from returning to work; reduced immigration; and government benefits that gave people without jobs more time to search for a good match. Still-present health risks also made potential workers cautious, especially when new virus variants—notably the Delta variant in the summer and the Omicron variant later in the year—fueled a renewed surge in U.S. COVID-19 cases over the summer. (Because of the risks posed by the variant, the Fed's 2021 Jackson Hole meeting was held virtually, for the second year in a row.) And, perhaps after a year and a half away from regular work routines, many people were reconsidering their choices of careers and the balance between work and other activities, including schooling, staying home with children, or retiring.

Inflation posed another, increasingly worrying, threat. Some economists, including Larry Summers, Olivier Blanchard (the former chief economist of the IMF), and Jason Furman (former head of Obama's CEA), voiced their concerns that the combination of powerful fiscal stimulus, accumulated household savings, and easy monetary policy would overheat the economy, leading either to the return of 1970s-style inflation or to a hasty tightening by the Fed that would disrupt the economy and markets. Inflation did pick up much faster than FOMC participants had expected, with core PCE inflation over the prior twelve months approaching 5 percent by late 2021. (As measured by the better-known consumer price index, inclusive of food and energy prices, inflation that month reached a shocking nearly 40-year high of 7 percent.)

By mid-2021, Fed officials had acknowledged that inflation was moving higher than they had anticipated but argued that the surge was largely the result of temporary factors related to the reopening of the economy, including the reversal of price declines in sectors hit hard during the pandemic (hotel rates, airfares), supply-chain bottlenecks (such as a global shortage of computer chips that slowed automobile production, pushing up the prices of new and used cars), and increases in the prices of oil and some other commodities as economic activity resumed.

Moreover, Fed officials argued, there were also important differences between 2021 and the inflationary 1960s and 1970s. Given that, before the pandemic struck, unemployment had been as low as 3.5 percent without generating inflation pressures, it was unlikely that the Committee was underestimating the natural rate of unemployment to the extent that policymakers of the earlier era had. The supply shocks of 2021, including the disruptions to supply chains and to labor supply, seemed likely to ease with the passage of time and better control of the virus. And the Federal Reserve of 2021 was better positioned than it had been in the 1960s and 1970s, with inflation expectations better anchored and closely monitored and its policy independence not in question. Supporting the Fed's view that the inflation surge was likely to be temporary, medium-term inflation expectations (as measured by surveys of households and businesses and the yields on inflation-indexed government bonds) generally remained moderate in 2021 despite the pickup in the rate of price increases.

Nevertheless, the unexpectedly high inflation readings caused rising anxiety on the FOMC and in the White House, and the Committee shifted toward an increasingly hawkish posture as the year went on. The September 2021 dot plot showed half the Committee—nine participants—anticipating that the first rate increase would occur by the end of 2022 (up from four in March and seven in June), and the minutes of the July meeting reported that many participants expected the tapering of asset purchases to begin "this year."[20] The beginning of the taper was indeed announced in November, and, at the December meeting, the Committee sped up the process, putting asset purchases on pace to end by March 2022. The announcement opened the possibility of rate rises beginning as early as March. The December 2021 dot plot showed all eighteen FOMC participants anticipating at least one rate increase by the end of 2022, and twelve participants expecting at least three rate increases.

Overall, the highly unusual recovery from the pandemic recession posed a difficult test for the Fed's new framework. The record fiscal stimulus, the uneven reopening, and the unusual behavior of both employment and inflation made forecasting and public communication particularly challenging. Medium-term inflation expectations seemed well controlled, but, depending on how people interpreted the burst of inflation in 2021, the possibility that inflation expectations would become unanchored—leading in turn to more-sustained inflation—could not be ruled out. Under its FAIT framework, the FOMC had sought a temporary overshoot of its inflation target. The risk was that the overshoot would go too far and persist for too long. Avoiding that outcome would test both the Fed's forecasting ability and its credibility.

Powell's term was due to end in early 2022. He was widely praised by both Democrats and Republicans for his handling of monetary policy before and during the pandemic, for his response to the March 2020 panic, and for his leadership and political skills. A monetary novice when he joined the Board, as chair he had proved a consummate 21st century central banker, proactively deploying a wide range of tools and strategies that his 20th century predecessors would not have anticipated. He had also made the Fed more open, reaching out to broad audiences in his press conferences and through programs like Fed Listens.

Nevertheless, reappointment was not a certainty. Senator Elizabeth Warren (D-Massachusetts) led criticism from the left that Powell had not been aggressive enough in regulatory matters, and the revelation that some FOMC participants had made questionable securities trades during 2020 threatened to tarnish the image of institutional integrity that Powell had tried to project.

Three days before Thanksgiving, President Biden announced he would nominate Powell as chair. Lael Brainard, the only remaining Obama nominee on the Board, was nominated to be vice chair, replacing Clarida, whose term would end in early 2022. Brainard had emerged as a serious contender for the top spot. Although her monetary policy views were similar to Powell's, progressive Democrats saw her as tougher on financial regulation and on climate issues. In choosing Powell, Biden opted for continuity and for returning to the tradition of reappointing successful Fed leaders of the opposite party. The president followed his nominations of Powell and Brainard by nominating Sarah Bloom Raskin, a former Board member and Treasury official, to serve as vice chair for supervision, and named economists Lisa Cook and Philip Jefferson to the two remaining vacant seats on the Board.

To be given four more years as chair was gratifying, but Powell would have no time for a victory lap. Confronted by high inflation and economic threats posed by new variants of the virus, Powell and his colleagues would once again have to find a way to bring the economy to a soft landing.

PART IV

21st CENTURY MONETARY POLICY

■

What Lies Ahead

11

THE FED'S POST-2008 TOOLKIT

Quantitative Easing and Forward Guidance

TWENTY-FIRST CENTURY MONETARY POLICYMAKERS face a different world than their 20th century predecessors—a "new normal," in which inflation that is too low can be as concerning as inflation that is too high, and in which a low neutral interest rate, by limiting the space for short-term rate cuts, severely reduces the potency of traditional monetary policies. What options do policymakers have for responding to these challenges? During and after the 2007–2009 financial crisis, the Federal Reserve (and other major central banks) used two alternative tools after conventional rate cuts were exhausted: large-scale quantitative easing to lower longer-term interest rates and increasingly explicit forward guidance, aimed at influencing financial conditions by shaping market expectations of future monetary policy. During the pandemic the Federal Reserve and many other central banks again leaned heavily on these tools.

How well do these alternative tools work? What costs and risks do they create? With neutral interest rates much lower than in the past, will QE and forward guidance be enough? When we introduced these tools at the Fed during the financial crisis, we were forced to make our best guesses, based on the evidence available. Now, with considerable experience behind us, both in the United States and abroad, we know much more about these tools and how to use them.

The bottom line is that the bulk of the evidence—derived from both formal research and practical experience—confirms the effectiveness of the alternative monetary policy tools adopted after 2008. They add significant stimulative power when short rates can be cut no further, and, importantly, their side effects are manageable. They have thus, appropriately, become permanent additions to the monetary policy toolkit, both in the United States and in an increasing number of other economies. On the other hand, the Fed's post-2008 tools are unlikely to be sufficient in all circumstances, particularly in very severe recessions or when the neutral interest rate is quite low. This naturally raises the question of what else might be done to make monetary policy, and economic stabilization policy more generally, more consistently effective.

QUANTITATIVE EASING

The term *quantitative easing* has been used to describe different types of programs. Here I'll define QE as large-scale purchases by the central bank of longer-term securities, aimed at reducing longer-term interest rates, easing financial conditions, and, ultimately, achieving macroeconomic objectives such as full employment and price stability.

This definition excludes, for example, the Bank of Japan's securities purchases begun in 2001. Although that program was the first to be called "quantitative easing" and did have macroeconomic objectives—mainly, the conquest of deflation—it involved mostly purchases of shorter-term securities and was intended to increase bank reserves and the money supply, rather than reduce longer-term interest rates. (The Japanese were relying on a flawed and over-simplified monetarist doctrine that posits a direct relationship between the money supply and prices.) My definition of QE also excludes securities purchases narrowly aimed at stabilizing particular financial markets, such as the European Central Bank's targeted purchases of troubled countries' debt during the European sovereign debt crisis or the Powell Fed's purchases of Treasury securities and government-guaranteed MBS in its role as buyer of last resort in March 2020. As the last example illustrates, however, a purchase program that begins as a market stabilization measure can evolve into a tool of economic stabilization as well, so the line between the two types of programs is not always sharp.

At the time of its introduction in the United States, QE was something of a last-ditch measure, with great uncertainty about both its likely effectiveness and its possible costs and risks. It also faced intense political criticism. Nevertheless, as QE proved to be useful without dire side effects, its acceptance grew. Strikingly, nearly $5 trillion in large-scale securities purchases by the Powell Fed during the pandemic recession and recovery received relatively little pushback from members of Congress or others. Likewise, the pandemic emergency triggered new securities purchases by the Bank of England and the European Central Bank, programs that were broadly supported within those institutions and accepted by politicians and the public. (The Bank of Japan, which had never ended its asset purchases, continued them throughout the period.) And central banks that had not used QE at all during the global financial crisis or the Great Recession—including the Bank of Canada, the Reserve Bank of Australia, and even some developing-economy central banks—adopted the tool during the pandemic.[*]

How Does QE Work?

Economists have extensively debated how QE works—and, indeed, if it works at all. When the FOMC first began discussing securities purchases, some economists argued that QE—which, after all, is simply a swap of one set of financial assets (bank reserves) for another (longer-term securities)—should have little or no effect on asset prices or the economy.[1] As I would put it in 2014, "The problem with QE is it works in practice, but it doesn't work in theory."[2]

But QE does indeed appear to work in practice, affecting financial markets—and, through them, the economy—via two broad channels:

---

[*] Rebucci, Hartley, and Jiménez (2020) study pandemic-era QE announcements in twenty-one countries. They find that QE has not lost effectiveness in advanced economies and that its impact on long-term bond yields is actually much stronger in emerging markets.

the portfolio-balance channel and the signaling channel.[3] We actively discussed both channels—which are complements, not alternatives—as we planned the Fed's first QE in 2008 and 2009.

The *portfolio-balance channel* is the intuitive idea that central-bank purchases of longer-term securities reduce the supply of those securities held by the public, driving their prices up and their yields down. The underlying premise is that many investors care not only about the risks and expected returns of their financial assets, but also about other features of those assets. If people are indifferent between apples and pears—a fruit is a fruit—then changes in the relative supplies of apples and pears will not affect their prices. But if some people prefer the tang of apples and others like the sweetness of pears, then a reduction in the supply of pears will raise the price of pears relative to the price of apples. By the same token, if some investors have *preferred habitats*—that is, because of specialized expertise, transactions costs, regulations, liquidity or maturity preferences, or other reasons, they prefer to hold certain classes of assets—then changes in the relative supplies of those assets will affect their prices.[*]

Many investors do prefer specific classes of assets, for reasons other than risk and return alone. For example, pension fund managers, knowing they will have to make fixed payments to retired workers far in the future, prefer long-maturity assets that pay safe and predictable returns, like long-term government debt. Money market mutual funds primarily hold short-term liquid assets, like Treasury bills and high-grade commercial paper, to satisfy regulators and because they can be sold easily to meet unexpected withdrawals by their shareholders. Investment banks tend to hold assets, such as Treasuries and MBS, that are easily used as collateral for short-term borrowing, and so on.

In its QE, the Fed bought large quantities of longer-term Treasury

---

[*] This is not quite the end of the story, since even if some investors have motives other than risk and return for holding certain assets, others may not. The latter group has an incentive to buy higher-yielding assets and sell lower-yielding assets, thus arbitraging away some of the effects of QE. However, as shown for example by Vayanos and Vila (2021), these effects will be limited if, realistically, arbitrageurs are unwilling or unable to take on unlimited amounts of risk.

securities and government-guaranteed MBS, usually paying for them by creating bank reserves.* Just as the relative price of pears rises when the supply
declines, central-bank purchases that reduce the net supply of longer-term
Treasuries or MBS should cause investors to bid up their prices. Moreover,
as investors who sell Treasuries or MBS move into similar securities, such
as high-quality, longer-term corporate debt, their prices should be bid up as
well. Again, bidding up the price of a security is the same as bidding down
its yield, which moves inversely to price. This is the essence of the portfolio-
balance channel: QE's ability to influence longer-term yields by forcing
investors to adjust their holdings in response to changes in the supply of
different assets. Even with short-term rates stuck at zero, QE enabled policymakers to reduce longer-term rates, which, in the United States at least,
remained well above zero (indeed, above 1.5 percent) throughout the Great
Recession and the subsequent recovery.

A caveat to this intuitive argument is that the outstanding supply of
U.S. Treasuries and MBS is huge—trillions of dollars. Federal government
deficits during and after the financial crisis further increased the supply of
Treasuries, including longer-term securities. Consequently, to move longer-
term interest rates by enough to make a difference to the economy, the
Fed and other major central banks had to purchase enormous quantities.
For example, when the Fed concluded QE3 in October 2014, its total net
securities purchases under all its QE programs were about $3.8 trillion. Its
holdings of Treasury securities, at about $2.5 trillion in October 2014, were
about 37 percent of the U.S. government debt held by the public. The Fed's
securities holdings took another major step up as the Powell Fed responded
to the pandemic recession. Figure 11.1 shows the evolution of the Fed's
holdings of Treasury securities and MBS since 2007.

Besides its effects on the relative supply of securities in private hands,
QE also works through what has become known as the *signaling channel*. The announcement of a large QE program can strongly signal that

---

* In its Maturity Extension Program, the Fed paid for its purchases of longer-term Treasuries by
selling or redeeming shorter-term Treasuries from its portfolio, rather than by creating bank reserves.

FIGURE 11.1.   THE FEDERAL RESERVE'S SECURITIES HOLDINGS, 2007–2021

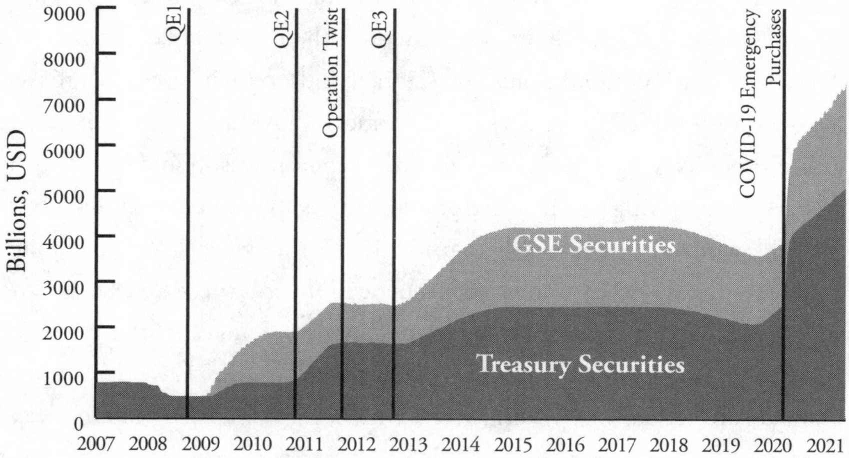

The figure shows Federal Reserve holdings of Treasuries and GSE-issued securities. Vertical lines show announcements of securities purchase programs. Source: Federal Reserve and FRED.

policymakers are committed to keeping policy easy and short-term rates low for a long time. Various explanations have been proposed for why QE seems to send this message of continued policy ease more convincingly than words alone. Some economists have noted that a big QE program is potentially costly for a central bank as an institution. It invites political criticism and risks capital losses if longer-term interest rates rise unexpectedly, resulting in a decline in the value of the bonds held by the central bank. In principle at least, a central bank's desire to avoid capital losses on its portfolio could motivate policymakers not to tighten policy prematurely. So, investors may see QE as evidence of a central bank's seriousness about providing sustained support to the economy.[4]

Although this explanation is logical and may have some merit, in my experience much of the signaling effect of QE appeared to have a more prosaic source: investors' beliefs about how central banks will sequence their policies. Market participants tend to believe that central banks will not raise short-term interest rates so long as securities purchases continue. After all, it wouldn't make sense for a central bank to tighten with one hand (by raising rates) while loosening with the other (by continuing securities purchases). Since QE programs typically last quarters, if not years, and are rarely ended prematurely (since doing so would hurt policymakers' credibility), initiating or extending QE often pushes out the expected date of the first increase in the short-term policy rate. Quantitative easing announcements can thus be an effective form of forward guidance, reinforcing policymakers' commitments to keep rates low. Observing this signal that short rates will be kept lower for longer than expected, investors have an additional reason to bid down longer-term rates.

When QE brings down longer-term interest rates, whether through portfolio-balance or signaling effects, it stimulates the economy through roughly the same channels as monetary easing during more normal times. For example, lower mortgage rates should increase the demand for housing, or increase current homeowners' disposable income by allowing them to reduce their mortgage payments by refinancing. Lower corporate bond rates reduce the cost of capital and make investments in plants or equipment more attractive. Lower long-term rates also tend to raise asset prices, including house and stock prices, which, by making people feel wealthier, tends to stimulate consumer spending—the *wealth effect*.[5] And, all else equal, lower interest rates, by reducing investment inflows to the United States, reduce the exchange value of the dollar, which in turn promotes U.S. exports. The combined effect of these developments increases demand for domestically produced goods and services, which helps put underutilized capital and labor back to work.

In laying out what QE is and how it works, it's also worth discussing what QE is not. Quantitative easing is *not* the same as government spending, since the central bank is purchasing interest-bearing financial assets, not goods or services. During my time as chair I found it intensely frustrating when journalists added QE purchases and government spending to determine the "cost" of the monetary and fiscal programs used to support the economy. This exercise made no sense. Quantitative easing is not analogous to a household spending money on groceries or car repairs; it is more like the same household buying a government bond that adds to its savings.

By the same token, as noted earlier, QE is not the same as "printing money." It has no direct effect on currency in circulation, which is determined by the amount of cash that people want to hold. It also does not necessarily increase broad measures of the money supply, whose growth depends on several factors, including the behavior of banks and households. For example, the so-called M2 measure of the money supply (which includes currency and total balances in checking accounts, savings accounts, and money market mutual funds) grew only modestly during the Fed's post-crisis QE programs, but the same measure rose sharply in 2020 as people put funds received through government programs into their bank accounts.

QE Event Studies: Some Initial Evidence

Theoretical arguments aside, the effectiveness of QE is ultimately an empirical question. Most of the evidence we have on QE comes from the Great Recession, although evidence on pandemic-era QE has also begun to arrive.[6]

Early evidence on QE came from event studies—a basic research tool. In financial economics, a typical event study compares asset prices just after some event or announcement with the same asset prices just before. Asset prices tend to react quickly to new information, so this before-and-after comparison provides a useful measure of how investors assess the economic consequences of an event. Announcements of early QE programs, at least, had large and wide-ranging effects. For example, the Fed's November 2008 announcement that it would buy mortgage-backed securities powerfully affected the yields on those securities, which ultimately translated into a significant decline in mortgage rates. Moreover, as the portfolio balance theory would suggest, the announcement also sharply reduced yields on longer-term Treasury securities, which are close substitutes for MBS.

Since information about policy initiatives may not arrive all at once, some event studies look at the cumulative change in asset prices over several key dates. A staff memo presented to the FOMC in March 2010 evaluated the effects of QE1 by looking at changes in asset prices on days when relevant information was released by the Fed.[7] The events examined included our announcement of MBS purchases on November 25, 2008; my speech of December 1, 2008,

TABLE 11.1. RESPONSES OF ASSET PRICES AND YIELDS TO QE1 ANNOUNCEMENTS	
2-year Treasuries	−0.57
10-year Treasuries	−1.00
30-year Treasuries	−0.58
Mortgage-backed securities	−1.29
AAA corporate bonds	−0.89
S&P 500 stock price index	2.32

Note: Daily responses, summed over five announcement dates identified by Gagnon, Raskin, Remache, and Sack (2011). Entries show yield changes for Treasuries, mortgage-backed securities, and corporate bonds, and changes in the level of stock prices, all in percentage points. Author's calculations.[8]

that raised the possibility that the Fed would buy Treasury securities; and the March 18, 2009, FOMC statement that announced the significant expansion of QE1. The memo also considered other relevant FOMC meeting dates, including at least one meeting (January 2009) when the Fed surprised markets by taking no action when action was expected. Table 11.1 reports the total effects on key asset prices and yields on five dates when important information was made public. The first five rows show changes in yields, in percentage points, and the last row shows the percent change in stock prices.

The table shows that information released about QE1 in late 2008 and early 2009 had large effects, including (over the five key dates) a full percentage point decline in ten-year Treasury yields and more than a percentage point decline in the yields on GSE-issued mortgage-backed securities. These responses are many times the size of normal daily movements in these prices and yields and would be expected to have significant economic effects. Assets—such as corporate bonds and stocks—that were not purchased by the Fed, but which are nevertheless sensitive to the prevailing level of longer-term interest rates and to monetary policy in general, also showed large post-announcement moves. The exchange value of the dollar (not shown in the table) also moved sharply downward after QE1. Event studies of the Bank of England's introduction of QE at about the same time found quantitatively similar effects, with yields on British longer-term government bonds falling in total about a percentage point over key announcement dates.[9]

The strong market reactions to the first rounds of QE in the United States and the United Kingdom encouraged policymakers, and they certainly refuted predictions that central-bank asset purchases would have little or no effect on financial conditions. However, economists have been cautious about simply extrapolating these results to all QE programs, for at least two reasons.[10]

First, in contrast to the strong results for the Fed's QE1, event studies of later QE rounds have found less dramatic effects. For example, financial economists Arvind Krishnamurthy and Annette Vissing-Jorgensen looked at the market reactions to the announcement of QE2 in November 2010.[11] Examining asset price changes on two key announcement dates, they found a total decline in the ten-year Treasury yield of a relatively moderate 0.18 percentage points, less than the estimated effect of QE1, even considering that QE2 securities purchases, at $600 billion, were only about a third of QE1 purchases. Event studies of other later-round QE programs, in both the United States and in other countries, have also tended to find smaller financial effects. One interpretation of these findings is that the earliest programs, like QE1, had large effects mainly because they were introduced during periods of exceptional financial volatility, which they helped calm. If this interpretation is correct, QE might be of limited use during more normal times.

A second reason for caution about event studies is that, by their nature, they capture market reactions over only short periods.* Perhaps market participants need longer to digest information about novel policies like QE, so that the very short-term asset price responses measured by event studies do not reflect QE's longer-term effects. If so, and if the effects of QE are in fact mostly temporary, then, once again, securities purchases would provide little sustained help for the economy.

---

* Table 11.1 shows full-day responses. Some event studies look at windows around announcements of as little as thirty minutes, which has the advantage of reducing the influence of other, non-policy–related events that may have occurred over the day, but also assumes that markets incorporate policy information quite quickly.

A variant of this "QE effects might be temporary" argument, which takes a slightly longer-term perspective, begins by pointing out that longer-term Treasury yields, despite their large initial reaction to QE1 announcements, did not consistently decline while the Fed was actually making its promised purchases. Indeed, when we completed QE1 purchases in early 2010, the ten-year Treasury yield was about a half percentage point *higher* than before expanded purchases were announced in March 2009. Perhaps investors came to appreciate that asset purchases would not be effective? Again, if QE effects don't last, they won't do much for the economy.

These critiques of QE event studies are important. But, as much subsequent research confirms, ultimately these arguments don't undercut the case for QE effectiveness. As the next sections explain, when researchers control for the fact that later rounds of QE were largely anticipated by markets, the evidence shows that QE continues to work well, even when markets are functioning normally. Moreover, evidence from our best available models of interest-rate determination confirms that the effects of QE on longer-term interest rates are long lasting, not temporary, making it a useful tool whenever short-term rates are constrained by the lower bound.

Were Later Rounds of QE Really Less Effective?

The first reservation raised by event studies is that later rounds of QE had smaller effects per dollar than earlier rounds, suggesting that QE may only be effective when financial markets are in crisis. For QE to be part of the standard monetary toolkit, we need assurance that it will lower interest rates and ease financial conditions generally even when markets are functioning normally.

A key assumption underlying the event-study approach is that the event or announcement surprised markets. Since markets are forward looking and incorporate available information, the announcement of a widely anticipated event should not have much effect on asset prices, even if the event itself is highly consequential. By this reasoning, the weaker results found for later QE could simply reflect that the later programs were better anticipated, and consequently priced in by investors, who by then knew more about the tool and central banks' willingness to use it.

Later rounds of U.S. QE after the financial crisis—in contrast to QE1—were in fact widely anticipated at the times they were announced, as contemporary surveys of market participants show. Eight times a year, prior to each regularly scheduled FOMC meeting, the New York Fed asks primary dealers (which make the market in government securities) about their expectations for monetary policy, including securities purchases. Before the announcement of QE2 in November 2010, for example, dealers placed an 88 percent probability on the Fed adopting the program, in part reflecting public foreshadowing by me and other FOMC members. Moreover, on average, the dealers expected the program to be larger than what the Fed ultimately chose.[12] It should not be surprising, then, that the market reaction was small on the day of the announcement.

Can the event-study approach be adjusted to account for shifting market expectations? In principle, we could measure the full market effect of a QE program by including not only the day of the formal announcement, but also all the days in which *any* information bearing on the program became publicly available. In practice, however, many days would fit that criterion—including, for example, any day when economic data or other news changed market views of the outlook and, consequently, the likelihood of new QE. Including every possibly relevant day in an event study might capture all the news influencing market expectations about QE, but it would also incorporate much news unrelated to QE. Because this approach would not isolate the effects of QE expectations on asset prices, it would not provide much clarity.

A more promising approach is to try to control directly for the market's policy expectations in the event study. Suppose we knew the market's expectation for the size, composition, and timing of the next QE program. If the central bank then announced a materially different program, the response of asset prices to the *unexpected* aspects of the announcement could help us infer the effect of the overall program. Of course, that approach requires a reasonably accurate measure of market expectations.

The Fed's survey of primary dealers provides one source for such expectations. But researchers also can construct expectations measures using investor surveys and media reports. For example, a study by Roberto De Santis of the European Central Bank used articles from the financial press to estimate the market effects of the ECB's first foray into large-scale QE, announced in January 2015 in response to increased worries about the threat of deflation.[13] Commentary from ECB policymakers and the media over the prior six months had strongly hinted the program was coming, so its formal announcement—like the announcement of later rounds of QE in the United States—had only modest market effects. Moreover, additional news about the program arrived over time, including details of its implementation and changes in its size and expected duration. To control for market expectations, De Santis counted the stories by Bloomberg News that contained certain key words relating to the ECB and quantitative easing. From this he created an index of media and market attention to QE before and after the ECB's announcement.

De Santis used this index to measure the markets' policy expectations and then estimated the response of longer-term interest rates to only the unexpected part of policy announcements. He found that the ECB's 2015 QE program cumulatively reduced average ten-year sovereign debt yields by 0.63 percentage points. This reduction is economically quite significant and comparable to estimates from event studies of early U.S. and U.K. QE, after adjusting for the differences in the sizes of the programs. The market impact occurred even though European financial markets were not distressed in early 2015, as they had been a few years earlier.

Studies like De Santis's rely on there being a meaningful difference in the overall size of a QE program, when announced, and what investors expected, which may not always be the case. However, even if investors anticipate the overall size of a QE program, they may still be unsure about *which* specific securities, or classes of securities, the central bank will buy. Because QE works partly by affecting the relative supplies of different assets—the portfolio-balance effect—news about the specific securities that will be purchased in the greatest quantities should raise the prices and lower the yields of those assets, relative to securities that are not targeted. Measuring these differential effects is another way to assess the strength of the portfolio-balance channel.

A good deal of research has been built on this insight, forming a body of work that draws on data from various episodes and countries.[14] For example, in a comprehensive 2013 study, Fed staff members Michael Cahill, Stefania D'Amico, Canlin Li, and John Sears used within-day data on the prices of every outstanding Treasury security to study the market effects of announcements about the *mix* of securities to be purchased under various QE programs. To identify unanticipated shifts in the Fed's plans, they used the Primary Dealer Survey and market commentaries.

To illustrate their approach: On November 3, 2010, the FOMC announced $600 billion of Treasury securities purchases (QE2). Because markets largely anticipated QE2, not surprisingly, its announcement had little visible effect on Treasury yields overall, as already noted. However, at the same time, the New York Fed released information about how it planned to allocate the $600 billion across securities of different maturities. It surprised market participants by revealing that bonds with maturities between ten and thirty years would make up only about 6 percent of planned purchases, compared with 15 percent in QE1. What happened next is evidence that the portfolio-balance channel works. The news about the Fed's planned mix of purchases was quickly followed by a rise in prices and a decline in yields of securities with maturities of less than ten years—the securities whose share of purchases would be greater than expected—relative to the prices and yields of the longer-maturity bonds, which investors learned would be relatively disfavored by QE2.

Applying this approach more broadly, Cahill and coauthors found, in particular, that QE2 and the Maturity Extension Program (Operation Twist) were as effective at lowering longer-term yields as QE1, even though financial markets were not in crisis when the later programs were implemented. These results, which have been replicated in other studies including several for the United Kingdom, again suggest that QE is effective, even when markets are functioning normally.[15]

The Fed's QE purchase programs differed not only in their relative emphasis on Treasuries of different maturities, but also in the relative quantities bought of Treasuries and GSE-guaranteed mortgage-backed securities. For example, the majority of QE1 purchases were of MBS and GSE debt, but in both QE2 and the Maturity Extension Program the Fed bought Treasuries only. If portfolio-balance effects are at work, and the changing emphasis on Treasuries versus MBS was not fully anticipated, then QE1 should have led to a relatively larger reduction in MBS yields than the later programs. That seems to have been the case, as shown for example in the earlier-referenced paper by Krishnamurthy and Vissing-Jorgensen that compared QE1 and QE2.

In the same vein, researchers have also looked at the relative effects of Fed QE on the yields of MBS issued by the GSEs, which were legally eligible for Fed purchases, and the yields on securities backed by "jumbo" (large-principal) mortgages, which GSEs are not allowed to buy and which were therefore not eligible to be purchased by the Fed. As predicted by the portfolio-balance effect, Fed QE programs that included significant MBS purchases (like QE1) lowered yields on GSE-issued MBS considerably more than the yields on securities backed by jumbo mortgages. Meanwhile, QE programs (like QE2) that did not purchase any MBS did not differentially affect yields on the two types of mortgage-backed securities.[16] All these findings back the idea that the portfolio-balance channel continued to operate through later rounds of postcrisis QE.

Although the portfolio-balance channel has been more heavily researched, QE is also thought to work by sending the message that short-term interest rates will remain lower for longer—the signaling effect. Some event studies have documented the importance of this channel by showing that unexpected QE announcements tend to be associated with changes in the market's expected path of short-term interest rates, as measured for example in futures markets, where participants can bet on the expected course of rates.[17] The "taper tantrum" of 2013 was itself a sort of event study of signaling effects, if an unintentional one. When my comments alerted market participants that our securities purchases might slow soon, investors also brought forward the date they expected the first increase in the federal funds rate, leading to a rise in longer-term rates as well. The taper tantrum showed that the signaling effects of QE can be powerful indeed.

Are QE Effects Temporary?

So far we've seen that, once we control for the fact that markets substantially anticipated later rounds of QE, the effects of QE did not diminish as financial conditions improved or as central-bank balance sheets grew. That still leaves the second broad objection to the event-study evidence—that these studies prove only that QE announcements had short-run effects on asset prices and yields. If those effects were purely temporary, then QE would be ineffective in stimulating the broader economy.

A major flaw in that argument is that it implies that market participants during the post–financial crisis era were systematically ignoring attractive profit opportunities, which would be highly unlikely. If the effects of QE announcements on stock and bond prices were really known or expected to be short lived, then smart investors could have profited by betting on the reversal of those effects. There is little evidence that such speculation occurred; if it had, it would have tended to quickly reverse the observed effects of QE on interest rates, which did not happen. In this respect, investors were aligned with professional forecasters, most of whom also saw QE as having large and long-lasting effects on Treasury yields (and on other yields as well, such as corporate bond yields).[18]

Alternatively, perhaps investors thought at first that QE effects would persist, but over time they learned that was not the case, leading to a reversal of the initial effects on yields. For example, as I've noted, ten-year Treasury yields increased on net rather than declined from March 2009, when the Fed expanded QE1, to early 2010, when QE1 ended.

One response to this argument is that longer-term interest rates, and asset prices generally, respond to many factors other than monetary policy, including fiscal policy, global economic conditions, and sentiment changes. As I told the FOMC in June 2009, I saw the rise in yields as QE1 was being implemented not as a sign of failure but rather as an indication that our policies—together with other measures including the Obama administration's fiscal stimulus and the successful stress tests of major banks—were increasing public confidence in the economy. Based on comparisons with the yields on inflation-protected securities, much of the increases in ten-year yields during the implementation of QE1 (and QE2 as well) reflected higher inflation expectations—a desired outcome, given our concerns about inflation falling too low.

For a deeper response to this critique, however, it helps to think more carefully about how we should expect longer-term interest rates to be related to central-bank securities purchases. The critics' argument assumes that, if QE works, then longer-term interest rates should be lower when the central bank is actively buying securities than at other times. Under this assumption—sometimes called the *flow view* because it posits that longer-term interest rates are determined by the flow of new central-bank purchases—the failure of longer-term rates to fall when the Fed was carrying out QE1 purchases shows that QE is ineffective.

However, if QE works through the portfolio-balance channel, which most evidence supports, then the link between QE and longer-term interest rates is more complicated than a simple flow view suggests. According to the portfolio-balance theory, securities purchases by the central bank affect longer-term yields by changing the available supply—that is, the stock outstanding—of longer-term bonds. In this *stock view* of QE, the effect of securities purchases on yields at a point in time depends not on the current pace of purchases, but on the total amount of securities the central bank has accumulated and how long it is expected to hold them. Because financial markets are forward looking, the portfolio-balance theory and the associated stock view imply that, at any point in time, longer-term rates also depend on markets' expectations for *future* central-bank purchases.[19]

The implication of the portfolio-balance theory, that expected as well as current central-bank securities holdings matter for longer-term yields, makes empirical analysis of the effects of QE more difficult. Still, a lot of careful research has taken on this task. One approach, rather than relying on event studies, uses sophisticated models of Treasury yields at all maturities (the *term structure* of Treasury yields). This research basically asks the question: Given what we know about the factors that determine interest rates at different maturities, such as macroeconomic conditions and the stocks of outstanding securities, where would we have expected the term structure of Treasury yields to have been in the years after the financial crisis *in the absence of QE?* The difference between the actual levels of rates at different maturities and the model forecasts provides an estimate of the effects of QE on the Treasury market.

Jane Ihrig, Elizabeth Klee, Canlin Li, and Joe Kachovec of the Board staff, in a 2018 paper, used this approach to study how Treasury yields relate to both the Fed's accumulated and expected future holdings of Treasury securities.[20] They developed reasonable measures of market expectations of future QE purchases.[21] They also incorporated estimates of new Treasury debt issuance, which partially offset the effects of the Fed's purchases on the net supply of government debt available to investors.[22] And they relied on models developed using precrisis data, so that the benefits of QE in helping to calm the financial panic and improve market functioning were excluded from their estimates. (Their analysis also ignored signaling effects.)

Putting these elements together, these researchers found the Fed's securities purchases had significant and long-lasting effects on Treasury yields. Their estimates suggested that QE1 persistently reduced the ten-year yield by 0.34 percentage points and that, together, QE2, the Maturity Extension Program, and QE3 reduced yields by an additional 0.73 percentage points initially, and by more over time when the Fed announced plans to replace maturing securities on its balance sheet. These estimates, like other research, show that later QE programs were no less effective per dollar than the earliest ones.[*] Although the effect of any given QE program decayed over time, as securities purchased under the program matured and ran off

---

[*] These results are smaller than the QE1 event-study results in Table 11.1, but, taking statistical uncertainty into account, they are consistent with the event-study literature as a whole. They also suggest that the effects of QE are economically significant as well as long-lasting.

the Fed's balance sheet, the authors estimated that the cumulative effect of the Fed's purchases on the ten-year Treasury yield exceeded 1.2 percentage points when QE ended in October 2014 and was still about 1 percentage point at the end of 2015. Other research based on the stock view of QE has found quite similar results, for both the United States and other countries.[23]

Because many economic decisions—such as a household's purchase of a house or a company's investment in new plant and equipment—depend on longer-term interest rates, a given decline in long-term rates provides more stimulus than the same reduction in the very short-term federal funds rate. A rule of thumb derived from empirical macroeconomic models is that a percentage point reduction in the ten-year yield has the stimulative power of a 3 percentage point reduction in the funds rate.[24] On that approximation, the Fed's QE after the financial crisis provided additional stimulus at the effective lower bound equivalent to 3–4 percentage point cuts in the funds rate.

In short, current research indicates that the relationship of longer-term interest rates to central-bank securities purchases is complex, with both past and expected future purchases affecting rates. But when these relationships are taken into account, the evidence shows a long-lasting and economically significant effect of QE on longer-term rates. Moreover, the significance of *expected* purchases implies, once again, that central bankers' communication matters. A credible commitment to continue QE as long as the economy needs it is generally more effective than an approach that avoids clarity and commitment.

FORWARD GUIDANCE

In addition to QE, in recent years the Fed and almost all other major central banks have relied heavily on forward guidance, or communication by policymakers about how they expect the economy and policy to evolve. Central-bank communication takes many forms and occurs in many contexts, including policymakers' speeches and testimonies, the minutes of policy meetings, and regular publications like the Fed's semiannual *Monetary*

Policy Report to the Congress or the Bank of England's quarterly *Inflation Report*. However, for the Federal Reserve, the most powerful and closely watched guidance is the FOMC's post-meeting statement, as explained and elaborated upon by the chair in the press conference.

The basic insight motivating forward guidance is that financial conditions depend not only on the current short-term policy rate but also on market expectations of future rates. If market participants come to believe that the funds rate will move higher, they will bid up long rates as well, tightening financial conditions. By the same token, if they come to expect a lower funds rate in the future, they will bid down longer-term rates. To the extent that forward guidance influences expectations, it can become an additional policy lever.

Although most forward guidance is aimed at financial markets, in principle central-bank pronouncements could affect broader public expectations as well. For example, an announcement of plans to ease policy could in principle make households and firms more optimistic about growth, leading them to increase spending, investment, and hiring today. For this reason, as well as for transparency and democratic accountability, central banks around the world have in recent years been speaking more often and more directly to the general public about their outlook and policy plans. However, while this effort may someday bear fruit, for now the evidence suggests that the expectations of people who are not active investors are more likely to be shaped by personal experience—in the labor market, for example, or with price changes of the goods and services they typically buy.[25] When Fed staff simulate the effects of forward guidance in their economic models, they often do so under two alternative assumptions, the first being that both market participants and average citizens hear and understand the guidance, the second that only market participants—people actively engaged in investing and trading financial assets—do.[26] Conservative assessments of the likely effects of guidance put greater weight on the simulations that assume that only market participants pay attention.

Central bankers have long understood that expectations of future policy matter, but before the mid-1990s, Fed officials rarely actively tried to influence those expectations.[27] The FOMC began issuing post-meeting statements during Greenspan's tenure, initially only when it changed rates. Over time it added language that hinted at how policymakers were leaning. Forward guidance during the Greenspan era was qualitative and often indirect, but it nevertheless appeared to significantly affect market expectations and financial conditions. A 2005 paper by Refet Gürkaynak, Brian Sack, and Eric Swanson estimated that, from 1990 to 2004, more than three-fourths of the changes in five- and ten-year Treasury yields following FOMC statements and other Fed communications resulted, not from unexpected changes in the funds rate itself, but from new guidance (explicit or implicit) about the *future direction* of the funds rate.[28] As we've seen, the FOMC's reliance on forward guidance became much greater after 2008 when the lower bound limited the ability of policymakers to add stimulus through short-term rate cuts.

Forecasts versus Promises

In practice, central-bank guidance varies on many dimensions. Federal Reserve Bank of Chicago President Charles Evans and Chicago Fed economists Jeffrey Campbell, Jonas Fisher, and Alejandro Justiniano, in a 2012 paper, introduced the useful distinction between Delphic and Odyssean forward guidance.[29] *Delphic* guidance (after the oracles at the Temple of Apollo at Delphi) is intended only to inform, to help the public and markets better understand policymakers' economic outlook and provisional plans for policy. In short, Delphic guidance is an economic and policy *forecast* by the central bank (or, perhaps, by an individual policymaker), not a promise or commitment to take any particular action. In contrast, as Odysseus bound himself to the mast to avoid the temptations of the sirens, *Odyssean* guidance attempts to bind policymakers to a metaphorical mast by stating a *commitment*, or at least a very strong predilection, to conduct policy in a specific way in the future.

Delphic guidance can be helpful at any time, whether interest rates are constrained by the lower bound or not. Indeed, since about 1990, the desire to offer better Delphic guidance has helped to motivate the global trend toward central-bank transparency. The basic rationale for Delphic guidance is that greater openness should help markets better anticipate how policymakers will react to changes in the outlook, thereby reducing uncertainty and increasing policymakers' ability to influence financial and economic conditions. When the post-meeting statement or the meeting minutes indicate that FOMC policymakers are more pessimistic than expected about the economy, for example, markets can infer that policy is likely to be easier, at least for a while. The Fed's *Summary of Economic Projections* (SEP), like similar forecasts and reports provided by other central banks, is another channel for conveying policymakers' economic and policy outlooks. These forms of guidance are Delphic, in that they reflect only the central bank's best guesses about the future, involving no promise or commitment.

Because Delphic guidance is a forecast, it should change with the arrival of new data or other information bearing on the economic outlook. A sometimes-controversial example of Delphic guidance, discussed earlier, is FOMC participants' projections of the funds rate as reported in the SEP—the so-called dot plot, for the dots in the figure that show individual rate projections. FOMC participants submit their projections independently, before the meeting, so the dot plot is a summary of how individual participants—not necessarily the Committee as a whole— believe monetary policy should evolve over the next few years, given each participant's current assessment of the outlook and their individual policy preferences. Commentators have sometimes interpreted the dot plot as reflecting a policy commitment, but that's not correct. The FOMC's rate projections are conditional on the current economic outlook and change when the outlook changes, as policy forecasts should. That is, even putting aside that the dot plot reflects the views of individual participants and not the Committee as a whole, the dot plot is Delphic (a forecast, subject to change), not Odyssean (a promise or commitment). More generally, Delphic guidance is intended to show the factors underlying policymakers' own analyses of the economy, and it invites market participants and others to think along with the central bank.*

In contrast, Odyssean guidance is useful primarily when short rates are at the lower bound. When short-term rates cannot be reduced further, policymakers can still put downward pressure on longer-term rates by persuading market participants that they intend to keep the short-term policy rate low for longer than market participants may have previously thought—a so-called *lower-for-longer* policy. Odyssean guidance can make lower-for-longer commitments clear and, if credible, shift market expectations in a way that promotes easier financial conditions even at the lower bound.

Because Odyssean guidance is a commitment, or at least a strong statement of intention, to conduct policy in a certain way, it is likely to be more effective if it is explicit and verifiable—rather than vague. The FOMC's forward guidance in the immediate aftermath of the global financial crisis was qualitative, using phrases like "extended period." The lack of specificity made the guidance less effective, as many forecasters expected the FOMC to raise rates sooner than most Committee members intended. Eventually, the FOMC pushed back against the excessively hawkish expectations with more precise and forceful Odyssean guidance, including a commitment, initially, not to raise rates until at least a certain date (time-dependent guidance) or, subsequently, until the unemployment rate had fallen at least to a certain level (state-contingent guidance). The stronger guidance had the desired effect on market policy expectations and, consequently, on financial conditions. Professional forecasters reacted to the Fed's more-explicit guidance by repeatedly marking down the unemployment rate at which they expected the Committee to approve its first rate increase, suggesting the message of greater policy patience was getting through.[30]

---

* The debate over the usefulness of the dot plot has a parallel in the question of whether the FOMC participants—nineteen of them, when the Committee is at full strength—help or hurt the Fed's messaging by frequently giving talks or interviews that highlight their personal views on the economic and policy outlook. While the diversity of views can muddy the Committee's guidance at times, on net I think multiple voices help the public understand the nuances of the ongoing debate and provide assurance that a range of views is being considered.

The FOMC's forward guidance during the pandemic continued the trend toward stronger, often more-explicit guidance. Beginning in September 2020, the Committee said that it would not raise the funds rate from its near-zero level until "labor market conditions have reached levels consistent with the Committee's assessment of maximum employment and inflation has risen to 2 percent and is on track to moderately exceed 2 percent for some time." Supplemented by the Committee's individual projections for unemployment and inflation in the SEP, as well as by policymakers' speeches and testimony, this guidance provided considerable information about the conditions under which rates would be raised and how they would move subsequently.[31] The early evidence suggests that the Fed's communication, together with the broader policy framework announced in August 2020, had its intended effects. For example, the Fed's surveys showed that, following the new guidance, primary dealers and market participants expected significantly higher inflation and lower unemployment at the time when the FOMC lifts rates from the lower bound.[32] This episode further confirmed that forward guidance can affect policy expectations well into the future, as markets at the time projected that rates would be kept low for several years.*

Although the FOMC provided substantial detail in September 2020 about aspects of its plans for the funds rate, it was vague on others. Notably, the Committee declined to define the terms "moderately" and "some time," leaving the size and duration of the inflation overshoot to the discretion of future policymakers. Also, in December 2020, when adding guidance on its securities purchases, the Committee tied them—in a manner reminiscent of QE3—to achieving "substantial further progress" toward its goals, a less-explicit criterion. These ambiguities reflect a trade-off apparent in many examples of Odyssean guidance. On the one hand, a highly specific commitment is clearer to markets and, because violations of a clear

---

* The surge of inflation would lead to an earlier tightening than was expected in August 2020. That's not inconsistent with the guidance, which was state-contingent, tying future policy to developments in the economy.

statement of intent are more apparent, makes it more difficult for policy-makers to renege. On the other hand, in an uncertain world, policymakers are understandably reluctant to cede their ability to respond to unexpected or unusual circumstances. Odyssean guidance thus often includes escape clauses, like the FOMC's September 2020 statement that it was prepared to adjust policy "if risks emerge that could impede the attainment of the Com-mittee's goals"—presumably a reference to financial-stability risks such as an excessive buildup of debt—or its provision in 2012 that, in determining how long to pursue QE3, the Committee would take account of the "likely efficacy and costs" of the program. Central bankers are still learning how to balance the trade-off between commitment and flexibility.

Overall, the Fed's experience since the financial crisis illustrates the more general point that central banks, collectively, have been learning how to better use communication as a policy tool. The most powerful central-bank signal of the post–financial crisis era was undoubtedly Mario Draghi's promise in July 2012 to "do whatever it takes" to save the euro, but the European Central Bank and other foreign central banks have also made extensive use of more-conventional guidance. The ECB began its formal guidance in July 2013, saying—in a statement reminiscent of the Fed's ear-lier "extended period" language—that it expected key rates to remain "at present or lower levels for an extended period of time."[33] From this begin-ning, the ECB's guidance grew more elaborate, encompassing not only the ECB Governing Council's expectations for its various policy rates but also its securities purchases, reinvestment of maturing securities, special bank lending programs, and the relationships among its policy tools.

The Bank of Japan—a precrisis pioneer in forward guidance—has also relied heavily on guidance in recent years, including long-term com-mitments to keep rates low and a promise to overshoot its 2 percent infla-tion target. The Bank of England, the Bank of Canada, and other major central banks have also actively used more-explicit and more-Odyssean forms of guidance. Empirical studies of foreign central banks show that central-bank-speak can both reduce market uncertainty and add stimu-lus despite the constraint of the lower bound.[34] In a bit of exaggeration,

I often liked to say that monetary policy is 98 percent talk and 2 percent action. Certainly, one of the principal lessons of recent decades for central banks is that good communication makes for effective policymaking.

The Credibility of Guidance

To be effective in stimulating the economy, Odyssean guidance must signal that policymakers intend to keep rates lower for longer than market participants had previously expected. If markets see rates staying near zero for two years, for example, a promise by policymakers to keep rates at zero for a year would not ease financial conditions—indeed, it would probably tighten them.

Because, to be effective, Odyssean guidance may have to commit the central bank to actions far in the future, it raises the issue of the credibility of such commitments. Over a horizon of several years, economic circumstances may change, tempting policymakers to renege on their earlier promises. Or the policymakers themselves may change, as terms end and new people are appointed. If market participants are skeptical that the central bank's commitments will be carried out—if the Odyssean guidance is not credible—then they will not have the desired effect.

How can central banks enhance the credibility of their guidance? We have seen that explicit and verifiable commitments, which make reneging easy to detect, can help. But, in everyday life, we judge the credibility of promises more by the reputations of the promise-makers than by the exact words they use. The same principle applies to central-bank promises. Central-bank credibility depends in part on the personal reputations and communication skills of key policymakers, but since policymakers cannot irrevocably bind themselves or their successors, institutional reputation is important as well. Because of concerns about institutional reputation, policymakers have an incentive to follow through on promises, even those made by their predecessors. They know that, in doing so, they are preserving the central bank's reputation for following through and thus its ability to make credible promises in the future.[35]

Besides a record of clear guidance and consistent promise-keeping, at least two other factors help determine a central bank's credibility. First, it helps to have a broader policy framework, either implicit or explicit, that commands wide agreement within the institution and describes the principles that guide the central bank's approach. A framework puts individual episodes of guidance in a broader context, helps markets understand the rationale for specific pieces of guidance, and increases the costs to policymakers of deviating from their commitments. Think for example of the "constrained discretion" imposed on policymakers by inflation targeting and similar frameworks. The Powell Fed's unanimous adoption of flexible average inflation targeting in 2020 suggests that the FOMC will follow that broad approach even when the leadership of the Committee changes.

Second, central-bank independence from short-run political pressures enhances credibility. Partisan policymakers, facing regular elections and swings in political sentiment, would find it difficult, if not impossible, to make credible promises about policies three or four years in the future, nor do partisan policymakers have much incentive to follow through on commitments made by political opponents. Factors that promote Fed independence, such as the long terms of policymakers and its strong ethos of nonpartisanship, also increase the credibility of its commitments, even those reaching years into the future.

This chapter has discussed QE and forward guidance separately, but experience shows that the two are closely intertwined. On the one hand, QE works in part by signaling the likely path of policy rates (the signaling channel). Indeed, central banks have increasingly made the connection between QE and rates explicit, for example, by promising no rate increases until well after the conclusion of securities purchases. On the other hand, policymakers can also offer guidance about future QE or even tie the path of asset holdings to the level of rates. For instance, the FOMC indicated in June 2017 that it would begin to reduce the Fed's balance sheet only after raising the federal funds rate was "well under way." Because QE and forward guidance are so closely linked, separating their effects on asset prices is not straightforward. However, taken together, these tools provide monetary policymakers with valuable additional firepower when short-term rate cuts are no longer feasible.

12

IS THE FED'S TOOLKIT ENOUGH?

EVEN AS CENTRAL BANKERS BECOME increasingly confident that QE and forward guidance can ease financial conditions at the effective lower bound, critical questions remain. First, can these tools also help policymakers achieve significantly better employment and inflation outcomes, compared with the alternative of cutting rates to a low level and taking no further action? In other words, can these extra tools compensate—and if so, to what extent—for the limits on monetary policy created by the lower bound? Second, with possible side effects taken into account, do the tools pass a cost-benefit test? Or do the costs and risks of these tools limit their usefulness?

THE EFFECTS OF QE AND FORWARD GUIDANCE ON ECONOMIC PERFORMANCE

One way in which researchers have tried to assess the economic benefits of QE and forward guidance is to look at the (admittedly limited) historical experience. In the United States and other countries where these tools have been actively used, has economic performance been materially better than it would have been otherwise?

QE, Forward Guidance, and the Great Recession

With the recovery from the pandemic recession still playing out, most work to date has focused on the Great Recession and the subsequent recovery, when both the Fed and other major central banks first extensively used QE and increasingly explicit forward guidance.

Despite the use of these tools, as we know, the recession was severe and the recovery slow, and, in most cases, inflation remained stubbornly below central-bank targets. On the other hand, even in the precrisis era, when the lower bound was not a problem, monetary policy was never able to avoid recessions, only to mitigate them and speed recovery. Moreover, monetary policy was only one determinant of the pace of expansion after the Great Recession. In the United States, many factors contributed to the slow recovery, including the depressing effects of the housing bust on new construction, spillovers from the European sovereign debt crisis on U.S. trade and financial markets, premature austerity following the 2009 fiscal package, and slowing productivity growth. The recovery, though not rapid, was unusually sustained, ultimately becoming the longest expansion in U.S. history. The question remains, given this mixed record: How much did the new tools help?

Unsurprisingly, economists disagree. Some work suggests that QE and forward guidance substantially overcame the constraint of the lower bound after the financial crisis. According to this research, monetary policy was about as effective as usual in helping to put labor and capital back to work after the Great Recession, despite the lower bound. In a paper presented at the Brookings Institution in 2017, John Fernald, Robert Hall, James Stock, and Mark Watson found that the slow pace of the recovery can be explained largely by subdued productivity growth and declines in labor-force participation related to the aging of the baby boom generation.[1] Both of these trends were in place before the crisis. These authors also noted that indicators of resource utilization like the unemployment rate—which are more influenced by monetary policy than is potential growth—recovered at a relatively normal pace.* If the speed of recovery from the Great Recession was not historically unusual, given the size of the shock and the economy's underlying growth potential, then perhaps monetary policy, including the additional tools, was not severely hamstrung by the lower bound.

Most evaluations of the postcrisis response, however, draw more mixed conclusions. An example is a 2015 paper by Federal Reserve Board staffers Eric Engen, Thomas Laubach, and David Reifschneider.[2] They used the Board's principal forecasting model of the U.S. economy, known as FRB/US, to simulate the economic effects of the Fed's policies after the crisis. A detailed economic model like FRB/US allows researchers to control for factors other than monetary policy, such as fiscal policy and developments in foreign economies. This team found that, taken together, QE and forward guidance eased financial conditions, but that they did not meaningfully boost the pace of the recovery (beyond what was achieved by rate cuts alone) before 2011. Engen and his coauthors pointed to three reasons for the limited economic benefits of the new tools in 2009 and 2010: The Fed's early forward guidance was not effective in persuading markets that rates would stay lower for longer; the effects of QE accumulated only gradually as the Fed's holdings of securities grew and investors began to expect still-more asset purchases; and, importantly, monetary policy—whether conventional or not—always takes time to have its full effect.

However, by 2011, these authors found, the new tools had begun to speed the recovery appreciably. The tools led to an unemployment rate in early 2015 about 1.25 percentage points lower and, slightly later, to inflation about a half percentage point higher than would have been the case if the Fed had cut rates to zero but had not used QE or forward guidance. These effects are significant, even though delayed. For example, in the Fed's

---

* For example, from its peak in 2009 until 2019, the unemployment gap (the unemployment rate minus the Congressional Budget Office estimate of the natural rate) fell 0.14 percentage points per quarter, about the same as in previous postwar recessions. The prime-age employment-to-population ratio rose about 0.12 percentage points per quarter in the decade after its low point, noticeably slower than in the recoveries from the deep 1973–75 and 1981–82 recessions but similar to other recoveries, including those following the recessions of 1990–91 and 2001.

FRB/US model, a 1 percentage point decline in the federal funds rate is predicted to lower the unemployment rate by less than a quarter of a percentage point, or about a fifth the estimated effect of the new policy tools.[3]

These two papers are just some of many that have looked at the recovery from the Great Recession, both in the United States and elsewhere. I draw two conclusions from this body of research—conclusions shared, by the way, in a Fed staff report written in 2020 as part of the FOMC's strategic review.[4] First, on the positive side, QE and forward guidance after the global financial crisis did ultimately produce meaningfully better economic outcomes, compared with the hypothetical alternative scenario in which rates were cut to zero but no further policy actions were taken. The Fed's new policy tools not only stimulated spending and hiring, but they also boosted confidence, risk-taking, and credit flows. International comparisons also show that countries that used the new tools early and proactively, notably the United States and the United Kingdom, had relatively stronger and more-sustained recoveries and came closer to reaching their inflation targets.

Second, however, it seems unlikely that the new tools entirely compensated for the constraint imposed by the lower bound. This reflected in part the inherent limitations of QE and forward guidance, but also how we used both tools. At the Fed, we were initially cautious, especially about QE. We weren't confident that the new tools would be effective, we worried about their possible costs and risks, and we remained exceptionally uncertain about the economic outlook, especially early on. Market participants in turn needed to understand the evolving policy strategies of the Fed and other central banks. Over time, as we better understood the new tools and recognized that we could and should do more to help the economy, we applied both QE and forward guidance with more force and greater effect.

While these observations imply that the early stages of the recovery from the Great Recession were probably somewhat weaker than they might have been, they also suggest that, with the benefit of experience, the new policy tools could prove even more effective. The Fed had a chance to implement the lessons it had learned in its response to the 2020 pandemic recession.

The New Monetary Tools in the Pandemic

The pandemic struck with little warning, derailing an economy that had been performing quite well. The Powell Fed responded to the upheaval in financial markets in March 2020 by serving as a buyer of last resort for Treasuries and mortgage-backed securities, establishing currency swap lines with foreign central banks, and restarting 2008 crisis–era programs to provide liquidity to key financial markets and institutions. With support from Congress, the Fed used its 13(3) emergency powers to backstop lending to corporations, municipalities, and medium-sized firms.

To cushion the economic blow, monetary policymakers used QE and forward guidance but deployed these tools more quickly and with greater force than we did in the financial crisis. After cutting the funds rate to nearly zero in March, the FOMC began purchasing large quantities of Treasury securities (of all maturities, not just longer-term) and GSE-issued mortgage-backed securities. In December 2020, it promised that securities purchases would continue "until substantial further progress" had been made toward its policy goals. Through increasingly detailed forward guidance, especially after the introduction of its flexible average inflation targeting framework in August, the FOMC also persuaded markets that the funds rate was likely to remain near zero for the foreseeable future. As Chair Powell put it in a press conference in the early stages of the pandemic, the FOMC was "not even thinking about thinking about raising rates."[5] Likely reflecting the Fed's actions and guidance, the yield on ten-year Treasury bonds, which had been just below 2 percent before the pandemic hit, remained well below 1 percent for the rest of 2020. The yield rose again in 2021 (though it remained quite low) as the increasing pace of vaccinations and strong fiscal action raised expectations for growth and inflation.

Did the Fed's monetary actions help the economy recover more swiftly? Any assessment will be complicated by the unique nature of the pandemic recession. In particular, FOMC members faced the question of whether easing financial conditions could do much good, given that many people's decisions not to work or shop had little to do with interest rates but instead reflected shutdown orders by governors and mayors and general fear of contracting the virus. And, even after vaccines became available, the uneven reopening process greatly complicated both monetary and fiscal policymaking, as new waves of infection, snarled supply chains, and hesitancy to return to work slowed growth and boosted inflation.

Nevertheless, early evidence suggests that the monetary response helped get the economy back on its feet. Notably, the recovery in the second half of 2020, before vaccines became available, was faster than almost anyone expected. The FOMC made no economic projections in March, during the short-lived financial panic, but in June it projected that real growth over the year (from fourth quarter 2019 to fourth quarter 2020) would be minus 6.5 percent, and that the unemployment rate in the fourth quarter would be 9.3 percent. In early July, the Congressional Budget Office projected similar numbers: 2020 growth at minus 5.9 percent and fourth-quarter unemployment at 10.5 percent.[6] These forecasts, which accounted for the expected effects of the CARES Act, passed in March, were similar to private forecasts.

The economy performed substantially better than the forecasts. Despite a sharp increase in virus cases and hospitalizations in the fall and winter, and the absence of any new fiscal action until the last days of the year, real GDP only fell about 2.5 percent over the course of 2020—about 4 percentage points better than expected—and the unemployment rate in the fourth quarter dropped below 7 percent. Of course, these were still weak numbers, and the lower unemployment rate partly reflected fewer people actively seeking work. But the performance relative to forecasts was encouraging, and the U.S. recovery outpaced those of most other advanced economies. Inflation fell in 2020 (from 1.6 percent over 2019, as measured by prices for personal consumption expenditures, to 1.3 percent in 2020), but inflation expectations remained reasonably close to the 2 percent target.

The better-than-expected performance in 2020 reflected several factors, including Americans' impatience to get back to work and school and possibly greater-than-expected benefits from the CARES Act. However, the influence of monetary policy can be clearly discerned. The recovery was led by strong gains in interest-sensitive sectors, most notably housing, which benefited from thirty-year mortgage rates that had fallen below 2.7 percent by late 2020. Other interest-sensitive sectors also recovered rapidly, in many cases exceeding pre-pandemic levels of activity. Among these sectors were manufacturing, trade (the dollar fell steadily through the second half of the year), business capital spending, and consumer durables. Strength in interest-sensitive sectors compensated for continued weakness in services, especially services dependent on personal contact such as leisure and hospitality.

Monetary ease also helped revive private credit markets and (together with fiscal actions) reduced financial stress—as measured, for example, by corporate bankruptcies and ratings downgrades, which proved less severe than expected.[7] Better access to credit for all types of borrowers supported growth and employment. In addition, the prices of stocks and other assets more than fully recovered from their initial plunges, strengthening the balance sheets of households and businesses and increasing their willingness and ability to spend.

Strong growth in output and employment continued in 2021, powered by new fiscal initiatives but supported by continued monetary policy ease. However, as we've seen, supply-side constraints (such as a global shortage of computer chips and shipping capacity) and continued fear of illness (including new variants of the virus) contributed to a burst of inflation and high uncertainty about economic prospects in the second half of the year. Following its earlier guidance, the FOMC announced its intention to begin withdrawing its policy support, starting with a wind-down of its securities purchases. The Committee's difficult challenge was to ensure that supply-shock-induced inflation did not become too persistent without snuffing out the ongoing recovery in the labor market.

More time and research will be needed to parse the sources of the strong recovery that began in mid-2020 and continued through 2021. Overall, however, the pandemic recession and recovery provide support for the view that, coming into the crisis, monetary policy was not out of ammunition, even though the Fed had only limited scope to cut the funds rate when the recession began.[8]

THE ROLE OF THE NEUTRAL INTEREST RATE IN DETERMINING POLICY SPACE

Historical perspective is valuable, but what about the future? After the recovery from the pandemic recession, how well will 21st century monetary policy—which combines short-term rate cuts, QE, forward guidance, and possibly other tools—meet the objectives of the Fed and other central banks? Although the effectiveness of new monetary tools depends on many factors, we have seen that a key determinant is the level of the (nominal) neutral interest rate, R^*. The neutral interest rate matters because it affects the amount of operating space available to monetary policymakers.

Suppose for example that the neutral short-term interest rate is 2.5 percent (again, in nominal or market terms, not inflation-adjusted)—its value as estimated by FOMC participants in recent years. If that level persists, then on average, in normal times, longer-term interest rates will also be about 2.5 percent, ignoring some complicating factors such as bond risk premiums (the extra yield investors demand to hold longer-term securities). Now suppose the economy is hit with a recessionary shock. If the neutral policy rate is 2.5 percent, then on average—again, in normal times—the central bank would have about 2.5 percentage points of room to cut short rates, assuming that the lower bound is zero. (In response to the pandemic recession in early 2020, the Powell Fed cut the funds rate about 1.5 percentage points, having already made 0.75 percentage points of "insurance cuts" in 2019.)

In the decades before the financial crisis, the Fed typically responded to recessions by cutting the funds rate by 5 to 6 percentage points. If the neutral rate is 2.5 percent, then conventional short-term rate cuts obviously would not provide enough ammunition to deal with a typical recession, especially if the funds rate happened to be below neutral when the recession hit. The question then becomes: Once the funds rate hits zero, how much *additional* policy room can be achieved with QE and forward guidance? This implicitly assumes, appropriately, that cutting the short-term interest rate to zero does not result in long rates also reaching zero. It's precisely because long rates typically remain above zero even when short rates are at the lower bound that QE and forward guidance can provide useful additional stimulus.

In a 2020 study I looked at this question using the Fed's FRB/US model to perform hundreds of simulations of the U.S. economy, assuming that it is randomly buffeted by shocks similar to those observed since 1970.[9] (The shocks that triggered the Great Recession are included, but the study ended before the pandemic.) In these simulations I assumed an historically normal response of monetary policy to economic downturns and inflation, except that I also assumed that, when the funds rate hits the lower bound, the Fed uses QE and forward guidance more forcefully than we did early in the recovery from the Great Recession, consistent with the growing consensus that proactive and forceful use is most effective.[10] I also assumed that the Fed uses forward guidance to tie future changes in the policy rate and securities purchases to inflation and unemployment (state-contingent guidance). For each simulation of the model, I measured how well the economy performed, on average, in meeting or exceeding the Fed's full employment goals and hitting the 2 percent inflation target.

My main finding was that QE, supplemented by forward guidance that commits policymakers to lower-for-longer rate policies, can provide the equivalent of about 3 additional percentage points of policy space. In other words, if the neutral interest rate is 2.5 percent, forceful use of QE and forward guidance can provide the Fed with total monetary firepower equivalent to roughly 5.5 percentage points of traditional rate cuts—close to its normal response to typical recessions before the lower bound became a problem. However, in a deeper-than-average recession that requires more than 5.5 percentage points of policy response, even forceful use of the new monetary policy tools would probably prove insufficient to compensate fully for the effects of the lower bound.

My 3-percentage-point rule of thumb is broadly consistent with the empirical literature, including studies of the portfolio balance and signaling effects of QE, as well as other work using FRB/US or similar economic models.[11] However, given the many assumptions that go into modeling the effects of QE and forward guidance, uncertainty is inevitable. It's possible that the policy space created by the new tools is less than 3 percentage points, and, moreover, that it may vary depending on the state of the economy or financial markets. That's grounds for prudence in planning future policy responses, and a motivation to continue seeking new approaches for increasing policy space.

On the other hand, many standard analyses of QE and forward guidance, including my work, may underestimate the tools' overall effect. For example, evidence suggests that QE strengthens bank balance sheets and leads to more lending, a possibility not usually included in conventional analyses, including mine.[12] Moreover, for simplicity, my simulations assumed that the Fed purchases only Treasury securities, ignoring the additional effects of MBS purchases, and I made conservative assumptions about the effects of forward guidance on market expectations (and ignored the signaling effects of QE altogether). As we'll see in Chapter 14, monetary policy may also affect the economy through a risk-taking channel that is not considered in most policy simulations. Overall, I see the 3-percentage-point rule of thumb as a reasonably conservative starting point.[13]

The value of the neutral interest rate, R*, which helps determine total monetary firepower, is however another source of uncertainty for policymakers. The value of R* can't be observed, only estimated, and, as we've seen, the Fed's estimates of this key variable have fallen substantially over time. For the United States, consistent with the Fed's 2021 estimate of 2.5 percent, most studies currently estimate the nominal neutral rate to be in the range of 2 to 3 percent—or, 0 to 1 percent in real, inflation-adjusted terms, assuming inflation expectations are close to the Fed's 2 percent target. However, if the downward trend in R* continues, or R* has been overestimated, that could be another reason why, even with QE and forward guidance available, the lower bound will limit monetary policy firepower.

My 3-percentage-point rule of thumb is based on simulations of a model of the U.S. economy and as such cannot apply directly to other economies. At a minimum, the evidence certainly suggests foreign central banks should include QE, forward guidance, and possibly other new tools in their toolkits, as indeed many of them have. Another critical lesson for other countries is that, for monetary policy to have the space to respond to downturns, the neutral interest rate cannot be too low. Since real (inflation-adjusted) rates of return are low globally, the best way to keep the neutral interest rate from falling too low is to keep inflation (and inflation expectations) from falling much below target.[14] In other words, hitting the inflation target is important not only for achieving price stability, but also for ensuring that monetary policy has the rate-cutting room it needs to respond effectively to adverse economic shocks.

Unfortunately, for some major foreign economies, consistently achieving inflation goals has been difficult. In the eurozone, at least prior to the pandemic supply shock, inflation and inflation expectations had for some years remained well below the ECB's inflation objective of below, but close to, 2 percent (recently changed to simply 2 percent).[*][15] Europe's inflation and inflation expectations have been lower, relative to the United States, because its sovereign debt crisis followed on the heels of the global financial crisis and because the ECB delayed using lower-for-longer forward guidance and QE. In Japan, decades of near-zero inflation or deflation have conditioned people to expect inflation to remain very low. Shifting those expectations has proved extremely difficult, despite very active monetary policy since about 2013. In Europe and Japan, greater fiscal support may be needed in the future to bring inflation and inflation expectations closer to target, which in turn would raise the neutral interest rate and increase the potency of monetary policy.

---

* As in the United States, inflation in most advanced economies, notably the United Kingdom and the euro area, jumped in 2021, the result of pandemic-related supply-side constraints and higher energy prices. If those factors recede, inflation in those economies could well fall back below target.

COSTS AND RISKS OF THE NEW POLICY TOOLS

The additional firepower that QE and strong forward guidance can provide must be weighed against unintended costs and risks. Quantitative easing in particular raised concerns both inside and outside the Fed when it was first used after the global financial crisis. The FOMC continued to discuss possible costs and risks throughout the recovery from the Great Recession, including risks to financial stability, the possibility that inflation or inflation expectations could become unanchored, potential difficulties in managing the eventual exit from QE, possible adverse effects on the functioning of key securities markets, and the risk of capital losses on the Fed's large securities portfolio. Some FOMC participants worried that these risks could be amplified by lower-for-longer forward guidance that might keep the funds rate near zero for years. Now that we can draw on substantial experience, both in the United States and other economies, what can we say about these potential costs and risks of the new monetary tools?

Many of the concerns about QE and lower-for-longer forward guidance have proved to be unfounded. Dire warnings notwithstanding, those policies have not led to sustained excessive inflation. (The increase in inflation in 2021 reflected a number of factors besides QE, including fiscal policy and supply-side effects associated with the pandemic.) To the contrary, from 2008 to 2020, inflation in the United States and other major economies generally remained too low, reflecting economic slack and the effects of the lower bound.

Exiting from QE has also not been a problem thus far, at least from a technical perspective. When the Yellen Fed began to tighten policy, the Fed's ability to pay interest on reserves allowed it to raise the funds rate with little difficulty, despite the large size of its balance sheet. Once the funds rate had moved above zero, the Fed then allowed its balance sheet to shrink by ending reinvestment of repayments of principal on its securities holdings. Judging by the flare-up in repo markets in September 2019, the Fed probably reduced its balance sheet and the supply of bank reserves, if anything, by somewhat too much. In that sense, the Fed's balance sheet can be said to have fully normalized by 2019, at a level consistent with its new ample-reserves operating framework, until the pandemic crisis forced new securities purchases in 2020. The Bank of England, the other major central bank that quickly adopted QE after the financial crisis, also experienced no technical problems in raising rates at the appropriate time.

Nor is there evidence that QE has impeded the functioning of U.S. securities markets, by crowding out private buyers and sellers, for example, or by creating shortages of particular bond issues. To the contrary, by adding liquidity, promoting confidence, and strengthening financial institutions' balance sheets, QE likely improved market functioning during the global financial crisis and the European sovereign debt crisis. In the early days of the 2020 pandemic shock, Fed securities purchases—though not technically QE, at least initially since their goal was not to provide monetary stimulus—helped return financial and credit markets to normal functioning. And, although the risk of losses on the Fed's portfolio remains, it is moderate. If future losses do occur, they should be weighed against the more than $800 billion in net returns that the Fed remitted to the Treasury in the decade before the pandemic, the higher tax revenues generated by a stronger economy, and the lower cost of financing government debt.[16] In any case, the purpose of monetary policy is to help achieve high employment and price stability, not to make profits for the Treasury.

Although these frequently cited risks now appear negligible, or at least insufficient to prevent the use of QE and lower-for-longer guidance when needed, debate on other issues continues. I'll discuss four here: the purported link between the new monetary tools and financial instability; the perception that QE, and easy money generally, promotes economic inequality; the complaint that QE distorts capital market signals; and the concern that easy money creates zombie firms.

Financial Instability

The relationship between easy money and financial stability is a large and controversial topic. In brief, the evidence does suggest that sustained monetary ease may promote private risk-taking, which can help speed recovery in a depressed economy but may also increase the risk of dangerous financial instability over time. Most economists and policymakers agree that financial-stability risks should be addressed primarily with targeted tools, such as financial regulation and supervision, leaving monetary policy free to pursue its price stability and employment goals. The main controversies concern whether regulation and other targeted tools are sufficient and, if not, whether and to what degree monetary policymakers should take financial-stability concerns into account when setting rates.

Deferring the broader issue to a later chapter, the narrower question taken up here is whether QE and forward guidance are *particularly* likely to increase financial risks. Is there anything about these alternative tools, other than the fact that they are associated with persistently low interest rates, that should be particularly worrisome for financial stability? At least so far, the answer appears to be no.

At least two principal arguments are made for why QE and forward guidance might stimulate more risk-taking than other forms of monetary easing. First, QE works in part by inducing private investors to rebalance their portfolios. The investors who sell Treasuries and MBS to the Fed presumably use some of the proceeds to buy other assets, some of which are riskier than the assets sold to the Fed. This portfolio rebalancing allows QE to influence the prices of securities, like corporate bonds, that are not purchased by the central bank. The rebalancing effect also explains why many investors perceive QE as enhancing market liquidity: QE purchases provide liquid funds that the sellers of securities use to buy other, possibly riskier assets.

While QE does leave some investors with riskier portfolios, on net it can actually reduce financial risk in the private sector, in two ways. First, QE injects reserves into the banking system and removes longer-term securities in equal amount. Longer-term securities are riskier than (safe, liquid) bank reserves because their values can change sharply when longer-term interest rates change. Economists Ricardo Caballero and Gunes Kamber found that, after the financial crisis, QE allowed the Fed to absorb, on net, risk previously held by investors, reducing the risk of the typical private portfolio.[17] Second, by lowering longer-term interest rates and strengthening corporate borrowers' balance sheets, QE also typically lowers the riskiness of existing corporate bonds and similar assets.[18] The stabilizing effects of QE-type policies were particularly evident during March 2020, when the Fed's large-scale purchases of Treasuries and MBS provided needed liquidity and calmed market volatility.

Another argument linking the new monetary tools to financial instability begins with the observation that lower-for-longer forward guidance—and QE, in its rate-signaling effects—assures investors that short-term rates will be kept low for some time. Lower-for-longer guidance, this argument goes, emboldens investors to take undue risks because they no longer have to worry about near-term changes in the policy rate. For example, lower-for-longer guidance might lead investors to plunge into so-called *carry trades*—borrowing short-term to hold higher-yielding, longer-term investments. A similar contention, incidentally, holds that the predictability of the long sequence of rate increases between 2004 and 2006 was likewise destabilizing, by making investors too confident of the future rate path and thus less inclined to be cautious.

This reasoning misses the important point that, even in a lower-for-longer rate environment, most financial and real assets have expected maturities well beyond the horizon of policymakers' forward guidance. Thus, even if short rates are guaranteed (or at least highly likely) to stay low for a time, most asset prices will still move in response to economic news relevant to the longer-term outlook. A paper by John Williams, then the president of the Federal Reserve Bank of San Francisco and now the head of the New York Fed, and Eric Swanson showed that, even after the Fed dropped the funds rate to near zero in 2008, longer-term interest rates rose and fell in response to jobs reports and other economic news much as they had before the crisis.[19] For this reason, in practice forward guidance does not eliminate the financial risks inherent in carry trades and similar strategies. To the contrary, these trades have been likened to picking up nickels in front of a steamroller. Most of the time they yield a small profit, but occasionally (when the prices of longer-term assets move unexpectedly) they lead to a large loss. The profit opportunities from carry trades are further reduced by the fact that any reduction in uncertainty resulting from credible forward guidance is likely to be already priced into longer-term assets. In particular, guidance should lower the risk premium that investors earn on longer-term assets, reducing the potential profit of carry trades. In short, lower-for-longer forward guidance provides no evident incentive for excessive risk-taking, over and above those created by low-interest-rate policies generally.

I conclude that QE and forward guidance do not pose significant additional financial-stability risks, relative to easy money in general. Indeed, they are most likely to be used during times of crisis or severe economic weakness, when private risk-taking is typically too low rather than too high. In those circumstances, the new tools—by improving confidence, strengthening balance sheets, and increasing access to credit—are as likely to reduce as to increase financial-stability risks.

Economic Inequality

The FOMC's discussions sometimes allude to the distributional effects of monetary policy, but in practice the Fed's mandate and the bluntness of its policy instruments lead the Committee to focus on overall economic performance. Some critics have argued that the relative neglect of the distributional consequences of monetary policy is a problem. They contend that easy-money policies, including QE and lower-for-longer forward guidance, tend to increase economic inequality and should accordingly be used sparingly.

Although often heard, this critique is not persuasive. Monetary policies that promote economic recovery have broad benefits, including increasing employment, wages, capital investment, and tax revenues. Given the widespread gains from a strong economy, as well as the reduced risk of unwanted disinflation or even a deflationary trap, easy monetary policies in a downturn could be justified even if they did increase inequality.

However, most research finds that, once all the channels of monetary policy are considered, expansionary policies have small distributional effects and may even reduce inequality on net, especially inequality measured in terms of income or consumption. Perhaps most importantly, much evidence suggests that "hot" labor markets disproportionately benefit minority and lower-income communities, whereas extended recessions increase economic inequality by reducing employment opportunities for people in those communities, as well as for workers with fewer skills or less experience.[20] This point came through loud and clear in the Fed Listens sessions conducted by the Powell Fed. That feedback helped to motivate the shift to a policy framework that puts a greater emphasis on achieving and maintaining high levels of employment. Because of the broad-based benefits of strong labor markets, pro-worker groups tend to favor expansionary monetary policies when demand is weak and see easy money as helping, not hurting low- and middle-income people.

Two questions are frequently raised in response to these arguments: First, aren't retirees and other savers living on interest income hurt by easy money? And second, doesn't easy money, including QE, worsen wealth inequality by raising stock prices?

On the first question, some retirees and other savers do depend heavily on interest income—and are thus vulnerable to low rates—but their situation is not typical. According to the national income accounts, as of mid-2021, net interest income made up only about 8 percent of total personal income. (The comparable figure at the beginning of 2019, when the funds rate was at its recent peak and QE was not being used, was 9 percent.) Among retirees, the least-well-off depend primarily on government programs like Social Security and Medicare, whose payments are not sensitive to changes in interest rates.* More broadly, in a 2013 study, Richard Kopcke and Andrew Webb estimated the reductions in investment income (both interest and dividends) of families with heads aged 60–69 during the period 2007–2013, a time when the economy was weak and monetary

---

* Social Security has effectively stabilized the ratio of retirement income to preretirement income for most older Americans and reduced poverty among the elderly to low levels. See Devlin-Foltz, Henriques, and Sabelhaus (2016).

policy was radically eased.[21] They found that, relative to 2007 income, declines in investment income across wealth quintiles ranged from near zero to 6 percent, with the greater reductions suffered by relatively well-off families (who own more financial assets).

These relatively moderate effects of easy money result in part from the fact that many families enter retirement with at least some assets whose values typically rise or remain stable when interest rates are low: For example, as of 2019, about 60 percent of working-age families (and just under 40 percent of families in the bottom half of the income distribution) had a company pension or retirement plan, and about 65 percent of families (50 percent in the bottom half of the income distribution) owned their own home. Stock ownership is more concentrated than other assets, but 53 percent of families (and 31 percent in the bottom half of the distribution) owned at least some stocks in 2019, either directly or in a retirement plan.[22]

In addition, savers, including retirees, typically have many economic roles, which benefit from appropriately easy money. For example, they may have children helped by an improving labor market, or they may want the option to hold a job themselves. They may also hope to sell a home or family business, which is easier when the economy is healthy. Or they may be borrowers as well as savers, benefiting from lower rates—for example, by refinancing a mortgage. Once again, evaluating the impact of monetary easing requires consideration of all of its economic effects.

On the second question, higher stock prices do tend to increase wealth inequality (as opposed to income inequality), since richer people are more likely to own stocks, either directly or indirectly in retirement plans.[*] However, higher stock prices are the likely consequence of almost any economic policy that increases economic growth and employment, not only monetary policy. Disqualifying any government policy that has a positive effect on stock prices would make no sense. Moreover, while it is true that higher-income people own the most stock, other forms of wealth—such

---

[*] About 90 percent of families in the top income decile own stocks directly or indirectly, according to the Fed's *Survey of Consumer Finances*.

as housing or a stake in a small business—are important assets for many middle-class families, as already noted. A stronger economy and lower interest rates also boost these other forms of wealth. In any case, for those concerned (appropriately) with the long-run increase in wealth inequality in the United States, there is a much more direct and effective solution than neutering monetary policy, which is to raise the tax on capital gains. It is telling that those who criticize the Fed for increasing wealth inequality rarely propose this much more direct solution to the problem.*

To be clear, none of this is intended to downplay the problem of the widening gulf between the rich and poor. Large and persistent racial differences in wealth—the result of many years of discrimination, including by the government itself—are particularly concerning.[23] However, inequality has been rising in the United States since at least the 1970s, regardless of the ups and downs of interest rates. This long-term trend is primarily the result of slowly evolving forces, including technological change, globalization, and changes in labor markets that reduce workers' bargaining power. As such, inequality can be most effectively addressed by comprehensive government policies, including fiscal programs (taxes, transfers, and other spending) that provide more help to lower-income people, as well as policies that broaden access to housing, health care, and education generally. Monetary policy's greatest contribution to reducing inequality is promoting economic recovery and helping to keep unemployment low.

Market Distortions

Some critics, such as the authors of the well-publicized open letter to the FOMC in 2010, claim that easy-money policies, and especially QE, harm economic efficiency by "distorting" interest rates and other market signals.

---

* A more subtle point is that even as lower interest rates have pushed up stock values, lower rates also imply lower returns; that is, stock owners receive less dividend income from each dollar's worth of stock. Reflecting this lower return, despite much higher stock prices, personal income receipts from assets have fallen from 17 percent of GDP in 1990 to around 13 percent today, according to the St. Louis Fed's FRED database.

In this view, the Fed should allow the market to set interest rates and asset prices, without interference.

However, in a fiat-money system—one in which money is not backed by a physical commodity such as gold—it is not possible for a central bank to leave asset prices and yields entirely to the free market.* It must set *some* policy regarding interest rates and the money supply, which in turn inevitably influence market outcomes. Moreover, monetary policy is not unique in affecting interest rates and asset prices. Government spending and taxation, the Treasury's decisions about the maturities of the debt it issues, financial regulation, and many other government policies all contribute as well.† In modern economies, there is no such thing as a "pure" market outcome in which asset prices and yields are entirely free of all policy influence.

Perhaps the critics are arguing that monetary policy should be more passive. For example, the Fed could simply fix the quantity of reserves in the banking system and not respond to changes in prices and employment. Possibly, that would simplify the lives of bond traders by reducing, at least somewhat, the amount of information—including central bank communication—that they must process. However, it's hard to see why the Fed's abandoning its maximum employment and price stability mandate, as a purely passive policy would almost surely demand, would lead to better allocation of capital or preferable economic outcomes. Indeed, the most basic requirement for economic efficiency is that the economy's resources, including the labor force, be fully employed.

---

* In practice, even under the pre-Depression gold standard, central banks had some scope to manage interest rates, especially if their gold reserves were high enough that outflows posed no threat to maintaining convertibility between currency and gold at the established rate.

† Of these, QE is closest to the Treasury's decisions about debt maturities. If you think of the government as having a consolidated balance sheet, combining the assets and liabilities of the Treasury and the Fed, QE amounts to a swap of short-term government liabilities (interest-paying bank reserves) for longer-term government liabilities (government bonds). From this perspective, the effects of QE on asset prices are similar to those of a decision by the Treasury to shorten the average maturity of the debt it issues.

Zombie Companies

A variant of the market distortion argument is the claim that extended easy money promotes the survival of so-called *zombie companies*. Zombie companies are firms that are fundamentally insolvent—their assets, including the present value of future profits, are less than their liabilities—but that nevertheless continue to operate. Zombie firms were first identified as a problem in Japan, although subsequent work has argued that the phenomenon occurs in other countries as well.[24] With interest rates very low for many years, an increasing number of fundamentally insolvent firms in Japan were nevertheless still able to make the required interest payments on their debts, which in turn allowed their bankers to avoid declaring their loans in default—a practice known as "evergreening." Zombie firms are a problem for economic growth and efficiency not only because they themselves have low productivity, but because they take market share away from more-efficient firms, reducing the efficient companies' profitability, investment, and hiring.

In general, if interest rates are low, some lower-productivity firms that would not otherwise be funded may receive financing. However, that outcome does not necessarily imply that capital is misallocated. If interest rates are low because desired global saving exceeds the high-return investments available, for example, then some saving will necessarily flow to lower-return investments, which are its best available use. Likewise, if interest rates are low because the economy is in recession and monetary policy is easy, then the alternative to devoting resources to lower-return investments is to leave those resources unemployed. The funding of low-productivity firms thus does not automatically misallocate capital. We have to ask, what is the best alternative use? Misallocation requires that, for some reason, there are higher-productivity alternatives that are *not* being funded. Low interest rates on their own should ease, not block, the funding of high-return investments.

Low interest rates promote "zombie-ism" and the associated misallocations only if there are other, accompanying problems in the financial system and financial regulation. In the case of Japan, the main problem was the combination of undercapitalized banks (earlier bank reforms had been incomplete) and weak bank supervision. This regulatory breakdown led banks to allocate too much capital to zombie firms instead of more productive investments. Undercapitalized banks had an incentive not to recognize loan losses, since doing so would reduce their reported capital and lead to penalties—hence the evergreening, which postponed the formal recognition of losses. For their part, effective supervisors would have forced the banks to hold adequate capital and to promptly recognize and write down bad loans. (Political pressures from the banks and the zombie firms themselves may help explain supervisors' passivity.) In short, while low interest rates may have made evergreening easier, the deeper problem in Japan's case lay in inadequate bank capital and bank supervision. Addressing issues of regulatory or market failure, rather than raising interest rates above the level consistent with full employment and price stability, is the most direct way of dealing with the zombie problem. Recent research finds that "zombie-ism" is not a major issue in the United States, although programs designed to help firms through the pandemic risk increasing the problem in the future.[25]

In summary, QE and forward guidance have substantial ability to add stimulus when the policy rate can be cut no further. And the costs of these policies appear manageable.[26] The Fed and all other major central banks now view QE and forward guidance as basic elements of the policy toolkit, available not only in crises but whenever additional stimulus is needed. However, these tools may not always be enough, particularly in a deep economic downturn. Monetary policymakers therefore continue their search for new tools and strategies.

13

MAKING POLICY MORE POWERFUL

New Tools and Frameworks

QUANTITATIVE EASING AND FORWARD GUIDANCE, used forcefully and in coordination, can deliver stimulus that I estimate to be roughly equal to 3 percentage points of additional cuts in the federal funds rate at the lower bound. However, that additional firepower, as useful as it is, will not be enough in all circumstances, particularly if the nominal neutral interest rate, R*—and thus the Fed's policy space—proves to be lower than current estimates. Policymakers must continue to explore additional options for responding to shortfalls in employment and inflation.

Some options are promising, though political issues (including, possibly, the necessity of getting new legal authority from Congress) might complicate their adoption. For example, central banks abroad have used tools that the Federal Reserve might consider, including negative interest rates and yield curve control. And alternative policy frameworks, building on the developments of the past few years, could add clarity and credibility to forward guidance.

Still, even with an enhanced toolkit, monetary policy in the future will likely have to partner with fiscal policy to tackle deep downturns, as it did during the pandemic recession. Fiscal policy is hampered by a cumbersome political process, but it has the advantages of being powerful even when (or especially when) the neutral interest rate is low; and, to a much greater degree than monetary policy, it can more precisely target groups or sectors that need help. More-exotic possibilities for monetary-fiscal cooperation include so-called helicopter money and Modern Monetary Theory, which recommends that monetary and fiscal policy reverse their standard roles.

NEW TOOLS: LEARNING FROM
THE FOREIGN EXPERIENCE

Like the Federal Reserve, other leading central banks—notably, the Bank of England, the European Central Bank, and the Bank of Japan—have confronted the challenges of 21st century monetary policy, including the global financial crisis, the ensuing Great Recession, and the shock of the pandemic. The ECB also contended with a sovereign debt crisis and an imperfectly integrated eurozone, and the Bank of Japan came into the global financial crisis having already grappled since the mid-1990s with persistently low inflation and interest rates.

The four major central banks reacted similarly to 21st century crises, with some differences in timing. All responded to both the financial crisis of 2007–2009 and the pandemic panic in the spring of 2020 by serving as active lenders of last resort, seeking to stabilize financial conditions and financial institutions, and developing or expanding programs to help backstop private credit markets. Each of the central banks, having exhausted the conventional monetary policy ammunition of short-term rate cuts, looked for other methods to add stimulus. All have used Fed-style QE, purchasing longer-term securities to bring down longer-term interest rates and ease financial conditions generally. All relied on increasingly explicit forward guidance, communicating their plans for their short-term policy rate and for securities purchases as well.

Foreign central banks have also devised policy tools that have *not* been used by the Fed. That raises the possibility that the Fed, learning from its peers, could further expand its policy arsenal. The Fed could consider at least four alternative tools used by foreign central banks: QE purchases of a broader range of financial assets, funding-for-lending programs, negative interest rates, and yield curve control.[1] Although none of these alternatives will displace QE and forward guidance, under the right circumstances each could add useful policy space.

QE Purchases of a Broader Range of Financial Assets

Except when the Federal Reserve invokes its Section 13(3) emergency lending powers, available only when private credit markets are severely disrupted, it faces relatively tight restrictions on the securities it can buy. The Fed in its QE programs has purchased only Treasury securities and government-guaranteed, mortgage-related securities issued by GSEs like Fannie Mae and Freddie Mac.[*] Using its 13(3) authority, the Fed did acquire other securities, including commercial paper during the 2007–2009 crisis and in 2020 and corporate bonds, municipal bonds, and bank loans in 2020. However, the Fed's purchases of alternative assets in those two episodes were comparatively quite modest in size, were aimed at preventing breakdowns in specific credit markets, and were kept legally and conceptually separate from QE and monetary policy.

The QE programs by the other major central banks, like those of the Fed, also mostly involved purchases of government securities or government-guaranteed debt. But, facing fewer legal constraints, foreign central banks have also routinely bought other types of assets, including corporate bonds, commercial paper, covered bonds (a type of mortgage-backed security issued by European banks), and—in the case of the Bank of Japan—even the stock of private companies and shares in real estate investment trusts. The logic of buying, say, corporate bonds, was the same as the logic behind the Fed's purchases of mortgage-backed securities during and after the global financial crisis. In both cases, central-bank purchases reduce the yields on the targeted securities, encouraging borrowing and spending— on capital investment, in the case of corporate bond purchases, and on housing and other real estate, when MBS are bought. And, as government

---

[*] The Fed also has authority, which has not been used in its QE programs, to buy certain short-term municipal securities.

bond purchases affect the yields of related assets, the effects of central-bank purchases of other securities likewise spill over more broadly. Buying high-grade corporate bonds, for example, also lowers yields on other types of bonds such as municipal debt, issued by states and localities, and higher-risk corporate debt.

As noted, purchases of financial assets other than government debt have generally been only a small part of foreign QE, leaving limited empirical evidence on their effects. But what evidence exists suggests that including a wider range of securities enhances the power of QE. For example, research by Stefania D'Amico and Iryna Kaminska found that the Bank of England's purchases of corporate debt reduced the spread between corporate bond yields and U.K. government debt yields and stimulated new corporate bond issuance.[2] These effects are similar to the effects of the Fed's MBS purchases, which lowered the spread between mortgage yields and Treasury yields, promoting mortgage refinancing and housing sales and construction.

As mentioned, unlike other major central banks, the Fed does not have the authority to buy a broader range of assets as part of routine monetary policy. To purchase corporate or most municipal securities, non-GSE mortgages, and other alternative assets as part of a noncrisis QE program, the Fed would need permission from Congress. Should it seek that permission?

The strongest argument for expanding the list of QE-eligible assets is that it could help make the Fed's securities purchases both more targeted and more effective. It was fortunate that the Fed had the authority to buy mortgage-related securities during and after the global financial crisis—a crisis driven by the breakdown of mortgage markets. But the trouble during some future crisis or recession could be concentrated in a sector other than housing. Moreover, Congress's willingness to authorize, even temporarily, Fed purchases of corporate bonds, municipal bonds, and bank loans in the 2020 CARES Act suggests that legislators may be more open to expanding the Fed's authorities than I would have thought a decade ago.

On the other hand, routine noncrisis purchases of, say, corporate bonds as part of QE would cross lines that the Fed has tried to preserve. First, the FOMC has tried when possible to avoid directly allocating credit, which would inevitably favor some borrowers over others. For this reason, the Committee agreed after the Great Recession to hold primarily Treasury securities in the longer term and run its mortgage-related holdings down to minimal levels so as not to create a long-run bias in favor of housing over other types of investment. Second, buying private-sector or municipal debt—unlike buying Treasuries or government-guaranteed MBS—involves taking on credit risk, which the Fed is reluctant to do on the grounds that any losses would reduce the profits it sends to the Treasury.

These concerns do not sink the case for expanding the range of allowable purchases. To minimize the risk of favoring certain firms or sectors when buying, say, corporate bonds, the Fed could buy broad, well-diversified portfolios of those securities, as it did in its 13(3) corporate bond facility in 2020. (However, that approach would still favor large corporations over smaller firms, which generally cannot issue bonds.) Broad diversification, and the fact that the private-sector securities the Fed would purchase during periods of stress would earn a higher-than-usual yield, should also minimize the Fed's exposure to credit losses. In addition, the evidence suggests that yields on private-sector debt, such as corporate bonds, rise much more in recessions or during periods of financial instability than is justified by increases in default risk.[3] Monetary easing may also reduce corporate default risk, and thus the risk to the Fed of acquiring corporate bonds.[4]

All that said, the Federal Reserve probably will not press Congress any time soon for the authority to buy private-sector debt in QE programs, unless policy space becomes considerably more constrained. The purchases of Treasuries and MBS alone, through spillover effects, already give the Fed significant leverage over municipal and private-sector yields. And having the power to buy a wide range of financial assets might compromise the Fed's independence if it caused Congress to pressure the Fed to buy securities issued by borrowers with political influence, or to avoid the securities of disfavored companies.[5] Probably for this reason, Chair Powell frequently emphasized during the pandemic crisis that the Fed's programs to buy corporate and municipal securities were limited and temporary. The debate in Congress in late 2020 about whether to renew the Fed's 13(3) lending facilities under the CARES Act suggests that giving the Fed permanent authority to purchase a wider range of assets would be politically controversial, with conservatives opposing any broader role for the Fed in financial markets.

Funding for Lending

Besides buying a variety of financial assets in QE, major foreign central banks also subsidized bank lending. Following the terminology introduced by the Bank of England, these programs are often known as *funding-for-lending* schemes. A principal goal was to help household or small-business borrowers, who can't access stock or bond markets and rely heavily on bank credit.

The original Funding-for-Lending Scheme was announced jointly by the Bank of England and the U.K. Treasury in July 2012. Under it, the Bank of England provided funding—at a rate as low as 0.25 percent, for up to four years—to banks that increased their lending to households and nonfinancial businesses, with the amount of low-cost funding depending on how much that lending increased. The original program was expanded several times, closed in January 2018, then revived in modified form in response to the pandemic.

The European Central Bank's funding-for-lending program evolved from its lender-of-last-resort activities during the global financial crisis and the subsequent sovereign debt crisis. In October 2008, the ECB established long-term refinancing operations (LTROs). Banks were allowed to borrow from the ECB with no limit—as long as they had adequate collateral—at a fixed interest rate. Initially, the rate charged was 4.25 percent and the maximum term of the loan was six months, but over time the ECB lowered the rate, extended the term, and eased collateral requirements. These loans to banks did not initially include restrictions on how they were to be used, but in June 2014, under Mario Draghi, the ECB began to tie the terms of LTRO loans to banks' new lending. Under Draghi's targeted LTRO program (TLTRO), banks could borrow for up to four years at a low rate, but—as with the British program—the amount a bank could borrow at the most favorable rates depended on its net increase in lending to nonfinancial businesses and households.

The TLTRO program was expanded several times, with increasingly generous terms. In response to the pandemic, the ECB, under Draghi's successor Christine Lagarde, provided long-term funding to banks at rates as low as *minus* 1 percent, again under the condition that the cheap funds be used for new loans. The Bank of Japan also operated a diverse set of programs, including low-cost funding for banks and direct loans to businesses. Evidence suggests that funding-for-lending programs have been an important supplement to other monetary policy tools. Take-up, as measured by bank borrowing and net increases in lending, has been large, especially in Europe, and studies find that these programs lowered the costs of bank funding, increased lending to the private sector, and improved the passthrough of other monetary actions to the economy.[6]

The Federal Reserve, alone among the major central banks, did not introduce a funding-for-lending program during the recovery from the Great Recession. The Board and the FOMC considered the possibility but were dissuaded after discussions with bank and market contacts. The main constraint on new lending, we heard, was not the cost of funding—American banks, having been recapitalized after the crisis, could borrow cheaply on private markets—but a lack of creditworthy borrowers and tighter postcrisis credit standards. Consequently, for better or worse, we did not pursue the idea.

The 2020 pandemic, however, significantly increased the Fed's role in credit markets, at least for a time. With fiscal support from Congress and the Treasury, the Fed used its 13(3) authority to create several temporary facilities to keep credit flowing to businesses, state and local governments, and other borrowers. These included the Main Street Lending Program, which, like foreign funding-for-lending programs, was intended to increase lending to bank-dependent borrowers.

However, the structure of the Main Street program differed importantly from the foreign programs. Overseas funding-for-lending facilities provided cheap funding but left the loans made to households and businesses on the balance sheets of the lending banks. Instead, in the Main Street facility, the Fed proposed to buy and hold 95 percent of each loan made, shouldering most of the risk of non-repayment (on behalf of the Treasury, which put up funds for this purpose). Because it was taking credit risk on behalf of the taxpayer, the Fed put numerous conditions on borrower eligibility and on the terms of loans. Likely because these terms and conditions were not sufficiently attractive, either to borrowers or banks, relatively few Main Street loans were made. In addition, for banks with adequate capital and ability to bear risk—a category that included most U.S. banks in 2020—the Fed's risk-sharing plan did not provide much incentive to make loans they would not otherwise have made. Treasury Secretary Steven Mnuchin shut down all of the 13(3) programs approved through the CARES Act at the end of 2020.

The Fed thought of its lending programs during the pandemic as emergency financial-stability facilities rather than as part of monetary policy. That distinction was underscored by the programs' reliance on 13(3) authority and on Treasury funds specially appropriated by Congress. Conceivably, though, special lending programs could supplement existing monetary policy tools in the future. For example, when tight credit is hampering economic recovery, or if bank funding markets are under stress, the Fed might extend cheap, long-term funding to banks in the amount that they increase their lending to, say, households and small businesses, taking the loans made as collateral. These loans to banks could be provided through the Fed's discount window and under most circumstances would require neither 13(3) authority nor Treasury capital. (The Fed cannot lend directly to corporations or other nonbank borrowers without invoking its 13(3) emergency authority.)

This approach could be implemented as needed and, importantly, would have the virtue of simplicity. The only terms to be specified would be the Fed's lending rate and the categories of loans eligible for cheap Fed funding. The principal drawback of funding-for-lending is that, if the lending rate is below the interest rate paid on bank reserves, as would be expected, the implied subsidy to bank lending would reduce the Fed's prof-its and, ultimately, its payments to the Treasury. Whether the Treasury and Congress would object to the Fed providing an implicit subsidy would probably depend on the economic circumstances. A related issue is that, if short-term rates are near zero, the Fed might have to explicitly pay banks to increase their lending—for example, by charging a negative interest rate on the funding it provides—as the ECB did during the pandemic. In that situation, an alternative to setting an explicitly negative interest rate on discount-window loans that fund new lending would be to pay participat-ing banks a higher interest rate on an amount of their reserves equal to their increase in lending.

Negative Interest Rates

The ECB, the Bank of Japan, and the central banks of several European countries outside the eurozone (including Sweden, Denmark, and Swit-zerland) have reduced their short-term policy rates below zero. The neg-ative rates are enforced by charging banks a fee on their reserves held at the central bank, which is equivalent to a negative interest rate. To avoid the charge, banks try to switch to other assets, driving down the yields on those assets as well, sometimes even into negative territory. Since people and businesses can avoid negative returns by holding currency, which pays zero interest, negative rates can only go so low. But because transacting and saving in, say, $20 bills or $100 bills can be inconvenient or costly for consumers and businesses, let alone for banks that must settle hundreds of very large transactions each day, it appears that rates can fall modestly below zero without creating a large-scale shift to cash.* For example, short-term (three-month) interest rates have fallen as low as minus 0.75 per-cent in Sweden and minus 0.85 percent in Switzerland. Among the major central banks, the ECB has relied most heavily on negative rates. It first

---

* As Kenneth Rogoff has argued in his 2017 book, *The Curse of Cash: How Large-Denomination Bills Aid Crime and Tax Evasion and Constrain Monetary Policy,* even more negative rates would be possible if the government worked to reduce the use of cash, particularly large bills, which are less costly to store.

introduced negative rates in 2014 and, in increments, lowered the rate it pays to banks on their reserves until it reached minus 0.50 percent in September 2019.[7]

Within the limited range experienced so far, negative policy rates appear to have achieved their purpose. They've resulted in lower interest rates on bank loans, lower money market rates, and lower longer-term interest rates. And they've eased financial conditions generally. So negative rates can add at least a moderate amount of monetary policy space by lowering the effective lower bound on short-term interest rates. The lower bound seems likely to be a perennial concern, so that extra space could prove useful.

Negative rates are controversial, though. Many people would view the idea of receiving fewer dollars back from their bank than they deposited as unfair, or find it confusing that borrowers may receive rather than pay interest. However, negative rates are not so paradoxical when we recognize that, for most economic decisions, the relevant measure of the return to investment or the cost of borrowing is not the nominal (or market) interest rate, but the real interest rate, equal to the nominal rate less the rate of inflation. Historically, negative real interest rates are not uncommon; that happens whenever inflation exceeds nominal interest rates. For example, in late 2021, with headline CPI inflation over 6 percent and the funds rate near zero, the *real* federal funds rate was roughly minus 6 percent. Moreover, for an investor, the difference between a return of, say, 0.1 percent and a return of minus 0.1 percent is negligible. Nevertheless, people's anxiety or confusion about negative rates often translates into political opposition, which makes central bankers reluctant to use them.

A more substantive objection asserts that negative rates may increase financial-stability risks. For example, banks complain that negative rates reduce their profits and ultimately their capital and lending capacity. The banks' primary concern is that they may not be able to pass on the negative rates they receive on their reserves. Depositors rebel at negative rates on checking and savings accounts, forcing the banks to make up the difference. Indeed, some economists have argued that a "reversal rate" of interest may exist, below which the adverse effects of a negative rate on bank capital and bank lending could make the policy economically con-tractionary on net.[8]

In practice, negative rates do not seem to have seriously damaged bank profits, at least so far.[9] In fact, negative rates can improve bank profitabil-ity. If negative rates, by giving the central bank more policy space, lead to a stronger economy, banks will benefit from increased revenues and lower credit losses. Lower interest rates also tend to increase the value of assets in banks' portfolios while reducing their funding costs from sources other than deposits, such as wholesale funding and the bonds they issue. More-over, central banks have found ways to mitigate the effects of negative rates on bank profits. For example, the Bank of Japan and the ECB charge banks a fee only on reserves above a certain level, a practice known as "tiering."

Should the Fed consider negative rates? Fed officials believe they have the authority to impose negative short-term rates (by charging a fee on bank reserves) but so far have shown little appetite for the idea. In 2010, we briefly discussed and rejected the option. We thought at the time that the benefits of negative rates would be quite limited. A staff memo esti-mated that, because Americans would likely hoard cash if rates got too negative, the funds rate could probably not be reduced below about minus 0.35 percent.[10] We also had financial-stability concerns, less about banks than about money market mutual funds, which are a more important part of the financial system in the United States than elsewhere. We worried they could face investor runs if negative returns on the assets they held forced them to "break the buck"—that is, return less than a dollar for each dollar invested. Discussions under Chairs Yellen and Powell have similarly not found much or any support for negative rates, at least as long as other options are available.

While I understand this reluctance, it is unwise to categorically rule out negative rates. I don't expect the United States to fall into a persistent low-inflation trap, but, if it does, negative rates could prove useful. Even short of that extreme, ruling out negative short-term rates could have the unintended consequence of limiting the Fed's ability to bring longer-term rates to very low levels, through QE or other means.[11] Because longer-term rates are typically a bit higher than the short-term rates that markets expect to see in the future, a credible commitment by monetary policymakers to keep short rates at or above zero could effectively set a floor under longer-term rates as well. Maintaining at least some constructive ambiguity about the possibility of negative policy rates seems a better strategy, though admittedly one that risks political pushback.

Yield Curve Control

A final policy option used abroad that the Fed might consider is *yield curve control*, introduced by the Bank of Japan in September 2016. Yield curve control, as the name suggests, involves controlling interest rates on government debt across a range of maturities by both pegging the short-term policy rate (as in traditional policymaking) and targeting a range for the yield on longer-term bonds. For example, the Bank of Japan announced in 2016 that it would keep the yield on ten-year Japanese government bonds in a range around zero, enforcing that target by standing ready to purchase bonds at a price consistent with a zero yield. In traditional QE, the central bank announces the quantity of securities it intends to buy, and the resulting pattern of interest rates is determined by the market. Yield curve control can be thought of as a form of QE that reverses the standard approach: Policymakers set a target for the yield on bonds but leave it to the market to determine the quantity of bonds that must be purchased to enforce that yield.

Yield curve control has several potential advantages over standard QE. First, because it targets longer-term interest rates, which directly affect many investment and spending decisions, it may allow policymakers to gauge more precisely the amount of stimulus they are providing. Second, if market participants believe the central bank is firmly committed to its yield targets, then bond yields may settle at their targets without the central bank actually having to buy significant quantities of securities.* In effect, the

---

* This consideration helped motivate the Bank of Japan's adoption of yield curve control, since at the Bank's ongoing rate of purchases it risked running out of government debt to buy.

announcement of a plan to peg bond yields may act as a form of forward guidance, guidance made more credible by the central bank's commitment to use its balance sheet to enforce it.

The Fed engaged in what amounted to yield curve control from 1942 until the 1951 Treasury-Fed Accord. To reduce the cost of financing the government's war debt, during that decade the Fed pegged the short-term Treasury bill rate (at 0.375 percent for most of the period) and enforced a ceiling of 2.5 percent on long-term government bonds. During my term as chair, the FOMC studied that episode carefully to see if it carried lessons for policy at the effective lower bound.[12] We concluded that, notwithstanding the pre-1951 experience, pegging or capping very long-term bond yields is probably not feasible, or at least not advisable, in the contemporary United States.

Suppose for example that the Fed tried to peg the ten-year government yield at 1 percent. That could work provided market participants believed that, under almost any circumstances, the Fed would keep short-term rates around 1 percent for the next ten years. But ten years is a long time, and a change in the economic outlook or in central-bank communication that caused market participants to suspect that the Fed might shift course over the next decade would bring the credibility of the peg into doubt. For example, what if an unexpected increase in inflation led markets to believe that the Fed would raise the funds rate to 2 percent and hold it there? The yield on longer-term bonds would then also tend toward 2 percent, notwithstanding the Fed's announced yield target. The Fed would then either have to abandon its announced yield target or buy a large share of outstanding bonds to enforce it—purchases that could severely complicate the eventual exit from the policy and expose the Fed to large capital losses.

How then was the pre-1951 Fed, or today's Bank of Japan, able to peg longer-term yields without massive bond purchases? The difference lies in the depth and liquidity of the markets for government debt in the contemporary United States. For example, many Japanese government bonds are held by banks and other institutions for regulatory or other reasons, rather than solely for their return, and the amount of trading of Japanese bonds tends to be quite low, relative to the outstanding stock. Pre-1951 Treasury markets were likewise much less liquid and active than they would ultimately become. In contrast, U.S. Treasuries today are traded globally in heavy volume. Because of the depth and liquidity of Treasury markets, a small inconsistency between a hypothetical Fed target for the longer-term Treasury yield and market expectations of future funds rates could force the Fed to buy massive amounts of securities.

Although targeting (say) the ten-year yield is probably off the table for the Fed, pegging Treasury yields at a horizon of two to three years would be feasible, as the FOMC could plausibly commit to a path of short-term rates over that horizon. An explicit peg of two- to three-year yields at a rate close to the lower bound could powerfully reinforce forward rate guidance—a form of putting your money where your mouth is. In its 2020 strategic review, the Fed explored medium-term interest-rate targets or caps, enforced by a commitment to buy securities at the desired yield.[13] Although medium-term yield curve control does not add much if markets are already persuaded that the Fed will keep its policy rate low for some time, I expect the Committee would seriously consider this approach if it believed its forward guidance for the funds rate wasn't working.

ALTERNATIVE POLICY FRAMEWORKS

Yield curve control is one way to strengthen forward guidance. Another is to embed forward guidance in a broader policy framework that lays out how policymakers plan to react to a wide range of economic conditions. With a clear policy framework, market participants will have a better sense of the form that guidance is likely to take, even before it is given. They will understand the circumstances that might cause policy to deviate from the guidance, and how. And they can be more confident that guidance, once given, will not be lightly abandoned. In short, a good policy framework can increase the coherence and predictability of policy in general, and guidance in particular.

Through the years, the Fed has followed a variety of monetary doctrines and frameworks, from the gold-standard orthodoxy of its early years to Greenspan's risk-management approach. But the FOMC did not adopt a formal policy framework until January 2012, when it established the 2 percent inflation target and explained its "balanced approach" to price stability and employment.[14] The flexible average inflation targeting (FAIT) approach endorsed by the FOMC in 2020 built on the foundations of the 2012 framework. It specified that, to keep inflation and inflation expectations near target on average, temporary overshoots of the target would compensate for undershoots. Under the new framework, the FOMC also foreswore pre-emptive strikes on inflation based only on falling unemployment.

The Fed adopted FAIT in response to a changing economic environment, including the declining neutral rate of interest, which increased the likelihood that the lower bound could constrain policy, as well as the growing realization that unemployment rates can be sustained at lower levels than in the past without fueling inflation. The economic environment will continue to change, of course, which may lead to further evolution of the Fed's framework (Notably, much will depend on how persistent the inflation surge in 2021 turns out to be, and on how the neutral interest rate evolves.) In announcing FAIT, Chair Powell noted that the Fed plans to review its framework every five years. In these coming debates, some alternative policy frameworks will likely command the Committee's attention. And, although the FOMC in the last review ruled out increasing its inflation target, some economists outside the Fed continue to advocate increasing the target to address the lower-bound problem.

Variants of Inflation Targeting

Many policy frameworks, including those in use (like FAIT) and others still on the drawing board, involve targets for the level or rate of change of consumer prices. For this discussion, we can think of these as variants of inflation targeting. Each of the leading variants comes with its own strengths and weaknesses.

The framework adopted by the FOMC in January 2012 (which I'll call here *standard inflation targeting*) remains, with minor differences across countries, the dominant framework globally. Central banks using this framework announce a specific numerical target or target range for inflation, to be achieved over the medium term—a term of art, but usually referring to a period of two to three years. (The effective lower bound on policy rates caused many central banks to undershoot their targets for much longer than that, however.) All standard inflation-targeting central banks take a flexible approach in practice, meaning that they pursue other goals besides price stability. Our 2012 principles emphasized that the FOMC would pursue maximum employment as well as price stability, consistent with the Fed's dual mandate. We saw the two goals as usually complementary. In particular, low and stable inflation improves the functioning of the economy and the labor market. And if keeping inflation near target helps anchor inflation expectations, monetary policymakers increase their ability to respond forcefully to declines in employment without destabilizing inflation. In cases in which the goals conflicted, we said that we would take a balanced approach in weighing each against the other.

One of the most important goals of inflation targeting in general is promoting accountability and transparency. Inflation-targeting central banks typically provide extensive information about their economic forecasts, policy analyses, and policy expectations. The numerical inflation goal, together with openness about policy plans and their rationales, imposes discipline and predictability without entirely removing central bankers' ability to respond to unforeseen circumstances. To use the phrase that I coined in my work with Rick Mishkin, inflation targeting and similar regimes allow monetary policymakers to exercise "constrained discretion."[15]

An inflation-targeting central bank tries to keep the inflation rate near the announced goal, but policy mistakes, recessions, supply shocks, or other factors can push the inflation rate away from the target. How should monetary policymakers respond when that happens? The answer helps differentiate variants of inflation targeting.

Under standard inflation targeting, the answer is relatively simple. Inflation misses either above or below target are equally concerning—the inflation target is "symmetric." So, in the standard approach, when inflation deviates from the target for any reason, policymakers aim to gradually return it to target. How gradually they do that can vary, depending on the state of the labor market, the risks to the outlook, the proximity of interest rates to the lower bound, and other factors. Importantly, though, under standard inflation targeting policymakers do not attempt to compensate for the size or duration of the earlier target miss. From whatever the starting point, the goal is just to get back to the target in a reasonable time. Bygones are bygones.

An alternative form of inflation targeting called *price-level targeting*— much studied by economists but so far not adopted by any central bank— articulates a different response. Under this framework, a central bank would try to keep the *level* of prices—not the inflation rate itself—close to a fixed, typically upward-sloping, path. (As with standard inflation targeting, in practice a price-level-targeting central bank would also consider employment and other goals in making its policy decisions, but I'll ignore that complication.)

Suppose the initial price of a basket of consumer goods is $100, and that a price-level-targeting central bank's goal is to have the price of that basket rise by 2 percent per year. If all goes according to plan, then the price of the consumer basket, equal to $100 in year one, will be $102 in year two, $104 (approximately) in year three, and so on. Now suppose that, unexpectedly, the price of the basket rises not to $102 in year two, but only to $101—that is, the inflation rate between periods one and two is 1 percent rather than 2 percent. What should the central bank do?

Following the miss, a standard inflation-targeting central bank would simply try to return the inflation rate to 2 percent. From the realized price level of $101 in year two, it would aim to get prices to $103 in year three, roughly 2 percent higher. (In year four it would aim for $105, and so on.) Under price-level targeting, however, the central bank aims to keep prices as close as possible to the *original* target path. So, after prices rise only to $101 in year two, this central bank would aim to get the price level to $104 in year three, bringing prices back to the original path. In inflation terms, the price-level-targeting central bank would compensate for the 1 percent inflation rate in year two by aiming for a (roughly) 3 percent rate in the following year. By fully offsetting deviations of inflation from 2 percent, the price-level-targeting central bank works to keep average inflation at 2 percent, even over long periods.*

Proponents point out several advantages of price-level targeting.[16] First, by targeting a specific level of prices at all future dates, and by fully offsetting any deviations of prices from their target path, this approach greatly reduces uncertainty about the long-run cost of living, which should make household and business planning easier. Second, if booms and recessions are caused mostly by shifts in total demand (for example, changes in consumer or government spending), then price-level targeting may help stabilize the economy more effectively than standard inflation targeting.

To illustrate the second point, suppose a decline in demand causes a recession; and, following the previous numerical example, assume that, for the usual Phillips-curve reasons, the recession is accompanied by a decline in inflation, from 2 percent to 1 percent. Under standard inflation targeting, the central bank would ease policy, aiming to return inflation to 2 percent, as well as to offset job losses. But a central bank targeting the price level would ease by even more, because (as in the numerical example) it would want to compensate for the initial inflation shortfall by raising inflation *above* 2 percent for long enough to return the price level to its original path. This more powerful easing policy under price-level targeting—and market expectations of that policy—would presumably help to return the economy to full employment more quickly as well. The lower-for-longer policy implied by price-level targeting would be particularly helpful when short rates are pinned to the lower bound, since then it's especially important to convince markets that policy will remain easy for an extended period.

Price-level targeting has some disadvantages. It may be harder to explain to markets and the public than standard inflation targeting,

---

* The example assumes the make-up period is one year. In practice, the central bank could return to the original price-level path more slowly or more quickly, depending on considerations like the state of the labor market.

making it both less effective and less credible. Also, price-level targeting may perform poorly in downturns caused by inflationary supply shocks such as a sharp increase in oil prices or the pandemic-era disruption of supply chains. Because a price-level-targeting central bank would aim to fully offset the upward jump in the price level resulting from the supply shock, which in turn would require driving inflation temporarily *below* its long-run average, it might have to tighten policy significantly even if the supply shock had also pushed the economy into recession.

This last disadvantage is addressed by a third variant of inflation targeting, known as *temporary price-level targeting* (TPLT). I proposed this approach in 2017 and evaluated a modified variant in a 2019 paper with Michael Kiley and John Roberts of the Federal Reserve Board.[17] As the name suggests, TPLT is like price-level targeting, but it applies in only a specific circumstance—when short-term interest rates are at the lower bound. I argued that, when the funds rate is at the lower bound, the Fed— in the spirit of price-level targeting—should commit to keeping it there at least until prior shortfalls of inflation from the target had been made up, returning average inflation to 2 percent. Once average inflation was back to 2 percent, in my proposal, the Fed could raise the funds rate from the lower bound.* Probably, the delay in tightening would imply that inflation would overshoot its target for a time, but under TPLT ultimately the Fed would aim to return inflation to 2 percent.

Temporary price-level targeting implies a powerful lower-for-longer rate policy at the lower bound, comparable to what ordinary price-level targeting would provide. At the same time, under TPLT, inflation target overshoots do not require a subsequent undershoot, avoiding the unattractive implication of ordinary price-level targeting that inflation overshoots caused by supply shocks must be fully reversed. Also, TPLT might

---

* Under TPLT, the return of average inflation to 2 percent is a necessary condition for lifting the funds rate from the lower bound. The Fed might choose to hold the rate at the lower bound for longer if labor market conditions did not sufficiently improve. The Fed would also want to be sure that average inflation had sustainably returned to 2 percent before raising the funds rate.

be easier to explain than ordinary price-level targeting because policy is expressed in terms of goals for the inflation rate rather than the price level.

Temporary price-level targeting requires that, when the funds rate is at the lower bound, inflation must be returned to 2 percent on average before the FOMC considers raising the funds rate. Over what period should the inflation average be calculated? My original proposal suggested that the entire shortfall of inflation since the policy rate first hit the lower bound should be made up before the funds rate is increased. However, Fed Board member Lael Brainard pointed out that such a plan could require the Fed to accept sustained overshoots of the inflation target, which in turn might destabilize inflation expectations.[18] My subsequent work with Kiley and Roberts, using simulations of the Fed's FRB/ US economic model, suggested that waiting only until inflation averaged 2 percent over the prior year before lifting the funds rate from the lower bound worked well. The strategy produced good results on average for both inflation and unemployment.

The Fed's 2020 FAIT framework, as implemented in the September 2020 FOMC statement, adopts elements of each of these variants of inflation targeting. Following the standard approach adopted in 2012, FAIT retains the 2 percent inflation target, the flexibility to respond both to inflation and employment goals, and transparency about the Committee's outlook and policy plans. However, the Committee's 2018–2020 strategic review concluded that standard inflation targeting does not adequately address the problems raised by the decline in the neutral interest rate and the more-frequent encounters with the lower bound that result. In particular, if the constraint imposed by the lower bound makes the Fed less effective at fighting recessions and low inflation—even with QE and other new tools—then, under standard inflation targeting, inflation might remain below its target most of the time. Chronically too-low inflation might in turn lower inflation expectations, which would further reduce the neutral interest rate and constrict the Fed's policy space.

The Fed's new framework addresses the downward bias in inflation under standard inflation targeting by combining elements from both

TPLT and ordinary price-level targeting.[19] When the funds rate is at the lower bound, the FOMC will follow the TPLT strategy, committing to refrain from tightening until average inflation has reached 2 percent. The Committee also specified that conditions in the labor market will have to be consistent with full employment before rate liftoff, which helps ensure that the return of inflation to 2 percent is sustainable.

Once liftoff occurs, under FAIT the Fed would manage the funds rate so that inflation moderately exceeds the target for some time, with the goal of keeping inflation near 2 percent on average and so anchoring inflation expectations near that level. The general principle that policymakers will try to compensate for periods of below-target inflation by subsequent overshoots is in the spirit of price-level targeting. A difference between FAIT and ordinary price-level targeting is that, under FAIT, the FOMC does not intend to compensate for *overshoots* of inflation by intentionally undershooting the target. This asymmetric policy, which on its own would tend to push inflation higher on average, is intended to offset the downward bias in inflation created by the constraint of the lower bound.

The FAIT framework, designed for a low-inflation world, was challenged by the large pandemic-induced supply shock in 2021, which raised inflation well above target. In those circumstances, the implications of FAIT are similar to those of standard inflation targeting. So long as inflation expectations remain anchored, monetary policymakers can be patient, allowing the supply shock to subside. However, if inflation expectations show signs of becoming dislodged, then policy must balance the need to keep inflation and inflation expectations near target with the goal of promoting recovery in the labor market.

Overall, the adoption of FAIT reflects the FOMC's concern that— with a low neutral interest rate, a flat Phillips curve, a low natural rate of unemployment, and a high risk of encountering the lower bound— inflation may often be too low (below the 2 percent target) rather than too high. The experiences of Japan and, to a lesser extent, the euro area, demonstrate the problems that very low inflation can cause. When the Fed next revisits its policy framework, the recent behavior of inflation—high, low, or on target—will be an important factor in determining whether FAIT is retained or modified.

Nominal GDP Targeting

Inflation targeting and its variants are not the only possible policy frameworks. A leading alternative, which the FOMC will likely discuss when it next reconsiders its framework, is *nominal GDP targeting*. (Nominal GDP is the total dollar value of goods and services produced within the country's borders.) Although nominal GDP targeting comes in several variants, the main idea—apparent from the name—is that the central bank sets policy to target nominal GDP rather than inflation. I'll focus here on the case in which a central bank sets a fixed target for the growth rate of nominal GDP and, in analogy to standard inflation targeting, does not try to make up for past undershoots or overshoots of the target.*

The growth rate of nominal GDP equals, by definition, the sum of the growth rate of real output and the rate of inflation (where inflation here is measured in terms of the prices of all the goods and services that make up the GDP, not just consumer prices). Targeting this variable, rather than inflation, has several potential advantages.

First, the central bank can more clearly signal that it cares about both real growth (and hence growth in employment) and inflation—a particularly relevant consideration for the Fed, with its dual mandate. Although flexible inflation-target advocates also take employment into account, supporters of nominal GDP targeting argue that, by explicitly including growth in the target, the central bank can underscore its commitment to supporting ongoing expansion of jobs and incomes. Indeed, for people who must make fixed dollar payments, like rent or mortgage payments, stability of nominal incomes may be more important than stability of inflation.

---

* The previously discussed variants of inflation targeting contrasted frameworks in which the central bank targets inflation (the rate of change of the price level) with an approach in which the target is the price level itself. Analogously, nominal GDP targeting can involve targeting either the growth rate or the level of nominal GDP, alternatives that raise issues similar to the choice between inflation targeting and price-level targeting.

Second, targeting nominal GDP generally tends to push monetary policy in the right direction after shocks to the economy. For example, if a recession causes real growth to slow, keeping nominal GDP growth on track will require higher growth and inflation, and thus easier monetary policy. Alternatively, a stagflationary supply shock that raises inflation and lowers real growth will not necessarily prompt the central bank to tighten, because in that case the effects of higher inflation and lower growth on nominal GDP growth are offsetting.

Third, targeting nominal GDP growth may help the central bank cope with declines in the neutral rate of interest. The neutral interest rate, measured in real terms, tends to move up or down with the economy's trend growth rate, since the real returns to capital investments are higher in a faster-growing economy. Now consider what happens if trend growth and the real neutral interest rate decline—for example, if each declines by 1 percent. For a central bank with a fixed inflation target, a 1 percent decline in the real neutral interest rate implies a 1 percent decline in the nominal neutral interest rate, R^*, as well, which further constrains the central bank's ability to ease policy. However, because nominal GDP growth is the sum of real output growth and inflation, a central bank that targets nominal GDP growth would compensate for a 1 percent decline in trend economic growth by aiming for an inflation rate that is 1 percent higher over time. With higher inflation and inflation expectations, then—notwithstanding the decline in trend growth—the nominal neutral interest rate, R^*, should not fall, preserving the available space for rate cuts.

In the midst of the slow recovery from the Great Recession, at its November 2011 meeting, the FOMC considered—and rejected—adopting a nominal GDP target.* We concluded that there should be a high bar for making such a dramatic change in our framework; and that the potential advantages of nominal GDP targeting, relative to standard inflation targeting—the framework that the FOMC had used implicitly and

---

* Most of the Committee's discussion centered around setting a target for the level of nominal GDP, rather than its rate of growth, but many of the FOMC's reservations would apply to either approach.

formally adopted two months later—were more apparent than real. In particular, standard inflation targeting allowed the FOMC to flexibly balance its inflation and employment goals as appropriate, whereas a nominal GDP target effectively assigns equal weight to inflation and growth at all times. On this point, Federal Reserve Bank of New York President Bill Dudley pointed out that hitting a nominal GDP target would not by itself guarantee that the FOMC was satisfying the dual mandate. For example, 5 percent nominal GDP growth is consistent with 3 percent real growth and 2 percent inflation, a satisfactory outcome, but it is also consistent with zero growth and 5 percent inflation, which is far from satisfactory.

FOMC participants also pointed out a practical measurement concern: Nominal GDP data are calculated quarterly, are available only with considerable lags, and are often extensively revised, all problems for timely policy-making. Despite these concerns, nominal GDP targeting in various forms has over the years attracted support from many economists.[20]

Raising the Inflation Target

Another way to address a low neutral interest rate and lower-bound constraints would be to retain standard inflation targeting but increase the target. If the Fed successfully targeted inflation at, say, 4 percent instead of 2 percent, then (by the Fisher principle) the general level of nominal interest rates should rise by about 2 percentage points as well, as investors demanded extra compensation for inflation. If the neutral interest rate, R*, were 2 percentage points higher, then the Fed would have significant additional policy space, allowing it to respond more effectively to deeper recessions with traditional rate cuts, reducing its need for QE or other new policy tools.[21]

The simplicity of increasing the inflation target is appealing but it would entail significant costs and uncertainties. Permanently higher inflation is itself costly for the economy (although economists disagree about how costly). It adds noise to the price system at the heart of the market economy and makes long-term planning (for individuals saving for retirement and businesses contemplating capital investments, for example) more difficult.

As a practical matter, many in Congress would likely see an increased inflation target as inconsistent with the Fed's mandate for price stability.

The transition to the higher target might also prove tricky. For example, inflation expectations—which, based on many years of experience, have become anchored near the Fed's 2 percent target—could become volatile, possibly creating financial and economic instability. Further, if people infer that the target will be changed periodically in response to changes in economic conditions, or other factors, then inflation expectations might be difficult to re-anchor at the new target. It is also not clear that a higher inflation target would be credible, given that the Fed has had chronic problems (the unusual circumstances of 2021 excepted) in getting inflation up to its current 2 percent target. If the higher target were not credible, or if market participants expected the target increase to be temporary, the desired increase in the neutral interest rate might not occur.

For these reasons, in its strategic review the FOMC ruled out in advance any increase in its inflation target. However, the FAIT framework that the Committee ultimately adopted, by allowing for temporary and moderate overshoots of the 2 percent inflation target, effectively took a step in this direction. Under the standard inflation targeting regime in place since 2012, after a period at the lower bound, the FOMC would try to return inflation to 2 percent. Under FAIT, given the same circumstances, the Committee will aim for inflation above 2 percent, at least for a time.

MONETARY-FISCAL COORDINATION

Reasonable people can disagree about whether attempts to increase monetary policy's effectiveness near the lower bound would be fruitful, or whether they would be past the point of diminishing returns. These questions aside, there is widespread consensus, including among central bankers, that, in light of the increased relevance of the lower bound, fiscal policy—changes in government spending and taxes—should be more often deployed to stabilize the economy, especially in deep downturns. Some economists go further and argue that, given the limitations of monetary policy when low interest rates prevail, fiscal policy should become the principal recession-fighting tool, with monetary policy playing at most a supporting role.[22]

Fiscal policy has several advantages as a stabilization tool. First, unlike monetary policy, fiscal policy is not less effective when the neutral interest rate is low. Instead, low interest rates, by reducing the cost of financing government debt, make expansionary fiscal policies more attractive. Relatedly, a traditional concern about expansionary fiscal policies is that government borrowing to finance spending or tax cuts, by absorbing some of the pool of available saving and pushing interest rates higher, might "crowd out" other uses of saving, such as business investment in factories and equipment. However, when interest rates are already very low, worthy private investments have little difficulty getting financing and crowding out is less of an issue. Moreover, any increase in longer-term interest rates triggered by expansionary fiscal policy may also have benefits, including higher returns for savers and the increase in monetary policy space afforded by a higher neutral interest rate.

Compared with monetary policy, fiscal policy can also better target the people or sectors of the economy most in need. For example, during the pandemic, the $2.2 trillion CARES Act not only supported the economy generally, it also allocated funds specifically for public health (aid to hospitals, vaccine development) and to groups hit especially hard by the crisis, including unemployed workers and small businesses. By contrast, monetary policy can only strengthen the overall economy, in the hope that better macroeconomic conditions will benefit those workers and businesses most in need.

As a countercyclical tool fiscal policy also has drawbacks. Unlike monetary policy, which can be adjusted quickly as needed, government spending and tax policies are not as easy to change. The federal budget comprises thousands of line items, reflecting diverse objectives, long-term commitments, and carefully worked-out compromises, all of which make fiscal policy less flexible in the short run. For example, given long project-planning horizons, it is difficult to quickly scale up spending on infrastructure or defense, and frequent changes in tax policies distort economic decision-making and complicate household and business planning. Transfer payments, such as unemployment insurance or grants to states and localities, can typically be increased more quickly, but even here bureaucratic and logistical challenges may delay funds reaching intended recipients. Most recently, the distribution of the extended unemployment insurance provided by the CARES Act was complicated by disparate and, in some cases, antiquated state unemployment insurance systems.

The more serious problem with using fiscal policy to target inflation and unemployment is that government spending and tax policies are made in a complex political environment. In the United States, fiscal action often requires fraught, protracted negotiations, followed by the assent of the administration and both houses of Congress, which may be controlled by different political parties. Recent experience suggests that our political system can deliver large fiscal programs in major emergencies—examples being the American Recovery and Reinvestment Act, signed by President Obama in 2009, and the CARES Act, approved by President Trump in 2020—but is otherwise prone to partisan gridlock and delay.[23] In stark contrast, a nonpartisan and politically independent central bank can adjust monetary policy quickly and proportionately in response to changes in the economic outlook. For this reason, relying entirely on fiscal policy for economic stabilization is unwise.

Nevertheless, it seems clear that—if the effective lower bound remains a significant constraint on monetary policy, as expected—fiscal policy will need to assume greater responsibility for offsetting economic downturns. The question arises, then, should monetary policy and fiscal policy be coordinated? And if so, how? (I take as given that central banks will work closely with the rest of the government during major financial crises, pandemics, and other national emergencies.)

The most basic form of monetary-fiscal coordination is informal consultation. The Fed chair and the Treasury secretary meet regularly, and their discussions include economic and financial developments as well as possible legislative initiatives. Consultations with the administration and Congress help the Fed anticipate potential changes in fiscal and other

economic policies, which then informs the FOMC's own economic forecasts and policy thinking. The Fed leadership in turn keeps Congress and
the administration informed about the Fed's views on the economy and
broad policy strategy.

In general, in contemporary Fed-Congress relations, Congress leads
and the Fed follows, meaning that the FOMC generally takes fiscal policy initiatives as given and adjusts monetary policy accordingly. The active
involvement by the Fed chair in the details of fiscal policy planning during
the Burns and Greenspan eras would no longer be considered appropriate,
at either the White House or the Fed. However, recent Fed chairs have
spoken out when they believed monetary policy alone was insufficient to
respond to an economic emergency. During the pandemic crisis, for example, Chair Powell repeatedly called for additional fiscal support beyond the
initial CARES Act. I did the same on several occasions when Congress
pivoted from supportive fiscal policies to austerity during the recovery from
the Great Recession. But, like Powell, I was careful not to endorse specific
measures or propose dollar amounts.

Powell's and my caution reflected the fact that comments by Fed leaders about fiscal policy inevitably involve a balancing act. On the one hand,
legislators, not unelected central bankers, are responsible for fiscal decisions
and could well resent what looked like Fed overstepping. On the other
hand, central bankers, with their analytical resources and information
about the economy, are well placed to offer advice on whether fiscal action
is needed, advice that fiscal policymakers are free to ignore. Moreover, fiscal
policy decisions bear directly on the Fed's ability to meet its dual mandate.
The right balance, I believe, is for the Fed to speak publicly when fiscal
action is needed to help stabilize the economy but to avoid taking sides in
partisan debates about the details of fiscal programs.

Monetary-fiscal coordination can also occur when lawmakers—either
implicitly (as a consequence of powers already granted to the Federal
Reserve) or through new legislation—delegate fiscal authority to the Fed.
All monetary policy has a fiscal element, if only because changes in interest rates affect the cost of financing government debt. Overall, though, the

Federal Reserve has less fiscal discretion, implicit or explicit, than most major central banks. For example, as we have seen, many central banks, as part of their normal operations, can buy securities, such as corporate bonds, that bear credit risk. These purchases have fiscal implications, because gains or losses on these assets affect the profits that central banks send to their national treasuries. (The Federal Reserve bears the risk of holding longer-term securities, which can change in value when interest rates change, but does not bear credit risk in its normal monetary policymaking.) The European Central Bank's use of some of its profits to subsidize commercial-bank lending, through its targeted long-term refinancing operations (TLTROs), is another example of fiscal discretion by a central bank. The general point is that the dividing line between monetary policy and fiscal policy is fluid. It depends, in practice, on politics, norms, and institutional arrangements. The legislature also can shift the line if circumstances warrant.

The CARES Act, which appropriated funds to backstop several Fed emergency lending programs, was a precedent-breaking example of Congress delegating fiscal discretion to the Federal Reserve (together with the Treasury). This backstop allowed the Fed, using its 13(3) lending authority, and with Treasury approval, to buy securities and make loans (some via the banking system) on terms that might lead to losses. This subsidized lending gave the Fed an additional tool to help calm financial markets in the early months of the pandemic. Importantly, the Fed had sufficient discretion to design these programs, including determining who would be eligible to borrow, to feel comfortable that the new assignment did not put its policy independence at risk.

However, these lending programs were explicitly temporary, both because of limits imposed by the CARES Act and because they were set up under 13(3) emergency authority. Also, Republicans opposed continuing the programs beyond 2020, perhaps because they feared that, under President Biden, the Fed might lend for purposes of which they disapproved. The debate about the programs made clear that, in U.S. politics, the question of where to draw the line between monetary and fiscal policy remains contentious.

Several policy tools used by foreign central banks—such as funding-for-lending or buying a broader range of securities in QE—would at least implicitly involve additional fiscal discretion for the Fed (the authority to buy a broader range of securities would require an explicit statutory change). Given the constraints imposed by the lower bound, the case for adding these tools is reasonably solid on economic grounds. But, from a political perspective, the Fed likely would not seek to increase its fiscal flexibility unless it believed certain conditions would be met. First, that Congress understood and accepted the potential implications of any increase in the Fed's fiscal discretion—for example, for the Fed's remittances to the Treasury. Second, that no strings would be attached to any new authorities that would endanger the Fed's monetary policy independence or divert it from the pursuit of its dual mandate. In particular, Fed policymakers would want to be assured that any new tools would be intended for use only to improve the broad functioning of credit markets and the performance of the economy as a whole, not to allocate credit to favored borrowers.

Helicopter Money

Some economists have advocated more-comprehensive forms of monetary-fiscal coordination than the limited types already familiar to advanced economies. I don't think we'll see more exotic forms of coordination any time soon, at least in the United States. But these alternative policies could become relevant under extreme conditions.

A classic example is *helicopter money*. The phrase and the idea were the brainchild of Milton Friedman.[24] Imagine a future—not so different from the current situation in Japan—in which the economy is suffering from persistently low inflation or even deflation, and, because both short-term and long-term interest rates are already close to zero, monetary policy alone has been unable to reach its goals. Suppose then, following Friedman's original thought experiment, that the authorities sent helicopters to drop newly minted currency from the sky, which of course people would quickly gather. When people spent the new cash, Friedman argued, prices would rise, ending deflation.

If we make Friedman's fanciful example more realistic, we can understand the conditions under which helicopter money would—or would not—be an effective response to a deflationary threat. To be implemented in a modern economy like the United States, a helicopter drop would proceed in two steps. In the first step, Congress would approve a large tax rebate, payable immediately to a wide swath of the population. Suppose for concreteness that the rebate program totals $500 billion. Under normal circumstances, the Treasury would pay for the rebate by issuing $500 billion in additional government debt, to be sold to private investors. But let's suppose that instead, in the second step, the Fed finances the rebate directly. In practice, this could be done simply by crediting the Treasury's account at the Fed with an extra $500 billion. The Treasury could then draw on that balance to send people checks. Alternatively, and equivalently, the Treasury could issue $500 billion in zero-interest, perpetual debt, which the Fed would buy, depositing its payment for the new debt in the Treasury's account at the Fed. These two steps together—a tax cut financed by an expansion of the Fed's balance sheet—are a realistic equivalent of Friedman's thought experiment.

How would a (realistic) helicopter drop affect an economy at the lower bound? The tax rebate, the first step, is standard fiscal policy, with well-understood effects. By raising people's incomes, the rebate should stimulate spending and economic activity. But does the fact that the tax rebate is financed by the Fed, rather than by the usual method of selling new government debt to the public, provide additional stimulus? Perhaps surprisingly, the use of Fed finance may not add very much.[25]

One reason to downplay the effects of Fed participation in the helicopter drop is that, despite being financed by the Fed, in the long run the tax rebate is not really "free money" for the Treasury. The reason is subtle. It has to do with how the Fed controls the funds rate. Whether people spend or save their rebates, the extra money they receive will eventually end up in the banking system in the form of reserves. So, in our example, bank reserves are ultimately $500 billion higher after the helicopter drop.

At some point—probably sooner than it had planned because the rebate will improve the outlook—the Fed will want to raise the funds rate from zero, which it does by paying interest on bank reserves, including on the extra $500 billion in reserves created by the rebate. The interest payments the Fed makes to banks reduce the profits it has left over to send to the

Treasury, so indirectly the Treasury bears the extra interest cost.* In effect, despite its use of Fed financing, the Treasury still pays interest on the funds it used for the rebate. Indeed, since the interest rate the Fed pays banks on their reserves is usually close to the rate on Treasury bills (short-term government debt), the Treasury enjoys only limited cost-saving by using Fed financing, relative to the case where it pays for the rebate simply by issuing Treasury bills directly to the public. Nor does a Fed-financed rebate (as opposed to a rebate financed by a standard debt issuance) look any different to the recipients of the tax break. In short, in the United States today, a tax rebate financed directly by the Fed should not have markedly different stimulative effects than an ordinary, debt-financed tax rebate of the same size.

There are some qualifications to this conclusion. First, the previous argument implicitly assumes that the government's alternative to Fed financing is issuing short-term debt, which pays an interest rate close to the rate the Fed pays on reserves. If the government pays for the rebate instead by issuing new long-term debt to the public, rather than issuing short-term bills, the increase in the supply of longer-term debt could raise the yield on that debt, increasing the cost of borrowing to both the government and the private sector. The Fed could undo that effect through QE purchases of longer-term securities, avoiding any crowding out effects of higher interest rates that would work against the effects of the rebate. Note that, overall, this means of implementing helicopter money does not necessarily involve an especially high degree of monetary-fiscal coordination: It boils down to tax rebates by the government combined with sufficient Fed QE to avoid follow-on increases in longer-term interest rates.

Second, the announcement of Fed financing might have psychological effects. For example, a commitment by the Fed via QE to prevent long-term rates from rising might lead fiscal policymakers to legislate bigger rebates than they otherwise would, or induce people to expect higher inflation,

---

* Following procedures now used by the Bank of Japan and the ECB, the Fed might be able to control the funds rate by paying no interest on bank reserves below a certain level. That would reduce the Treasury's implicit financing cost, but only through an implicit tax on banks, which Congress, if it chose, could impose directly.

even absent other changes in the economic fundamentals. Another possibility is that the announcement of the combined monetary-fiscal action would convince markets that the Fed will keep rates lower for longer than previously thought, perhaps on a supposition that the Fed cares about the government's financing costs as well as inflation. These psychological effects are hard to predict.

An alternative approach would cut the fiscal authorities out altogether. Proposals have been made for so-called *people's QE*, in which the central bank distributes cash directly to the public. People's QE is economically equivalent to a helicopter drop, so its effects would be similar to a Fed-financed tax rebate of the same size. A possible argument for people's QE, nevertheless, is that the central bank might be better able than the legislature to judge the amounts and timing of needed stimulus. However, people's QE is illegal in all jurisdictions, to my knowledge, reflecting the principle that the distribution of public funds is the prerogative of legislators, not the central bank. In practice, for understandable reasons, it is highly unlikely that legislatures would delegate that authority.

The conclusion that the effects of a helicopter drop would be similar to those of a conventional, debt-financed tax rebate, perhaps supplemented by QE to offset any increases in longer-term rates, is surprising. We are used to hearing about countries, from 1920s Germany to Venezuela in recent years, in which government spending or tax cuts financed by money creation leads to high inflation, or even hyperinflation. The difference is that, in these examples, the central bank is not independent but is subservient to the government. An independent central bank, with a commitment to price stability, will stop accommodating the government's spending and begin to tighten policy when the bank's inflation goals are threatened. A nonindependent central bank does not have that option but must continue to create money and keep rates low as long as the government demands it. In that case, if the government prioritizes its fiscal needs over price stability, the result can be out-of-control inflation. A situation in which the government, rather than an independent central bank, controls monetary policy and subjugates price stability to its own fiscal requirements is called *fiscal dominance.* With fiscal dominance, helicopter money is inflationary. However, we are far from such a situation in the United States today.

In theory, one can imagine intermediate cases between a fully independent central bank and fiscal dominance that could make helicopter money effective without risking hyperinflation. Suppose, for example, the government passed a law that allowed the central bank to operate independently only when inflation had sustainably reached a critical level, say 3 percent.* When inflation is below 3 percent, in this example, the central bank must finance the government deficit in unlimited amounts at zero interest, but once inflation passes 3 percent the central bank becomes free to raise interest rates to prevent further inflation. While that approach could work in principle, in practice it raises significant concerns. The government might not restore the central bank's independence as promised. Or, even if the government fully intended to restore the central bank's independence, fear that it might not do so could destabilize inflation expectations.

Modern Monetary Theory

Most economists believe fiscal dominance—usually associated with countries wracked by war, disaster, or political instability—should be avoided. However, proponents of *modern monetary theory* (MMT) argue that a form of fiscal dominance is the best way to manage the economy.[26]

Modern monetary theory has received attention from some progressive Democratic politicians, including Senator Bernie Sanders (I-Vermont) and Representative Alexandria Ocasio-Cortez (D-New York). Modern monetary theory is a mixture of theoretical propositions and policy recommendations (including that the government provide a universal job guarantee). Here I discuss only how some proponents see the relationship between monetary and fiscal policy.

Effectively, MMT supporters would eliminate central-bank independence and institutionalize fiscal dominance. In their view, monetary policy

---

* For this approach to work, the critical level of inflation would have to be higher than the level the central bank would choose if allowed to make policy with full independence.

should keep interest rates fixed at a low level at all times. If that level is zero, then the distinction between money-financed and debt-financed government spending is essentially eliminated, as all government liabilities would pay zero interest. Meanwhile, fiscal policy would be charged with, among its other goals, ensuring economic stability, including price stability. The fiscal authorities would promote economic stability through tax and spending policies—for example, higher taxes, by reducing private spending power, could help control inflation—but also through other policies, including price controls and the jobs guarantee.

It is correct, as MMT advocates note, that in this arrangement the precise level of the government budget deficit in a given year is not particularly important. The deficit would not be important from a budgetary point of view because—if the central bank keeps interest rates at zero indefinitely—financing government debt is cost free. If we also assume (as MMTers do) that the government, through all its policies taken together, is able to maintain high employment and low inflation, then the current deficit is not important for economic stabilization either. So far, so good.

However, some observers have misinterpreted the MMT conclusion that "budget deficits are not important" as implying that the government can spend essentially unlimited amounts without economic consequences, including the need to impose higher taxes. That is incorrect. Although economic policies can affect the economy's potential, ultimately the nation's productive capacity is limited. As a matter of arithmetic, if the government uses large amounts of resources, less will be left over for the private sector. And if the total demand for goods and services, both public and private, greatly exceeds the economy's capacity to produce, then inflation is inevitable—unless wage and price increases are suppressed by controls. But, in that case, the demand pressure will show up as shortages and bottlenecks, as it did when the Nixon administration tried price controls in the 1970s. In short, the MMT assumption that the government will use fiscal policy to stabilize the economy—and, in particular, to keep inflation low—implies that there are definite limits to what the government can spend.

Additionally, as a practical matter, making the fiscal authorities alone responsible for economic stabilization, with monetary policy in a purely passive role, is ill advised. Fiscal policy has some strengths as a stabilization tool, and when neutral interest rates are low, it makes sense to rely relatively more heavily on fiscal policy. However, because of the complexities of political decision-making, fiscal policy is unlikely to respond flexibly and promptly to changes in the economic outlook. Thus, a system that requires the Fed to keep rates permanently at zero and abdicate its responsibility to fight recession and inflation would likely destabilize the economy or result in high inflation. Both monetary and fiscal policies have roles to play in keeping the economy on an even keel.

In sum, monetary policymakers could pursue many means of increasing the potency of their tools and frameworks, as well as ways to cooperate with fiscal policymakers. Improved frameworks can make monetary policy more powerful and more predictable. The Fed could also consider several tools used by foreign central banks. The main uncertainties about alternative tools are not about their technical feasibility, but about politics and governance. Legislators and the central bank will need to agree on where to draw the line between monetary policy, managed by an independent central bank, and fiscal policy, which is the province of Congress and the administration.

It also seems likely that, so long as the effective lower bound constrains monetary policy, fiscal policy will have to play a larger role than in the past in maintaining full employment and avoiding too-low inflation. Fiscal policy's effectiveness could be increased by greater use of *automatic stabilizers*, changes in government spending or taxes that are linked to economic indicators and are put in place before they are needed. For example, Congress could legislate in advance increases in unemployment insurance that kick in automatically when the unemployment rate exceeds a predetermined level. Because they are triggered when warranted by economic conditions, automatic stabilizers could make fiscal policy more responsive and proportionate and less vulnerable to political stalemates. Congress has shown relatively little interest in this approach, however. Barring a major effort to increase the flexibility of countercyclical fiscal policy, monetary policy will continue to be an important stabilization tool.

14

MONETARY POLICY AND FINANCIAL STABILITY

THE FED WAS FOUNDED IN 1913 not to make monetary policy in the modern sense—the gold standard still held sway—but rather in large part to prevent financial panics and to serve as a lender of last resort. As Walter Bagehot's dictum prescribes, when bank depositors and other short-term lenders lose confidence and withdraw their cash, it's the central bank's job to "lend freely" to financial institutions, taking their good loans and other unimpaired assets as collateral. By replacing the lost private funding, this last-resort lending can avoid costly failures of solvent banks, reduce the incentives of the remaining depositors to run, limit fire sales of bank assets, give banks breathing space to raise new capital, and calm the panic.

Though the basic logic remains the same, the Fed's lender-of-last-resort strategy has evolved with the structure of the U.S. financial system. When the Fed was founded, credit was provided mostly by banks, and bank runs were the primary threat to stability. By 2007, however, most credit flowed through securities markets and nonbank financial institutions, the so-called shadow banking system. During the global financial crisis, the Fed accordingly broadened its lender-of-last-resort role, using its emergency powers to lend to a wide range of financial markets and institutions, and even in some cases to nonfinancial businesses. During the short but sharp financial crisis of March 2020, the Fed went still further, serving as a buyer of last resort for Treasuries and other securities, and also—with congressional support—backstopping credit to corporations, municipalities, and medium-sized businesses.

Although the global financial crisis and the pandemic each required particularly powerful and wide-ranging responses, the Fed has long monitored the financial system and dealt with emerging stability threats. However, historically, the Fed's interventions tended to be *ad hoc* and kept in a separate intellectual box from monetary policy—except when policymakers used monetary tools to offset the effects of financial disruptions on the economy, as during the Asian crisis of the 1990s. In the 21st century, however, thinking about the Fed's role in promoting financial stability has shifted. The expansion of the Fed's traditional lender-of-last resort role is one aspect of that shift. More fundamentally, with explosive growth, innovation, and deregulation in the financial sector, financial instability—in conjunction with the decline in the neutral rate of interest, which limits the ability of monetary policy to counter shocks—has become an increasingly concerning threat to the Fed's dual mandate. Indeed, many policymakers now see maintaining financial stability as the *de facto* third element of the mandate because, without it, there is little hope of sustainably achieving maximum employment and price stability.

These changes have intensified the debate, both within and outside the Fed, about the causes of financial instability and the appropriate responses. Swings in market sentiment, financial innovation, and regulatory failure are acknowledged sources of instability, but what about monetary policy? Can monetary policy create or amplify risks to the financial system? If so, should the conduct of monetary policy change? Can nonmonetary policies, such as financial regulation, control systemic financial risks and substitute for a monetary policy response? These questions are among the most difficult that central bankers face.

FINANCIAL INSTABILITY AND ITS
ECONOMIC CONSEQUENCES

For years, the Alphaville column of the *Financial Times* (*FT*) has featured pieces titled "This is nuts. When's the crash?" that cover what *FT* writers see as anomalous or irrational behavior in financial markets. Reporting on these developments is entertaining and sometimes instructive. Do these examples signal broader financial risks, though, as the Alphaville pieces sometimes imply? It is true that excesses in specific assets or trades are more likely when overall risk-taking is high. Still, it is striking that, even though financial crises are rare, idiosyncratic asset pricing puzzles are not, as the *FT* column demonstrates.[*] That suggests that the signal from these anomalies is weak. Indeed, a certain amount of volatility and hard-to-explain pricing in specific financial markets is normal and entirely consistent with a healthy economy.

In contrast, financial instability that is *systemic*—that threatens the functioning of the financial system as a whole, with significant potential spillovers to the real (nonfinancial) economy—is very much a policy concern. Systemic financial events, like the global financial crisis or the March 2020 panic, are rare but can wreak enormous damage. Clearly, reducing the probability of systemic events, and ameliorating their effects when they occur, should be high priorities for policymakers.

To prevent or respond to a systemic financial event, though, we have to know one when we see it. What kinds of events pose the greatest risks to stability? The future will doubtless reveal new threats. Cyberattacks on the financial system are one worrisome possibility. Rather than speculating about new risks, though, here I'll compare two types of events that have been historically important and get lots of attention from the public and the media: stock-market bubbles and credit booms and busts. Both,

---

[*] A well-known example is the so-called January effect, the observed tendency for stocks to outperform in that month. Like many such anomalies, this effect seems to have waned once researchers called attention to it.

if severe enough, pose risks to the broader economy. However, historical evidence suggests that credit booms and busts, particularly if associated with bubbles in commercial or residential real estate, are the much more dangerous phenomena.

Stock-Market Bubbles

Stock-market booms and crashes (often labeled as bubbles after the fact, and sometimes even during the boom) are dramatic and, if severe enough, historic events.* For many people the 1929 stock crash symbolizes the Great Depression. Likewise, the collapse of the tech bubble in 2001 is often perceived as the turning point between the ebullient 1990s and the lackluster 2000s.

The sources of stock bubbles are typically both psychological and economic. As such they are hard to predict or identify. Rapid and sustained stock-price increases are often driven by widespread optimism and the belief that the economy is entering a new era. In the 1920s, an avalanche of new mass-produced consumer goods, as well as large increases in wages and leisure time, fueled the optimism. The late 1990s bubble likewise reflected the popular belief that the internet revolution would foster whole new industries and revolutionize old ones. In retrospect, the optimists in the 1920s and the 1990s weren't entirely wrong. In each case, the new technologies eventually did have enormous social and economic impacts—and proved highly profitable. But in both cases the optimism was premature or was derailed by intervening events, and sharp stock-price declines followed.

Other factors affect stock prices, including monetary policy. Easier monetary policy tends to raise stock prices—by improving the outlook for the economy (and hence for corporate profits), by lowering the interest rate at which future profits are discounted, and, as we'll see in this chapter, by

---

* There are many definitions of "bubble." A standard definition is that, in a bubble, people buy an asset based solely on their belief that its price will continue to rise, rather than because of favorable fundamentals.

increasing investors' tolerance for risk. Indeed, easier money affects the real economy, in part, through higher asset prices. That said, empirical studies find, in most circumstances, that monetary policy has only relatively modest direct effects on stock prices (in contrast to indirect effects over time arising from an improved economy).[1] Ironically, the strongest direct effects are often seen when tight money contributes to a stock-price crash, as happened in 1929 and 2001.

What risks do stock bubbles pose to the economy as a whole, as opposed to the portfolios of individual stock investors? Large swings in asset prices do have economic effects, of course. Higher stock prices raise household wealth and sentiment, which in turn affects consumer spending. And high stock prices, by making it easier for firms to raise funding, may also spur increased capital investment. By the same token, a sharp decline in the stock market would be expected to slow spending and investment. That said, historical evidence strongly suggests that booms and busts in stock prices, though certainly a concern, are by no means the most dangerous form of financial instability, so long as they are not associated with a wider breakdown in credit markets.

For example, a 2003 study by Frederic Mishkin and Eugene White identified fifteen crashes in U.S. stock markets since 1900, each involving a drop of at least 20 percent in equity prices over a span of a year or less.[2] Despite their magnitudes, many of the drops had surprisingly limited economic effects. Some were not associated with subsequent economic slowdowns at all, including a 25 percent drop in stock prices in 1946–47, a 23 percent fall in 1961–62, and the 23 percent one-day decline that confronted new Fed Chair Greenspan in October 1987. Other sharp declines were associated with only mild recessions, including a 30 percent drop in 1969–70 and the 2000–2001 decline of about 23 percent. Though it came after the Mishkin-White study, the more-than-30-percent decline in stock prices in early 2020 was clearly an effect rather than a cause of the pandemic crisis, and in any case was quickly reversed, with the market hitting new highs later that year.

On the other hand, not every collapse in stock prices has been innocuous. The 1929 crash was followed by the Great Depression and stock prices fell sharply in 2008–2009, before the Great Recession. Why are some stock crashes followed by economic contractions while others are not? It depends, according to Mishkin and White, on whether the crash is an isolated event—an episode of "irrational exuberance," perhaps—or is instead accompanied by broad-based stress in banking and credit markets.* A decline in stock prices without a credit-market breakdown, as in 1987, will have some economic effects, on household wealth and confidence for example, but the overall impact will likely be limited. In contrast, if a stock-market crash is caused by, or leads to, extensive stress in the broader financial system, including banking and credit markets, then a sharp and protracted recession is much more likely.

The 1929 and 2008–2009 experiences illustrate the importance of looking at the broader context of stock-market busts. Despite the popular perception, most economic historians do not believe the 1929 boom and crash, despite its drama, was a singular cause of the Depression. The economy slowed after the crash but did not plunge until the banking system, both in the United States and abroad, imploded in 1930 and 1931. As discussed earlier, rather than the 1929 crash, most economic historians now believe that the main causes of the Depression were the instability of the international gold standard and recurring banking crises.[3] The collapse of the gold standard led to the deflation of consumer prices in countries that tied their currencies to gold, an effect exacerbated by the Fed's misguided policy tightening (aimed, ironically, at cooling the stock market) in the latter 1920s. Bank runs, which began in the United States in late 1930 and in Europe in the spring of 1931, intensified the collapse of the money supply, which worsened the deflation, and constricted credit availability to households and businesses. Thus, although the 1929 stock-market crash signaled the onset of the Great Depression and, through its effects on wealth and

---

* Mishkin and White measure financial stress by the spread between yields on low-risk and high-risk corporate bonds. Increases in that spread, which reflect reduced willingness or ability to lend to higher-risk borrowers, correlate with worsening credit conditions.

confidence, doubtless worsened the downturn, it was not the primary cause of the economic collapse.

In 2008–2009, a deep recession followed the sharp stock-price decline—stocks fell by almost half between May 2008 and March 2009. However, like the 1929 crash, this decline did not occur in isolation. Rather, the stock-price drop both reflected and amplified a much broader breakdown in credit markets, triggered by the subprime mortgage crisis and runs on wholesale funding. The 2008–2009 stock-market crash was not an independent cause of the Great Recession, but rather a mirror of other forces.

Credit Booms and Busts

Historically, greater economic dangers are posed by credit booms and busts. In credit booms, lending and leverage increase rapidly, often along with rapid rises in commercial or residential real estate prices. Like stock-price increases, an expansion in lending may be driven by less-than-rational psychological factors, be justified by the fundamentals, or perhaps some combination of both. Telling a "good" credit boom from a "bad" one, like identifying whether an increase in stock prices is a bubble, can be difficult. However, when credit booms go bust, the risks to the economy can be high, especially when the bust is tied to collapsing real estate prices.

Historical experience again provides key evidence. For example, in a series of studies of seventeen advanced economies, using data back to 1870, economic historians Òscar Jordà, Moritz Schularick, and Alan Taylor found a significant link between credit booms, especially booms driven by real estate speculation, and subsequent financial crises, which in turn were often followed by deep recessions and slow recoveries.[*4] A credit and housing boom gone wrong is, of course, an apt description of the 2007–2009 global financial crisis.

Why should a boom and bust in real estate and related credit markets

---

* These authors also confirmed, for their long time frame and large sample of countries, the Mishkin-White result that stock market crashes reliably forecast subsequent recessions only when they occur in conjunction with major credit-market disruptions.

have more severe economic consequences than a stock-price crash? One reason is that stocks are held primarily by richer people, often in separate retirement accounts. In contrast, in the United States at least, most families are homeowners; and for those families, housing wealth is typically a large share of their total wealth. Because people of more-modest means tend to spend a higher proportion of their wealth, changes in home equity on average have a larger effect on aggregate consumer spending than do changes in stock values of similar size.[5] In the lead-up to the global financial crisis, the ability of U.S. homeowners to tap their home equity, through home equity loans or cash-out refinancing, for example, tied housing wealth closely to consumer spending.

Even more important than these wealth effects, however, is that housing and other types of real estate are frequently financed by borrowing, much more so than stockholdings. For most households, the mortgage on their home is by far their biggest liability, while loans collateralized by residential and commercial real estate make up a large share of the assets of most banks and other lenders.[6] A collapse in the prices of housing or other real estate, especially if it exposes poor lending practices, will likely cause much wider financial distress than a decline in stock prices. To continue making house payments, homeowners with declining income, heavy mortgage burdens, and vanishing home equity have little choice but to sharply reduce their spending on consumer durables and other goods.[7] The decline in demand in turn reduces output and employment, exacerbating the initial effect and spreading distress beyond the housing sector. Similarly, losses on mortgages and other real estate loans hurt financial institutions' profits and capital, reducing their capacity and willingness to lend. In the worst case, as in 2007–2009, a financial panic can erupt. Short-term funding providers pull back, forcing insolvencies and fire sales that further depress lending and asset prices.

In short, stock-market declines, in the absence of other financial stresses, affect the economy primarily by making stockowners feel poorer, which leads them to spend less. A credit and real estate bust of similar magnitude has a larger direct effect on spending, but it also has potentially powerful second-round effects as escalating financial distress leads both borrowers and lenders to retrench. In the worst case, a credit bust can trigger a full-blown financial panic, resulting in enormous economic damage.

How should policymakers respond? The two main approaches are not mutually exclusive. One is to use monetary policy to try to defuse threats to financial stability. The alternative is to use regulation and supervisory oversight to try to forestall dangerous buildups in risk.

MONETARY POLICY AND RISK-TAKING

The case for using monetary policy to respond to threats to financial stability rests on an apparent link between monetary policy and private-sector risk-taking.

In traditional macroeconomic analyses, monetary policy is assumed to work in large part by affecting the cost of borrowing.* All else equal, a lower cost of capital makes investing in a new factory more profitable, for example, while a lower mortgage rate makes buying a house more affordable. In traditional models, changes over time in the willingness of people to take risks—which in principle should also affect their borrowing and investing decisions—are typically not considered.

However, growing evidence suggests that the propensities of lenders, borrowers, and investors to take risks do vary over time and are influenced by monetary policy, with easier policy associated with greater risk-taking. The tendency of monetary easing to promote risk-taking has become known as the *risk-taking channel of monetary policy*. For example, many researchers have found that, all else equal, easier monetary policy makes banks more willing to lend to risky borrowers.[8] Easier money also appears to make investors more willing to hold risky assets, in that the extra yield that investors demand to hold those assets tends to fall when interest rates

---

* In standard macro models like the Fed's FRB/US model, monetary policy also works through wealth effects and by affecting the exchange value of the dollar.

are low. In work that I did in 2005 with Kenneth Kuttner, we found that monetary easing raises stock prices in part by lowering the risk premium investors demand to hold stocks.[9] Similarly, a 2015 paper by Samuel Hanson and Jeremy Stein found that a cut in the federal funds rate reduces the compensation that investors require for the risk of holding longer-term securities, amplifying the effect of policy easing on longer-term yields.[10]

Why does easier monetary policy increase people's willingness to take risk? Several mechanisms are at work. First, if policy ease improves economic conditions and raises people's actual or prospective incomes, they will feel more financially secure, which in turn makes them less concerned about the potential downside of risk-taking. For example, investors are more likely to buy risky stocks if they feel that they can afford to take the loss if things go badly. An investor with a smaller financial cushion, in contrast, is more likely to be conservative. Moreover, monetary policy can reinforce the increased willingness of investors to make risky investments in good times by making the economic environment feel safer. For example, policy ease, if accompanied by assurances of continued support, should reduce investors' fears of worst-case scenarios, encouraging additional investment in risky assets.

Second, easier monetary policy, by increasing asset values, improves the balance sheets of both lenders and borrowers, promoting the flow of new credit, including to riskier borrowers. Stronger bank balance sheets ease regulatory constraints on new lending and increase banks' ability to attract low-cost, uninsured funding. Similarly, borrowers' creditworthiness improves when their balance sheets strengthen. Homeowners with more equity in their home (because home values have increased) will have an easier time qualifying for a second mortgage or home equity loan, for example, while a corporation with more collateral to post will be able to borrow on better terms. Changes in the strength of balance sheets over the business cycle are central to what Mark Gertler, Simon Gilchrist, and I once dubbed the *financial accelerator*.[11] The basic idea is that an economic upswing tends to improve the financial conditions of households, firms, and banks, which in turn encourages greater lending, borrowing, and investment.

As the discussion thus far suggests, the tendency of monetary easing to increase risk-taking is not always a problem. During recessions—especially recessions following financial crises—private-sector risk-taking is typically too low rather than too high. It is important to encourage banks and other investors to take reasonable risks, rather than hoard cash and hunker down. That's why policymakers often talk about the need to restore public confidence as a prerequisite to recovery. But it's also possible to have too much of a good thing—to have monetary or other economic policies that induce more risk-taking than is healthy for longer-term financial stability. Just as easy money can help restore risk-taking from levels that are too low, it can lead to an increase in risk-taking that ultimately overshoots.[12]

One reason that risk-taking, once ignited, can become excessive is that, in the real world, people are not the fully informed, rational actors of economics textbooks. Many have short memories (or limited experience) and tend to extrapolate recent trends or interpret evidence selectively—to better fit with their prior beliefs, for example. If stock or house prices have risen rapidly for a while, investors or homeowners may infer that those increases will continue.[13] More generally, short memories and extrapolative thinking may lead people to believe that, if economic conditions have recently been stable, they will continue to be stable. The economist Hyman Minsky famously argued that long periods of relative calm are potentially dangerous, because people will erroneously assume that calm conditions must continue and load up on risk—until a large adverse event, or a "Minsky moment," shakes them out of their complacency.[14]

Critics of these psychologically grounded arguments sometimes contend that because sophisticated investors can take advantage of the cognitive errors of others, markets can be collectively rational even if many, or most, investors are not. I mentioned earlier Michael Lewis's book *The Big Short*, which tells the story of a small number of investors who bet against subprime mortgages in advance of the global financial crisis—actions which, if widely imitated, might have helped cool the market fever.[15] But, as that story also shows, if the more hardheaded investors have only limited resources to back their views, or if they believe that they are smart enough to "ride the bubble" and get out before it bursts, then less rational players may still dominate market outcomes.

Another reason that risk-taking can overshoot is bad incentives, stemming from factors such as poorly structured government regulations or flawed compensation schemes for traders, asset managers, and lenders.[16] Traders in large financial institutions may earn bonuses based on their trading gains but share less than proportionally in losses—they always have the option to leave the firm if things go badly. These arrangements incentivize traders to take larger risks. Similarly, money market mutual funds that report higher returns can attract more investors and earn more management fees. To achieve the higher returns, fund managers may take additional risks, including risks that are not easily observed by investors (because they involve the use of complex or opaque financial instruments, for example). One might think that our market system would weed out inefficient and risk-promoting arrangements once they are recognized, but rapid financial innovation and slowly adapting financial regulations reduce the market's power to detect and eliminate dangerous incentive structures.[17]

In some situations, irrational beliefs and poorly structured incentives may work in combination. For example, it is commonly observed that investors may "reach for yield" when interest rates are low, taking on more risk than desirable in an effort to achieve historically average returns. This behavior may have a significant psychological component if investors see historically average returns as "normal" or "fair" and thus take on undue risks to achieve them. Alternatively, an insurance company or pension fund might reach for yield because it has long-term contractual commitments, perhaps agreed to during a time when rates were higher, that can be met only by earning a high return. Earning a safe but low return guarantees failure in such cases, so (barring adequate regulatory oversight) their incentive is to take the risks needed to earn the necessary return, even if those risks are greater than policyholders or pensioners would prefer.[18]

There is much yet to learn about reach-for-yield behavior. For example, does reach-for-yield behavior persist when interest rates remain low for many years? If rates are low for a long time, then it seems that the "normal" rate perceived by investors should also decline, reducing the pressure to reach for yield. Similarly, when low rates persist, pension funds and insurance companies have strong incentives to reset the contracts they offer to reflect the new normal. Financial institutions do not seem to be especially prone to excessive risk-taking in Japan, where interest rates have been near zero for decades. Likewise, it's not always clear whether investors measure "normal" rates in nominal or real (inflation-adjusted) terms. Investors should care about real rates in principle, but in comparing current rates with the rates they are used to, they may nevertheless think in nominal terms. A clear understanding of the effects of lower-for-longer monetary policies on risk-taking will require getting a better handle on these issues.

Yet another reason risk-taking overshoots is that borrowers, lenders, and investors lack incentives to take account of the possible effect of their decisions on the overall stability of the system. For example, home buyers or companies who borrow heavily in good times may have to sharply cut back their spending in a crisis. In making their borrowing decisions, households and firms have no incentive to consider their individual contributions to the risk of a general pullback in spending that may worsen a subsequent recession. Similarly, broker-dealers who finance risky credit with short-term borrowing do not consider the possibility that, in a crisis, their need to sell their holdings quickly will affect returns for all investors. Because people understandably ignore the effects of their own risk-taking on overall financial stability, they may take too much risk from a social perspective.*

In short, the risk-taking channel of monetary policy can help promote economic recovery by encouraging investors, lenders, and borrowers to come out of their defensive crouch and take appropriate risks. However, for psychological and institutional reasons, risk-taking set off by monetary

---

* This is an example of what economists call an *externality*: a situation in which people or firms lack incentives to take the general good into account, as when a factory owner decides to pollute a river without considering the effects on people downstream.

ease can ultimately become excessive. Does that imply that central bankers should refrain from using easy money to fight recessions, or at least use it less often or less forcefully?

MACROPRUDENTIAL POLICIES

Some would argue yes, but the answer is not so clear. The fact that monetary policy affects risk-taking does not necessarily imply that it is either a principal source of financial crises or the most effective tool for preventing them. For example, the recurring banking panics of the 19th century, as well as the global crisis that helped touch off the Great Depression, occurred mostly under the gold standard, before the advent of modern, activist monetary policies. The long period between the 1951 Treasury-Fed accord and the 2007–2009 financial crisis featured both activist monetary policy and relatively few episodes of crises severe enough to threaten macroeconomic stability, at least in advanced economies. Moreover, as discussed earlier, most economists believe that monetary policy was at best a minor source of the 2007–2009 crisis. Overall, while monetary policy does seem to influence risk-taking, other factors—such as the structure of the financial system, the effectiveness of financial regulation, and mass psychology—also affect the frequency and severity of crises.

Moreover, while foregoing activist monetary policies may or may not help prevent or mitigate financial crises, the costs of diverting monetary policy from its economic goals are clear. If managed well, monetary policy is an effective and flexible tool for stabilizing the economy. More-passive monetary policies could produce too-high inflation or too-low employment without doing much to promote financial stability.

For these reasons, before we change how we use monetary policy, we should ask whether more-targeted policies are available to address systemic financial risks. Policies (other than monetary policy) aimed at promoting the stability of the financial system as a whole are known collectively as *macroprudential policies*.[19] In contrast, traditional regulatory policies, now sometimes referred to as *microprudential policies*, aim to promote stability, efficiency, and fairness in individual financial firms and markets, without explicit consideration of system-wide stability. Both types of policies have roles to play in promoting a well-functioning and stable financial system.

While some countries had included macroprudential elements in their regulatory frameworks before the 2007–2009 crisis, interest in the approach has exploded since then. Official committees with new powers to implement macroprudential policies have been established in many countries, and international regulatory bodies have promulgated best practices and worked to coordinate initiatives globally. In the United States, substantial progress has been made, but troubling gaps in macroprudential regulation remain.

Macroprudential Policies in the United States

American financial regulation has been reformed since the global financial crisis in an attempt to address deficiencies in the U.S. regulatory framework. Owing to a combination of politics, historical accident, and the constant evolution of our financial markets, financial oversight in the United States in the run-up to the crisis was fragmented and uneven. Some financial institutions and markets had multiple regulators with overlapping jurisdictions, while some had no effective regulators. In certain cases, regulators opted not to prioritize or impose limits on excessive risk-taking.

Beyond the gaps and duplications, the precrisis regulatory system suffered from a fundamental conceptual flaw: Each regulatory agency covered only a narrowly defined set of institutions or markets, with no responsibility outside its fiefdom. Meanwhile the crisis exposed weaknesses that spanned the system and did not fit neatly under the regulatory purview of any single agency. No regulator was responsible for understanding the broader risks of securitization, for example, or for gaming out the implications of the failure of an investment bank like Lehman Brothers or of runs on money market mutual funds. No one was responsible for the system as a whole.

After the financial crisis, legislators and regulators around the world strengthened regulation generally but also recognized that siloed oversight of each constituent part of the financial system cannot ensure overall stability. They responded by creating new macroprudential frameworks to monitor and promote the stability of the system without sacrificing the still-vital tasks of ensuring the safety, efficiency, and fairness of individual firms or markets. The new macroprudential policies came in two broad categories. *Structural* policies, also called through-the-cycle policies, are intended to enhance the overall resilience of the financial system against shocks. Once in place, structural policies do not change with the business cycle or market developments. In contrast, *cyclical* policies are supposed to vary in response to evolving economic and financial conditions or the emergence of new threats to stability.

In the United States, the 2010 Dodd-Frank Act adopted a macroprudential perspective in many of its provisions. For example, the realization that deceptive subprime lending had consequences for financial system as a whole was one motivation for Dodd-Frank's creation of the Consumer Financial Protection Bureau and for bans on certain mortgage-lending practices. From a macroprudential vantage point, however, an especially crucial provision was the creation of a new council of regulators, the Financial Stability Oversight Council (FSOC), charged with monitoring and responding to financial-stability risks.

Headed by the Treasury secretary, the FSOC coordinates the efforts of key regulators like the Federal Reserve, the Securities and Exchange Commission (SEC), and the FDIC. (The FSOC has ten voting members in all.) Several of these agencies in turn greatly increased the resources dedicated to monitoring the financial system. The Fed's Division of Financial Stability, created after the crisis, analyzes risks to the financial system and briefs the Board and the FOMC. Both the FSOC and the Fed issue regular public reports on financial-stability risks and planned policy responses. The Dodd-Frank Act also created a new Office of Financial Research within the Treasury that collects and analyzes data to support the FSOC's work and publishes its own annual report.

The financial system is constantly changing in response to demand, innovation, and regulatory incentives, presenting a perennial challenge for regulators. For example, one might think that tightening regulations on bank lending would make the system safer, but that may not be true if tougher rules on banks only serve to push risky lending into less regulated parts of the system. To help regulation keep up with an evolving financial industry, Congress empowered the FSOC to designate individual nonbank financial firms or activities as systemically important and thus subject to additional oversight by the Fed. In addition, the FSOC has the power to pressure individual regulatory agencies by making "comply or explain" recommendations. The agencies must either adopt the FSOC recommendations or provide an explanation of why they did not.

Dodd-Frank also established a legal framework, known as the *orderly liquidation authority*, for dealing with a systemically critical financial firm on the brink of collapse—the next Lehman Brothers. In standard bankruptcy proceedings, the goal is to maximize the ultimate recovery by the failing firm's creditors. In contrast, the orderly liquidation authority empowers the Fed, the FDIC, and other agencies to unwind a failing financial firm in ways that also account for the risks that an uncontrolled failure may pose to the stability of the system. Firms covered by this provision must provide regulators with *living wills* showing how the firm could be safely unwound in a crisis. Firms must also issue special forms of debt that can be converted into equity when the firm is liquidated or restructured. This more orderly liquidation process will not eliminate the systemic impact of a large firm's collapse, but it should result in a far less chaotic process than Lehman's failure in 2008.

In another key macroprudential reform, an international agreement called Basel III (after the city in Switzerland where it was negotiated) and the Dodd-Frank Act together substantially increased bank capital and liquidity requirements, reflecting the central role of banks in most financial systems. Basel III also requires large, systemically critical banks to hold more capital and liquid assets than other banks. In the United States, bank capital requirements were further strengthened by subjecting banks to regular stress tests to determine whether they have enough capital to meet regulatory minimums and continue to lend even in extremely bad economic and financial scenarios. (The Fed relied on bank stress tests during the 2020 pandemic to decide whether to allow banks to pay dividends or buy back shares, both of which reduce bank capital.) Unlike the general increases in bank capital and liquidity, which are structural macroprudential policies, capital requirements based on stress tests are cyclical policies because the stress tests are based on scenarios reflecting economic and financial risks that regulators currently find most concerning. Another cyclical macroprudential policy—available to the Federal Reserve but not used, even during the long expansion preceding the pandemic—allows bank supervisors to require banks to increase their capital during economic expansions. Once built up, this countercyclical capital buffer can be drawn down during a crisis or recession.

Taken together, these and other reforms have strengthened macroprudential oversight in the United States. Are they enough?

SHORTCOMINGS OF U.S. MACROPRUDENTIAL POLICY

Despite notable progress, U.S. macroprudential policy still has significant shortcomings, which leave the financial system at risk. Most could be remedied, but doing so would take a real commitment by legislators and regulators.

The Structure and Powers of the Financial Stability Oversight Council

Dodd-Frank intended the FSOC to lead efforts to monitor the financial system and to coordinate responses to potential risks. (The Obama administration had proposed giving the Fed those responsibilities, but the political blowback from the Fed's role in unpopular bailouts during the financial crisis sunk that idea.) But the structure of the FSOC, as well as limits on its powers, hampers its ability to carry out its mandate. Notably, the FSOC is headed by the Treasury secretary, which perhaps confers political legitimacy, but also means that the council may be more or less active, depending on the secretary's priorities and the political winds.[20] Under Treasury

Secretary Steven Mnuchin, for example, the FSOC took a deregulatory approach, consistent with the Trump administration's priorities but a step backward in terms of making the financial system safer.

Significantly, during the Trump administration, the FSOC did not use the authority it was granted by the Dodd-Frank Act to designate specific nonbank financial firms or activities as systemically important. Indeed, the administration did not appeal a questionable court decision in a suit brought by the insurance company MetLife that made such designation of financial firms considerably more difficult. At the end of the Trump administration, not a single firm was designated as systemically important. (Several firms have had that designation removed after changing their structure or operations.)

Another weakness of the FSOC is that it is not a separate agency but instead a council of regulators, each retaining its independent authority. The agency heads meet once a quarter or so to share views and information, and, as mentioned, the Council can pressure an individual agency to take specific actions. But this consultative process slows any potential responses to emerging risks.

Moreover, a recalcitrant agency can ignore recommendations aimed at promoting financial stability, even if backed by all other members of the Council. The FSOC's efforts during the Obama administration to reform money market mutual funds, which suffered devastating runs in 2008 and required emergency assistance from the Treasury and the Federal Reserve, are a case in point. Money funds are regulated by the SEC. The FSOC proposed reforms to eliminate run risk at the money funds, but the SEC—which has no financial stability mandate and, for historical reasons, has generally not seen limiting risk-taking as part of its mission—dragged its feet, argued that it lacked sufficient authority, and ultimately implemented a limited set of changes that did not solve the problem.* Economists at the

---

* For example, the SEC's reforms included the institution of "gates," which allowed the funds to suspend investor redemptions in the face of a run. But the gates only increase the incentive to run before the gate is shut. Moreover, reforms were applied only to funds used by institutional investors, not funds open to retail investors.

Fed, Treasury, and other agencies well understood that the SEC's reforms were inadequate and that the incentive for money fund investors to run had not been eliminated. And, indeed, some money funds experienced runs during the March 2020 crisis. Further reforms are clearly needed, but, barring new legislation, the SEC's active cooperation will be required.*

Housing and Mortgage Markets

The FSOC and its member agencies, collectively, also lack adequate tools to contain credit booms in housing and commercial real estate. To be sure, it is never easy to determine whether a boom is economically justified but— as 2007–2009 starkly demonstrated—a credit boom gone bust can destabilize the financial system, clog the flow of new credit, and force financially stressed borrowers to cut their spending. A comprehensive macroprudential framework should provide regulators—perhaps in coordination with the Treasury or FSOC—with the tools to moderate credit booms and help ensure that the system can survive busts.

The U.S. macroprudential policies enacted after the crisis—including tough bank capital standards, bank stress tests (which may include credit boom-and-bust scenarios), and the orderly liquidation authority—have undoubtedly helped make the system more resilient. The Dodd-Frank Act also toughened mortgage-lending standards in general, required securitizers of lower-quality mortgages to retain partial ownership ("skin in the game"), and created the Consumer Financial Protection Bureau. Those are meaningful accomplishments.† Nevertheless, I worry that U.S. regulators still lack tools tailor-made to address an emerging housing and credit bubble.

Many other countries, including both emerging markets and advanced economies, have adopted macroprudential policies targeting excesses in real estate prices and mortgage lending. For example, some countries not only set maximum loan-to-value or debt-to-income ratios for mortgage

---

* As of this writing, the SEC under Chair Gary Gensler is considering further reforms aimed at reducing the threat of runs on money funds.
† Depending on their future status, the GSEs could also play a role in adjusting mortgage rules and requirements to help moderate booms and busts. The GSEs' regulator is a member of the FSOC.

borrowers but also allow those limits to vary in response to economic developments. Other regulations used abroad limit the proportion of low-down-payment or high debt-to-income mortgages a given lender can make, cap overall bank lending growth, or permit regulators to increase capital requirements when they become concerned about rapid increases in house prices or credit. The evidence suggests that policies of this type can—with modest overall economic costs—slow growth in house prices, mortgage lending, and bank credit, thus reducing crisis risk.[21]

Shadow Banking

An especially troubling weakness of the U.S. macroprudential framework is the still-inadequate oversight of the shadow banking sector. Excessive risk-taking in shadow banking was at the heart of the 2007–2009 crisis. When the short-term funding of investment banks (like Bear Stearns and Lehman Brothers) and other holders of credit assets (like off-balance-sheet special-purpose vehicles) evaporated, the resulting asset fire sales affected virtually all forms of private credit, not only mortgages.

Some progress has been made, through both legislation and changes in the market, in reducing the risks posed by shadow banking. Of the five major investment banks operating before the financial crisis, one failed (Lehman), two were acquired by large banks (Bear Stearns and Merrill Lynch), and two (Morgan Stanley and Goldman Sachs) became bank holding companies, bringing them into the orbit of federal bank regulators. The Federal Reserve also took actions to improve the operation of the repo market, regulators pressed banks to reduce risky corporate lending through off-balance-sheet vehicles, and the Financial Stability Board (an international group of regulators) began regularly monitoring shadow banking worldwide. Dodd-Frank also improved the safety and transparency of markets for financial derivatives, which are heavily used by shadow banks. Still, there are reasons to worry that the reforms were incomplete, and that serious risks remain.*[22]

---

* Among those expressing concern (in 2018) was Janet Yellen, who as Treasury secretary in 2021

The events of March 2020, after markets realized the threat posed by the pandemic, validated these concerns. In that month, the shadow banking sector experienced runs and fire sales akin to the disruptions in 2008, generating extreme volatility and market dysfunction—even in what is usually the safest and most liquid financial market, the market for U.S. Treasury securities. As noted earlier, in an echo of 2008, investors ran from money market mutual funds, confirming that the SEC's earlier reforms were inadequate. Runs also occurred at some bond funds, mutual funds that hold relatively illiquid corporate bonds while assuring investors that they can withdraw cash at will. Certain types of hedge funds, whose repo market borrowing allowed them to achieve debt-to-equity ratios of nearly a hundred-to-one, were forced by losses to dump securities, adding to selling pressure. Only dramatic measures by the Fed, including emergency lending and massive purchases of Treasuries and mortgage-backed securities, stabilized the markets. Emergency interventions by the Fed, which create moral hazard (incentives for excessive risk-taking in the future) and uncertainty, may be necessary to protect the economy in the short run, but they are no substitute for adequate before-the-fact regulation that prevents crises from occurring in the first place.

The 2020 panic highlighted specific problems in shadow banking, some of which might have been addressed under existing legal authority. The broader problem is that the shadow banks, taken together, function as a banking system—providing liquidity and a return to investors and credit to borrowers—but they are not regulated like a banking system. For example, the postcrisis reforms that strengthened the capital and funding security of commercial banks do not generally apply to shadow banks, and regulatory oversight of their investments and lending remains limited. That asymmetry is not justified; in fact, it encourages risky activities to migrate into the sector. Shadow banks that hold risky assets (like investment banks or hedge funds) should be subject to capital requirements or leverage limits that reflect the riskiness of their portfolios, and those that promise investors quick access to cash (like money market funds or bond

---

would lead the FSOC.

funds) should either hold significant liquid reserves or structure their offerings in a way that provides investors no incentive to run.[23]

Crisis-Fighting Tools

Although macroprudential policies should reduce the frequency and severity of crises, we can never eliminate them. We accordingly need adequate tools for dealing with crises when they occur. In the United States, Dodd-Frank's orderly liquidation authority allows regulators to handle a failing systemic nonbank financial firm in a predictable manner that considers financial stability. Other jurisdictions have also created new tools for resolving failing firms, and countries are working together to prepare for the failure of a multinational firm, through joint role-playing exercises for example. That is all to the good. On the other hand, the orderly liquidation authority to resolve nonbank firms is less flexible than the FDIC's authority to resolve a failing bank. And regulators cannot draw on a preexisting insurance fund to resolve nonbanks, as the FDIC can when closing or selling a bank. Any costs borne by the government would instead be made up after the fact by assessing fees on the financial industry. Although it is a clear improvement over what we had in 2008, the liquidation authority remains untested.

The state of other crisis-fighting tools is mixed.[24] After the 2008–2009 bailouts, Congress curtailed several tools that the Fed, Treasury, and other policymakers had used to control the crisis. The Dodd-Frank Act restricted the Fed's 13(3) emergency lending authority by prohibiting it from lending to a single stressed firm (as opposed to a lending program open to all borrowers within a class). All 13(3) lending programs now require the approval of the Treasury secretary, as well as the Fed's Board. Dodd-Frank also required the Fed to disclose information on discount-window borrowers (with a two-year lag) and borrowers from 13(3) programs (within a year of the termination of the program). Congress's desire for more transparency is understandable, but these tougher reporting requirements will increase the stigma of borrowing from the Fed, making it more difficult for the central bank to serve its classic role of lender of last resort in a crisis. Likewise, successful crisis-era measures like an FDIC program guaranteeing newly issued bank debt and the Treasury's insurance program for money market funds have been eliminated or subjected to extensive new constraints.

Of course, Congress can reinstate emergency powers as needed, as it did when it expanded the Fed's 13(3) lending programs under the 2020 CARES Act. Nevertheless, financial crises move fast, and economic effects that legislators can see typically lag financial market disruptions. Legislative delay or political stalemate could greatly increase a future crisis's ultimate economic and fiscal costs.

More positively, the Fed (as well as the Treasury and other regulators) learned a great deal from the 2007–2009 and 2020 crises. These lessons were particularly evident in 2020, when the Fed moved quickly and proactively. It invoked its 13(3) powers even before Congress expanded its lending capacity. Building on actions taken during the global financial crisis, the Powell Fed also aggressively used a range of existing authorities, including currency swaps with foreign central banks to ensure global access to dollars, trillion-dollar repo operations to maintain market liquidity, and large-scale purchases of Treasuries and mortgage-backed securities to backstop those markets. Thus, despite new legislative constraints, the Fed—by using existing tools in new and creative ways—has effectively expanded its crisis-fighting toolkit.

Macroprudential policy in the United States, which for practical purposes was nonexistent before the 2007–2009 crisis, has come a long way. For the first time, risks to financial stability are routinely monitored and analyzed, the implications of new financial products or regulatory measures for the broader system are considered, and tools like the orderly liquidation authority are available.[25] The banking system is much stronger and the government has tools, if not yet fully deployed, to bring systemically risky shadow banking firms and activities under the umbrella of regulation. At the same time, the United States—with the world's most sophisticated and diverse financial system—lags many other countries in the development and application of macroprudential tools. The fact that the government has had to intervene massively in markets twice in less than a decade and a half suggests that the problems are deep. The good news is that diverse international examples provide useful models for further development of the U.S. framework for anticipating and responding to financial emergencies.

MONETARY POLICY VERSUS MACROPRUDENTIAL POLICY

The shortcomings of macroprudential policy again raise the question of whether monetary policy should focus more on financial stability. Should monetary policymakers take emerging financial risks into account when deciding where to set interest rates? Should they limit the use of easy-money policies in general, even in the absence of clear risks, on the grounds that easy money increases the potential for future instability?

For most policymakers and ex-policymakers, including me, the answer is: In principle, yes. But, in practice, very cautiously and not very often. Why the reluctance? I made the basic case for skepticism in my first speech as a Fed governor, in October 2002.[26] Because the internet bubble had recently popped, contributing to the 2001 recession, I framed my arguments around the question of whether the Fed should try to identify and prick emerging stock-market bubbles through rate increases, but my reasoning also applies to other financial risks. In my speech I highlighted three reasons why I saw monetary policy as a poor tool for forestalling risks to financial stability.

First, I argued, the Fed cannot reliably identify bubbles (or, by extension, other unhealthy risk buildups) with any confidence, and in any case should not try to be the arbiter of the "correct" level of the prices of stock or other assets. Second, our understanding of the links between monetary policy and stability risks is too limited to usefully guide policy. Historically, for example, attempts to use monetary policy to prick bubbles have often led to a crash rather than a gentle descent, a leading example being the Fed's attempt to cool stock prices in the late 1920s, which culminated in the 1929 plunge. Finally, monetary policy is a blunt tool: Changes in interest rates affect the entire economy and cannot target a narrow set of

markets or a few overheated sectors. As Benjamin Strong, leader of the
Federal Reserve Bank of New York in the 1920s, once said, it makes no
sense to spank all one's children when one of them is bad.[27] Attempts to use
monetary policy to pop bubbles or address other financial-stability risks are
as likely to hurt as help the broader economy, because the degree of policy
tightening needed to control a bubble is also likely to depress jobs, growth,
and inflation in the near term.

I emphasized this last point. Bubbles and lending booms occur because
investors expect outsized returns to continue. Accordingly, I argued, a sharp
monetary tightening would be needed to cool rapid increases in the prices
of stocks or other assets. But a sharp tightening would have unwanted economic side effects. A paper delivered years later, at the Fed's 2010 Jackson
Hole conference, by Bank of England economists Charles Bean, Matthias
Paustian, Adrian Penalver, and Timothy Taylor provided an illustration.
They estimated what might have happened if, in response to the housing
bubble, the Fed had kept the fed funds rate 2 percentage points higher from
2003 to 2006. After accounting for the indirect effects of slower growth
as well as the direct effects of higher rates, they concluded that credit and
house prices, driven by other factors, would have grown only modestly
less than otherwise.[28] Yet, a tightening of monetary policy by 2 percentage
points starting in 2003 would certainly have seriously impeded the recovery from the 2001 recession and increased deflationary risks. Consistent
with these results, economists Òscar Jordà, Moritz Schularick, and Alan
Taylor estimated that avoiding the entire housing bubble during 2002–
2006 would have required the Fed to raise the funds rate by as much as 8
percentage points.[29]

While rejecting routine use of monetary policy as a financial-stability
tool, my 2002 speech still acknowledged the central importance of maintaining financial stability. I argued instead that we should use "the right
tool for the job" to control financial risks—in most cases regulatory, supervisory, and lender-of-last resort powers.

Two decades later, I remain comfortable with much of what I said in
that speech. Nevertheless, a great deal has happened since, most obviously

the devastating 2007–2009 crisis, which regulators failed to prevent. And, although financial regulation has been strengthened since the crisis, we are far from where we need to be. We also know more today than we did in 2002 about the risk-taking channel of monetary policy, the sources and economic effects of financial crises, and the constraints that the effective lower bound put on postcrisis monetary policy. A fresh look at these issues is certainly warranted.

Lean-against-the-Wind Policies

An alternative view to the one in my 2002 speech holds that, in addition to responding to changes in the outlook for jobs and inflation, central bankers should also use monetary tools to lean against buildups of financial risks— or what are often called, generically, "financial imbalances." This so-called lean-against-the-wind (LATW) approach had advocates even before the global financial crisis. Claudio Borio and William White of the Bank for International Settlements (BIS) laid out the key ideas at the Fed's Jackson Hole conference in 2003.[30] Since 2008 the approach has naturally received greater attention.

For the most part, LATW supporters do not see themselves as advocating major changes to the traditional policy framework. They agree that the ultimate goals of monetary policy should be price stability and high employment. Indeed, they acknowledge that recessions and excessive inflation can themselves become sources of financial instability, for example, by weakening the banking system, increasing borrower defaults, or adding to market volatility. However, they argue that the traditional approach is deficient because it considers only the short-term effects of easy monetary policies, ignoring the possibility that in the longer term financial risks created by easy money could jeopardize the economy. They see the use of monetary policy to pre-empt threats to financial stability as consistent with the Fed's dual mandate, so long as policymakers take a sufficiently long-term view.

LATW supporters also generally agree with traditionalists that macroprudential and other regulatory policies should be the first line of defense against financial instability, used whenever possible to increase the resilience of the financial system and address emerging risks. However, they are pessimistic that regulatory policies will ever be sufficient to eliminate the risk of crises, implying that other tools—including monetary policy, imperfect though it may be—may also be needed. Advocates of LATW also tend to be skeptical that the increases in interest rates needed to contain financial-stability risks would be as large as those suggested by the calculations I cited. They argue that when investors realize that monetary policymakers will not ignore threats to stability, risk-taking will become less excessive.

So, in practice, how would LATW monetary policies be different from more traditional approaches? It's useful to distinguish between two broad types of LATW policies. Supporters of what I'll call *always-on* LATW contend that growing financial risks are often invisible, so that monetary policy should *always* be set with potential financial imbalances in mind. Under this approach, policymakers should try to avoid extended periods of easy money, even when no threats to financial stability are evident.[31] In contrast, under what I'll call *situational* LATW, monetary policy responds primarily to observable indicators of risk-taking, such as unusually rapid growth in house prices, stock prices, or credit. (It was situational LATW I had in mind in my 2002 speech, when I discussed the potential use of monetary policy to prick an apparent stock-market bubble.)

Always-On LATW Policies

Advocates of always-on LATW policies urge caution in the use of easy-money policies, even if economic performance falls short of desired levels and serious financial risks are not evident. In this view, easy monetary policy is analogous to a medicine that is powerful and effective but also has uncertain and possibly dangerous side effects and should therefore be used only when absolutely necessary.

Consistent with the always-on approach, then-Fed governor Jeremy Stein, in an influential 2013 speech, argued that too-frequent use of lower-for-longer monetary policies may increase fragility in the financial system.[32] Stein emphasized that, in practice, excessive borrowing and risk-taking may be quite difficult for policymakers to detect in a timely way. For example, hedge funds and other asset managers can use complex financial derivatives to achieve the functional equivalent of high leverage, or to make large and risky bets, in ways that are too subtle for regulators to reliably identify and limit. From this perspective, the advantage of the always-on LATW approach, which calls for more limited use of low-rate policies, is that higher interest rates reduce the incentive to borrow to finance all manner of risky investments. As Stein put it, higher interest rates can "get in all the cracks," reducing excessive risk-taking throughout the system, even in places where regulators have poor visibility or limited authority.

Stein was correct that excessive risk-taking may be difficult to detect or address in some cases. But, for such risks, I think that it's too soon to give up on macroprudential and regulatory policies. Regulators could improve their ability to monitor shadow banking, for example, by requiring improved disclosures or stress-testing asset managers' portfolios. Even absent such steps, existing policies that improve financial resilience broadly—for example, by ensuring that the banking system and other key financial institutions are well capitalized—can help the system withstand even unanticipated shocks.

Another question is whether the type of risk-taking that worried Stein threatens overall economic stability, which is the Fed's primary concern. Threats to financial stability large enough to cause a serious economic downturn don't usually come from nowhere, but are almost always reflected in economic data, such as large increases in credit and house prices.* Policymakers are more likely to be presented with a false positive—a rise in stock or home prices that is not, in fact, a systemic risk—than a false negative, in which a destabilizing shock arrives with no prior indication of danger.

Another argument for always-on LATW can be summarized as "stability breeds instability." According to this view, which has been formalized in research at the IMF, there is a trade-off between short-run and long-run economic stability.[33] In particular, if the central bank is "too successful"

---

* The exceptions are threats originating outside the system, like the 2020 pandemic or, perhaps in the future, a large-scale cyberattack.

in hitting its employment and inflation targets in the near term, making the economy and markets more stable, investors may become complacent and take risks that fuel financial and economic instability in the longer term. This view is reminiscent of arguments that the so-called Great Moderation—the long period of relative economic stability between the mid-1980s and the global financial crisis—helped promote the excessive risk-taking that set off that crisis.[34] It also evokes Hyman Minsky's argument that long financial cycles of growing complacency would be followed by crisis. The policy implication drawn by always-on LATW advocates is that the Fed should less aggressively pursue its inflation and employment targets in the short run. If the Fed's willingness to accept more near-term instability reduces investor complacency, and thus the risk of destabilizing financial crises, then the net result could be an economy that, paradoxically, is more stable in the longer term.

There may be some truth to the view that economic stability in the short run breeds financial instability in the long run, although the existing evidence remains murky. Even assuming this premise is true, I would not advocate that monetary policymakers purposefully accept more short-term economic volatility. Stated baldly, the stability-breeds-instability view holds that one portion of the economy—the financial sector—periodically creates extreme risk for the rest of the economy, and that the only way to control that risk is for monetary policymakers to limit investor complacency by *intentionally* accepting inferior economic performance in the short run. I think most people would see that as putting the cart before the horse. In their previously cited 2003 article, LATW proponents Borio and White themselves pointed out that a significant portion of the increase in the risk of financial instability appears to be the product of a global trend, starting in the 1970s, toward financial deregulation and liberalization. If the financial sector is truly so dangerous, then believers in the stability-breeds-instability hypothesis, rather than focusing on monetary policy, should be devoting their energies to more consistently and forcefully demanding comprehensive financial regulatory reform.

We can also draw an analogy between always-on LATW policies and pre-emptive inflation strikes. Before 2020, the Fed typically began to raise rates when the economy and labor market heated up, but before inflation had increased. Fed leaders at the time believed that this pre-emptive policy, by reducing the risk that the Fed would have to respond to an inflation overshoot, would result in more-stable growth and employment in the longer term. In 2020, however, the FOMC disavowed pre-emptive inflation strikes on the grounds that they created too great a risk of tightening policy prematurely. Always-on LATW amounts to pre-emptive policy tightening, sacrificing employment gains today to reduce the risk of financial instability in the future. Since financial instability is less predictable than inflation and can be addressed to some degree by other tools, the Fed's argument against pre-emptive inflation strikes—that a strong labor market today is too valuable to trade for speculative future reductions in inflation—should apply even more to always-on LATW policies. Indeed, consistent use of always-on LATW policies could lead to an economy in which employment and inflation are chronically below target, with inflation expectations drifting downward.

Situational LATW Policies

The alternative to the always-on approach, situational LATW, would link monetary policy to observable indicators of financial risk, such as rapid credit growth. Under this approach, monetary policy only responds when policymakers see significant financial-stability risks that can't be managed by other tools.

In my previously cited 2002 speech, I was skeptical that the Fed could identify market bubbles or other precursors of financial crises reliably enough for such policies to be useful. Since then, the evidence has led me to shift my views. Identifying risks to systemic financial stability is difficult, but our ability and commitment to monitor them have improved. Economists inside and outside the Federal Reserve have developed systematic frameworks and new metrics for assessing potential risks.[35] I've cited here historical research, using data beginning in the 19th century, that finds that credit booms often (though certainly not always) precede financial crises and deep recessions. Similarly, another study, by a Harvard team that includes Robin Greenwood, Samuel Hanson, Andrei Shleifer, and Jakob Sørensen, used data since 1950 from 42 countries.[36] They showed that rapid growth in credit and asset prices over the prior three years increased the probability of a crisis in the succeeding three years.

In general, asset bubbles, unhealthy credit booms, and other financial risks cannot be identified in real time with anything approaching certainty—on this point I think my 2002 speech is still correct—but evidence is now accumulating that, in some cases and with many statistical caveats, we can estimate whether the risk of a crisis at a given time is relatively high or low. If severe financial instability is at least somewhat predictable, if macroprudential or other regulatory policies are unable to mitigate these risks sufficiently, and if monetary policy can be used to meaningfully reduce the risk of a crisis, then situational LATW policies could make sense. That is, in theory. To put this approach into practice, we would need to know much more, including how strongly and for how long monetary policy should respond to particular risk indicators.

Ideally, to obtain this guidance, we would look at historical examples. But there are few if any clear cases of monetary policy alone successfully deflating a boom or a bubble, without precipitating a crash and damaging the economy. In 2010, the Swedish central bank, the Riksbank, raised interest rates despite high unemployment and low inflation, because of concerns about rising house prices and household debt. However, this attempt to lean against the wind collapsed as the economy slowed in response. The Riksbank reversed itself, cutting rates into negative territory and undertaking quantitative easing. In a more ambiguous case, in 2012, the Norwegian central bank, the Norges Bank, announced that, for financial-stability reasons, its policies would reflect not only its inflation target but also the extent to which interest rates deviated from normal levels.[37] Specifically, when macroeconomic conditions called for easy monetary policy, it would keep rates slightly higher than it otherwise would to reduce the risk of financial instability. It's hard to know whether this policy had any benefits. The Norges Bank reversed the policy in 2017, asserting that financial-stability risks had decreased. Whether risks had in fact decreased, and if so by how much, is difficult to say. In 2021, the New Zealand government told the central bank to consider house prices in setting monetary policy; however, the government's motivation was concerns about housing affordability rather than financial stability. The Reserve Bank of New Zealand (correctly) argued that targeting house prices for affordability reasons would make meeting its overall economic goals more difficult, and that a much better response would be to enact policies to increase housing supply. In short, history provides few if any clear success stories and little to guide us on the implementation or effectiveness of LATW monetary policies. In contrast, international examples of the effective use of macroprudential policy to moderate credit and housing booms are now common.

As an alternative to historical examples, economists have used econometric models to examine situational LATW. Many of these studies are based on comparisons of the expected costs and benefits of LATW. The principal cost of a proactive LATW policy tightening is worse near-term inflation and employment outcomes.* The benefit is the assumed reduction in the risk that a future crisis will inflict longer-term damage on the economy. In principle, we could determine the optimal degree of leaning against the wind by finding the policy that best balances these costs and benefits. Unfortunately, the costs and especially the benefits of LATW remain difficult to quantify.

An influential early analysis was done by Lars Svensson, an academic economist who also served as a monetary policymaker in his native Sweden.[38] (As a policymaker, Svensson strongly opposed the Riksbank's attempt to apply LATW.) To study the effects of LATW, Svensson used the Riksbank's primary economic model to estimate the effects of monetary policy on unemployment as well as on credit growth, which Svensson treated as

---

* Although not typically included in economic models, other possible costs include ending an increase in credit or asset prices that is not a bubble but is justified by fundamentals; or triggering a crash more severe than justified by fundamentals.

a proxy for the risk of a financial crisis. He added assumptions—based on historical evidence—about the frequency of financial crises in the absence of LATW policies, the average duration of a crisis, the effect of a crisis on unemployment, and the effect of credit growth changes on the probability of a crisis. Putting these elements together, he estimated the expected economic effects of a LATW-style, pre-emptive policy tightening. He then evaluated its costs (higher near-term unemployment) and benefits (lower crisis risk). He found that, quantitatively, the costs of LATW policies far outweigh the benefits. Studies using models of the U.S. economy also generally find that active use of monetary policy to promote financial stability is not justified by comparisons of costs and benefits.[*]

Svensson's work captures the intuition of my 2002 speech, that rate increases large enough to restrain a stock bubble or excess credit growth are also likely to impose heavy near-term economic costs. However, a potential weakness of this logic is that, while we have good estimates of the effects of monetary policy on current economic conditions, we know much less about both the effects of monetary tightening on the risk of future crises and about the economic costs of crises.[39] For example, Svensson assumed that the effects of a crisis on the economy, though severe, are ultimately temporary. But the slow recoveries in many countries after the global financial crisis raise the possibility that the economic effects of a crisis can be quite long-lasting. If so, then the benefits of avoiding a crisis may be considerably larger than Svensson assumed.[40] On the other hand, as Svensson himself noted, tightening policy could itself make the economic effects of a crisis worse, by slowing the economy just as the effects of the credit contraction are being felt.

This lack of clarity is discouraging. Based on what we know now, I draw two provisional conclusions. First, in most circumstances, regulatory and macroprudential policies are the most effective, best understood,

---

[*] For example, in a 2019 study, Andrea Ajello, Thomas Laubach, David López-Salido, and Taisuke Nakata of the Federal Reserve Board staff found, in their baseline simulations, that the optimal monetary policy response to financial-stability risks is close to zero.

and best-targeted tools for dealing with risks to financial stability. These tools can enhance the overall resilience of the financial system, they can be tailored to specific threats, and their spillover effects on the economy are typically limited. Policymakers should actively use these targeted tools and, where they are insufficient, should be vocal about the need for expanded authority.* In particular, every financial regulatory agency should have financial stability as part of its mandate, and excessive risk-taking should be monitored and addressed no matter where in the financial system it occurs.

But second, given our current state of knowledge, we can't confidently rule out circumstances when monetary policy might supplement other tools to deal with financial-stability risks. These instances likely will be rare and, in any case, should reflect a careful analysis of the trade-offs involved.

In that spirit, the FOMC's 2020 statement on policy goals and strategy does not treat financial stability as a goal on par with unemployment and inflation. However, it does stipulate that "risks to the financial system that could impede the attainment of the Committee's goals" should be included in the overall balance of risks that policymakers weigh. That formulation suggests the FOMC will not make large changes in monetary policy in response to perceived financial risks, nor is it specific about the nature of the risks that might spur a monetary response. But it does leave open the possibility that, in the context of an otherwise close policy call, the Committee might take out some insurance by leaning against risks to financial stability.

INTERNATIONAL FINANCIAL CONTAGION

Financial conditions among countries are linked, in part, by the monetary policies of major central banks. The Fed's actions are particularly influential

---

* In a 2019 paper presented as part of the Fed's strategy review, Anil Kashyap and Caspar Siegert called for a congressional commission to comprehensively review the tools available for preventing or responding to financial crises. Hubbard and Kohn (2021) present the results of a task force on financial stability sponsored by the Brookings Institution and the Chicago Booth School of Business.

and emerging-market economies are often among those most affected. The taper tantrum of 2013, although an extreme example, illustrates a more general phenomenon.

Hélène Rey has documented what she calls the global financial cycle: the tendency of risky assets around the world, from Mexican corporate bonds to South African stocks, to move together.[41] Rey and others also found that changes in U.S. monetary policy significantly influence the global cycle. When Fed policy eases, risk-taking around the world increases, risky asset prices rise, and capital flows push into emerging markets. When Fed policy tightens, that all reverses.

It's not hard to see why Fed policy would affect global financial conditions.[42] The U.S. economy is big and its capital markets are the largest and most liquid in the world. To access those markets, many foreign governments and corporations borrow in dollars, which means that their financial health is affected by changes in the value of the dollar or in U.S. interest rates. Most international reserves held by governments around the world are in dollars, and much international trade—even when neither trading partner is American—is invoiced in dollars as well. Tobias Adrian and Hyun Shin, currently top economic advisers at the IMF and BIS respectively, have documented that when U.S. monetary policy eases, international banks tend to increase their leverage and lend more, in dollars, to risky borrowers—an international version of the risk-taking channel of monetary policy.[43] The resulting flow of dollars, particularly to emerging-market borrowers, strengthens foreign currencies and raises the prices of risky foreign assets. When U.S. monetary policy tightens, however, international banks cut back on dollar lending, leading to falling foreign currencies and capital outflows.

Although the Fed's mandate is to focus on the U.S. economy, the Fed has a clear interest in avoiding actions that will lead to excessive volatility abroad that in turn will spill back into our economy and markets. To avoid or minimize volatility, the Fed tries to clearly communicate its policy plans, allowing time for foreign markets and policymakers to adjust. And, during periods of financial stress such as March 2020, the Fed's outsized influence and the global role of U.S. markets makes a strong policy response particularly important.

Emerging-market countries can also act to reduce their vulnerability in the global financial cycle. Most directly, they can mitigate wide swings in capital flows by improving their economic fundamentals. Over the past few decades, many countries have strengthened their economies by reducing fiscal and trade deficits, protecting the independence of their central banks, improving financial regulation, allowing greater exchange-rate flexibility, and undertaking structural reforms. These types of changes help persuade investors that a country can continue to grow even when global financial conditions are tight.

Macroprudential policies can also reduce the risks of the global financial cycle. For example, the IMF traditionally pressed emerging markets to allow unrestricted capital flows across their borders, on the grounds that foreign investment fosters development. However, since the financial crisis, the IMF has become more sympathetic to emerging-market economies using targeted capital controls—restrictions on inflows and outflows of financial capital—to mitigate the global cycle's effects. Likewise, emerging-market policymakers have increased their oversight of dollar-based borrowing by their banks and nonfinancial corporations. Through organizations like the G20 and the Financial Stability Board, advanced and emerging-market economies are working together to monitor global risks and strengthen the resilience of the global system.

For the Federal Reserve, the international dimension makes preserving financial stability that much more challenging. Macroprudential policy is more difficult in an international context because U.S. regulators have limited ability to observe or respond to risks originating from abroad. And the need to coordinate with regulators from many countries creates additional complexity. Attempts to use an LATW monetary policy strategy also become more complicated when policymakers must account for its effects on global as well as domestic markets.

In general, our understanding of the links between monetary policy, regulatory policy, and financial stability remains much more limited than we would like. Researchers and policymakers have a lot of work left to do. Policymakers and legislators also need to appreciate that the work of redesigning our regulatory system to better anticipate and prevent financial crises has only just begun. I don't expect that maintaining financial stability will become a formal part of the Fed's legal mandate, along with price stability and maximum employment, as some have suggested. However, for the foreseeable future, financial instability will be a central concern for 21st century central bankers.

15

THE FED'S INDEPENDENCE AND ROLE IN SOCIETY

To MEET ITS ECONOMIC AND FINANCIAL-STABILITY goals, the Fed likely will continue to innovate and experiment. Beyond the technical policy challenges, however, the Fed also faces substantial challenges as an institution. Will it retain its cherished independence? Should it? And how will it respond to broader societal changes, including technological advance, climate change, and increasing demands for social justice?

THE FED'S INDEPENDENCE

The Federal Reserve is often described as independent. That doesn't mean that it is fully autonomous, democratically unaccountable, or divorced from politics. To the contrary, the Fed is a product of the political system. Its powers and structure—its very existence—are dictated by the Federal Reserve Act, which Congress can amend at any time. The Fed's Board members are political appointees, and its chair and other leaders keep legislators informed about the Fed's actions and plans through testimony, formal reports, and personal contacts. As I put it in my final press conference as chair, when asked to give advice to my successor: "Congress is our boss."[1]

With its influence over the economy and the financial system—serving sometimes as a savior, sometimes as a scapegoat—the Fed is a subject of intense interest for politicians.

Notwithstanding the real political constraints on the Fed, in practice it *is* independent—up to a point. Congress sets the Fed's goals—price stability and maximum employment—and provides broad oversight and accountability.* However, the Fed has long enjoyed considerable *de facto* policy independence, setting rates and taking other actions in pursuit of its mandated goals with, for the most part, limited political interference.

Unlike many countries, the United States does not have a law that explicitly guarantees the independence of the central bank. However, in practice the Fed's policy independence is protected by several legal provisions, many established in the Fed's early days. These include the long terms of Board governors, the fact that the president cannot fire governors over policy differences, and the Fed's ability (subject to congressional oversight) to finance itself out of the returns to the securities it holds, as opposed to relying on Congress to fund it. Continued support for those provisions reflects the long-standing belief by most in Congress and, with few exceptions—notably Trump—by presidents after Nixon that an independent central bank provides both economic and political benefits. The Federal Reserve System's national footprint also supports its independence. The presidents and boards of directors of the regional Reserve Banks develop close relationships with local political and business leaders, who at crucial moments have helped defend the Fed's autonomy.

Looking to the future, the Fed's independence raises at least two questions. First, in today's economic and political environment, does Fed policy independence remain justified? And, assuming that it does, will the Fed be able to defend that independence against political opposition?

While the doctrine of central-bank independence has deep roots, the

---

* The Fed has some flexibility in practice in interpreting its goals. For example, the FOMC defined "price stability" as 2 percent inflation in 2012 and, in 2020, emphasized the "broad-based and inclusive" nature of its employment goal.

current consensus in its favor was strengthened by the experience of the Great Inflation. The damaging effects of the Burns Fed's lack of independence from the Nixon administration were evident. Based on that experience, and the subsequent success of the fiercely independent Volcker Fed in quelling inflation, the Fed's independence is often seen as a bulwark against the temptation of politicians to overstimulate the economy in the short term.

The idea that independent central bankers are better equipped than politicians to take the economy's long-run interests into account still rings true. But the specific argument that independence is required to avoid excessive inflation doesn't seem as strong today. Notwithstanding the rise in inflation during the recovery from the pandemic, 21st century monetary policymakers have more often worried about too-low, rather than too-high, inflation. And, while the Trump administration's pressure on the Powell Fed to cut rates prior to the pandemic was a notable exception, much of the political opposition faced by central banks in recent years has come from those who wanted them to do less rather than more. Examples include Republicans' criticism of quantitative easing after the financial crisis and German opposition to the European Central Bank's QE programs.

However, avoiding another Burns-Nixon scenario is not the only rationale for continued Fed independence. Congress has good reasons—both technical and political—for continuing to delegate monetary policy decisions to an independent central bank.

From a technical perspective, monetary policymaking requires specialized skills and knowledge. Being a good chair or FOMC member does not require a PhD in economics—some of the best did not have one—but it does require an appreciation of complex economic issues and ideas combined with a full-time commitment to monitoring the economy and financial markets. Also, monetary policy is often time sensitive. It must respond quickly and accurately to changing economic and financial conditions, particularly during emergencies. And it requires consistent, coherent, and timely communication with markets and the public. It is no criticism to say that legislators have neither the time nor the training to manage monetary policy successfully. Congress employs the Fed to make monetary policy in part for the same reason that I hire professionals to fix my plumbing. While I hold the plumbers accountable for the results, I don't second-guess their decisions about how to get the job done. Monetary policy is difficult, and the Fed makes mistakes, but there is no other agency in Washington that can call on the depth of economic talent and policymaking experience available to the central bank.

The technical argument alone is not enough, however. Those concerns might be addressed by having the Treasury or another political agency develop the requisite expertise to run monetary policy. In the United Kingdom and Japan, for example, finance ministries have overseen monetary policy as recently as the 1990s. Potential arguments in favor of Treasury control of monetary policy include greater democratic accountability, more careful consideration of the fiscal implications of monetary policy, and increased monetary-fiscal coordination. Still, political control of monetary policy—which would, in practice, give the president the final word on interest-rate decisions—is a bad idea.

Monetary policy operates with substantial lags and policy easing or tightening can play out over a span of years. (The easing of policy and its reversal following the global financial crisis spanned more than a decade.) Accordingly, policy continuity and coherence demand that monetary policymakers maintain a longer-term perspective. Treasury secretaries, who serve at the pleasure of the president, may turn over too quickly. As Fed chair I worked with four Treasury secretaries, two Republicans and two Democrats, and Greenspan worked with seven. More generally, our political system, with elections every two years and ever-churning media cycles, does not favor long-horizon policymaking. An independent central bank is better able than a political agency to firmly anchor inflation expectations, issue credible forward guidance, and establish predictable and consistent policies and policy frameworks.

A politicized monetary authority also would face greater scrutiny and potential skepticism about the motivations for and timing of its actions. Would its economic forecasts be viewed as objective and credible? Would a politicized agency be tempted to time interest-rate moves for short-term political benefit? With political control, would the influence of powerful interest groups override the interests of the economy as a whole? As was the case before the 1951 Treasury-Fed Accord, would the political agency change interest rates to manage the costs of government debt rather than to promote high employment and price stability? Considering current levels of partisan polarization and distrust, the case for insulating monetary policy from politics seems, if anything, stronger than in the past. Congress's decision to delegate major pandemic-era lending programs to the Fed reflected legislators' confidence in both the central bank's expertise and its apolitical approach to policymaking.

I am moderately optimistic that the Fed can defend its policy independence, even as it remains accountable for achieving its objectives. The Fed's independence and authority survived both the post–financial crisis blowback and Trump's assault by Twitter. That's evidence that its independence—though in principle revocable by Congress at any time—is not so fragile in practice. Biden's nomination of Powell to a second term, returning to the tradition of reappointing chairs originally appointed by a president of a different party, is another hopeful sign. That said, the risks to Fed independence in the 21st century are greater than they have been in some time. The financial crisis damaged the central bank's reputation on both the left and the right—on the left, for perceived favoritism to Wall Street in the bailouts; on the right, for monetary policies seen as risky and experimental; and on both sides, for failure to prevent the crisis in the first place. The rise of populism, with its conspiracy theories and distrust of elites, poses a particular threat to technocratic, nonpartisan institutions like the Fed.

Fed leaders have always recognized that the institution exists in a political context and that they play a political role. Developing personal connections with politicians, giving them the chance to ask questions and voice concerns, is an important part of the Fed chair's job. Alan Greenspan had close relationships with presidents and congressional leaders of both parties, and Jay Powell "wore out the carpets" in the halls of Congress. But in recent years the Fed has also been changing its institutional style, to embrace greater transparency and public outreach.

As chair, my early motivation for working to increase the Fed's transparency was to improve communication with markets, to make monetary policy more predictable and thus more effective. But in the political maelstrom that followed the financial crisis, I realized that transparency and public outreach could serve the broader goal of explaining, and thereby (I hoped) building support for, our policies. With the help of our public affairs office, headed by Fed veteran Michelle Smith, I worked to expand our audience beyond financial market participants and Washington insiders. My successors expanded the Fed's outreach, explaining policy decisions in more plainspoken terms and working to show how the Fed's policies help people on Main Street. The Fed will certainly continue to use more plain language to explain its actions and look for opportunities for dialogue, in the belief that, if people understand better what the Fed is and what it does, they will be more likely to support its independence. The twelve Reserve Banks, with their strong roots in local communities, have been and will be instrumental in this effort.

THE FED'S BROAD REACH: FROM NEW TECHNOLOGIES TO SOCIAL ISSUES

Additional challenges lie ahead for the Fed, including keeping up with new technologies and engaging with pressing social issues, from climate change to racial inequality.

New Technologies and the Fed

The Fed is a sophisticated agency, well positioned to embrace evolving technologies that help it to do its job better. For example, Fed staff are increasingly monitoring the economy through large, quickly available data sets on credit card charges, passengers cleared through airport security, restaurant seatings, online search topics, and many other measures. Microlevel "big data" like these were particularly useful for measuring economic activity during the pandemic.

The Fed is also strengthening its high-tech expertise as a bank regulator. For example, it is overseeing banks' deployment of machine-learning algorithms to screen potential borrowers and manage risks.[2] Are these and other artificial intelligence tools reliable and sufficiently transparent? Are they biased against minority credit applicants? The Fed has been particularly concerned about the increasing frequency of sophisticated cyberattacks on banks and other financial institutions. The banking system, by its nature, is highly interconnected, which creates many potential entry points for hackers. To help protect the system, Fed bank supervisors work with cybersecurity experts in the Treasury and other agencies to test banks' defenses.*[3]

The Fed plays a crucial role in the payments system. It serves as the fiscal agent of the Treasury, handling most payments made by the government to households and businesses. It oversaw the delivery of most of the relief payments authorized by the 2020 CARES Act, for example, including via direct deposits, checks, and prepaid debit cards.[4] The Fed has also long cleared checks for banks, moving funds from the checkwriter's bank to the recipient's bank. At one time that required large check-sorting operations at the Reserve Banks, as well as a fleet of planes to fly checks around the country. Today, check clearing is entirely electronic.

Although few people are aware of the Fed's role in ensuring that they receive money owed them, they do notice delays between when a check is issued and when they have access to the money. For a family living paycheck to paycheck, or a small business carefully managing its cash flow, delays can create hardship. To eliminate delays, the Fed is developing a service, called FedNow, to provide nearly instantaneous payments through any bank in the country, twenty-four hours a day.[5] Among other benefits, the service would ensure that government relief payments—to victims of a natural disaster, for example—would be immediately available.

More speculatively, the Fed could create a "digital dollar" as an alternative to paper currency. A digital currency system could be structured in

---

* The Fed has to protect itself from cyberfraud as well. In 2016, hackers penetrated the Central Bank of Bangladesh, sending phony payment orders to the Bangladeshi account at the New York Fed.

many ways, including (most likely) arrangements in which the Fed collaborates with the existing banking system or new fintech companies specializing in payments. For example, people might have access to central bank digital payments through their existing commercial bank accounts. In the conceptually simplest model—although one that would be challenging to administer in practice—every household and business could opt to have what amounts to a checking account at the Fed. Balances at the Fed would be as good as cash and could be used for immediate payment to any business or individual with a Fed account, for example through a cellphone app. Unlike cash transactions, digital dollar transactions would presumably leave a record, although allowing anonymous or untraced accounts is a possibility. A Fed-sponsored digital currency would have important advantages relative to cash or checks, including safety; convenience; and the immediate, guaranteed transfer of funds. It would likely speed and reduce the cost of international payments, including remittances from foreigners working in the United States to families in their home countries. A digital dollar could also promote financial inclusion, if people who do not have accounts at banks—out of concerns about fees, for example—could be persuaded to enroll in a Fed-sponsored system.

Many central banks are considering digital currencies, although only the People's Bank of China has progressed as far as conducting field tests. The Fed is studying the technological feasibility of a digital currency but has indicated that it plans to move forward only cautiously, with guidance from Congress. Technological and design issues only partly explain this deliberative approach. Fed policymakers also must consider the potential implications of this innovation for the financial system and the economy. For example, a digital currency with recorded transactions, if it ultimately replaced currency, would cut down on tax evasion, money laundering, the drug trade, and other illicit transactions—but potentially at the sacrifice of privacy. Some worry that digital cash could lead to financial instability since investors could find it easy to run to the (ultrasafe) digital currency at the first whiff of risk in the financial system. The Fed also will need to understand how digital cash would interact with existing payment systems, such as credit card networks, and how competition between digital currency and traditional bank deposits would affect banks' profitability and access to funding.

Another issue is how a digital currency would affect monetary and fiscal policy. It offers some clear advantages. If everyone had an account at the Fed, for example, tax rebates, tax refunds, relief payments, and other government payments could be delivered instantaneously. If the digital accounts were set up to pay interest, the Fed could speed up and strengthen the effects of its interest-rate decisions by varying the rate paid on digital money.

A central-bank digital currency is very different from bitcoin and other so-called cryptocurrencies. Cryptocurrencies are typically created and managed through a decentralized technology (a blockchain), rather than by a central bank. Since the introduction of bitcoin in 2009, the value of many cryptocurrencies has skyrocketed and their advocates tout them as an alternative to central-bank currencies, such as the dollar and euro.* Do bitcoin and similar assets have significant implications for monetary policy?

The answer is almost certainly not, at least for the foreseeable future. Cryptocurrencies like bitcoin have become accepted as a speculative asset, like gold, but they are not really money. A successful money, like the dollar, must be usable in ordinary transactions and have a relatively stable value, measured in terms of the things that consumers buy. Leading cryptocurrencies don't come close to satisfying either condition. People don't buy groceries with bitcoin (bitcoin transactions are quite expensive, relative to, say, ordinary credit card purchases), and the prices of ordinary goods and services, when measured in bitcoin, swing wildly. The dollar and other major

---

* The discussion in the text applies to cryptocurrencies, like bitcoin, with variable, market-determined values. Unlike bitcoin, some cryptocurrencies have values pegged to the dollar or other fiat currencies, or to assets denominated in fiat currencies. These so-called stablecoins may become the basis of new payment methods, but since they are tied to existing currencies, they do not threaten to replace those currencies. Important questions also remain on how stablecoins will be regulated to protect users and help ensure that they do not become a source of financial instability.

fiat currencies are therefore not in danger of being supplanted by floating-value cryptocurrencies like bitcoin as the principal means of payment.* Even if, improbably, bitcoin or a similar cryptocurrency did displace the dollar in many private transactions, the fact that the government requires taxes to be paid in dollars and makes its own payments in dollars ensures continuing demand for U.S. currency. So long as dollars are widely used, monetary policy would still work in the accustomed way, with the values of cryptocurrencies responding to Fed actions much as other asset values do.

In the extremely unlikely event that a cryptocurrency like bitcoin were to displace the dollar, what would happen then? In that scenario, the economy would effectively return to a version of the 19th century gold standard, except with bitcoin playing the role of gold (although without official government sanction or central-bank involvement). The prices of ordinary goods and services, measured in terms of bitcoin, would depend on the supply of and demand for bitcoin, just as the supply of and demand for gold determined the prices of goods and services under the gold standard. If the supply of bitcoin grew more slowly than the economy, for example, then the bitcoin prices of ordinary products would decline over time. Under a bitcoin standard, monetary policies aimed at stabilizing prices or employment would no longer be feasible, since central banks would have no control over the supply of money. Because the public expects the government to try to stabilize the economy, a bitcoin standard would likely be unsustainable politically, just as the gold standard—which also limited activist use of monetary policy—proved untenable in the 1930s.

The Federal Reserve and Society

The Fed's prominent role in stabilizing the economy and financial system raises the question of whether it can assist in addressing other pressing challenges. For example, the environmental, societal, and economic costs

---

* Bitcoin and similar assets have additional drawbacks: Their creation uses large amounts of energy and, because they are often used for illicit activities, from money laundering to ransomware, they face the risk of much heavier regulation in the future.

of climate change are becoming increasingly evident. In another sphere, the pandemic crisis spotlighted deep fissures in American society. Among these are increasingly wide inequalities in income and wealth, limited economic and social mobility, and persistent disparities in access to health care, education, and economic opportunity. Black people, Hispanic people, and other minority groups have suffered the greatest disadvantages. Can the Fed help solve problems like these?

On the one hand, as powerful as the Fed can be in some dimensions, its ability to ameliorate major social problems is constrained by its congressional mandate and by the limits of its tools. In a democracy, elected representatives, not appointed officials like Fed governors, should set national priorities. Solving our most difficult social problems lies well beyond both the Fed's capacity and its remit. On the other hand, when the Fed has the opportunity, the means, and the legal authority to contribute constructively, consistent with the direction set by political leaders and the public, it should do so.

On climate change, for example, potentially useful policies—such as carbon taxes or carbon trading, subsidies for carbon-reducing technologies, and retrofitting buildings and utilities—are not the Fed's decisions. They are decisions for Congress (and some agencies that Congress designates, such as the Environmental Protection Agency). The Fed can nevertheless contribute to the collective effort. For example, the Fed has sponsored research and conferences on climate change. As a bank regulator, following the lead of the Bank of England and other major central banks, the Fed has also begun to introduce climate risks as a factor in its evaluation of bank portfolios and capital needs. Once in place, this practice could force banks to write down assets at risk from climate change (properties in flood plains or hurricane zones, for example) or that would be affected by policies to limit warming (such as bonds issued by oil and gas companies). Another possible action, adopted by the European Central Bank and others, would be to avoid purchasing the bonds of corporations that are major contributors to warming. However, the Fed—unlike most major central banks— does not buy corporate securities in the course of normal policymaking, so the issue is of limited practical importance in the United States. To this point, the Fed has not tried to incorporate the effects of climate change in its economic projections or monetary policy analyses, since those effects have been viewed as unpredictable and mostly very long term, but that may change as the near-term effects of the changing climate on growth and productivity become more evident.

On issues of inequality and social mobility, as we have seen, the Fed can make one exceedingly important contribution—using monetary policy to promote consistently high levels of employment. Hot labor markets disproportionately benefit minorities, lower-paid, and less experienced workers. A healthy demand for workers also brings more people off the sidelines into the labor force, where they can gain experience and develop connections that will serve them well, even if the labor market weakens.

Beyond monetary policy, the Fed has other tools for promoting a more equal society. For example, it maintains regular relationships with community development organizations, including community development financial institutions and minority-owned banks. The Fed helps these institutions better serve their constituents through training programs and technical assistance.[6] The Fed is also among the agencies that implement the Community Reinvestment Act of 1977, which requires that depository institutions meet the broad credit needs of the communities where they do business.[7] Fed researchers in Washington and at the Reserve Banks also collect data and conduct research on the labor market and inequality, including racial and ethnic disparities. For example, the Fed's regular *Survey of Consumer Finances* is a basic source for data on U.S. wealth and income inequality.

The Fed can also advance equity by increasing its own diversity, to ensure that all points of view are represented in policy decisions and, more generally, to make the economics profession more inclusive. The Fed has made diversity a formal goal for some time with at best fair results. From 1990 to 2021, nineteen men (one of them Black) and eight women have served on the Fed's Board. (Two of the women, Janet Yellen and Alice Rivlin, and the Black man, Roger Ferguson, also served as Board vice chair. Yellen served as become the third woman to serve as vice chair; Lisa Cook and Philip Jefferson, both Black economists, were nominated that same year to fill Board seats.) Board members are chosen by the president, not the Fed itself, so the composition of the staff may be a better indicator of the Fed's diversity efforts. Among staff, according to a 2019 Brookings study, around 24 percent of the PhD economists in the Federal Reserve System were female and around 25 percent were minorities.[8] However, the definition of minorities used by the Brookings study is broad. A 2021 *New York Times* article by Jeanna Smialek pointed out that the Board employed only two Black PhD economists.[9] This lack of diversity reflects in part trends in the economics profession as a whole. Economics has fallen behind other fields, including scientific and engineering disciplines, in attracting, developing, and promoting women and underrepresented minorities. However, as a public agency and one of the world's largest employers of economists, the Fed has a special responsibility to try to improve this situation. It should redouble its commitment to attracting a diverse staff and build a pipeline that will bring more talented minority and women students into the field.

THE FED: PAST AND FUTURE

The title of a famous painting by Paul Gauguin asks, "Where do we come from? What are we? Where are we going?" This book has tried to answer these questions about America's central bank. As illustrated by its extraordinary actions during the pandemic crisis, the Federal Reserve has changed enormously since the days of William McChesney Martin and Arthur Burns. It has radically revamped its policy toolkit, its strategy, and its communications. It has navigated changing political winds, protected its policy independence, and, at the same time, worked with administrations and Congress to respond to crises and support other national priorities.

The remarkable changes in the Fed's policy arsenal and approach from Martin to Powell are not, for the most part, the result of changes in its powers or mandate or of revolutions in economic thinking. Rather, as the historical account demonstrates, long-term economic and political developments have reshaped the Fed and its policies over the past seventy years.

The changing behavior of inflation, resulting both from shifts in the Fed's policies and changes in the structure of the economy, is the first such key development. Paul Volcker's victory over inflation in the 1980s reestablished the primacy of monetary policy for controlling inflation, restored the Fed's credibility, and demonstrated the benefits of Fed policy independence. Aided by favorable changes in the structure of the economy, including an apparent decline in the sustainable rate of unemployment, Alan Greenspan locked in Volcker's gains, further stabilizing inflation and anchoring inflation expectations. During my term, the Fed established a formal framework describing how it would achieve both its inflation target and maximum employment and, under Jay Powell, updated the framework.

Will the control of inflation continue to play a central role in U.S. monetary policymaking? The Fed has been criticized in recent years for putting too much emphasis on inflation at the expense of employment. There is some truth to this criticism. The Great Inflation of the 1960s and 1970s made monetary policymakers averse to even moderate increases in inflation, which they feared might unanchor expectations and, over time, lead to a more serious inflation problem. Over the years, these concerns led to some hawkish policy errors. Likewise, some have argued that the Fed's "balanced approach," as laid out in its 2012 policy principles, and which gave approximately equal weight to the two sides of the mandate, did not sufficiently value the social benefits of high employment and a hot labor market. The Fed's reworking of its policy framework in 2020 responded to these concerns. In particular, in its abandonment of pre-emptive inflation strikes, the Powell Fed indicated it was willing to allow more volatile inflation and temporary overshoots of its inflation target to achieve high employment more consistently.

The broad and lasting benefits of hot labor markets should certainly be reflected in the Fed's framework and policies. That said, the Fed will not—and should not—neglect the price stability half of its mandate. Keeping inflation well controlled is not only economically beneficial in itself—because it allows markets to function better and facilitates long-term planning, for example—but it is also critical for fostering consistently high levels of employment. Stable inflation and well-anchored inflation expectations support employment by giving monetary policy greater flexibility to respond to shocks that put the labor market at risk. For example, a central bank that is credible on inflation has greater ability to "look through" supply shocks (such as increases in oil prices or the supply chain disruptions of the pandemic) or to more forcefully ease policy in a recession, with greater confidence that any increases in inflation will not be sustained.* The Fed may retain its FAIT framework, or it may modify it in the future, but, in the interest of promoting a healthy economy and job market in the long run, it should be careful to maintain its hard-won credibility on inflation.

The second development shaping the Fed and its policies has been the long-term decline in the neutral rate of interest, R*. This decline partly reflects lower inflation and inflation risk, but real (inflation-adjusted) rates also have fallen substantially, by roughly 3 percentage points since the mid-1980s.[10] A low-interest-rate environment has many economic consequences, most directly for lenders and borrowers. For the Fed and other central banks, confronted with the effective lower bound, the decline in the neutral rate has limited the ability to support a weak economy through the traditional method of cutting short-term rates. Fortunately, new policy tools, including quantitative easing and more-explicit, long-horizon forward guidance, have proved effective, adding firepower roughly equivalent to 3 percentage points of cuts in the federal funds rate (according to my simulations), with limited unwanted side effects. That said, even with the new tools, at current levels of R* monetary policy alone is unlikely to be able to deal with a deep recession.

Much will depend on how the neutral interest rate evolves. Bond

---

* More generally, a sound monetary framework must have what economists call a *nominal anchor*, a policy target that helps pin down the general price level over time. Currently, the inflation rate is the nominal anchor in all major economies. As discussed in Chapter 13, alternative nominal anchors that monetary policymakers might consider include the price level (as opposed to the inflation rate) or nominal GDP. For some countries, a fixed value of the exchange rate provides the nominal anchor. History shows that the choice of nominal anchor is important, as it helps shape monetary policy and the resulting behavior of the economy.

markets see interest rates as likely to remain low for many years, judging that the demographic and technological factors that caused the neutral rate to decline will persist. If the neutral rate does stay low, I expect the Fed will continue to develop new monetary tools, or adapt tools developed by other central banks. For example, the Fed could strengthen its forward guidance by reinforcing rate promises with yield curve control; it could develop subsidized lending programs for use in bad economic times; and it could leave open the possibility of setting moderately negative short-term rates. If the neutral rate remains low or falls even lower, however, greater reliance on fiscal policy in deep recessions seems inevitable. Although perhaps politically unlikely now, further development of fiscal automatic stabilizers—tax and spending provisions triggered automatically when the economy weakens—could pick up some of the slack resulting from less potent monetary policy.

It is not certain, however, that the neutral rate will remain low or decline further. Somewhat higher inflation, the need to finance large government deficits in the United States and abroad, and increased compensation for the risk of holding longer-term securities are all possible reasons for a higher neutral rate in the future. More speculatively, many new technologies—from artificial intelligence to new green energy technologies to quantum computing to advances in biotechnology—have the potential to help reverse the slowdown in productivity and end the dearth of investment opportunities. Most importantly, improved productivity would result in more-rapid growth in output and living standards. But, additionally, the increase in the neutral rate created by higher trend growth and investment would provide greater scope for monetary policy.

Increased risk of dangerous financial instability, the third long-term trend shaping the Fed's tools and strategies, is perhaps the most concerning development. Many factors fueling that risk will be hard to reverse or repair, including weaknesses (even following postcrisis reforms) in the structure of financial regulation, rapid financial innovation, and the ever-increasing complexity, opacity, and interconnectedness of the global financial system. To help preserve financial stability, and to avoid the economic damage that a financial crisis can cause, the Fed has expanded its tools for fighting crises, as demonstrated by its responses to the global financial crisis and the March 2020 panic. It has also adopted a macroprudential perspective, systematically monitoring the overall financial system—including markets and institutions for which it has no direct regulatory responsibility—and working to identify risks to its stability. And it has continued to study the links between monetary policy and private risk-taking.

Legislators and regulators deserve credit for progress made since the global financial crisis, but critical regulatory gaps remain, as the events of March 2020 demonstrated. U.S. regulators continue to lack the powers and mandates they need to protect against important systemic risks, especially in housing and shadow banking. Given its expertise and credibility, the Fed should do more to highlight the remaining gaps and press Congress and the other members of the FSOC for action. In particular, as risk-taking will always migrate to the least-regulated parts of the system, the principle that financial firms that perform similar functions should be regulated similarly should be taken much more seriously. From the Fed's perspective, stronger macroprudential regulation would make active use of monetary policy safer and more effective by reducing possible financial-stability side effects.

Beyond its economic and policy challenges, the Fed has also had to contend with its increased public visibility. Its leading role in dealing with recent financial and economic crises has thrust the once-obscure institution into the national spotlight. In this respect, the world has changed a great deal since 1996, when former Board Vice Chair Alan Blinder said, "I have been told that millions of Americans still think that the Federal Reserve System is a system of government-owned forests and wildlife preserves where, presumably, bulls and bears and hawks and doves frolic together in blissful harmony."[11] Fed leaders will need to engage even more closely with all Americans—to listen to their concerns, to explain the Fed's policies, and to show that apolitical, independent, and objective policymaking serves the long-run interest of the economy. The Fed will doubtless make mistakes, as it has in the past. But, as Jay Powell put it, it must continue to show that it will not make mistakes of character or integrity.

AN INVITATION TO COMMENT

I am eager to hear from readers of *21st Century Monetary Policy*. Are there important issues that I did not cover, or issues where my coverage was faulty? Are there topics that should have been explored in more depth? In light of the complex and ever-changing environment in which monetary policy is made, are there new questions that should be addressed? To ask questions or make comments about the book, please go to http://benbernankebook.com/feedback. Your suggestions will inform any future editions, and I will post responses to selected questions and comments on the public site. Thank you in advance for your feedback.

Ben S. Bernanke

ACKNOWLEDGMENTS

Many people provided help and encouragement on this project. Dave Skidmore, who worked closely with me on my memoir of the financial crisis, *The Courage to Act*, once again devoted his considerable editing skills and knowledge of the Federal Reserve to making this book clearer and more accurate. I thank him for his hard work and his invaluable ideas and suggestions. I also thank Michael Ng, Sage Belz, Finn Schuele, Tyler Powell, and Eric Milstein for outstanding research assistance, in support both of this book and of several independent research projects on which this book draws. It was a great pleasure to work with these talented young people. I am sure much more will be heard of them in the future.

Readers of early drafts of this book included Bill English, Mark Gertler, Anil Kashyap, Don Kohn, Debbie Lucas, Rick Mishkin, Angel Ubide, and David Wessel. I thank them, as well as participants in seminars at the Massachusetts Institute of Technology, for useful comments. I thank the Brookings Institution (where I am a Distinguished Senior Fellow at the Hutchins Center on Fiscal and Monetary Policy) and MIT (where I was a Fellow of the Golub Center for Finance and Policy during 2020–21) for their support.

I am grateful to the staff of W. W. Norton and especially my editor Brendan Curry—who also partnered with me on *The Courage to Act*—for comments on the manuscript and for shepherding the project through the publication process. My thanks for highly professional assistance go also to project editor Rebecca Homiski, production manager Anna Oler, art director Ingsu Liu, copyeditor Carla Barnwell, publicist Rachel Salzman, and editorial assistant Caroline Adams. My legal advisers and literary agents, Bob Barnett and Michael O'Connor, provided excellent advice and guidance.

This book was my pandemic project, written largely at home, which subjected my wife Anna even more intimately than usual to the ups and downs of the writing process, overlaid by the anxieties of that unusual year. As always, she provided unfailing support and empathy.

Finally, I express my appreciation to my friends and former colleagues at the Federal Reserve. The Fed is a remarkable institution whose efforts to strengthen and protect the American economy and financial system are, unfortunately, often not well understood or appreciated. I hope this book helps to remedy that situation, at least a little.

A NOTE ON SOURCES

This book draws on many sources, including public documents such as speeches, reports, news accounts, published books and articles, research papers, and economic data. The following are some general sources, with links, used frequently in the preparation of this book.

Federal Reserve Documents

The Federal Reserve Board's website, www.federalreserve.gov, provides extensive historical information as well as information on current policy.

- Information about the Federal Open Market Committee, including minutes of policy meetings, post-meeting statements and implementation notes, transcripts of the chair's press conferences, and quarterly economic projections by FOMC members: http://www.federalreserve.gov/monetarypolicy/fomccalendars.htm
- FOMC historical materials (including meeting transcripts and staff memos): http://www.federalreserve.gov/monetarypolicy/fomc_historical.htm
- Federal Reserve press releases, discount rate meeting minutes, explanations of asset purchase programs, and authorizations for

emergency facilities: https://www.federalreserve.gov/newsevents/
pressreleases.htm

- The Federal Reserve Board of Governors *Monetary Policy Report to
  Congress*, released twice a year with congressional testimony by the
  chair, discusses monetary policy and the economic outlook, and
  contains Fed staff analysis of developments in the financial sector:
  http://www.federalreserve.gov/monetarypolicy/mpr_default.htm

- Speeches by members of the Board of Governors from 2006
  onward: https://www.federalreserve.gov/newsevents/speeches.htm
  And from mid-1996 through 2005:
  https://www.federalreserve.gov/newsevents/speech/speeches-archive
  .htm

- Congressional testimony by members of the Board of Governors
  from 2006 onward: https://www.federalreserve.gov/newsevents/
  testimony.htm
  And from mid-1996 through 2005:
  https://www.federalreserve.gov/newsevents/testimony/testimony
  -archive.htm

- Federal Reserve Archival System for Economic Research (FRA-
  SER), Federal Reserve Bank of St. Louis: FRASER is a digital
  library of U.S. economic, financial, and banking history—particularly the history of the Federal Reserve System. Key documents
  available from FRASER, including laws and other documents relating to the Federal Reserve and Federal Reserve speeches and congressional testimony before 1996: https://fraser.stlouisfed.org/

- Federal Reserve oral history interviews: Transcripts of interviews
  with former FOMC members and Board staff, conducted in preparation for the Federal Reserve System's centennial in 2013: https://
  www.federalreserve.gov/aboutthefed/centennial/federal-reserve-oral
  -history-interviews.htm

- Essays on Federal Reserve history, and related resources:
  https://www.federalreservehistory.org/

Other Public Documents

- Transcripts of Senate and House hearings: http://www.gpo.gov/fdsys/browse/collection.action?collectionCode=CHRG

Data Sources

- FRED, Federal Reserve Bank of St. Louis: FRED is a database for financial and macroeconomic data. It also provides tools for graphing and manipulating data series. Key indicators available from FRED include unemployment and payrolls, gross domestic product (GDP), the consumer price index (CPI), the personal consumption expenditure (PCE) price index, personal income, oil prices, the S&P and Dow Jones Industrial Average stock-market indices, interest rates on Treasury securities, Treasury debt held by the public, and housing prices (as measured by the Case–Shiller 20-City Composite Home Price Index): https://research.stlouisfed.org/fred2/
- Data about the Fed's balance sheet come from the Federal Reserve Board's H.4.1 release: http://www.federalreserve.gov/releases/h41/
- Other data sources used in the book are specified in the endnotes.

NOTES

INTRODUCTION

1. Transcript of Powell's press conference, January 29, 2020, 1.
2. Transcript of Powell's press conference, January 29, 2020, 11.
3. Transcript of Powell's press conference, March 3, 2020, 1.
4. Powell (2020b).
5. Friedman and Schwartz (1963).
6. For further discussion of the role of the gold standard in the Depression, see Eichengreen (1992), Bernanke (2000), and Ahamed (2009).
7. Eichengreen and Sachs (1985).
8. Bernanke (2002b).
9. Fischer (1995). Fischer used the term *instrument independence* rather than policy independence.

CHAPTER 1: THE GREAT INFLATION

1. Phillips (1958). The basic idea of a relationship between wages and unemployment is older than Phillips's paper. It dates back at least to a 1926 paper by Irving Fisher, reprinted in 1973 (Fisher, 1973).
2. Samuelson and Solow (1960).
3. "John F. Kennedy on the Economy and Taxes." *John F. Kennedy Presidential Library and Museum*, accessed November 20, 2020, https://www.jfklibrary.org/learn/about-jfk/jfk-in-history/john-f-kennedy-on-the-economy-and-taxes.
4. *The American War Library*, accessed November 24, 2020, http://www.americanwarlibrary.com/vietnam/vwatl.htm.
5. Hooper, Mishkin, and Sufi (2020). The original Medicare law prohibited any intervention by the government in physicians' decisions about care, eliminating the possibility of cost-saving restrictions.
6. Fair (1978).
7. Dam and Shultz (1977).

8. Bernanke (2008a).

9. Friedman (1968).

10. Phelps (1968).

11. Gordon (2013) discusses empirical work on the contemporary model of inflation. See also Yellen (2015).

12. Hodgson (August 20, 1998).

13. For more on the story of the Accord, see Hetzel and Leach (2001) and Romero (2013).

14. In the Federal Reserve Archival System for Economic Research (FRASER), see "Joint Announcement by the Secretary of the Treasury and the Chairman of the Board of Governors, and of the Federal Open Market Committee, of the Federal Reserve System," March 4, 1951.

15. Binder and Spindel (2017).

16. Hetzel and Leach (2001).

17. Volcker (2018).

18. Martin's exact quote was, "Our purpose is to lean against the winds of inflation or deflation, whichever way they are blowing, but we do not make those winds." See, in FRASER, Martin's testimony to the Committee on Banking and Currency, U.S. Senate, January 20, 1956.

19. In FRASER, see Martin's address to the New York Group of the Investment Bankers Association of America, October 19, 1955.

20. In FRASER, see Martin's testimony before the Committee on Finance, U.S. Senate, August 13, 1957.

21. Romer and Romer (2002).

22. Hetzel (2008). Chapter 6.

23. Okun is cited in Orphanides and Williams (2013).

24. Current estimates of the Okun's Law coefficient are closer to 2 than 3. For a discussion of Okun's Law, see Owyang and Sekhposyan (2012).

25. Orphanides and Williams (2013) discuss the consequences of policymakers' strongly held beliefs about the natural rate during the Great Inflation. Orphanides (2003) was among the first to document the misestimation of u* during this period.

26. Binder and Spindel (2017).

27. Cited in Granville (June 13, 2017).

28. Granville (June 13, 2017).

29. Hetzel (2008). Chapter 7.

30. Federal Reserve Board Oral History Project: Interview with J. Dewey Daane, former Board member (June 1, 2006), 37.

CHAPTER 2: BURNS AND VOLCKER

1. For more on Burns's views, see Hetzel (1998) and Wells (1994).

2. Abrams (2006).

3. Ferrell (2010), 38.

4. Hetzel (1998).

5. Ferrell (2010), 34–35. Burns (1970) advocated controls in a speech at Pepperdine University.

6. Steelman (2013).

7. Burns (1979).

8. Silber (2012), 136.

9. Federal Reserve Board Oral History Project: Interview with Paul A. Volcker (January 28, 2008), 77–78.

10. Silber (2012), 146.

11. Volcker (2018), 102–4.

12. Mondale and Hage (2010), 272–73.

13. Rogoff (1985).

14. In FRASER, see Volcker's testimony before the Committee on Banking, Housing and Urban Affairs, U.S. House of Representatives, February 19, 1980.

15. Silber (2012), 168.

16. FOMC transcript, October 6, 1979, 19.

17. For more on the credit controls, see Schreft (1990).

18. Silber (2012), 190. Volcker (2018) writes, 111, that, at a Philadelphia garden party, Carter called the Fed's decision to focus on the money supply "ill-advised."

19. Volcker (2018), 118.

20. Silber (2012), 254.

21. Volcker (2018), 113.

22. "Failure of Continental Illinois." Federal Reserve History, https://www.federalreservehistory .org/essays/failure-of-continental-illinois.

23. Haltom (2013). For Volcker's recollections, see Volcker (2018), 125–28.

24. The bill was titled the Depository Institutions Deregulation and Monetary Control Act. See Robinson (2013).

25. See Goodfriend and King (2005) for a discussion.

26. Volcker (1990).

CHAPTER 3: GREENSPAN AND THE NINETIES BOOM

1. Mallaby (2016).

2. Mallaby (2016), 344–45.

3. Greenspan (2007), 108.

4. Transcript of ceremony commemorating the Centennial of the Federal Reserve Act, December 16, 2013, 5–7, https://www.federalreserve.gov/newsevents/press/other/20131216-centennial -commemoration-transcript.pdf.

5. FOMC transcript, December 16, 1987, 71–72.

6. See Freund, Curry, Hirsch, and Kelley (1997).

7. Peek and Rosengren (1992), 21–31.

8. It was a recess appointment. Greenspan would not be confirmed by the Senate until February 28, 1992. In the interim, the Fed Board named him "chairman pro tempore."

9. Mallaby (2016), 366.

10. Nelson (March 9, 1990).

11. Bush, State of the Union Address, January 29, 1991. The American Presidency Project, University of California-Santa Barbara, accessed November 27, 2021. https://www.presidency.ucsb .edu/documents/address-before-joint-session-the-congress-the-state-the-union-1.

12. Mallaby (2016), 398–400.

13. Blanchard (2019).

14. *Wall Street Journal* (August 25, 1998).

15. Blinder and Yellen (2001), 26.

16. In FRASER, see Greenspan's testimony before the Subcommittee on Economic Growth and Credit Formation of the Committee on Banking, Finance and Urban Affairs, U.S. House of Representatives, February 22, 1994.

17. Greenspan (2007), 155.

18. Boyle (1967), 217.

19. Bernanke, Laubach, Mishkin, and Posen (1999).

20. *Los Angeles Times* (September 27, 1987).

21. FOMC transcript, February 3–4, 1994, 29–30.

22. The minutes combined two previous documents—the Record of Policy Actions and the Minutes of Action—that had been released disjointedly. Previously, the Record had been released to the press and the Minutes of Action had been made available in the Board's Freedom of Information office—both on the Friday after the subsequent meeting.

23. Woodward (2000).

24. Uchitelle and Kleinfield (March 3, 1996).

25. FOMC transcript, February 4–5, 1997, 98.

26. For example, the initial data releases showed that output per hour worked (labor productivity) grew 0.8 percent in 1996 and 1.7 percent in 1997. See Productivity and Costs, Archived Press Releases, U.S. Bureau of Labor Statistics, accessed November 30, 2020, https://www.bls.gov/bls/news-release/prod.htm. Revised, the data show labor productivity growth of 2.1 percent in 1996 and 2.7 percent in 1997. Moreover, labor productivity growth was accelerating, rising to an impressive 3.3 percent in 1998. See Nonfarm Business Sector: Real Output Per Hour of All Persons, FRED (Federal Reserve Bank of St. Louis Database).

27. Worker attitudes are documented in Manski and Straub (2000). Actual job security in the 1990s was studied in Allen, Clark, and Schieber (2001) and in Stewart (2000). Likewise, little support for Greenspan's hypothesis was found, using worker surveys and regional comparisons, in Katz and Krueger (1999).

28. Blinder and Yellen (2001), 43–48.

29. The CBO estimates of the natural rate are 6.2 percent for 1980, 5.3 percent for 1997.

30. Katz and Krueger (1999).

31. Lexington (KY) Herald, November 1, 1915, page 7, column 4, cited by Barry Popik (April 18, 2012), https://www.barrypopik.com/index.php/new_york_city/entry/luck_is_the_residue_of_design_dodgers_executive_branch_rickey.

32. Net private investment from abroad into those five economies rose from $40.5 billion in 1994 to $93.0 billion in 1996. See Radelet and Sachs (2000), 2.

33. In congressional testimony two days after the market decline, he said, "Equity prices in the United States were primed to adjust. . . . The market's net retrenchment of recent days will tend to damp [the unsustainable reduction in labor market slack], a development that should help to prolong our six-and-a-half-year business expansion." See Greenspan's testimony before the Joint Economic Committee, U.S. Congress, October 29, 1997.

34. Greenspan (2007), 192.

35. Loomis (October 26, 1998).

36. Federal Reserve Oral History Project: Interview with Alan Greenspan (August 13, 2009), 68.

37. FOMC transcript, September 21, 1998, 98.

38. FOMC transcript, October 15, 1998, 29.

39. FOMC transcript, September 29, 1998, 29.

40. Greenspan (2007), 196.

41. FOMC transcript, February 3–4, 1994, 47.

42. FOMC transcript, February 22, 1994, 3.

43. Campbell and Shiller (1998).

44. Greenspan (1996).

45. This calculation represents the return from the S&P 500 over the period from December 1996 to December 2002 and uses data from Shiller (2000). Updated data were accessed through Shiller's online data repository.

46. For a review of models used to estimate the equity risk premium, see Duarte and Rosa (2015). The premium appears to have been roughly stable during the 1990s through 1996, declining

(and thus suggesting overvaluation) only in the period after Greenspan's "irrational exuberance" speech.

47. Greenspan (2007), 178–79.
48. Greenspan (2007), 199–200.

CHAPTER 4: NEW CENTURY, NEW CHALLENGES

1. Shiller (2019).
2. Willoughby (March 20, 2000).
3. Real personal consumption expenditures increased 11 percent from the Nasdaq peak in March 2000 to the index's bottom in October 2002, considerably less than the 19 percent increase during the comparable period leading up to the Nasdaq peak.
4. Ferguson (2003).
5. Wicksell (1936) referred to the "natural" rate of interest, which he defined as the interest rate at which prices tended to be stable.
6. Fisher (1930).
7. Laubach and Williams (2003) and Holston, Laubach, and Williams (2017).
8. Summers (2014).
9. Hansen (1939).
10. Rachel and Summers (2019).
11. Bernanke (2005). See also Bernanke (2015c, d, e).
12. Caballero, Farhi, and Gourinchas (2017). For further evidence see Del Negro, Giannone, Giannoni, and Tambalotti (2017).
13. Mian, Straub, and Sufi (2021).
14. Greenspan (2007), 229.
15. An important early contribution was Krugman (1998).
16. Bernanke (2002c) and Bernanke, Reinhart, and Sack (2004).
17. FOMC transcript, December 9, 2003, 89.
18. Blinder and Reis (2005), 13.
19. FRED, S&P/Case-Shiller U.S. National Home Price Index.
20. See "Factors Contributing to the 2008 Financial Crisis," October 17, 2017, University of Chicago Booth School of Business: The Initiative on Global Markets, https://www.igmchicago.org/surveys-special/factors-contributing-to-the-2008-global-financial-crisis/.
21. Glaeser, Gottlieb, and Gyourko (2013).
22. Kuttner (2012).
23. Bernanke (2010a).
24. Shiller (2007).
25. Bernanke (2015a), 96.
26. Gramlich (2007), 108–9.
27. The Board's authority to outlaw "unfair or deceptive" lending practices was established by the Home Ownership and Equity Protection Act (HOEPA). For a discussion, see Bernanke (2015a), 100–102.
28. Greenspan (2005).
29. Greenspan's testimony before the Committee on Oversight and Government Reform, U.S. House of Representatives, October 23, 2008.

CHAPTER 5: THE GLOBAL FINANCIAL CRISIS

1. Much of my research on the Depression is collected in Bernanke (2000).
2. The thirty-year mortgage rate rose only from about 6.3 percent to 6.6 percent in the two years from June 2004, despite increases in the funds rate of more than 4 percentage points over the same period. Greenspan referred to the modest response of mortgage rates and other longer-term rates to the fed funds increases as a "conundrum." I argued in a later speech (Bernanke, 2006) that foreign demand for apparently safe, longer-term dollar assets was a reason for the weak response. The rise in short-term rates did pressure borrowers with variable-rate mortgages, but as noted in the text, these made up less than 8 percent of U.S. mortgages by 2007.
3. Lewis (2010).
4. Bernanke's testimony before the Joint Economic Committee, U.S. Congress, March 28, 2007.
5. FOMC transcript, March 21, 2007, 67.
6. Bartlett (2018).
7. Gorton (2012).
8. Kacperczyk and Schnabl (2010).
9. Pozsar, Adrian, Ashcraft, and Boesky (2010).
10. Bernanke (2015a), 402.
11. Kacperczyk and Schnabl (2010).
12. Gorton and Metrick (2012).
13. Bernanke (2018).
14. Bagehot (1873).
15. For an extensive review of the U.S. government's crisis-era programs, their logic, and their outcomes, see Bernanke, Geithner, and Paulson (2020). I describe the events of the financial crisis, and my role in them, in more detail in my memoir, Bernanke (2015a).
16. Articles collected in Bernanke, Geithner, and Paulson (2020) provide citations and reviews of the evidence.
17. See Bernanke (2015a), 248–69, and Bernanke, Geithner, and Paulson (2019), 61–73.
18. For further details on monetary policy during the crisis, see Kohn and Sack (2020), 425.
19. Board of Governors, "Policy Tools: Interest on Reserve Balances," accessed November 20, 2021, https://www.federalreserve.gov/monetarypolicy/reserve-balances.htm.
20. For evidence on the effects of credit disruptions on the real economy, see Bernanke (2018). See Kohn and Sack (2020) on the Federal Reserve staff's overoptimistic forecasts for the economy early in the crisis.

CHAPTER 6: A NEW MONETARY REGIME

1. Bernanke (2008b).
2. FOMC transcript, December 15–16, 2008, 25.
3. See, for example, Correa and Davies (2008).
4. Bernanke (2009a).
5. Bernanke, Reinhart, and Sack (2004).
6. Furman (2020).
7. Kohn and Sack (2020).
8. FOMC transcript, March 17–18, 2009, 123.
9. FOMC transcript, March 17–18, 2009, 203.
10. FOMC transcript, April 28–29, 2009, 33.
11. Federal Reserve Board, press release, "Federal Reserve, OCC, and FDIC release results of

the Supervisory Capital Assessment Program," May 7, 2009, https://www.federalreserve.gov/newsevents/pressreleases/bcreg20090507a.htm.

12. Reinhart and Rogoff (2009).
13. Something close to that sequence was in fact adopted by the Committee in its 2014 statement of exit principles (foreshadowed by information provided in the June 2011 minutes) and in the actual policies under Chair Yellen and Chair Powell. See Policy Normalization Principles and Plans, September 16, 2014, https://www.federalreserve.gov/monetarypolicy/files/FOMC_PolicyNormalization.pdf. See also Board of Governors, Policy Normalization: History of the FOMC's Policy Normalization Discussions and Communications, accessed December 8, 2020, https://www.federalreserve.gov/monetarypolicy/policy-normalization-discussions-communications-history.htm.
14. The drawbacks of the eurozone were anticipated by several prominent economists, including Barry Eichengreen, Milton Friedman, Martin Feldstein, and Michael Mussa. See Jonung and Drea (2009).
15. Erceg, Linde, and Reifschneider (2010).
16. Bernanke (2010b).
17. Letter available at David M. Herszenhorn, "Dear Mr. Bernanke: No Pressure, but . . .", *New York Times*, November 17, 2010, https://thecaucus.blogs.nytimes.com/2010/11/17/dear-mr-bernanke-no-pressure-but.
18. *Wall Street Journal* (November 15, 2010).
19. *Wall Street Journal* (September 20, 2011).
20. Wheatley and Garnham (September 27, 2010).
21. Bernanke (2015a), 493.
22. For a discussion of the legislative battle, see Bernanke (2015a), 435–66.
23. Binder and Spindel (2017).
24. Perry's remark came while campaigning in Iowa on August 15, 2011, and Gingrich's in the Republican presidential debate on September 7, 2011. See Bernanke (2015a), 520–23, for more on the political blowback.
25. Bernanke (2009b).
26. Bernanke (2015b).

CHAPTER 7: MONETARY EVOLUTION

1. Reinhart and Rogoff (2009).
2. Fernald (2014).
3. Woodford (2012).
4. Femia, Friedman, and Sack (2013).
5. Swanson (2011).
6. Bernanke and Mishkin (1997).
7. The canonical Taylor rule is described in Taylor (1993). For discussion, see Bernanke (2015f).
8. Mallaby (2016), 380.
9. Mallaby (2016), 487–91.
10. Bernanke (2003a, b).
11. Bernanke (2015a), 538.
12. Draghi (2012).
13. Bernanke (2012).
14. FOMC meeting minutes, March 19–20, 2013, 8.
15. Bernanke (1999).

16. Bernanke's testimony before the Joint Economic Committee, U.S. Congress, May 22, 2013.

17. FOMC meeting minutes, April 30–May 1, 2013, 7. For a discussion of quantitative words used in the FOMC minutes (such as "most," "many," "several," and so forth) and their interpretation, see Meade, Burk, and Josselyn (2015).

18. Transcript of Bernanke's press conference, June 19, 2013, 5–6.

19. Bernanke (2014a).

CHAPTER 8: LIFTOFF

1. FOMC transcript, March 4, 2014, 4.

2. Transcript of Yellen's press conference, March 19, 2014, 14.

3. Federal Reserve Board, press release, Federal Reserve issues FOMC statement on policy normalization principles and plans, September 17, 2014, https://www.federalreserve.gov/newsevents/pressreleases/monetary20140917c.htm.

4. Williams (2017).

5. Das (2019).

6. Spicer (August 26, 2015).

7. Rosenfeld (August 28, 2015).

8. Transcript of Yellen's press conference, December 16, 2015, 4.

9. Irwin (September 29, 2018).

10. Mui (July 27, 2016).

11. Gordon (2016).

12. Daly, Hobijn, Şahin, and Valletta (2012).

13. Staiger, Stock, and Watson (1997).

14. Yellen (2014).

15. Jamrisko, Whiteaker, and Diamond (2018).

16. Bernanke (2016).

17. Nechio and Rudebusch (2016).

18. Studies that identify the 1990s break in the Phillips curve include: Blanchard, Cerutti, and Summers (2015); Blanchard (2016); and Del Negro, Lenza, Primiceri, and Tambalotti (2020).

19. See Kiley (2015) for a discussion.

20. Stock and Watson (2007) showed, using statistical methods, that after 1990 inflation is best modeled as transitory deviations around a permanent trend, whereas in earlier periods shocks to inflation tended to persist rather than to die away. Hooker (2002) showed that oil price shocks stopped passing through to core inflation in the 1980s.

21. Yellen (2017c) reviewed Fed thinking on inflation determination.

22. For cross-country studies, see Blanchard, Cerutti, and Summers (2015). Also see Forbes (2019) on international influences on inflation. For state-level studies, see Hooper, Mishkin, and Sufi (2020) and McLeay and Tenreyro (2020).

23. See, for example, Gilchrist and Zakrajšek (2019).

24. Mahedy and Shapiro (2017) discuss the case of health care. Stock and Watson (2020) show more generally that cyclically insensitive goods and services make up a bigger share of the consumer basket today than in the past. When they focus on cyclically sensitive prices, they find less flattening of the Phillips curve.

25. See Bernanke (2007) and Mishkin (2007). See also Roberts (2006) on how changes in monetary policy can help explain the flattening of the Phillips curve.

26. Harker (2017).

27. Appelbaum (April 4, 2017).

28. Bernanke (2015g).

29. Yellen (2017a)

30. Yellen's testimony before the Committee on Financial Services, U.S. House of Representatives, July 12, 2017.

31. Trump commented that Yellen was "a very political person" during a Bloomberg TV interview on October 16, 2016. His comment that Yellen should be "ashamed of herself" was during a CNBC interview on September 12, 2016.

32. See YouTube, "Donald Trump's Argument for America," November 6, 2016, https://www .youtube.com/watch?v=vST61W4bGm8.

33. Timiraos and Davidson (June 13, 2017).

34. Fleming (October 26, 2018).

35. Yellen (2017b).

CHAPTER 9: POWELL AND TRUMP

1. Powell (2015).

2. Transcript of Powell's swearing-in remarks, February 5, 2018, 1.

3. Powell's testimony before the Committee on Banking, Housing, and Urban Affairs, U.S. Senate, June 22, 2017, 1.

4. Transcript of Powell's press conference, March 21, 2018, 2–3.

5. Condon (2019) aggregates various Trump tweets about the Fed that are referenced in this chapter.

6. Powell (2018a).

7. Powell (2018b).

8. Transcript of Powell's press conference, December 19, 2018, 1–4.

9. Cox (October 3, 2018).

10. Transcript of Powell's press conference, December 19, 2018, 6.

11. *Wall Street Journal* (January 4, 2019).

12. Transcript of Powell's press conference, January 30, 2019, 13.

13. Federal Reserve Board, press release, "Statement on Chair Powell's and Vice Chair Clarida's meeting with the President and Treasury Secretary," February 4, 2019, https://www .federalreserve.gov/newsevents/pressreleases/other20190204a.htm.

14. For more see Tankersley (April 11, 2019) and Tankersley, Haberman, and Cochrane (May 2, 2019).

15. Amiti, Redding, and Weinstein (2020).

16. Weinraub (October 19, 2020).

17. Baker, Bloom, and Davis (2016).

18. Powell (2019a).

19. Transcript of Powell's press conference, June 19, 2019, 1.

20. Transcript of Powell's press conference, June 19, 2019, 6.

21. Transcript of Powell's press conference, July 31, 2019, 1.

22. Transcript of Powell's press conference, July 31, 2019, 4.

23. Powell (2019b).

24. Transcript of Powell's press conference, October 30, 2019, 1–3.

25. Federal Reserve Board, press release, November 15, 2018, https://www.federalreserve.gov/ newsevents/pressreleases/monetary20181115a.htm.

26. Clarida (2019).

27. An August 2019 survey of senior financial officers of banks holding roughly three-quarters of reserves indicated that their aggregate lowest comfortable level of reserves was $652 billion; by extrapolation, all reserve holders would be comfortable with roughly $900 billion: https://www .federalreserve.gov/data/sfos/aug-2019-senior-financial-officer-survey.htm.

CHAPTER 10: PANDEMIC

1. Transcript of Powell's press conference, January 29, 2020, 2.
2. Transcript of Powell's press conference, January 29, 2020, 12.
3. Taylor (March 17, 2020).
4. Federal Reserve Board, press release, "Statement from Federal Reserve Chair Jerome H. Powell," February 28, 2020, https://www.federalreserve.gov/newsevents/pressreleases/other20200228a .htm.
5. Ghebreyesus (2020).
6. Achenbach, Wan, and Sun (March 11, 2020).
7. Quarles (2020).
8. Baer (May 20, 2020). For discussions of the March disruptions in Treasury markets, see Schrimpf, Shin, and Sushko (2020); Duffie (2020); and Cheng, Wessel, and Younger (2020).
9. See Cetorelli, Goldberg, and Ravazzolo (2020) on the effectiveness of the swap lines.
10. FOMC call minutes, March 15, 2020, 6.
11. Bank of England, "Monetary Policy Summary for the special Monetary Policy Committee meeting on 19 March 2020," https://www.bankofengland.co.uk/monetary -policy-summary-and-minutes/2020/monetary-policy-summary-for-the-special-monetary-policy -committee-meeting-on-19-march-2020.
12. Bank of Japan, "Enhancement of Monetary Easing in Light of the Impact of the Outbreak of the Novel Coronavirus (COVID-19)," March 16, 2020, https://www.boj.or.jp/en/mopo/mpmdeci/ state_2020/k200316b.htm/.
13. Lagarde (2020a).
14. European Central Bank, "Pandemic emergency purchase programme (PEPP)," accessed December 19, 2020, https://www.ecb.europa.eu/mopo/implement/pepp/html/index.en.html.
15. European Central Bank, "Open market operations," accessed December 19, 2020, https://www .ecb.europa.eu/mopo/implement/omo/html/index.en.html.
16. Rankin (July 21, 2020).
17. Powell (2020a).
18. Samuels (May 13, 2020).
19. Powell (2020c).
20. FOMC meeting minutes, July 27–28, 2021, 5. Clarida (2021) presented the logic behind beginning rate hikes in late 2022 or early 2023, arguing that doing so was consistent with the Fed's new framework.

CHAPTER 11: THE FED'S POST-2008 TOOLKIT

1. Eggertsson and Woodford (2003).
2. Bernanke (2014b).
3. For surveys on the experience with and effects of QE, see Williams (2014); Gagnon (2016); Bhattarai and Neely (forthcoming); Kuttner (2018); Dell'Ariccia, Rabanal, and Sandri (2018); and Bernanke (2020). Much of this chapter and the next is drawn from Bernanke (2020), which was the author's presidential address to the American Economic Association.

4. Bhattarai, Eggertsson, and Gafarov (2015).

5. Kiley (2014) presents a model in which both short-term and long-term rates affect aggregate demand. An implication is that reductions in longer-term interest rates arising from QE, not accompanied by reductions in short rates, may be less powerful than the combination of lower short-term and lower longer-term rates that a traditional policy easing produces, away from the lower bound.

6. Rebucci, Hartley, and Jiménez (2020).

7. Gagnon, Raskin, Remache, and Sack (2011).

8. Asset-price responses in the table, calculated by the author, are very similar to those in the original staff memo. Gagnon, Raskin, Remache, and Sack (2011) also considered a larger set of eight announcement days. Using the larger set leaves the results essentially unchanged. More generally, a large related literature shows that these results are not sensitive to the exact set of days considered, or to whether shorter or longer windows of time around the key announcements are used.

9. Joyce, Lasaosa, Stevens, and Tong (2011).

10. See, for example, Greenlaw, Hamilton, Harris, and West (2018). A reply to their paper, Gagnon (2018), anticipates some of the points I make here.

11. Krishnamurthy and Vissing-Jorgensen (2011).

12. See Cahill, D'Amico, Li, and Sears (2013).

13. De Santis (2020).

14. D'Amico and King (2013) pioneered this approach, but their paper considered only QE1. For more U.S. results, see Cahill, D'Amico, Li, and Sears (2013); Meaning and Zhu (2011); and D'Amico, English, López-Salido, and Nelson (2012).

15. An interesting example of a British study is McLaren, Banerjee, and Latto (2014). These authors consider three "natural experiments," dates on which the Bank of England announced changes to the maturity distribution of its asset purchases for reasons unrelated to monetary policy plans or objectives. They find strong local supply effects (higher prices for assets favored by the changes in plans) that do not fade over time. Studies finding similar results for the United Kingdom include Meaning and Zhu (2011) and Joyce and Tong (2012).

16. See Di Maggio, Kermani, and Palmer (2020).

17. See, for example, Bauer and Rudebusch (2014).

18. Altavilla and Giannone (2017).

19. D'Amico and King (2013).

20. Ihrig and others (2018).

21. For a summary of this approach and its findings, see Bonis, Ihrig, and Wei (2017). This work builds on Li and Wei (2013) and Hamilton and Wu (2012). Hamilton and Wu find somewhat weaker effects of asset purchases. Several papers use regression methods to assess the effects of bond supply on term premiums; for example, Gagnon, Raskin, Remache, and Sack (2011). This line of research, typified by Ihrig and others (2018), is an attempt to impose greater structure (including the no-arbitrage condition) on this approach. See also Greenwood and Vayanos (2014).

22. On the competing effects of Treasury issuance and QE purchases, see Greenwood, Hanson, Rudolph, and Summers (2015).

23. For example, Wu (2014) credited Fed asset purchases with more than half of the 2.2 percentage point decline in ten-year Treasury yields between the fall of 2008 and the taper tantrum in 2013, similar to the Fed staff study. Altavilla, Carboni, and Moto (2015) and Eser and others (2019) found comparable effects for the ECB QE program announced in January 2015.

24. The three-to-one ratio was often cited by the Federal Reserve staff. See Chung, Laforte,

Reifschneider, and Williams (2012), who regress changes of the funds rate on ten-year yields and find a relationship of four-to-one. See also Laforte (2018).

25. See, for example, Coibion, Gorodnichenko, Knotek, and Schoenle (2020). The authors, in a survey experiment, found that most people were unaware or did not react to the Fed's announcement of its new policy framework in August 2020.

26. See, for example, Bernanke, Kiley, and Roberts (2019).

27. See Nelson (2021), and Lindsey (2003), and Feroli and others (2017).

28. Gürkaynak, Sack, and Swanson (2005).

29. Campbell, Evans, Fisher, and Justiniano (2012).

30. See Femia, Friedman, and Sack (2013). Using information from interest rate options, Raskin (2013) came to a similar conclusion. See also Bernanke (2020) for a summary of event studies of the effects of the Fed's announcements tying rate guidance to specific dates. More generally, Carvalho, Hsu, and Nechio (2016), counting particular words in magazine and newspaper articles to measure policy expectations, showed that unanticipated communications by the Fed influenced longer-term interest rates. Del Negro, Giannoni, and Patterson (2015) concluded that forward guidance positively affected inflation and growth expectations.

31. An example of a policymaker's speech providing extensive guidance is Clarida (2020b).

32. Bush, Jendoubi, Raskin, and Topa (2020).

33. Introductory statement to Draghi's press conference, July 4, 2013, https://www.ecb.europa.eu/press/pressconf/2013/html/is130704.en.html.

34. Charbonneau and Rennison (2015) provide a chronology and a review of the international evidence on postcrisis forward guidance. Altavilla and others (2019) used a statistical analysis to identify the key dimensions of ECB communication. A similar analysis was used by Gürkaynak, Sack, and Swanson (2005) and Swanson (2020). Hubert and Labondance (2018) found that the ECB's forward guidance persistently lowered rates over the entire term structure.

35. Institutional reputation is modeled theoretically in Nakata (2015).

CHAPTER 12: IS THE FED'S TOOLKIT ENOUGH?

1. Fernald, Hall, Stock, and Watson (2017).

2. Engen, Laubach, and Reifschneider (2015).

3. This calculation is based on Laforte (2018).

4. Caldara, Gagnon, Martínez-García, and Neely (2020).

5. Transcript of Powell's press conference, June 10, 2020, 10.

6. "An Update to the Economic Outlook: 2010 to 2030," Congressional Budget Office, July 2020, https://www.cbo.gov/system/files/2020-07/56442-CBO-update-economic-outlook.pdf.

7. For an analysis of business exits in 2020, see Crane and others (2020).

8. For estimates of the past and expected effects of the ECB's policies on GDP and inflation during the pandemic, see Lagarde (2020b).

9. Bernanke (2020).

10. Chung and others (2019).

11. Reifschneider (2016) and Kiley (2018) produce qualitatively similar results, whereas Chung and others (2019) are somewhat more pessimistic. See Bernanke (2020) for a discussion of the differences among these studies. Kim, Laubach, and Wei (2020) present a more optimistic picture of the macroeconomic benefits of the new tools.

12. Rodnyanksy and Darmouni (2017).

13. Kurtzman, Luck, and Zimmermann (2017) find that banks lowered lending standards and made riskier loans after both QE1 and QE3 MBS purchases. They estimate that the extra credit issuance was equivalent to a 1 percentage point cut in the Fed funds rate. They argue

that this increased risk-taking was beneficial to the recovery and not detrimental to financial stability.

14. If the real neutral rate is above zero, then hitting a 2 percent inflation target would raise the nominal neutral rate to 2–3 percent, providing some space for monetary policy. Except for Kiley (2019), who estimates real neutral interest rates are negative in many countries, most current estimates place the real neutral rate in major foreign economies above zero. For example, the New York Fed reports estimates—based on Holston, Laubach, and Williams (2017)—of the real neutral rates of Canada, the euro area, and the United Kingdom that, as of 2021, were all positive. Using the methods of Laubach and Williams (2003) as well as an econometric model, Okazaki and Sudo (2018) estimate the real neutral rate in Japan to be close to 1 percent. Estimates by Davis, Fuenzalida, and Taylor (2021) of the real neutral rate in six advanced economies range between roughly zero and modestly positive.

15. See ECB, press release, "ECB's Governing Council approves its new monetary policy strategy," July 8, 2021, https://www.ecb.europa.eu/press/pr/date/2021/html/ecb.pr210708-dc78cc4b0d .en.html.

16. See Federal Reserve Board, press release, "Federal Reserve Board announces Reserve Bank income and expense data and transfers to the Treasury for 2020," January 11, 2021, https:// www.federalreserve.gov/newsevents/pressreleases/other20210111a.htm. For a quantification of the effects of QE on the government's long-run debt, see Clouse and others (2013).

17. Caballero and Kamber (2019).

18. Gilchrist and Zakrajšek (2013).

19. Swanson and Williams (2014).

20. Studies have examined the distributional effects of monetary policy in various economies. For the United States, see Bivens (2015). For the euro area, see Slacalek, Tristani, and Violante (2020). For the United Kingdom, see Bunn, Pugh, and Yeates (2018). The benefits to lower-wage workers of a "hot" labor market are demonstrated in Aaronson, Daly, Wascher, and Wilcox (2019). The contribution of recessions to increased inequality is documented in Heathcote, Perri, and Violante (2020). See Bernanke (2015h) for further discussion.

21. Kopcke and Webb (2013).

22. Data on retirement plans, homeownership, and equity holdings are from "Changes in U.S. Family Finances from 2016 to 2019: Evidence from the Survey of Consumer Finances," *Federal Reserve Bulletin*, September 2020.

23. Bartscher, Kuhn, Schularick, and Wachtel (2021) find that easier monetary policy increases Black employment by more than White employment but also significantly worsens racial differences in wealth.

24. On Japan, see Caballero, Hoshi, and Kashyap (2008). McGowan, Andrews, and Millot (2018) discuss the incidence of zombie firms in advanced economies.

25. Favara, Minoiu, and Perez-Orive (2021).

26. For more discussion of alternative critiques of QE and easy-money policies, see Bernanke (2017a).

CHAPTER 13: MAKING POLICY MORE POWERFUL

1. For further discussion, see Dell'Ariccia, Rabanal, and Sandri (2018) and Potter and Smets (2019).

2. D'Amico and Kaminska (2019).

3. Gilchrist and Zakrajšek (2012).

4. Gilchrist and Zakrajšek (2012).

5. In March 2020, Janet Yellen and I argued that Congress should grant limited discretion to the Fed to buy high-grade corporate bonds to backstop credit flows to nonfinancial firms. See Bernanke and Yellen (2020). The CARES Act set up just such a facility, but—as Janet and I had proposed—the purpose of the facility was to improve credit market functioning rather than to increase the potency of monetary policy more generally.

6. See Andrade, Cahn, Fraisse, and Mésonnier (2019); Churm, Joyce, Kapetanios, and Theodoridis (2021); and Cahn, Matheron, and Sahuc (2017).

7. See Arteta, Kose, Stocker, and Taskin (2018) and Eisenschmidt and Smets (2018).

8. Brunnermeier and Koby (2018).

9. See Lopez, Rose, and Spiegel (2020) and Altavilla, Burlon, Giannetti, and Holton (2021).

10. Burke and others (2010).

11. See Grisse, Krogstrup, and Schumacher (2017).

12. See Bowman, Erceg, and Leahy (2010). For the pre-1951 experience, see Chaurushiya and Kuttner (2003).

13. See Brainard (2019) for an early supportive view. Clarida (2020a) characterized yield caps and targets as "not warranted in the current environment but [that] could remain an option . . . if circumstances changed markedly."

14. See "What is the Statement on Longer-Run Goals and Monetary Policy Strategy, and why does the Federal Open Market Committee publish it?" FAQ, Board of Governors, accessed January 26, 2021, https://www.federalreserve.gov/faqs/statement-on-longer-run-goals-monetary-policy-strategy-fomc.htm.

15. Bernanke and Mishkin (1997).

16. Svensson (1999) was an early proponent of price-level targeting. Eggertsson and Woodford (2003) argued that price-level targeting could be particularly useful when the lower bound is a frequent constraint on monetary policy.

17. See Bernanke (2017a) and Bernanke, Kiley, and Roberts (2019).

18. Brainard (2017).

19. Clarida (2020b) provides a detailed discussion.

20. For the Board staff's analysis of nominal GDP targets, see Erceg, López-Salido, and Tetlow (2011) and Erceg, Kiley, and López-Salido (2011). Christina Romer advocated nominal GDP targeting in a *New York Times* op-ed (October 29, 2011). Other early advocates include Carney (2012), Woodford (2012), and Sumner (2014). Recent support has come from Federal Reserve Bank of St. Louis president James Bullard (Bullard and DiCecio, 2019).

21. For a recent statement of the case for an increase in the inflation target, see Andrade, Galí, Le Bihan, and Matheron (2019). See also Blanchard, Dell'Ariccia, and Mauro (2010) and Leigh (2010).

22. See, for example, Furman and Summers (2020). This view is reminiscent of that of Keynesian economists of the 1950s and 1960s who, following Keynes himself, saw fiscal policy as the most effective stabilization tool. As in the post-2000 period, interest rates in the 1930s (when Keynes was developing his theories) were close to zero, which Keynes saw as limiting the scope of monetary policy.

23. Boushey, Nunn, and Shambaugh (2019).

24. Friedman (1969).

25. See Kocherlakota (2016) for further discussion.

26. For an overview of MMT and further references, see Matthews (2019). Mankiw (2020) provides a thoughtful mainstream critique.

CHAPTER 14: MONETARY POLICY AND FINANCIAL STABILITY

1. Bernanke and Kuttner (2005) find that a surprise cut of a quarter percentage point in the federal funds rate typically increases stock prices by about 1 percent. Reinhart and Reinhart (2011) find that the long-term relationship between the federal funds rate and asset prices is quite weak, especially after 1990 when foreign capital inflows to the United States increased in importance.
2. Mishkin and White (2003).
3. On the role of the gold standard in the Depression, see Eichengreen and Sachs (1985), Bernanke and James (1991), and Eichengreen (1992). The classic study by Friedman and Schwartz (1963) emphasized the effects of U.S. bank failures on the money supply and the price level. Bernanke (1983) discusses the effect of bank failures on credit. Bernanke (2018) provides recent references on the role of credit in the Depression. See Ahamed (2009) for an engaging popular treatment of the sources of the Depression.
4. See Jordà, Schularick, and Taylor (2013) and Jordà, Schularick, and Taylor (2015b).
5. Case, Quigley, and Shiller (2013).
6. For example, about half of the loans and leases held by FDIC-insured banks in 2020 were secured by real estate, higher than any other category. FDIC: https://www.fdic.gov/analysis/quarterly-banking-profile/qbp/2020sep/qbp.pdf.
7. Mian, Sufi, and Verner (2017).
8. See Paligorova and Sierra Jimenez (2012) for an overview of evidence and theory on the effects of easy money on bank lending.
9. Bernanke and Kuttner (2005).
10. Hanson and Stein (2015).
11. Bernanke, Gertler, and Gilchrist (1996).
12. For further discussion, see Borio and Zhu (2012) and Stein (2013).
13. Barberis, Greenwood, Jin, and Shleifer (2018).
14. Minsky (1986).
15. In the movie based on Lewis (2010), Nobel-winning behavioral economist Richard Thaler is shown explaining investors' behavioral biases to a character played by actress Selena Gomez.
16. Rajan (2005).
17. Stein (2013) makes this argument.
18. See Lu and others (2019).
19. For an introduction to macroprudential tools, see Yilla and Liang (2020). Crockett (2000) was among the first to call for the use of this class of policies.
20. Liang and Edge (2019) present international evidence on the trade-off between political considerations and effectiveness on macroprudential committees.
21. See, for example, Claessens (2015) and Richter, Schularick, and Shim (2019).
22. Yellen (2018).
23. Metrick and Tarullo (2021) argue for "congruent" regulation—roughly, that financial firms that perform similar functions should be regulated in similar ways.
24. See "Conclusion: The Fire Next Time" in Bernanke, Geithner, and Paulson (2019).
25. See, for example, the Program on Financial Stability at the Yale School of Management, https://som.yale.edu/faculty-research-centers/centers-initiatives/program-on-financial-stability. The program, founded after the global crisis, has conducted detailed analyses of dozens of financial crises around the world, and the responses of policymakers. The goal of these case studies, which are used to help train staff from central banks and finance ministries from around the world, is to improve future crisis prevention and management.

26. Bernanke (2002a).
27. Ahamed (2009), 276.
28. Bean, Paustian, Penalver, and Taylor (2010), 300.
29. Jordà, Schularick, and Taylor (2015a).
30. Borio and White (2003).
31. Agur and Demertzis (2013) argue that, if monetary policy includes a financial-stability objective, the best policy in the face of a weakening economy is to ease policy aggressively but reduce the time that rates are kept low to limit the buildup of risk.
32. Stein (2013).
33. See Adrian, Duarte, Liang, and Zabczyk (2020).
34. Bernanke (2004).
35. See, for example, Adrian and Liang (2018).
36. See Greenwood, Hanson, Shleifer, and Sørensen (forthcoming). In a speech after the one discussed in the text, Stein (2014) suggested using measures of bond risk premiums as indicators of financial risk.
37. English (forthcoming) discusses the Norwegian case.
38. See Svensson (2017a, b).
39. Adrian and Liang (2018).
40. This point is made by Gourio, Kashyap, and Sim (2018). Reinhart and Rogoff (2009) provided evidence that recessions following financial crises tend to be especially deep and protracted.
41. Rey (2013).
42. Other factors affect the global cycle as well. For a study that ascribes relatively less importance to Fed policy for determining international capital flows, see Clark, Converse, Coulibaly, and Kamin (2016).
43. Adrian and Shin (2010).

CHAPTER 15: THE FED'S INDEPENDENCE AND ROLE IN SOCIETY

1. Transcript of Bernanke's press conference, December 18, 2013, 39.
2. See Brainard (2021).
3. See Das and Spicer (July 21, 2016).
4. Brainard (2020) discusses the Fed's role as fiscal agent and its FedNow service for instant check clearing.
5. For more on FedNow, see Federal Reserve Board, FedNow Service, accessed October 9, 2021, https://www.federalreserve.gov/paymentsystems/fednow_about.htm.
6. Federal Reserve Board, "Preserving Minority Depository Institutions," accessed October 9, 2021, https://www.federalreserve.gov/publications/files/preserving-minority -depository-institutions-2020.pdf.
7. For more on the CRA, see Federal Reserve Board, Community Reinvestment Act, accessed February 26, 2021, https://www.federalreserve.gov/consumerscommunities/cra_about.htm.
8. Wessel, Sheiner, and Ng (2019). The Board's Office of Minority and Women Inclusion reports annually to Congress. See Federal Reserve Board, "How does the Fed foster diversity and inclusion in the workplace?" accessed February 26, 2021, https://www.federalreserve.gov/faqs/ how-does-the-fed-foster-diversity-and-inclusion-in-the-workplace.htm.
9. Smialek (February 2, 2021).
10. Holston, Laubach, and Williams (2017).
11. Blinder (1996).

BIBLIOGRAPHY

Aaronson, Stephanie R., Mary C. Daly, William L. Wascher, and David W. Wilcox. 2019. "Okun Revisited: Who Benefits Most from a Strong Economy?" *Brookings Papers on Economic Activity* (Spring): 333–404.

Abrams, Burton A. 2006. "How Richard Nixon Pressured Arthur Burns: Evidence from the Nixon Tapes." *Journal of Economic Perspectives* 20 (4): 177–88.

Achenbach, Joel, William Wan, and Lena H. Sun. 2020. "Coronavirus Forecasts Are Grim: 'It's Going to Get Worse.'" *Washington Post*, March 11.

Adrian, Tobias, Fernando Duarte, Nellie Liang, and Pawel Zabczyk. 2020. "Monetary and Macroprudential Policy with Endogenous Risk." IMF Working Paper No. 2020/236. Washington, DC: International Monetary Fund.

Adrian, Tobias, and Nellie Liang. 2018. "Monetary Policy, Financial Conditions, and Financial Stability." *International Journal of Central Banking* 14 (1): 73–131.

Adrian, Tobias, and Hyun Song Shin. 2010. "Liquidity and Leverage." *Journal of Financial Intermediation* 19 (3): 418–37.

Agur, Itai, and Maria Demertzis. 2013. "'Leaning against the Wind' and the Timing of Monetary Policy." *Journal of International Money and Finance* 35 (June): 179–94.

Ahamed, Liaquat. 2009. *Lords of Finance: The Bankers Who Broke the World*. New York: The Penguin Press.

Ajello, Andrea, Thomas Laubach, David López-Salido, and Taisuke Nakata. 2019. "Financial Stability and Optimal Interest-Rate Policy." *International Journal of Central Banking* 15 (1): 279–326.

Allen, Steven G., Robert L. Clark, and Sylvester J. Schieber. 2001. "Has Job Security Vanished in Large Corporations?" In *On The Job: Is Long-Term Employment a Thing of the Past?*, edited by David Neumark. New York: Russell Sage Foundation.

Altavilla, Carlo, Luca Brugnolini, Refet Gürkaynak, Roberto Motto, and Giuseppe Ragusa. 2019. "Monetary Policy in Action: Multiple Dimensions of ECB Policy Communication and Their Financial Market Effects." Center for Economic Policy Research. *VoxEU*, October 4.

Altavilla, Carlo, Lorenzo Burlon, Mariassunta Giannetti, and Sarah Holton. 2021. "Is There a Zero

Lower Bound? The Effects of Negative Policy Rates on Banks and Firms." *Journal of Financial Economics* (forthcoming July).

Altavilla, Carlo, Giacomo Carboni, and Roberto Motto. 2015. "Asset Purchase Programmes and Financial Markets: Lessons from the Euro Area." ECB Working Paper 1864. Frankfurt, Germany: European Central Bank.

Altavilla, Carlo, and Domenico Giannone. 2017. "The Effectiveness of Non-Standard Monetary Policy Measures: Evidence from Survey Data." *Journal of Applied Econometrics* 32 (5): 952–64.

Amiti, Mary, Stephen J. Redding, and David E. Weinstein. 2020. "Who's Paying for the US Tariffs? A Longer-Term Perspective." *AEA Papers and Proceedings* 110 (May): 541–46.

Andrade, Philippe, Christophe Cahn, Henri Fraisse, and Jean-Stéphane Mésonnier. 2019. "Can the Provision of Long-Term Liquidity Help to Avoid a Credit Crunch? Evidence from the Eurosystem's LTRO." *Journal of the European Economic Association* 17 (4): 1070–1106.

Andrade, Philippe, Jordi Galí, Hervé Le Bihan, and Julien Matheron. 2019. "The Optimal Inflation Target and the Natural Rate of Interest." *Brookings Papers on Economic Activity* (Fall): 173–255.

Appelbaum, Binyamin. 2017. "Richmond Fed President Resigns, Admitting He Violated Confidentiality." *New York Times*, April 4.

Arteta, Carlos, M. Ayhan Kose, Marc Stocker, and Temel Taskin. 2018. "Implications of Negative Interest Rate Policies: An Early Assessment." *Pacific Economic Review* 23 (1): 8–26.

Baer, Justin. 2020. "The Day the Coronavirus Nearly Broke the Markets." *Wall Street Journal*, May 20.

Bagehot, Walter. 1873. *Lombard Street: A Description of the Money Market*. London: Henry S. King & Co.

Baker, Scott R., Nicholas Bloom, and Steven J. Davis. 2016. "Measuring Economic Policy Uncertainty." *Quarterly Journal of Economics* 131 (4): 1593–1636.

Barberis, Nicholas, Robin Greenwood, Lawrence Jin, and Andrei Shleifer. 2018. "Extrapolation and Bubbles." *Journal of Financial Economics* 129 (2): 203–27.

Bartlett, Charles. 2018. "The Financial Crisis, Then and Now: Ancient Rome and 2008 CE." Harvard University, Weatherhead Center for International Affairs. *Epicenter* (blog), December 10. https:// epicenter.wcfia.harvard.edu/blog/financial-crisis-then-and-now.

Bartscher, Alina K., Moritz Kuhn, Moritz Schularick, and Paul Wachtel. 2021. "Monetary Policy and Racial Inequality." Staff Report 959. Federal Reserve Bank of New York.

Bauer, Michael D., and Glenn D. Rudebusch. 2014. "The Signaling Channel for Federal Reserve Bond Purchases." *International Journal of Central Banking* 10 (3): 233–89.

Bean, Charles, Matthias Paustian, Adrian Panalver, and Tim Taylor. 2010. "Monetary Policy after the Fall." In *Proceedings*. Jackson Hole, WY: Federal Reserve Bank of Kansas City.

Bernanke, Ben S. 1983. "Nonmonetary Effects of the Financial Crisis in Propagation of the Great Depression." *American Economic Review* 73 (3): 257–76.

———. 1999. "Japanese Monetary Policy: A Case of Self-Induced Paralysis?" Presented at the ASSA Meetings, Boston, MA, December. https://www.princeton.edu/~pkrugman/bernanke_paralysis .pdf.

———. 2000. *Essays on the Great Depression*. Princeton, NJ: Princeton University Press.

———. 2002a. "Asset-Price 'Bubbles' and Monetary Policy." New York, October 15.

———. 2002b. "Remarks on Milton Friedman's Ninetieth Birthday." Chicago, November 8.

———. 2002c. "Deflation: Making Sure 'It' Doesn't Happen Here." Washington, DC, November 21.

———. 2003a. "A Perspective on Inflation Targeting." Washington, DC, March 25.

———. 2003b. "Remarks." St. Louis, October 17.

———. 2004. "The Great Moderation." Washington, DC, February 20.

———. 2005. "The Global Saving Glut and the U.S. Current Account Deficit." Richmond, VA, March 10.

————. 2006. "Reflections on the Yield Curve and Monetary Policy." New York, March 20.

————. 2007. "Inflation Expectations and Inflation Forecasting." Cambridge, MA, July 10.

————. 2008a. "Remarks on Class Day 2008." Cambridge, MA, June 4.

————. 2008b. "Federal Reserve Policies in the Financial Crisis." Austin, TX, December 1.

————. 2009a. "The Crisis and the Policy Response." London, England, January 13.

————. 2009b. "The Chairman." Interview by Scott Pelley. *60 Minutes*. CBS, March 15.

————. 2010a. "Monetary Policy and the Housing Bubble." Atlanta, January 3.

————. 2010b. "The Economic Outlook and Monetary Policy." Jackson Hole, WY, August 27.

————. 2012. "Monetary Policy since the Onset of the Crisis." Jackson Hole, WY, August 31.

————. 2014a. "The Federal Reserve: Looking Back, Looking Forward." Philadelphia, January 3.

————. 2014b. "A Discussion on the Fed's 100th Anniversary." Washington, DC: Brookings Institution. January 16.

————. 2015a. *The Courage to Act: A Memoir of a Crisis and Its Aftermath*. New York: W. W. Norton.

————. 2015b. *The Federal Reserve and the Financial Crisis*. Princeton, NJ: Princeton University Press.

————. 2015c. "Why Are Interest Rates So Low?" Brookings Institution. *Ben Bernanke's Blog*, March 30.

————. 2015d. "Why Are Interest Rates So Low, Part 2: Secular Stagnation." Brookings Institution. *Ben Bernanke's Blog*, March 31.

————. 2015e. "Why Are Interest Rates So Low, Part 3: The Global Savings Glut." Brookings Institution. *Ben Bernanke's Blog*, April 1.

————. 2015f. "The Taylor Rule: A Benchmark for Monetary Policy?" Brookings Institution. *Ben Bernanke's Blog*, April 28.

————. 2015g. "Warren-Vitter and the Lender of Last Resort." Brookings Institution. *Ben Bernanke's Blog*, May 15.

————. 2015h. "Monetary Policy and Inequality." Brookings Institution. *Ben Bernanke's Blog*, June 1.

————. 2016. "The Fed's Shifting Perspective on the Economy and Its Implications for Monetary Policy." Brookings Institution. *Ben Bernanke's Blog*, August 8.

————. 2017a. "Monetary Policy in a New Era." In *Rethinking Macroeconomic Policy*. Washington, DC: Peterson Institute for International Economics. https://piie.com/system/files/documents/bernanke20171012paper.pdf.

————. 2017b. "Temporary Price-Level Targeting: An Alternative Framework for Monetary Policy." Brookings Institution. *Ben Bernanke's Blog*, October 12.

————. 2018. "The Real Effects of Disrupted Credit: Evidence from the Global Financial Crisis." *Brookings Papers on Economic Activity* (Fall): 251–342.

————. 2020. "The New Tools of Monetary Policy." *American Economic Review* 110 (4): 943–83.

Bernanke, Ben S., Timothy F. Geithner, and Henry M. Paulson, Jr. 2019. *Firefighting: The Financial Crisis and Its Lessons*. New York: Penguin Books.

————, eds. 2020. *First Responders: Inside the U.S. Strategy for Fighting the 2007–2009 Global Financial Crisis*. New Haven, CT: Yale University Press.

Bernanke, Ben S., Mark Gertler, and Simon Gilchrist. 1996. "The Financial Accelerator and the Flight to Quality." *Review of Economics and Statistics* 78 (1): 1–15.

Bernanke, Ben S., and Harold James. 1991. "The Gold Standard, Deflation, and Financial Crisis in the Great Depression: An International Comparison." In *Financial Markets and Financial Crises*, edited by R. Glenn Hubbard, 33–68. Chicago: University of Chicago Press.

Bernanke, Ben S., Michael T. Kiley, and John M. Roberts. 2019. "Monetary Policy Strategies for a Low-Rate Environment." *AEA Papers and Proceedings* 109 (May): 421–26.

Bernanke, Ben S., and Kenneth N. Kuttner. 2005. "What Explains the Stock Market's Reaction to Federal Reserve Policy?" *Journal of Finance* LX (3): 1221–57.

Bernanke, Ben S., Thomas Laubach, Frederic S. Mishkin, and Adam S. Posen. 1999. *Inflation Targeting: Lessons from the International Experience*. Princeton, NJ: Princeton University Press.

Bernanke, Ben S., and Frederic S. Mishkin. 1997. "Inflation Targeting: A New Framework for Monetary Policy?" *Journal of Economic Perspectives* 11 (2): 97–116.

Bernanke, Ben S., Vincent R. Reinhart, and Brian P. Sack. 2004. "Monetary Policy Alternatives at the Zero Bound: An Empirical Assessment." *Brookings Papers on Economic Activity* (Fall): 1–100.

Bernanke, Ben, and Janet Yellen. 2020. "The Federal Reserve Must Reduce Long-Term Damage from Coronavirus." *Financial Times*, March 18.

Bhattarai, Saroj, Gauti B. Eggertsson, and Bulat Gafarov. 2015. "Time Consistency and the Duration of Government Debt: A Signalling Theory of Quantitative Easing." Working Paper 21336. Cambridge, MA: National Bureau of Economic Research.

Bhattarai, Saroj, and Christopher J. Neely (forthcoming). "An Analysis of the Literature on International Unconventional Monetary Policy." *Journal of Economic Literature*.

Binder, Sarah, and Mark Spindel. 2017. *The Myth of Independence: How Congress Governs the Federal Reserve*. Princeton, NJ: Princeton University Press.

Bivens, Josh. 2015. "Gauging the Impact of the Fed on Inequality during the Great Recession." Hutchins Center Working Paper 12. Washington, DC: Brookings Institution.

Blanchard, Olivier. 2016. "The Phillips Curve: Back to the 60s?" *American Economic Review* 106 (5): 31–34.

———. 2019. "Public Debt and Low Interest Rates." *American Economic Review* 109 (4): 1197–1229.

Blanchard, Olivier, Eugenio Cerutti, and Lawrence Summers. 2015. "Inflation and Activity—Two Explorations and Their Monetary Policy Implications." Working Paper 21726. Cambridge, MA: National Bureau of Economic Research.

Blanchard, Olivier, Giovanni Dell'Ariccia, and Paolo Mauro. 2010. "Rethinking Macroeconomic Policy." IMF Staff Position Note. Washington, DC: International Monetary Fund.

Blinder, Alan S. 1996. "Central Banking in a Democracy." *Federal Reserve Bank of Richmond Economic Quarterly* 82 (4): 1–14.

Blinder, Alan S., and Ricardo Reis. 2005. "Understanding the Greenspan Standard." In *The Greenspan Era: Lessons for the Future*. Jackson Hole, WY: Federal Reserve Bank of Kansas City.

Blinder, Alan S., and Janet L. Yellen. 2001. *The Fabulous Decade: Macroeconomic Lessons from the 1990s*. New York: Century Foundation Press.

Bonis, Brian, Jane Ihrig, and Min Wei. 2017. "Projected Evolution of the SOMA Portfolio and the 10-Year Treasury Term Premium Effect." Board of Governors of the Federal Reserve System. *FEDS Notes*, September 22.

Borio, Claudio, and William White. 2003. "Whither Monetary and Financial Stability? The Implications of Evolving Policy Regimes." In *Monetary Policy and Uncertainty: Adapting to a Changing Economy*. Jackson Hole, WY: Federal Reserve Bank of Kansas City.

Borio, Claudio, and Haibin Zhu. 2012. "Capital Regulation, Risk-Taking and Monetary Policy: A Missing Link in the Transmission Mechanism?" *Journal of Financial Stability* 8 (4): 236–51.

Boushey, Heather, Ryan Nunn, and Jay Shambaugh, eds. 2019. *Recession Ready: Fiscal Policies to Stabilize the American Economy*. Washington, DC: Brookings Institution: The Hamilton Project, Washington Center for Equitable Growth.

Bowman, David, Christopher Erceg, and Mike Leahy. 2010. "Strategies for Targeting Interest Rates Out the Yield Curve." Staff Memo. Washington, DC: Board of Governors of the Federal Reserve System.

Boyle, Andrew. 1967. *Montagu Norman: A Biography*. London: Cassell.

Brainard, Lael. 2017. "Rethinking Monetary Policy in a New Normal." Washington, DC, October 12.

————. 2019. "Federal Reserve Review of Monetary Policy Strategy, Tools, and Communications: Some Preliminary Views." New York, November 26.

————. 2020. "The Future of Retail Payments in the United States." Washington, DC, August 6.

————. 2021. "Supporting Responsible Use of AI and Equitable Outcomes in Financial Services." Washington, DC, January 12.

Brauer, David. 2007. "The Natural Rate of Unemployment." Working Paper 2007-06. Washington, DC: Congressional Budget Office.

Brunnermeier, Markus K., and Yann Koby. 2018. "The Reversal Interest Rate." Working Paper 25406. Cambridge, MA: National Bureau of Economic Research.

Bullard, James, and Riccardo DiCecio. 2019. "Optimal Monetary Policy for the Masses." Working Paper 2019-009. Federal Reserve Bank of St. Louis.

Bunn, Philip, Alice Pugh, and Chris Yeates. 2018. "The Distributional Impact of Monetary Policy Easing in the UK between 2008 and 2014." Staff Working Paper 720. London: Bank of England.

Burke, Chris, Spence Hilton, Ruth Judson, Kurt Lewis, and David Skeie. 2010. "Reducing the IOER Rate: An Analysis of Options." Staff Memo. Washington, DC: Board of Governors of the Federal Reserve System.

Burns, Arthur F. 1970. "The Basis for Lasting Prosperity." Speech delivered at Pepperdine University, Los Angeles, December 7.

————. 1979. "The Anguish of Central Banking." Per Jacobsson Lecture, Belgrade, Yugoslavia, September 30. http://www.perjacobsson.org/lectures/1979.pdf.

Bush, Ryan, Haitham Jendoubi, Matthew Raskin, and Giorgio Topa. 2020. "How Did Market Perceptions of the FOMC's Reaction Function Change after the Fed's Framework Review?" Federal Reserve Bank of New York. *Liberty Street Economics*, December 18.

Caballero, Ricardo J., Emmanuel Farhi, and Pierre-Olivier Gourinchas. 2017. "The Safe Assets Shortage Conundrum." *Journal of Economic Perspectives* 31 (3): 29–46.

Caballero, Ricardo J., Takeo Hoshi, and Anil K. Kashyap. 2008. "Zombie Lending and Depressed Restructuring in Japan." *American Economic Review* 98 (5): 1943–77.

Caballero, Ricardo J., and Gunes Kamber. 2019. "On the Global Impact of Risk-off Shocks and Policy-Put Frameworks." Working Paper 26031. Cambridge, MA: National Bureau of Economic Research.

Cahill, Michael E., Stefania D'Amico, Canlin Li, and John S. Sears. 2013. "Duration Risk versus Local Supply Channel in Treasury Yields: Evidence from the Federal Reserve's Asset Purchase Announcements." Working Paper 2013-35. Finance and Economics Discussion Series. Washington, DC: Board of Governors of the Federal Reserve System.

Cahn, Christophe, Julien Matheron, and Jean-Guillaume Sahuc. 2017. "Assessing the Macroeconomic Effects of LTROs during the Great Recession." *Journal of Money, Credit and Banking* 49 (7): 1443–82.

Caldara, Dario, Etienne Gagnon, Enrique Martínez-García, and Christopher J. Neely. 2020. "Monetary Policy and Economic Performance since the Financial Crisis." Working Paper 2020-065. Finance and Economics Discussion Series. Washington, DC: Board of Governors of the Federal Reserve System.

Campbell, Jeffrey R., Charles L. Evans, Jonas D. M. Fisher, and Alejandro Justiniano. 2012. "Macroeconomic Effects of Federal Reserve Forward Guidance." *Brookings Papers on Economic Activity* (Spring): 1–80.

Campbell, John Y., and Robert J. Shiller. 1998. "Valuation Ratios and the Long-Run Stock Market Outlook." *Journal of Portfolio Management* 24 (2): 11–26.

Carney, Mark. 2012. "A Monetary Framework for All Seasons." Speech delivered at the U.S. Monetary Policy Forum, New York, February 24.

Carvalho, Carlos, Eric Hsu, and Fernanda Nechio. 2016. "Measuring the Effect of the Zero Lower Bound on Monetary Policy." Working Paper 2016-06. Federal Reserve Bank of San Francisco.

Case, Karl, John Quigley, and Robert Shiller. 2013. "Wealth Effects Revisited 1975–2012." *Critical Finance Review* 2 (1): 101–28.

Cetorelli, Nicola, Linda S. Goldberg, and Fabiola Ravazzolo. 2020. "Have the Fed Swap Lines Reduced Dollar Funding Strains during the COVID-19 Outbreak?" Federal Reserve Bank of New York. *Liberty Street Economics*, May 22.

Charbonneau, Karyne, and Lori Rennison. 2015. "Forward Guidance at the Effective Lower Bound: International Experience." Staff Discussion Paper 15. Ottawa, Ontario: Bank of Canada.

Chaurushiya, Radha, and Ken Kuttner. 2003. "Targeting the Yield Curve: The Experience of the Federal Reserve, 1942–1951." Staff Memo. Washington, DC: Board of Governors of the Federal Reserve System.

Cheng, Jeffrey, David Wessel, and Joshua Younger. 2020. "How Did COVID-19 Disrupt the Market for U.S. Treasury Debt?" Washington, DC: Brookings Institution. May 1.

Chung, Hess, Etienne Gagnon, Taisuke Nakata, Matthias Paustian, Bernd Schlusche, James Trevino, Diego Vilan, and Wei Zheng. 2019. "Monetary Policy Options at the Effective Lower Bound: Assessing the Federal Reserve's Current Policy Toolkit." Finance and Economics Discussion Series 2019-003. Washington, DC: Board of Governors of the Federal Reserve System.

Chung, Hess, Jean-Philippe Laforte, David Reifschneider, and John C. Williams. 2012. "Have We Underestimated the Likelihood and Severity of Zero Lower Bound Events?" *Journey of Money, Credit and Banking* 44 (1): 47–82.

Churm, Rohan, Michael Joyce, George Kapetanios, and Konstantinos Theodoridis. 2021. "Unconventional Monetary Policies and the Macroeconomy: The Impact of the UK's QE2 and Funding for Lending Scheme." *The Quarterly Review of Economics and Finance* 80: 721–36.

Claessens, Stijn. 2015. "An Overview of Macroprudential Policy Tools." *Annual Review of Financial Economics* 7 (1): 397–422.

Clarida, Richard H. 2019. "The Federal Reserve's Review of Its Monetary Policy Strategy, Tools, and Communication Practices." Presented at the 2019 U.S. Monetary Policy Forum, New York, February 22.

———. 2020a. "The Federal Reserve's New Monetary Policy Framework: A Robust Evolution." Washington, DC, August 31.

———. 2020b. "The Federal Reserve's New Framework: Context and Consequences." Washington, DC, November 16.

———. 2021. "Outlooks, Outcomes, and Prospects for U.S. Monetary Policy." Washington, DC, August 4.

Clark, John, Nathan Converse, Brahima Coulibaly, and Steven Kamin. 2016. "Emerging Market Capital Flows and U.S. Monetary Policy." Washington, DC: Board of Governors of the Federal Reserve System. *IFDP Notes*, October 18.

Clouse, Jim, Bill English, Jon Faust, Jane Ihrig, Jeff Huther, Beth Klee, Mike Leahy, David Reifschneider, and Julie Remache. 2013. "Fiscal Implications of Additional Large-Scale Asset Purchases for the Federal Government and the Federal Reserve." Staff Memo. Washington, DC: Board of Governors of the Federal Reserve System.

Coibion, Olivier, Yuriy Gorodnichenko, Edward S. Knotek II, and Raphael Schoenle. 2020. "Average Inflation Targeting and Household Expectations." Working Paper 27836. Cambridge, MA: National Bureau of Economic Research.

Condon, Christopher. 2019. "Key Trump Quotes on Powell as Fed Remains in the Firing Line." Bloomberg, December 17.

Correa, Ricardo, and Sally Davies. 2008. "Implications of the Health of the Japanese Banking Sector for the Effectiveness of Monetary Policy." Staff Memo. Washington, DC: Board of Governors of the Federal Reserve System.

Cox, Jeff. 2018. "Powell Says We're 'A Long Way' from Neutral on Interest Rates, Indicating More Hikes Are Coming." CNBC, October 3.

Crane, Leland D., Ryan A. Decker, Aaron Flaaen, Adrian Hamins-Puertolas, and Christopher Kurz. 2020. "Business Exit during the COVID-19 Pandemic: Non-Traditional Measures in Historical Context." Finance and Economics Discussion Series 2020-089. Washington, DC: Board of Governors of the Federal Reserve System.

Crockett, Andrew. 2000. "Marrying the Micro- and Macro-Prudential Dimensions of Financial Stability." Speech at the Eleventh International Conference of Banking Supervisors, Basel, Switzerland, September 20.

Daly, Mary C., Bart Hobijn, Ayşegül Şahin, and Robert G. Valletta. 2012. "A Search and Matching Approach to Labor Markets: Did the Natural Rate of Unemployment Rise?" *Journal of Economic Perspectives* 26 (3): 3–26.

Dam, Kenneth, and George Shultz. 1977. "Reflections on Wage and Price Controls." *Industrial and Labor Relations Review* (January): 139.

D'Amico, Stefania, William English, David López-Salido, and Edward Nelson. 2012. "The Federal Reserve's Large-Scale Asset Purchase Programmes: Rationale and Effects." *Economic Journal* 122 (564): 415–46.

D'Amico, Stefania, and Iryna Kaminska. 2019. "Credit Easing versus Quantitative Easing: Evidence from Corporate and Government Bond Purchase Programs." London: Bank of England Working Paper 825.

D'Amico, Stefania, and Thomas B. King. 2013. "Flow and Stock Effects of Large-Scale Treasury Purchases: Evidence on the Importance of Local Supply." *Journal of Financial Economics* 108 (2): 425–48.

Das, Krishna N., and Jonathan Spicer. 2016. "How the New York Fed Fumbled over the Bangladesh Bank Cyber-Heist." Reuters, July 21.

Das, Sonali. 2019. "China's Evolving Exchange Rate Regime." Working Paper 19/50. Washington, DC: International Monetary Fund.

Davis, Josh, Cristian Fuenzalida, and Alan M. Taylor. 2021. "The Natural Rate Puzzle: Global Macro Trends and the Market-Implied R*." Working Paper 26560. Cambridge, MA: National Bureau of Economic Research.

De Santis, Roberto A. 2020. "Impact of the Asset Purchase Programme on Euro Area Government Bond Yields Using Market News." *Economic Modelling* 86 (March): 192–209.

Del Negro, Marco, Domenico Giannone, Marc P. Giannoni, and Andrea Tambalotti. 2017. "Safety, Liquidity, and the Natural Rate of Interest." *Brookings Papers on Economic Activity* (Spring): 235–94.

Del Negro, Marco, Marc Giannoni, and Christina Patterson. 2015. "The Forward Guidance Puzzle." Staff Report 574. Federal Reserve Bank of New York.

Del Negro, Marco, Michele Lenza, Giorgio E. Primiceri, and Andrea Tambalotti. 2020. "What's Up with the Phillips Curve?" *Brookings Papers on Economic Activity* (Spring): 301–73.

Dell'Ariccia, Giovanni, Pau Rabanal, and Damiano Sandri. 2018. "Unconventional Monetary Policies in the Euro Area, Japan, and the United Kingdom." *Journal of Economic Perspectives* 32 (4): 147–72.

Devlin-Foltz, Sebastian, Alice M. Henriques, and John E. Sabelhaus. 2016. "The Role of Social Security in Overall Retirement Resources: A Distributional Perspective." Washington, DC: Board of Governors of the Federal Reserve System. *FEDS Notes*, July 29.

Di Maggio, Marco, Amir Kermani, and Christopher J. Palmer. 2020. "How Quantitative Easing Works: Evidence on the Refinancing Channel." *The Review of Economic Studies* 87 (3): 1498–1528.

Draghi, Mario. 2012. "Remarks at the Global Investment Conference." London, England, July 26.

Duarte, Fernando, and Carlo Rosa. 2015. "The Equity Risk Premium: A Review of Models." Staff Report 714. Federal Reserve Bank of New York.

Duffie, Darrell. 2020. "Still the World's Safe Haven? Redesigning the U.S. Treasury Market after the COVID-19 Crisis." Hutchins Center Working Paper 62. Washington, DC: Brookings Institution.

Eggertsson, Gauti B., and Michael Woodford. 2003. "The Zero Bound on Interest Rates and Optimal Monetary Policy." *Brookings Papers on Economic Activity* (Spring): 139–235.

Eichengreen, Barry. 1992. *Golden Fetters: The Gold Standard and the Great Depression 1919–1939.* Oxford and New York: Oxford University Press.

Eichengreen, Barry, and Jeffrey Sachs. 1985. "Exchange Rates and Economic Recovery in the 1930s." *Journal of Economic History* 45 (4): 925–46.

Eisenschmidt, Jens, and Frank Smets. 2018. "Negative Interest Rates: Lessons from the Euro Area." In *Monetary Policy and Financial Stability: Transmission Mechanisms and Policy Implications,* edited by Álvaro Aguirre, Markus Brunnermeier, and Diego Saravia, 13–42. Santiago: Central Bank of Chile.

Engen, Eric M., Thomas Laubach, and David Reifschneider. 2015. "The Macroeconomic Effects of the Federal Reserve's Unconventional Monetary Policies." Finance and Economics Discussion Series 2015-005. Washington, DC: Board of Governors of the Federal Reserve System.

English, William. (forthcoming). "Monetary Policy and Financial Stability." In *The Handbook of Financial Stress Testing,* edited by J. Doyne Farmer, Alissa Kleinnijenhuis, Til Schuermann, and Thom Wetzer.

Erceg, Chris, Jesper Linde, and David Reifschneider. 2010. "Macroeconomic Consequences of a European Sovereign Debt Crisis." Staff Memo. Washington, DC: Board of Governors of the Federal Reserve System.

Erceg, Christopher, Michael T. Kiley, and David López-Salido. 2011. "Alternative Monetary Policy Frameworks." Staff Memo. Washington, DC: Board of Governors of the Federal Reserve System.

Erceg, Christopher, David López-Salido, and Robert Tetlow. 2011. "Adopting an Alternative Monetary Policy Framework." Staff Memo. Washington, DC: Board of Governors of the Federal Reserve System.

Eser, Fabian, Wolfgang Lemke, Ken Nyholm, Sören Radde, and Andreea Liliana Vladu. 2019. "Tracing the Impact of the ECB's Asset Purchase Programme on the Yield Curve." ECB Working Paper 2293. Frankfurt, Germany: European Central Bank.

Evans, Charles L. 2012. "Monetary Policy in a Low-Inflation Environment: Developing a State-Contingent Price-Level Target." *Journal of Money, Credit and Banking* 44 (s1): 147–55.

Fair, Ray C. 1978. "The Effect of Economic Events on Votes for President." *Review of Economic and Statistics* 60 (2): 159–73.

Favara, Giovanni, Camelia Minoiu, and Ander Perez-Orive. 2021. "U.S. Zombie Firms: How Many and How Consequential?" Washington, DC: Board of Governors of the Federal Reserve System. *FEDS Notes,* July 30.

Femia, Katherine, Steven Friedman, and Brian Sack. 2013. "The Effects of Policy Guidance on Perceptions of the Fed's Reaction Function." Staff Report 652. Washington, DC: Federal Reserve Bank of New York.

Ferguson, Jr., Roger W. 2003. "September 11, the Federal Reserve, and the Financial System." Nashville, TN, February 5.

Fernald, John G. 2014. "Productivity and Potential Output before, during, and after the Great Recession." In *NBER Macroeconomics Annual 2014.* Vol. 29: 1–51. Cambridge, MA: National Bureau of Economic Research.

Fernald, John G., Robert E. Hall, James H. Stock, and Mark W. Watson. 2017. "The Disappointing Recovery of Output after 2009." *Brookings Papers on Economic Activity* (Spring): 1–58.

Feroli, Michael, David Greenlaw, Peter Hooper, Frederic S. Mishkin, and Amir Sufi. 2017. "Language after Liftoff: Fed Communication Away from the Zero Lower Bound." *Research in Economics* 71 (3): 452–90.

Ferrell, Robert H. 2010. *Inside the Nixon Administration: The Secret Diary of Arthur Burns, 1969–1974*. Lawrence: University Press of Kansas.

Fischer, Stanley. 1995. "Central-Bank Independence Revisited." *American Economic Review* 85 (2): 201–6.

Fisher, Irving. 1930. *The Theory of Interest*. New York: The Macmillan Co.

———. 1973. "I Discovered the Phillips Curve: A Statistical Relation between Unemployment and Price Changes." *Journal of Political Economy* 81 (2): 496–502.

Fleming, Sam. 2018. "Janet Yellen on Trump, Fed Politics and Nurturing Recovery." *Financial Times*, October 26.

Forbes, Kristen J. 2019. "Inflation Dynamics: Dead, Dormant, or Determined Abroad?" *Brookings Papers on Economic Activity* (Fall): 257–338.

Freund, James, Timothy Curry, Peter Hirsch, and Theodore Kelley. 1997. "Commercial Real Estate and the Banking Crises of the 1980s and Early 1990s." In *History of the Eighties: Lessons for the Future*, Vol. 1: *An Examination of the Banking Crises of the 1980s and Early 1990s*, Chapter 3. Washington, DC: Federal Deposit Insurance Corporation. https://www.fdic.gov/bank/historical/history/137_165.pdf.

Friedman, Milton. 1968. "The Role of Monetary Policy." *American Economic Review* 58 (1): 1–17.

———. 1969. *The Optimum Quantity of Money and Other Essays*. Chicago: Aldine Publishing Company.

Friedman, Milton, and Anna Jacobson Schwartz. 1963. *A Monetary History of the United States: 1867–1960*. Princeton, NJ: Princeton University Press.

Furman, Jason. 2020. "The Fiscal Response to the Great Recession: Steps Taken, Paths Rejected, and Lessons for Next Time." In *First Responders: Inside the U.S. Strategy for Fighting the 2007–2009 Global Financial Crisis*, 451–88. New Haven, CT: Yale University Press.

Furman, Jason, and Lawrence Summers. 2020. "A Reconsideration of Fiscal Policy in the Era of Low Interest Rates." Discussion Draft. Washington, DC: Brookings Institution.

Gagnon, Joseph E. 2016. "Quantitative Easing: An Underappreciated Success." Policy Brief PB16-4. Washington, DC: Peterson Institute for International Economics.

———. 2018. "QE Skeptics Overstate Their Case." Peterson Institute for International Economics. *Realtime Economic Issues Watch*, July 5.

Gagnon, Joseph, Matthew Raskin, Julie Remache, and Brian Sack. 2011. "The Financial Market Effects of the Federal Reserve's Large-Scale Asset Purchases." *International Journal of Central Banking* 7 (1): 3–43.

Ghebreyesus, Tedros Adhanom. 2020. "Opening Remarks at the Media Briefing on COVID-19." World Health Organization. March 11. https://www.who.int/dg/speeches/detail/who-director-general-s-opening-remarks-at-the-media-briefing-on-covid-19---11-march-2020.

Gilchrist, Simon, and Egon Zakrajšek. 2012. "Credit Spreads and Business Cycle Fluctuations." *American Economic Review* 102 (4): 1692–1720.

———. 2013. "The Impact of the Federal Reserve's Large-Scale Asset Purchase Programs on Corporate Credit Risk." *Journal of Money, Credit and Banking* 45 (s2): 29–57.

———. 2019. "Trade Exposure and the Evolution of Inflation Dynamics." Working Paper 2019-007. Finance and Economics Discussion Series. Washington, DC: Board of Governors of the Federal Reserve System.

Glaeser, Edward L., Joshua D. Gottlieb, and Joseph Gyourko. 2013. "Can Cheap Credit Explain the Housing Boom?" In *Housing and the Financial Crisis*, edited by Edward L. Glaeser and Todd Sinai, 301–59. Chicago: University of Chicago Press.

Goodfriend, Marvin, and Robert G. King. 2005. "The Incredible Volcker Disinflation." *Journal of Monetary Economics* 52 (5): 981–1015.

Gordon, Robert J. 2013. "The Phillips Curve Is Alive and Well: Inflation and the NAIRU during the Slow Recovery." Working Paper 19390. Cambridge, MA: National Bureau of Economic Research.

———. 2016. *The Rise and Fall of American Growth: The U.S. Standard of Living since the Civil War.* Princeton, NJ: Princeton University Press.

Gorton, Gary B. 2012. *Misunderstanding Financial Crises: Why We Don't See Them Coming.* New York: Oxford University Press.

Gorton, Gary, and Andrew Metrick. 2012. "Securitized Banking and the Run on Repo." *Journal of Financial Economics* 104 (3): 425–51.

Gourio, François, Anil K. Kashyap, and Jae Sim. 2018. "The Tradeoffs in Leaning against the Wind." *IMF Economic Review* 66 (March): 70–115.

Gramlich, Edward M. 2007. "Booms and Busts, the Case of Subprime Mortgages." *Federal Reserve Bank of Kansas City Economic Review* 109: 105–13.

Granville, Kevin. 2017. "A President at War with His Fed Chief, 5 Decades before Trump." *New York Times*, June 13.

Greenlaw, David, James D. Hamilton, Ethan Harris, and Kenneth D. West. 2018. "A Skeptical View of the Impact of the Fed's Balance Sheet." Working Paper 24687. Cambridge, MA: National Bureau of Economic Research.

Greenspan, Alan. 1996. "The Challenge of Central Banking in a Democratic Society." Washington, DC, December 5.

———. 2005. "Mortgage Banking." Palm Desert, California, September 26.

———. 2007. *The Age of Turbulence: Adventures in a New World.* New York: Penguin Press.

Greenwood, Robin, Samuel G. Hanson, Joshua S. Rudolph, and Lawrence H. Summers. 2015. "Debt Management Conflicts between the U.S. Treasury and the Federal Reserve." In *The $13 Trillion Question: How America Manages Its Debt*, 43–89. Washington, DC: Brookings Institution Press.

Greenwood, Robin, Samuel G. Hanson, Andrei Shleifer, and Jakob Ahm Sørensen. (forthcoming). "Predictable Financial Crises." *Journal of Finance.*

Greenwood, Robin, and Dimitri Vayanos. 2014. "Bond Supply and Excess Bond Return." *Review of Financial Studies* 27 (3): 663–713.

Grisse, Christian, Signe Krogstrup, and Silvio Schumacher. 2017. "Lower-Bound Beliefs and Long-Term Interest Rates." *International Journal of Central Banking* 13 (3): 165–202.

Gürkaynak, Refet S., Brian Sack, and Eric T. Swanson. 2005. "Do Actions Speak Louder Than Words? The Response of Asset Prices to Monetary Policy Actions and Statements." *International Journal of Central Banking* 1 (1): 55–93.

Haltom, Renee. 2013. "Failure of Continental Illinois." *Federal Reserve History*, November 22. https://www.federalreservehistory.org/essays/failure-of-continental-illinois.

Hamilton, James D., and Jing Cynthia Wu. 2012. "The Effectiveness of Alternative Monetary Policy Tools in a Zero Lower Bound Environment." *Journal of Money, Credit and Banking* 44 (1): 3–46.

Hansen, Alvin H. 1939. "Economic Progress and Declining Population Growth." *American Economic Review* 29 (1): 1–15.

Hanson, Samuel, and Jeremy C. Stein. 2015. "Monetary Policy and Long-Term Rates." *Journal of Financial Economics* 115 (3): 429–48.

Harker, Patrick T. 2017. "Economic Outlook: The Labor Market, Rates, and the Balance Sheet." Presented at the Market News International (MNI) Connect Roundtable, New York, May 23.

Heathcote, Jonathan, Fabrizio Perri, and Giovanni L. Violante. 2020. "The Rise of US Earnings Inequality: Does the Cycle Drive the Trend?" *Review of Economic Dynamics* 37 (s1): S181–204.

Hetzel, Robert L. 1998. "Arthur Burns and Inflation." *Federal Reserve Bank of Richmond Economic Quarterly* 84 (1): 21–44.

———. 2008. *The Monetary Policy of the Federal Reserve: A History.* Studies in Economic History. Cambridge: Cambridge University Press.

Hetzel, Robert L., and Ralph F. Leach. 2001. "The Treasury-Fed Accord: A New Narrative Account." *Federal Reserve Bank of Richmond Economic Quarterly* 87 (1): 33–55.

Hodgson, Godfrey. 1998. "Obituary: William McChesney Martin." *The Independent,* August 20.

Holston, Kathryn, Thomas Laubach, and John C. Williams. 2017. "Measuring the Natural Rate of Interest: International Trends and Determinants." *Journal of International Economics* 108 (S1): S59–75.

Hooker, Mark A. 2002. "Are Oil Shocks Inflationary? Asymmetric and Nonlinear Specifications versus Changes in Regime." *Journal of Money, Credit and Banking* 34 (2): 540–61.

Hooper, Peter, Frederic S. Mishkin, and Amir Sufi. 2020. "Prospects for Inflation in a High Pressure Economy: Is the Phillips Curve Dead or Is It Just Hibernating?" *Research in Economics* 74 (1): 26–62.

Hubbard, Glenn, and Donald Kohn, eds. 2021. *Report of the Task Force on Financial Stability.* Washington, DC: Brookings Institution.

Hubert, Paul, and Fabien Labondance. 2018. "The Effect of ECB Forward Guidance on the Term Structure of Interest Rates." *International Journal of Central Banking* 14 (5): 193–222.

Ihrig, Jane, Elizabeth Klee, Canlin Li, Min Wei, and Joe Kachovec. 2018. "Expectations about the Federal Reserve's Balance Sheet and the Term Structure of Interest Rates." *International Journal of Central Banking* 14 (2): 341–90.

Irwin, Neil. 2018. "The Most Important Least-Noticed Economic Event of the Decade." *New York Times,* September 29.

Jamrisko, Michelle, Chloe Whiteaker, and Jeremy Scott Diamond. 2018. "Yellen's Labor Market Dashboard." Bloomberg, February 2.

Jonung, Lars, and Eoin Drea. 2009. "The Euro: It Can't Happen, It's a Bad Idea, It Won't Last. US Economists on the EMU, 1989–2002." Economic Papers 395. Brussels, Belgium: European Commission.

Jordà, Òscar, Moritz Schularick, and Alan M. Taylor. 2013. "When Credit Bites Back." *Journal of Money, Credit and Banking* 45 (s2): 3–28.

———. 2015a. "Interest Rates and House Prices: Pill or Poison?" Federal Reserve Bank of San Francisco. *FRBSF Economic Letter,* August 3.

———. 2015b. "Leveraged Bubbles." *Journal of Monetary Economics* 76 (S): S1–20.

Joyce, Michael A. S., Ana Lasaosa, Ibrahim Stevens, and Matthew Tong. 2011. "The Financial Market Impact of Quantitative Easing in the United Kingdom." *International Journal of Central Banking* 7 (3): 113–61.

Joyce, Michael A. S., and Matthew Tong. 2012. "QE and the Gilt Market: A Disaggregated Analysis." *Economic Journal* 122 (564): 348–84.

Kacperczyk, Marcin, and Philipp Schnabl. 2010. "When Safe Proved Risky: Commercial Paper during the Financial Crisis of 2007–2009." *Journal of Economic Perspectives* 24 (1): 29–50.

Kashyap, Anil K., and Caspar Siegert. 2019. "Financial Stability Considerations and Monetary Policy?" In *Financial Stability Considerations and Monetary Policy.* Federal Reserve Bank of Chicago.

Katz, Lawrence F., and Alan B. Krueger. 1999. "The High-Pressure U.S. Labor Market of the 1990s." *Brookings Papers on Economic Activity* (Spring): 1–87.

Kiley, Michael T. 2014. "The Aggregate Demand Effects of Short- and Long-Term Interest Rates." *International Journal of Central Banking* 10 (4): 69–104.

———. 2015. "Low Inflation in the United States: A Summary of Recent Research." Board of Governors of the Federal Reserve System. *FEDS Notes*, November 23.

———. 2018. "Quantitative Easing and the 'New Normal' in Monetary Policy." Finance and Economic Discussion Series 2018-004. Washington, DC: Board of Governors of the Federal Reserve System.

———. 2019. "The Global Equilibrium Real Interest Rate: Concepts, Estimates, and Challenges." Finance and Economics Discussion Series 2019-076. Washington, DC: Board of Governors of the Federal Reserve System.

Kim, Kyungmin, Thomas Laubach, and Min Wei. 2020. "Macroeconomic Effects of Large-Scale Asset Purchases: New Evidence." Finance and Economics Discussion Series 2020-047. Washington, DC: Board of Governors of the Federal Reserve System.

Kocherlakota, Narayana. 2016. "'Helicopter Money' Won't Provide Much Extra Lift." Bloomberg, March 24.

Kohn, Donald, and Brian Sack. 2020. "Monetary Policy during the Financial Crisis." In *First Responders: Inside the U.S. Strategy for Fighting the 2007–2009 Global Financial Crisis*, edited by Ben S. Bernanke, Timothy F. Geithner, and Henry M. Paulson, Jr., 421–50. New Haven, CT: Yale University Press.

Kopcke, Richard W., and Anthony Webb. 2013. "How Has the Financial Crisis Affected the Finances of Older Households?" Working Paper. Boston, MA: Center for Retirement Research at Boston College. https://citeseerx.ist.psu.edu/viewdoc/download?doi=10.1.1.651 .2278&rep=rep1&type=pdf.

Krishnamurthy, Arvind, and Annette Vissing-Jorgensen. 2011. "The Effects of Quantitative Easing on Interest Rates: Channels and Implications for Policy." *Brookings Papers on Economic Activity* (Fall): 215–65.

Krugman, Paul R. 1998. "It's Baaack: Japan's Slump and the Return of the Liquidity Trap." *Brookings Papers on Economic Activity* (Fall): 137–205.

Kurtzman, Robert, Stephan Luck, and Tom Zimmermann. 2017. "Did QE Lead Banks to Relax Their Lending Standards? Evidence from the Federal Reserve's LSAPs." Finance and Economics Discussion Series 2017-093. Washington, DC: Board of Governors of the Federal Reserve System.

Kuttner, Kenneth N. 2012. "Low Interest Rates and Housing Bubbles: Still No Smoking Gun." In *The Role of Central Banks in Financial Stability: How Has It Changed?* Federal Reserve Bank of Chicago.

———. 2018. "Outside the Box: Unconventional Monetary Policy in the Great Recession and Beyond." *Journal of Economic Perspectives* 32 (4): 121–46.

Laforte, Jean-Philippe. 2018. "Overview of the Changes to the FRB/US Model (2018)." Washington, DC: Board of Governors of the Federal Reserve System. *FEDS Notes*, December 7.

Lagarde, Christine. 2020a. "Our Response to the Coronavirus Emergency." European Central Bank. *The ECB Blog*, March 19.

———. 2020b. "The Monetary Policy Strategy Review: Some Preliminary Considerations." Speech at the "ECB and Its Watchers XXI" conference, Frankfurt, Germany, September 30.

Laubach, Thomas, and John C. Williams. 2003. "Measuring the Natural Rate of Interest." *Review of Economics and Statistics* 85 (4): 1063–70.

Leigh, Daniel. 2010. "A 4% Inflation Target?" Center for Economic and Policy Research. *VoxEU*, March 9.

Lewis, Michael. 2010. *The Big Short: Inside the Doomsday Machine*. New York: W. W. Norton.

Li, Canlin, and Min Wei. 2013. "Term Structure Modelling with Supply Factors and the Federal Reserve's Large Scale Asset Purchase Programs." *International Journal of Central Banking* 9 (1): 3–39.

Liang, J. Nellie, and Rochelle M. Edge. 2019. "New Financial Stability Governance Structures and Central Banks." Hutchins Center Working Paper 50. Washington, DC: Brookings Institution.

Lindsey, David E. 2003. "A Modern History of FOMC Communication: 1975–2002." Staff Memo. Washington, DC: Board of Governors of the Federal Reserve System.

Loomis, Carol J. 1998. "A House Built on Sand." *Fortune*, October 26. https://archive.fortune.com/magazines/fortune/fortune_archive/1998/10/26/250015/index.htm.

Lopez, Jose A., Andrew K. Rose, and Mark M. Spiegel. 2020. "Why Have Negative Nominal Interest Rates Had Such a Small Effect on Bank Performance? Cross Country Evidence." *European Economic Review* 124 (May).

Lu, Lina, Matthew Pritsker, Andrei Zlate, Kenechukwu Anadu, and James Bohn. 2019. "Reach for Yield by U.S. Public Pension Funds." Finance and Economics Discussion Series 2019-048. Washington, DC: Board of Governors of the Federal Reserve System.

Mahedy, Tim, and Adam Shapiro. 2017. "What's Down with Inflation?" Federal Reserve Bank of San Francisco. *FRBSF Economic Letters*, November 27.

Mallaby, Sebastian. 2016. *The Man Who Knew: The Life and Times of Alan Greenspan*. New York: Penguin Press.

Mankiw, N. Gregory. 2020. "A Skeptic's Guide to Modern Monetary Theory." In *AEA Papers and Proceedings*, 110:141–44.

Manski, Charles F., and John D. Straub. 2000. "Worker Perceptions of Job Insecurity in the Mid-1990s: Evidence from the Survey of Economic Expectations." *Journal of Human Resources* 35 (3): 447–79.

Matthews, Dylan. 2019. "Modern Monetary Theory, Explained." *Vox*, April 16.

McGowan, Müge Adalet, Dan Andrews, and Valentine Millot. 2018. "The Walking Dead? Zombie Firms and Productivity Performance in OECD Countries." *Economic Policy* 33 (96): 685–736.

McLaren, Nick, Ryan N. Banerjee, and David Latto. 2014. "Using Changes in Auction Maturity Sectors to Help Identify the Impact of QE on Gilt Yields." *Economic Journal* 124 (576): 453–79.

McLeay, Michael, and Silvana Tenreyro. 2020. "Optimal Inflation and the Identification of the Phillips Curve." In *NBER Macroeconomics Annual*. Vol. 34. Cambridge, MA: National Bureau of Economic Research.

Meade, Ellen E., Nicholas A. Burk, and Melanie Josselyn. 2015. "The FOMC Meeting Minutes: An Assessment of Counting Words and the Diversity of Views." Washington, DC: Board of Governors of the Federal Reserve System. *FEDS Notes*, May 16.

Meaning, Jack, and Feng Zhu. 2011. "The Impact of Recent Central Bank Asset Purchase Programmes." *BIS Quarterly Review* (December): 73–83.

Metrick, Andrew, and Daniel Tarullo. 2021. "Congruent Financial Regulation." *Brookings Papers on Economic Activity* (Spring).

Mian, Atif, Ludwig Straub, and Amir Sufi. 2021. "What Explains the Decline in r*? Rising Income Inequality versus Demographic Shifts." In *Proceedings*. Jackson Hole, WY: Federal Reserve Bank of Kansas City.

Mian, Atif, Amir Sufi, and Emil Verner. 2017. "Household Debt and Business Cycles Worldwide." *Quarterly Journal of Economics* 132 (4): 1755–1817.

Minsky, Hyman P. 1986. *Stabilizing an Unstable Economy*. New Haven, CT: Yale University Press.

Mishkin, Frederic S. 2007. "Inflation Dynamics." *International Finance* 10 (3): 317–34.

Mishkin, Frederic S., and Eugene N. White. 2003. "U.S. Stock Market Crashes and Their Aftermath:

Implications for Monetary Policy." In *Asset Price Bubbles: The Implications for Monetary, Regulatory and International Policies*, edited by William B. Hunter, George G. Kaufman, and Michael Pormerleano. Cambridge, MA: MIT Press.

Mondale, Walter, and David Hage. 2010. *The Good Fight: A Life in Liberal Politics*. New York: Scribner.

Mui, Ylan Q. 2016. "Why the Federal Reserve Is Rethinking Everything." *Washington Post*, July 27.

Nakata, Taisuke. 2015. "Credibility of Optimal Forward Guidance at the Interest Rate Lower Bound." Washington, DC: Board of Governors of the Federal Reserve System. *FEDS Notes*, August 27.

Nechio, Fernanda, and Glenn D. Rudebusch. 2016. "Has the Fed Fallen behind the Curve This Year?" Federal Reserve Bank of San Francisco. *FRBSF Economic Letter*, November 7.

Nelson, Edward. 2021. "The Emergence of Forward Guidance as a Monetary Policy Tool." 2021-033. Finance and Economics Discussion Series. Washington, DC: Board of Governors of the Federal Reserve System.

Nelson, Jack. 1990. "Interest Rates Peril Fed Chief's Job, Sources Say." *Los Angeles Times*, March 9.

Okazaki, Yosuke, and Nao Sudo. 2018. "Natural Rate of Interest in Japan: Measuring Its Size and Identifying Drivers Based on a DSGE Model." Bank of Japan Working Paper 18-E-6. Tokyo: Bank of Japan.

Orphanides, Athanasios. 2003. "The Quest for Prosperity without Inflation." *Journal of Monetary Economics* 50 (3): 633–63.

Orphanides, Athanasios, and John Williams. 2013. "Monetary Policy Mistakes and the Evolution of Inflation Expectations." In *The Great Inflation: The Rebirth of Modern Central Banking*, edited by Michael D. Bordo and Athanasios Orphanides. Chicago: University of Chicago Press.

Owyang, Michael T., and Tatevik Sekhposyan. 2012. "Okun's Law over the Business Cycle: Was the Great Recession All That Different?" *Federal Reserve Bank of St. Louis Review* (September): 399–418.

Paligorova, Teodora, and Jesus A. Sierra Jimenez. 2012. "Monetary Policy and the Risk-Taking Channel: Insights from the Lending Behaviour of Banks." *Bank of Canada Review*, 23–30.

Peek, Joe, and Eric S. Rosengren. 1992. "The Capital Crunch in New England." *New England Economic Review* (May): 21–31.

Phelps, Edmund S. 1968. "Money-Wage Dynamics and Labor-Market Equilibrium." *Journal of Political Economy* 76 (4): 678–711.

Phillips, A. W. 1958. "The Relation between Unemployment and the Rate of Change of Money Wage Rates in the United Kingdom, 1861–1957." *Economica* 25 (100): 283–99.

Potter, Simon, and Frank Smets. 2019. "Unconventional Monetary Policy Tools: A Cross-Country Analysis." Committee on the Global Financial System Paper 63. Basel, Switzerland: Bank for International Settlements.

Powell, Jerome H. 2015. " 'Audit the Fed' and Other Proposals." Washington, DC, February 9.

———. 2018a. Interview with Kai Ryssdal, *Marketplace*, July 12. https://www.marketplace .org/2018/07/12/powell-transcript.

———. 2018b. "Monetary Policy in a Changing Economy." Jackson Hole, WY, August 24.

———. 2019a. "Opening Remarks." Presented at the Federal Reserve Bank of Chicago, Conference on Monetary Policy Strategy, Tools, and Communication Practices, Chicago, June 4.

———. 2019b. "Challenges for Monetary Policy." Jackson Hole, WY, August 23.

———. 2020a. "Current Economic Issues." Washington, DC, May 13.

———. 2020b. "Q&A with Alan Blinder." *Wall Street Journal*, May 29. https://www.wsj.com/ articles/transcript-fed-chief-jerome-powell-q-a-with-alan-blinder-11590779548.

———. 2020c. "New Economic Challenges and the Fed's Monetary Policy Review." Jackson Hole, WY, August 27.

Pozsar, Zoltan, Tobias Adrian, Adam Ashcraft, and Hayley Boesky. 2010. "Shadow Banking." Staff Report 458. Federal Reserve Bank of New York.

Quarles, Randal K. 2020. "What Happened? What Have We Learned from It? Lessons From COVID-19 Stress on the Financial System." Washington, DC, October 15.

Rachel, Łukasz, and Lawrence H. Summers. 2019. "On Secular Stagnation in the Industrialized World." *Brookings Papers on Economic Activity* (Spring): 1–54.

Radelet, Steven, and Jeffrey Sachs. 2000. "The Onset of the East Asian Financial Crisis." In *Currency Crises*, edited by Paul Krugman. Chicago: University of Chicago Press.

Rajan, Raghuram G. 2005. "Has Financial Development Made the World Riskier?" In *Proceedings*. Jackson Hole, WY: Federal Reserve Bank of Kansas City.

Rankin, Jennifer. 2020. "EU Summit Deal: What Has Been Agreed and Why Was It So Difficult?" *The Guardian*, July 21.

Raskin, Matthew D. 2013. "The Effects of the Federal Reserve's Date-Based Forward Guidance." Finance and Economics Discussion Series 2013-37. Washington, DC: Board of Governors of the Federal Reserve System.

Rebucci, Alessandro, Jonathan S. Hartley, and Daniel Jiménez. 2020. "An Event Study of COVID-19 Central Bank Quantitative Easing in Advanced and Emerging Economies." Working Paper 27339. Cambridge, MA: National Bureau of Economic Research.

Reifschneider, David. 2016. "Gauging the Ability of the FOMC to Respond to Future Recessions." Finance and Economics Discussion Series 2016-068. Washington, DC: Board of Governors of the Federal Reserve System.

Reinhart, Carmen M., and Vincent R. Reinhart. 2011. "Limits of Monetary Policy in Theory and Practice." *Cato Journal* 31 (3): 427–39.

Reinhart, Carmen M., and Kenneth S. Rogoff. 2009. *This Time Is Different: Eight Centuries of Financial Folly*. Princeton and Oxford: Princeton University Press.

Rey, Hélène. 2013. "Dilemma Not Trilemma: The Global Financial Cycle and Monetary Policy Independence." In *Proceedings*. Jackson Hole, WY: Federal Reserve Bank of Kansas City.

Richter, Björn, Moritz Schularick, and Ilhyock Shim. 2019. "The Costs of Macroprudential Policy." *Journal of International Economics* 118 (May): 263–82.

Roberts, John M. 2006. "Monetary Policy and Inflation Dynamics." *International Journal of Central Banking* 2 (3): 193–230.

Robinson, Kenneth J. 2013. "Depository Institutions Deregulation and Monetary Control Act of 1980." *Federal Reserve History*, November 22. https://www.federalreservehistory.org/essays/ monetary-control-act-of-1980.

Rodnyansky, Alexander, and Olivier M. Darmouni. 2017. "The Effects of Quantitative Easing on Bank Lending Behavior." *The Review of Financial Studies* 30 (11): 3858–87.

Rogoff, Kenneth S. 1985. "The Optimal Degree of Commitment to an Intermediate Monetary Target." *Quarterly Journal of Economics* 100 (4).

———. 2017. *The Curse of Cash: How Large-Denomination Bills Aid Crime and Tax Evasion and Constrain Monetary Policy*. Princeton, NJ: Princeton University Press.

Romer, Christina D. 2011. "Dear Ben: It's Time for Your Volcker Moment." *New York Times*, October 29.

Romer, Christina D., and David H. Romer. 2002. "A Rehabilitation of Monetary Policy in the 1950's." *American Economic Review* 92 (2): 121–27.

Romero, Jessie. 2013. "Treasury-Fed Accord." *Federal Reserve History*, November 22. https://www .federalreservehistory.org/essays/treasury-fed-accord.

Rosenfeld, Everett. 2015. "Fed's Fischer: Too Early to Decide on Sept Hike." CNBC, August 28.

Samuels, Brett. 2020. "Trump Calls Fed Chair Powell 'Most Improved Player.'" *The Hill*, May 13.

Samuelson, Paul, and Robert Solow. 1960. "Analytical Aspects of Anti-Inflation Policy." *American Economic Review*, Papers and Proceedings 50 (2): 177–94.

Schreft, Stacey L. 1990. "Credit Controls: 1980." *Federal Reserve Bank of Richmond Economic Review* 76 (Nov): 25–55.

Schrimpf, Andreas, Hyun Song Shin, and Vladyslav Sushko. 2020. "Leverage and Margin Spirals in Fixed Income Markets during the Covid-19 Crisis." BIS Bulletin 2. Basel, Switzerland: Bank for International Settlements.

Shiller, Robert J. 2000. *Irrational Exuberance*. Princeton, NJ: Princeton University Press.

———. 2007. "Understanding Recent Trends in House Prices and Homeownership." In *Proceedings*. Jackson Hole, WY: Federal Reserve Bank of Kansas City.

———. 2019. *Narrative Economics: How Stories Go Viral and Drive Major Economic Events*. Princeton, NJ: Princeton University Press.

Silber, William L. 2012. *Volcker: The Triumph of Persistence*. London: Bloomsbury Press.

Slacalek, Jiri, Oreste Tristani, and Giovanni L. Violante. 2020. "Household Balance Sheet Channels of Monetary Policy: A Back of the Envelope Calculation for the Euro Area." *Journal of Economic Dynamics and Control* 115 (June): 103879.

Smialek, Jeanna. 2021. "Why Are There So Few Black Economists at the Fed?" *New York Times*, February 2.

Spicer, Jonathan. 2015. "Market turmoil makes September rate hike 'less compelling'—Fed's Dudley." Reuters, August 26.

Staiger, Douglas O., James H. Stock, and Mark W. Watson. 1997. "How Precise Are Estimates of the Natural Rate of Unemployment." In *Reducing Inflation: Motivation and Strategy*, edited by Christina D. Romer and David H. Romer, 195–246. Chicago: University of Chicago Press.

Steelman, Aaron. 2013. "Full Employment and Balanced Growth Act of 1978 (Humphrey-Hawkins)." *Federal Reserve History*, November 22. https://www.federalreservehistory.org/essays/humphrey-hawkins-act.

Stein, Jeremy C. 2013. "Overheating in Credit Markets: Origins, Measurement, and Policy Responses." St. Louis, February 7.

———. 2014. "Incorporating Financial Stability Considerations into a Monetary Policy Framework." Washington, DC, March 21.

Stewart, Jay. 2000. "Did Job Security Decline in the 1990s?" Working Paper 330. Washington, DC: Bureau of Labor Statistics.

Stock, James H., and Mark W. Watson. 2007. "Why Has U.S. Inflation Become Harder to Forecast?" *Journal of Money, Credit and Banking* 39 (1): 3–33.

———. 2020. "Slack and Cyclically Sensitive Inflation." *Journal of Money, Credit and Banking* 52 (2): 393–428.

Summers, Lawrence H. 2014. "U.S. Economic Prospects: Secular Stagnation, Hysteresis, and the Zero Lower Bound." *Business Economics* 49 (2).

Sumner, Scott B. 2014. "Nominal GDP Targeting: A Simple Rule to Improve Fed Performance." *Cato Journal* 34 (2): 315–37.

Svensson, Lars E.O. 1999. "Price-Level Targeting versus Inflation Targeting: A Free Lunch?" *Journal of Money, Credit and Banking* 31 (3): 277–95.

———. 2017a. "Leaning against the Wind: The Role of Different Assumptions about the Costs." Working Paper 23745. Cambridge, MA: National Bureau of Economic Research.

———. 2017b. "Cost-Benefit Analysis of Leaning against the Wind." *Journal of Monetary Economics* 90 (October): 193–213.

Swanson, Eric T. 2011. "Let's Twist Again: A High-Frequency Event-Study Analysis of Operation Twist and Its Implications for QE2." *Brookings Papers on Economic Activity* (Spring): 151–88.

————. 2020. "Measuring the Effects of Federal Reserve Forward Guidance and Asset Purchases on Financial Markets." *Journal of Monetary Economics* 118: 32–53.

Swanson, Eric T., and John C. Williams. 2014. "Measuring the Effect of the Zero Lower Bound on Medium- and Longer-Term Interest Rates." *American Economic Review* 104 (10): 3154–85.

Tankersley, Jim. 2019. "Herman Cain's Fed Chances Dim amid Republican Senate Opposition." *New York Times*, April 11.

Tankersley, Jim, Maggie Haberman, and Emily Cochrane. 2019. "Trump Won't Nominate Stephen Moore for Fed Board." *New York Times*, May 2.

Taylor, Derrick Bryson. 2020. "A Timeline of the Coronavirus." *New York Times*, March 17.

Taylor, John B. 1993. "Discretion versus Policy Rules in Practice." *Carnegie-Rochester Conference Series on Public Policy* 39 (December): 195–214.

Timiraos, Nick, and Kate Davidson. 2017. "Wall Street Veteran Leads Search for Next Fed Chief." *Wall Street Journal*, June 13.

Uchitelle, Louis, and N. R. Kleinfield. 1996. "On the Battlefields of Business, Millions of Casualties." *New York Times*, March 3. https://archive.nytimes.com/www.nytimes.com/specials/downsize/03down1.html.

Vayanos, Dimitri, and Jean-Luc Vila. 2021. "A Preferred-Habitat Model of the Term Structure of Interest Rates." *Econometrica* 89 (1): 77–112.

Volcker, Paul A. 1990. "The Triumph of Central Banking?" Per Jacobsson Lecture, Washington, DC, September 23. http://www.perjacobsson.org/lectures/1990.pdf.

————. 2018. *Keeping At It: The Quest for Sound Money and Good Government*. New York: PublicAffairs: Hachette Book Group.

Weinraub, Mark. 2020. "Trump's Payments to Farmers Hit All-Time High ahead of Election." Reuters, October 19.

Wells, Wyatt C. 1994. *Economist in an Uncertain World: Arthur F. Burns and the Federal Reserve, 1970–1978*. New York: Columbia University Press.

Wessel, David, Louise Sheiner, and Michael Ng. 2019. "Gender and Racial Diversity of Federal Government Economists." Washington, DC: Brookings Institution: Hutchins Center on Fiscal and Monetary Policy.

Wheatley, Jonathan, and Peter Garnham. 2010. "Brazil in 'Currency War' Alert." *Financial Times*, September 27.

Wicksell, Knut. 1936. *Interest and Prices: A Study of the Causes Regulating the Value of Money*. R.S. Kahn, trans. New York: Sentry Press.

Williams, John C. 2014. "Monetary Policy at the Zero Lower Bound: Putting Theory into Practice." Hutchins Center Working Paper. Washington, DC: Brookings Institution.

————. 2017. "Speed Limits and Stall Speeds: Fostering Sustainable Growth in the United States." Sydney, Australia, June 26.

Willoughby, Jack. 2000. "Burning Up." *Barron's*, March 20.

Woodford, Michael. 2012. "Methods of Policy Accommodation at the Interest-Rate Lower Bound." In *The Changing Policy Landscape*, 185–288. Jackson Hole, WY: Federal Reserve Bank of Kansas City.

Woodward, Bob. 2000. *Maestro: Greenspan's Fed and the American Boom*. New York: Simon & Schuster.

Wu, Tao. 2014. "Unconventional Monetary Policy and Long-Term Interest Rates." IMF Working Paper 14/189. Washington, DC: International Monetary Fund.

Yellen, Janet L. 2014. "Labor Market Dynamics and Monetary Policy." Jackson Hole, WY, August 22.

————. 2015. "Inflation Dynamics and Monetary Policy." Amherst, MA, September 24.

————. 2017a. "The Economic Outlook and the Conduct of Monetary Policy." Stanford CA, January 19.

————. 2017b. "Financial Stability a Decade after the Onset of the Crisis." Jackson Hole, WY, August 25.

————. 2017c. "Inflation, Uncertainty, and Monetary Policy." Cleveland, OH, September 26.

————. 2018. "Keynote Address on the Tenth Anniversary of the Financial Crisis." Washington, DC, September 21.

Yilla, Kadija, and Nellie Liang. 2020. "What Are Macroprudential Tools?" Washington, DC: Brookings Institution. February 11.

INDEX

Note: Page numbers in *italics* refer to tables and figures. Footnotes and endnotes are indicated by *n* after the page number.